Migration, Diaspora, Exile

Migration, Diaspora, Exile

Narratives of Affiliation and Escape

Edited by
Daniel Stein, Cathy C. Waegner,
Geoffroy de Laforcade, and Page R. Laws

LEXINGTON BOOKS
Lanham • Boulder • New York • London

Published by Lexington Books
An imprint of The Rowman & Littlefield Publishing Group, Inc.
4501 Forbes Boulevard, Suite 200, Lanham, Maryland 20706
www.rowman.com

6 Tinworth Street, London SE11 5AL, United Kingdom

British Library Cataloguing in Publication Information Available

Library of Congress Cataloging-in-Publication Data
Names: MESEA (Organization). Conference (11th : 2018 : Universität Graz).
  | Stein, Daniel, 1975- editor. | Waegner, Cathy Covell, 1948- editor. |
  Laforcade, Geoffroy de, editor. | Laws, Page R., editor.
Title: Migration, diaspora, exile : narratives of affiliation and escape /
  edited by Daniel Stein, Cathy C. Waegner, Geoffroy de Laforcade, Page R. Laws.
Description: Lanham : Lexington Books, 2020. | Selected papers presented at
  the 11th biennial conference sponsored by MESEA (Society for
  Multi-Ethnic Studies: Europe and the Americas), held May 3-June 2, 2018,
  at the University of Graz, on the theme, "Ethnicity and Kinship:
  Interdisciplinary Approaches to Family, Community, and Difference." |
  Includes bibliographical references and index. | Summary: "Migration,
  Diaspora, Exile examines narratives of affiliation and escape that
  imagine migration to and in Europe and the Americas in terms of kinship,
  community, and refuge. They investigate a broad range of literary,
  cinematic, and civic interventions in past and present constructions of
  diasporic, migratory, or exilic identities"— Provided by publisher.
Identifiers: LCCN 2020007641 (print) | LCCN 2020007642 (ebook) | ISBN
  9781793617002 (cloth) | ISBN 9781793617019 (epub)
Subjects: LCSH: Ethnicity in literature—Congresses. | Emigration and
  immigration in literature—Congresses. | Exile in
  literature—Congresses. | Ethnicity—Congresses. | Emigration and
  immigration—Congresses. | Exile—Congresses.
Classification: LCC PN56.E735 M47 2018 (print) | LCC PN56.E735 (ebook) |
  DDC 809/.933552—dc23
LC record available at https://lccn.loc.gov/2020007641
LC ebook record available at https://lccn.loc.gov/2020007642

Contents

Migration, Diaspora, Exile: Narratives of Affiliation and Escape

Editors' Introduction

Migration is arguably the most volatile sociopolitical issue of our time, exacerbated by the disastrous ecological and economic effects wrought by man-made climate change with its storms, aridity, and rising seas. Of course, movements of peoples have long shaped human history. Through many past centuries, invaders, raiders, conquerors, settlers, and enslavers displaced groups in manifold ways; lack of sustainable land, as well as political and religious persecution, led to the search for new homelands. Altered geopolitical paradigms and increasing populations have added intensity to migration pressures. The rise of lucrative mercantilism in the sixteenth and seventeenth centuries was fueled by the systematically organized, horrific Middle Passage transport of Africans to the "New World," with the accompanying, ever-increasing east to west immigration of European[1] settlers and the resulting near genocide committed on the Indigenous population. At least since the 1970s, the paradigmatic east/west axis has pivoted to a south/north one, as the impoverished and desperate citizens of war-torn, economically exploited, and often increasingly dry lands of the "Global South" seek refuge in the flourishing, industrialized nations to the north, amid burgeoning and alarming controversy.

The amount of newly published literature on these patterns and their urgent ramifications is vast, but our volume, attentive to migration to and within Europe and the Americas, offers particular perspectives that might yield valuable insights. It considers specific literary, cinematic, and civic interventions[2] that point not only to injustices but also to redemptive strategies involved in the changing paradigms of migration. It centers on narratives of kinship and community as a prominent means through which these interventions take shape, and it traces these interventions across borders, suggesting that narratives of migration to and in Europe and the Americas share certain tropes despite regional and cultural differences.

As a distinctive entry to the complex topic, the book chooses the trope of "Mother of Exiles," which links migration to kinship, community, refuge, and hegemony. The phrase appeared in Jewish writer and activist Emma Lazarus's sonnet "The New Colossus," written for a fund-raising event in 1883 and engraved on a bronze plaque below the Statue of Liberty in New York City harbor in 1903.[3] "Mother of Exiles" has become an enduring "meme" in the popular identification of the United States as a hospitable land of opportunity for immigrants and refugees.[4] The history behind the statue and the belated application of the poem reveal the intricate interconnections of national myths and transnational migration narratives that appreciably shape the analyses in this book. Initially conceived by the Frenchman Édouard de Laboulaye as a celebration of the emancipation of the slaves and the abolition of slavery in the United States, the statue by Frédéric-Auguste Bartholdi, in an early model, carried a torch in her right hand and broken shackles in her left (Brockell, 2019).[5] Yet when the final version of the statue was finished and unveiled in 1886, the rent chains were placed inconspicuously at Lady Liberty's feet, and she appeared primarily as a beacon, promising enlightenment to nondemocratic countries and, as Lazarus's poem would suggest, "[g]low[ing] world-wide welcome" to immigrating "huddled masses yearning to breathe free."

In the twenty-first century, the "Mother of Exiles" trope has taken on significance in Europe-as-asylum, particularly in the person of the German chancellor Angela Merkel, who was nicknamed "Mama Merkel" by arriving migrants in 2015. The current escalation of discourse and action in the United States and Europe, however, concerning walls, secure borders, refugee camps beyond the closed borders, and deportations propels the "Mother of Exiles" metaphor into explicitly ironic dimensions. Indeed, when historical injustices and atrocities regarding displaced groups are considered, irony regarding "cordial (mother)lands" has long been encoded on both sides of the Atlantic. The "embracing mother" image also acknowledges the family and community dimensions of migrancy, with the deep ruptures of forced or voluntary diaspora. However, kinship groups and affiliations are often at least contingently re-sorted or replaced by new formations, as some of the case studies in our book will show. The figure of the "exile" transmogrifies in our chapters into the fugitive, the escapee, the refugee, the nomad, the Other, depending on the historical and story context. These figures moving "elsewhere" are stunningly embodied in our cover art, generously provided to us by the French artist Olivier Suire Verlay. His painting *Voyageurs* (Travelers) evokes a fractured landscape of sand and shadows, journeys and crossings, with lines of water in shades of blue. Individuals of all ages and in various groupings move in slow, possibly painful cadence toward an unknown destination, pausing furtively to glance back at a past when their identities once seemed fixed and grounded in time and space. Some carry baggage, others have canes as their sole possessions; some drift alone, perhaps lost, hands in their pockets, while others grasp at one another, as if determined to salvage or create some sense of community.[6]

Migration, Diaspora, Exile: Narratives of Affiliation and Escape was spearheaded by a transdisciplinary group of scholars from Norfolk State University, United States, and University of Siegen, Germany, joined by European members of MESEA (Society for Multi-Ethnic Studies: Europe and the Americas) in presentation at the 2018 MESEA conference in Graz/Austria, the conference theme being "Ethnicity and Kinship: Interdisciplinary Approaches to Family, Community, and Difference." Project papers were also presented at a symposium at the University of Siegen in June 2018. The individual studies divide up into three modes of migrancy intervention: literary, filmic, and civic.

DIASPORIZATION OF SOCIETY AND (IN)EQUITABLE BELONGING

Most of the recent literature on migrancy calls for alternatives in attitude and political undertaking to strict exclusion and the enforcement of territorialized and racialized borders in dealing with what Isolde Charim calls the "diasporization of society." Charim views the figure of the "nomad" as the potentially positive embodiment of the diverse mobilities and hybridity in the twentieth-first century (*Lebensmodell Diaspora*).[7] Kathleen Staudt offers theoretical background and practical applications for heading toward "a more equitable world" in *Border Politics in a Global Era* (1); she suggests changing the state practices for dealing with the thoroughly transcultural borderlands, which could be viewed as "bio-regions" that transcend national borderlines. Despite the crisis-oriented titles of a number of recent attention-gaining publications, such as *The Oxford Handbook of Migration Crises* (Menjívar et al., 2019)[8] and Jacqueline Bhabha's *Can We Solve the Migration Crisis?* (2018), the tenor of those books agrees with ours that contemporary migration need not be viewed as an unsolvable crisis, but rather as an urgent wake-up call for the industrialized countries to reduce their excesses in consumption and economic colonization that have contributed so significantly to the environmental, political, and familial instability of many nations to the south.

Two sociological publications can be named here that point directly to family issues in migration involving both severances and adjustments, on respective sides of the Atlantic: Leisy J. Abrego, *Sacrificing Families: Navigating Laws, Labor, and Love Across Borders* (2014), and Ionela Vlase and Bogdan Voicu, *Gender, Family, and Adaptation of Migrants in Europe: A Life Course Perspective* (2018). Together these books reflect the complex dialectic between "sacrificing" and "adapting" that individuals, families, and communities in our case studies must undergo in the wake of escape and exile.[9] One major focus of our book falls on Germany as a target country for migrant affiliative groups; Berthold Löffler's *Flucht nach Deutschland: Wie Migration Politik und Gesellschaft verändert* (2020; *Flight to Germany: How Migration Changes Politics and Society*) will support this accentuation.[10] Increasingly networking with each other and with their homelands via "new media" platforms, migrant kinship and ethnic groups in Europe are discovering new ways to adapt to and shape their nomadic existences, as the empirical investigations of Internet participation cogently show in Karim H. Karim and Ahmed Al-Rawi's *Diaspora and Media in Europe: Migration, Identity, and Integration* (2018). The geocultural concentration of migrancy in cities in Europe and the United States has profound implications for metropolitan governments and, above all, for the migrants themselves. Alex Sager's *Toward a Cosmopolitan Ethics of Mobility: The Migrant's-Eye View of the World* (2018) and Avner de Shalit's *Cities and Immigration: Political and Moral Dilemmas in the New Era of Migration* (2018) attest to the ethical and pragmatic transformations required when large numbers of often rural refugee family members are drawn to urban areas in search of work and inhabitable space.

In addition to our book's interest in twenty-first-century migrancy trends, *Migration, Diaspora, Exile: Narratives of Affiliation and Escape* includes chapters dealing with the *longue durée* of migration in historical developments and through the filters of recent aesthetic productions. The violent displacement of the North American Indigenous peoples, the unconscionable transatlantic shipping of humans that provided the basis for the slave system in the Americas, the perilous fleeing of slaves to points north—above all Canada—from the plantations in the Southern United States, including the repetition of this south-north pattern by the US military personnel choosing precarious fugitive life in Canada over service in the Iraq and Afghanistan wars: the unabated academic and aesthetic concern with such long-term historical sequences and their discourses takes on new angles when viewed, as in our chapters, through graphic or gothic novels, contemporary Native poetry, and—for social scientists—archival revelation or undercover interviews. The traumas of systemic historical injustice echo in the burdened sense of belonging evidenced in assertions by present-day descendants of migrants who were painfully on the move in the extended past.

LITERARY NARRATIVES: FROM THE *LONGUE DURÉE* OF MIGRATION TO NOVELISTIC "CITY-ZENS"

The first part of the book is devoted to literary and graphic works offering fresh insights into historical and more current movements of peoples that tore apart family and cultures and/or created new, transnational affiliations. Daniel Stein compares two deliberately unsettling works in a medium rapidly gaining academic attention: graphic narrative. "Recuperating the Black Family in Graphic Narrative: Tom Feelings's *Middle Passage* and Kyle Baker's *Nat Turner*" examines the experimental visual aesthetics that attempt to represent the devastating loss of personal freedom and tribal relations suffered by enslaved Africans arriving as "cargo" in the New World colonies, as well as the slaves' dangerous counteractions—aesthetics that serve to replace or refunctionalize the racist caricatures and sentimental iconography with which precarious African American slave families have traditionally all too often been depicted. The two graphic artists invoke racial communities contravening the eradication of black subjectivity through the Middle Passage and chattel slavery in the Americas by focusing substantial parts of their stories on black families and their forced fractures. They employ pictorial strategies that echo the hyperbole of superhero-genre conventions, such as positioning weapons or pained faces in penetrating graphic position, uncomfortably addressing the readership, or superimposing a historical diagram of how to efficiently pack a slave ship on the body of a larger-than-life African in chains. Thus challenging "legacies of racial representation," Feelings's and Baker's revisionary "graphic enunciation of black counterhistory" undercuts the "historically laden language" of white EuroAmerican hegemony, and attempts to "heal historical wounds by reopening the pains of the past for contemporary consideration" (Stein).

In "Generational Doubling as Eth(n)ic Narrative Strategy: Annie Proulx's *Barkskins* and Yaa Gyasi's *Homegoing*," Cathy C. Waegner continues the investigation into narrative treatment of the foundational injustices of New World colonization, not only the financially lucrative importation of slaves, but also the wholesale destruction of Indigenous peoples' band structures and their environments. In both novels, the epic material is structured through generations of intertwining families with contrasting mixtures of ethnicity, wealth, and choice, and both books inscribe the historical horrors into the gothic mode with haunting kinship, "transgothic" deviance (Zigarovich), and uncanny forms of transhistorical doubling. The twinning of material objects, such as tables and pendants, provides ethnic and ethical touchstones and prepares for possible healings. The matriarchal haunters and the unscrupulous exploiters in the novels call for the reader to radically reorient the trope of

Mother of Exiles who "glows world-wide welcome" in North America's master narrative, inviting him/her to re-imagine the "network of kinship between exiles and exploiters, between old and new homelands, among ethnic groups, between people and their environment" (Waegner).

Ludmila Martanovschi's "'As Much the Invader as the Native': Investigating Immigrant and Indigenous Family Ties in Wendy Rose's *Itch Like Crazy*" probes the dilemma of the contemporary Native American of mixed heritage for whom the blind spots and cruelties of that master narrative are woven into her own genealogy: "the deeper I delve into [my] various family histories, the more I find that the people from whom I come [German, English, Irish, and Scottish] were the perpetrators of those very acts that ignited my rage (and my art)" (Rose, *Itch Like Crazy*, 2002, Part 3). As an exile in her own land, Rose, or more precisely the speaker in her poem "These Bones," sees her role gothically and restoratively as a remembering Hopi/Miwok descendant in a place "where the living haunt the dead" (61). She empathetically imagines the disconnectedness felt by her ancestral EuroAmerican immigrant-settlers, but the images of transplantation, woundedness, and brokenness in her poetry "embody . . . the destruction engendered by colonizing practices" (Martanovschi).

Patrycja Kurjatto-Renard introduces her chapter with a detailed analysis of the historical contexts and interpretations of Lazarus's 1883 sonnet. The ambiguities of the ostensibly liberal sentiments in the poem being adopted for a national monument in a time of aggressive colonization and increasingly restrictive immigration policies are reflected in the polysemy of the 2014 novel by Ethiopian American Dinaw Mengestu, set in the early 1970s, as Kurjatto-Renard shows in "Mothers/Lovers of Exiles: Women Characters in Dinaw Mengestu's *All Our Names*." She sees further intertexts for this novel in, for example, Asian American fiction with its complex cross-cultural relationships, transition texts from the family idealism of the 1950s and 1960s to new feminist forms, migrant shipwreck reports and graphics, and Mengestu's other works. The protagonist Helen, a Midwestern social worker assigned to advise migrant Isaac, is viewed as a novelistic version of the Mother of Exiles, a helper, a storyteller, a builder of a potentially new world, and a strangely debilitated lover who cannot fathom the complications of a migrant existence.

Isabella Karlsson deals with three novels, Joseph O'Neill's *Netherland* (2008), Teju Cole's *Open City* (2011), and Atticus Lish's *Preparation for the Next Life* (2014), which portray the collision between migrants and political institutions in the aftermath of the September 11 terror attacks. As she shows in "The Securitized Migrant: Migrant Mobility and Kindred Alliances in Post-9/11 New York Novels," the migrants are treated as potentially dangerous for the nation in the paranoid atmosphere, but the novels also provide a counternarrative to the official stance with their depiction of the protagonists' labyrinthine movements through urban space. These movements enable the ethnic figures to form surprising relationships with local citizens and fellow migrants, thus stressing the lateral agency of the refugees rather than the passive protection by the Mother of Exiles in her iconic city. Karlsson's reading of the three novels is underpinned by de Shalit's appeal to discuss "the role of cities and locality in integrating immigrants" rather than exclusively the role of the state and the nation (*Cities* vii); de Shalit usefully coins the re-valuing term "city-zens" for the migrants—indeed a large majority—who choose to reside in metropolitan venues.

CINEMATIC NARRATIVES: CONTESTING OTHERED IDENTITIES ON SCREEN

The second part of our book attests to the power of film and its industry to intervene in public perceptions of historical and contemporary migration. We find support for this claim of power in Staudt's investigation of cross-regional borderlands migration; she features more than forty influential films in her interdisciplinary study mentioned earlier, *Border Politics in a Global Era*.[11] The first chapter in this part, Michele Rozga's "Mother(less) Exiles: The New Woman's Absence from the Migration of the Expressionists to Hollywood," addresses gender issues in film production and transfer. The creativity of the Weimar Republic in Germany between the World Wars, especially with regard to photography and film, opened up perspectives for artistic agency for (Jewish) "New Women," although they were seldom at the helm in, for instance, Bauhaus film experiments. With the rise of Hitler and his National Socialist Party, the Expressionist film industry migrated to Hollywood—but there women found themselves in their traditional roles as "muse, homemaker, and object" (Rozga). The ingenuity of German filmmaker Lotte Reiniger, who in the Weimar years used the female-marked technology of a pair of scissors to create Expressionist films featuring cut-out silhouettes, was not called for in the Mother of Exiles-Hollywood milieu, where the German or Austrian émigré directors were men: Fritz Lang, Robert Siodmak, Douglas Sirk, Billy Wilder. Referring to imaginative spaces created by, for example, banned Jewish Expressionist poet Else Lasker-Schüler, Rozga shows that "[a]rtists who are also women have often waged the battles of culture within their imaginative work, testing the boundaries of the legal, economic, and cultural countries they have called home, even when that home has been inhospitable" and even when forced into nomadic precarity.

In chronological consonance with Rozga's study, Cathy M. Jackson's "Go West, Young Men: Teutonic Myths and American Westerns Blazed Path for the Acceptance of Nazism in Germany" presents the possibly unexpected argument that the gender bias of American western movies to a certain extent influenced the rise of the German Nazi ideology: through the frontier images imagined by German novelist and con-man Karl May in the last decade of the nineteenth century, his novels wildly popular for readers of German, western heroes—modern versions of German mythical heroes like Siegfried and Barbarossa—became, as it were, "fathers of exiles" for German immigrants to the United States. These German settlers in turn wrote often public letters home, reinforcing May's imagination of the New World clash of "golden-haired, blue-eyed" victors (Jackson) and dark and ferocious but domitable Indigenes. In these accounts and in frontier novels by US authors such as James Fenimore Cooper, Owen Wister, and Zane Grey, as well as the crowd-pleasing Wild West performances abroad by "Buffalo Bill" and other show-entrepreneurs, only stereotypical nods were made to the New World roles of women and nonwhite people. The white male supremacist overtones of early western films found resonance in post-World War I Germany when these movies "migrated" to the Continent. As mirrored in the westerns, America's perceived exceptionalism and expansionism through achieved Manifest Destiny and its conquering of inferior "nonwhite" foes, notably Native Americans and Mexicans, fed easily into the propaganda trends of early National Socialist thought in Germany. Cathy Jackson's chapter delineates the migration of Native American images to Germany in its puzzling complexity, however, developing this observation: "It is ironic that an ideology—Nazism—immersed in decreeing its country's superiority over all people of color would embrace Native Americans."

The Othered identities of contemporary migrants struggling to arrive in Europe by boat are dealt with in an award-winning documentary film interpreted by Page R. Laws in "'What Pain It Was to Drown': Quotidian Meets Tragic in Gianfranco Rosi's *Fire at Sea*." The viewer of the 2016 "observational" movie must watch actively to cognize the implicit contrast between coming-of-age focalizer Samuele's comfortable middle-class family on the Italian island of Lampedusa and the incoming migrants traumatized by the deadly, chaotic situation at sea. Laws employs film and migration theory, as well as a discourse of water imagery, to provide contexts for the way the understated film shocks: "horror coexists so quietly and just out of sight" of the diurnal on the island of fishermen (Laws). A "father of exiles" figure, the town's empathetic doctor Bartolo is the human connector between indigenous Lampedusans, the migrant rescuers/processers, and the migrants themselves, each of whom places his or her hand into Dr. Bartolo's as he gently checks for indications of disease. Laws also outlines the very different strategy of Ai Weiwei's epic-scale migration film *Human Flow* (2017), in which the filmmaker takes on a participatory role.

The "cinematic interventions" part of our book concludes with a treatment of a decade-long film serialization probably not readily considered to depict migration and kinship patterns. Christopher Hansen's "Shifting Affiliations: Kinship Formation through Othering in the Marvel Cinematic Universe" reveals how the three phases of the MCU films provide divergent perspectives on the personal developments of singular characters, their dynamic relationships to others and larger organizations, as well as their modes of displacement and migration. Within the frame of a serialized narrative, shifting loyalties are not limited to a decisive plot twist, but arise from an evolution of personal associations and teams with a greater number of characters. Applying Edward Said's concept of Othering and Gayatri Spivak's notion of subalternity to MCU processes, Hansen finds patterns of ethnicity and hegemony within the MCU that refract "real-world parallel[s]," such as the discursive amassing of different hereditary, migratory, and cultural groups into "Latinxs," or US military veterans of Muslim faith frequently being "categorized as Other in public discourse" (Hansen). The deliberate "interpretive fluidity" of the films encourages the viewers to use a wide range of frames to construe the complex and constantly adjusting 'Self' and 'Other' configurations in these movies. Hansen draws the conclusion that "superheroes . . . emerge as Metamigrants: as fictional figures that encapsulate and embody universal elements of diverse migrant experiences."

MODES OF ASYLUM AND FORMATIONS OF AFFILIATION FOR ESCAPEES, FUGITIVES, AND EXILES

The third part of this book depicts actual programs and movements—historical and current—that deal concretely with disruptions brought on by political and economic unevenness or deliberate exploitation. The part begins with the dangerous "self-exile" of enslaved African Americans courageously seeking asylum. Historian Cassandra Newby-Alexander, who has created an encyclopedic database of the movements and narratives of Virginia slaves escaping to the North via the "Underground Railroad" (http://www.racetimeplace .com/ugrr/index.htm) clandestinely organized by opponents to chattel slavery, exposes the complex family choices and gender implications of secret flight in her "'Son, I Am Not Coming Here Anymore': Migration, Loss, Separation, Trauma, and the Underground Railroad." Sheridan Ford painfully continued his journey north although he had to abandon his wife, who had been imprisoned with their children to prevent her from aiding him to flee, in dire straits. Clarissa Davis failed to escape with her brothers, then finally succeeded through cross-dressing. These are two of many 1850s cases of the kinship costs of liberation and uneasy accomplishments within an inhumane, perniciously paternalistic socioeconomic system begun 400 years ago in 1619 with the first shipload of unfree Africans to Virginia. The helpers on the Underground Railroad, called "agents" in contemporary accounts, engaged themselves at tremendous personal peril: in years of activity Eliza Bains of Hampton Roads, Virginia, herself a slave, hid fugitives in her home and audaciously arranged for their passage north with the mariners of schooners in the nearby harbor. Newby-Alexander refers to trauma theory, the anthropological basis of "Negro spirituals," and concepts of freedom underlying the early US nationhood to highlight the difficult decisions that "allowed [the escaping slaves] to define their lives rather than continue to allow others to limit their freedoms."

In the twenty-first century, US military resisters to the wars in Iraq and Afghanistan fled from the United States, the conventionally perceived "Mother of Exiles," to its northern neighbor Canada, continuing the pattern put in place by those escaping slaves in the nineteenth century, as well as by Vietnam War objectors in the twentieth. For "Contested Affiliations: The Migration of US American War Resisters to Canada," Sarah J. Grünendahl conducted empirical research to trace and systematize the paths of and the personal consequences for those seeking asylum from military duty in the Iraq and Afghanistan wars, which has involved their separating from family members, ripping themselves out of professional and social contexts, and enduring an extremely uncertain legal status. Some of the asylum seekers have been able to develop new affiliations in Canada, but, on the whole, they lead precarious, nonparticipatory lives in their new mother country for fear of deportation. Local activists, among them US Vietnam War objectors who remained in Canada, seek to mediate. The US military resisters' adjustments with regard to language and culture might appear small in comparison to those of many other involuntary migrants, but, like the migrants who must exist in overfilled camps and shelters, often for years, the Afghanistan and Iraq War resisters suffer from liminal legality and deportability that "severely limit . . . their orientation toward the future," Grünendahl observes. Thus, she recommends a stance of involvement on the part of government officials: "immigration policy would do well to foster [refugee claimants'] involvement from the very beginning rather than create a climate of self-effacement and aloofness."

Like Newby-Alexander, sociologist Andreas Kewes re-examines the archives, often the "gray literature" of unpublished protocols and reports, to develop hypotheses about the reasons for present-day contradictory stances on migration in Germany. In "'No Asylum from the Germans': Policies of Deterrence and the Early West German Refugee Movement," he follows a "contentious politics approach" and applies discourse theory to public conversations on the waves of refugees in the late 1970s and early 1980s, from

Afghanistan, Turkey, Ethiopia, Sri Lanka, India, and Bangladesh, among others. Authorities and populist groups tended to view the asylum seekers as a bureaucratic burden and a threat to the economy regarding housing, jobs, and services; left-wing and church-group efforts to deal fairly with the refugees emphasized kinship as human beings with rights and dignity, propagating an "image of the foreigner as some kind of brother or sister" and creating "intersubjective certainty on state wrongdoing toward refugees and migrants" (Kewes). In 1980, however, 100,000 migrants applied for asylum, strengthening the governmental agenda to restrict refugee rights and deter migration. The right-wing agitation against migrants and their kindred groups as the source of national dis-ease is captured in the very title of Neeraj Kaushal's *Blaming Immigrants: Nationalism and the Economics of Global Movement* (2019). The refugee protectors, while insisting upon solidarity with asylum seekers, were and increasingly are a heterogeneous group, often with conflicting opinions: "Recently, the early German refugee movement and its most visible actor, the association *Pro Asyl*, have been criticized by younger activists for taking a positivist approach: for calling for a correct implementation of existing law instead of raising the political question of open borders" (Kewes).

In a diametrically opposed movement to that described by Grünendahl, one forced by the sending country, Mine Gencel Bek describes the ousting of regime-critical professionals from Turkey to its closest partner country Germany in the European Union in her chapter titled "Contesting Home, Nation, and Beyond: The Digital Space of New Migrants from Post-Gezi Turkey." Since the 1950s, when Germany encouraged the so-called guest workers from countries to the south to join in its economic upswing, Germany has been viewed as a "mother country" of jobs, but now it is serving as a sanctuary for outspoken high-achievers often compulsorily separated from their families. As one of those exiles herself, Gencel Bek even includes in her academic curriculum vitae the explicit information that she was "dismissed [in 2017] from her position as a professor at the Department of Journalism, Faculty of Communication, Ankara University, Turkey, . . . for signing the petition for peace [in 2016]." Gencel Bek examines the multiple forms of exiles' civic advocacy through their sophisticated use of the social media. The online contributions of exiled journalists objecting to President Erdoğan's autocratic policies and his conception of nation should not be taken for granted: "When writing even very classical liberal news articles can be a reason for so-called 'legal' punishments within Turkey, the recently established diasporic news platforms with their internationally visible dissent must be viewed as daring" (Gencel Bek). Creative blogs abound. New media alliances with non-Turkish groups transnationally strengthen the exiles' cause. Her case study adds a significant chapter to Karim H. Karim and Ahmed Al-Rawi's examples of transnational communication for professional, family, and activist purposes (*Diaspora*), and it productively troubles our titular notion of escape. If "home" and "nation" are already contested concepts, there is no stable place, however repressive, from which those living in exile could have escaped; by relocating to a new place, they are neither completely safe nor do they stop resisting their political persecution and forced exclusion from Turkey.

In "Religion, Family, Community, Difference: Immigrant Millennials in Cologne, Germany," Aprilfaye T. Manalang presents the findings of a transnationally supported, two-year project conducting surveys and in-depth interviews of vocational-college students with a migratory background. They are first-, second-, or even third-generation immigrants from a range of nations. The impacts of this background and their religious stance, ranging from religiosity to unbelief, on their educational, civic, and political engagement are deep and diverse, most strikingly for the children of Muslim families now "navigat[ing] life in one of the more secular countries in the world" (Manalang). She confirms Vlase and Voicu's findings that the dynamics of migrancy are "likely to break traditional life patterns and challenge belonging within bonding relationships" (6). However, the dramatic title of Abrego's *Sacrificing Families*, which focuses on migration from the countries south of the United States, applies on the whole less radically to the immigrant millennials in Germany. Exploring the role of religion in these students' lives offers clues, Manalang avers, not only to "transnational family and kinship models," but also to the "reasons for the persistent educational inequality among immigrants and their attainment of high school/college degrees" in Germany." The one-to-one and focus-group interviews, emphasizing themes from social networks and integration to religion and homosexuality, elicited strikingly candid responses from the millennials, reflecting their search for moral guidance, as well as connection to family and frequently tensely interwoven communities, often in the face of social and economic insecurity.

The concluding chapter by historian Geoffroy de Laforcade sweepingly draws the convoluted backstory of EuroAmerican hegemony, outlining with breadth and depth key patterns of space, time, and movement buried beneath the national narratives of identity, borders, roots, and destinies, beneath dominant concepts of race and ethnicity. The associations in his title to the speculative "space race" among technologically advanced nations to colonize distant planets and establish control over outer-space "aliens" are deliberate. In "'Space,' 'Aliens,' and the 'Race' to Belong: Changing Geographies and Moving Borders in Europe and the Americas," de Laforcade points out the "paternalistic" agenda of the standard Mother of Exiles paradigm: "Nineteenth-century élites cast nation-states as mythical kinship communities, in which those élites claimed to fulfill a 'parental' role by guaranteeing order, economic security, and social distribution, tapping into the emotional and moral needs of citizens undergoing the disruptive impact of capitalist modernization." Receiving societies continue to understand immigration narrowly as a "culturally and economically destabilizing tide that states should endeavor to stem, a kind of disruption in the family." A divergent view of the energy generated by "exilic or fugitive spaces" arises when focus is placed on the Caribbean as not only "the incubator of modernity in the western hemisphere but also the source of epic struggles to define freedom within it": "Its history vividly illustrates how chaotic and unbounded, and fancifully imagined, territory and identity actually have been." The transversal, nonlinear, hybrid affiliations, porous boundaries, and defiance of control that emerge in de Laforcade's narration of the history of the circumCaribbean region including Florida, New Orleans, and pre-USA Mexico dramatically counter the "modern sense of place, territoriality, fixed identities, physical boundaries, civilizational barriers, and bounded national communities" that are foregrounded in present-day migration discourse and lead to, for example, the Mexican being viewed in the United States as the "paradigmatic alien" (de Laforcade). The transborder activist movement *La Otra Campaña* (The Other Campaign) aims to regain a measure of those transversal affiliations and defiances of control, advocating transnational solidarity among a plethora of Indigenous, Hispanic, and migrant groups. De Laforcade identifies productive parallels to the Algerian as the paradigmatic alien of France, revealing damaging hierarchies of citizenship and belonging. Here too, the creation of fugitive spaces must be seen as amelioratingly undermining "the very narrative of modernity, which, while premised on universality, in reality has always been parochially Christian, European, and white" (de Laforcade).

OLD ECONOMY AND NEW SOCIALITY:
AESTHETIC AND ENGAGED INTERVENTIONS

De Laforcade shows that the "space race" is being modulated by the changing discourses of affiliation in Europe and the Americas that fracture received, coherent categories of belonging. He joins most other recent commentators on twenty-first-century migration paradigms in noting the systemic economic practices that serve to send people in search of viable living spaces and conditions. Obtaining hegemony over resources, encouraging monocultures that destroy environments and traditional agricultural networks, denying laborers subsistence-level wages are but a few. Pauline G. Barber and Winnie Lem point their finger at the capitalist basis of cultural and economic inequalities: "Throughout history, . . . capitalism ha[s] rendered populations as mobile and immobile, insiders and outsiders, citizens and denizens, and necessary and disposable, in different places and over time" (2).[12] In the present era of "post-industrial" capitalism, finance and speculation provide a "key dynamic of accumulation" under the "aegis of neoliberal forms of global transformations" (2). Indeed, neoliberalism has become a bashing term for many observers distressed with those "global transformations" that disadvantage and displace large population groups. Cultural critic-renegade Peter Fleming goes as far as to transform the word "neoliberalism" into "*nihi*liberalism," seeing the capitalist achievers' relentless striving after ever-increasing growth at the expense of fair and sustainable treatment of poorer people and countries as containing the seeds of its own destruction (20). His witty but well-documented and scathing book of prognosis is despairingly titled *The Worst Is Yet to Come: A Post-Capitalist Survival Guide* (2019). Anthropologist James G. Ferguson of Stanford University, whose work *Global Shadows: Africa in the Neoliberal World Order* (2006) has influenced the Cameroonian philosopher and political theorist Achille Mbembe, has long warned against the dangers, with regard to uncontrolled South–North migration, of using African lands as a reservoir for resources and, on the other end of the supply chain, as a dumping ground for outdated AmerEuropean products or simply waste. In outlining the challenges of the International Organisation for Migration (IOM) with its 172 member states, Fabian Georgi devotes a lengthy chapter in his book *Managing Migration?* (2019) to the effects of the 2008–2009 global financial meltdown in knotting the multifarious braid of economic causes of migrancy. Fleming would agree, opining that this financial crisis simply reinforced corporations' questionable practices instead of eliciting deep-seated changes in business strategies (38–9).

Fittingly for the undertaking in this book, Fleming turns to literary narrative for the "survival guidance" heralded in the title of his book. He adopts novelist W. G. Sebald's notion of "*revolutionary pessimism*" as propagated in Sebald's hybrid novel-memoir *The Rings of Saturn: An English Pilgrimage* (1998); according to Fleming, this notion turns the capitalist formula that "collective misery and individual optimism [especially for mega-rich CEOs] are just different sides of the same coin" on its head. Sebald and Fleming thus call for "generalized optimism and individual unease," the latter for those who fail to work toward far-sighted global "sociality" (Fleming, all quotes 39). The room for action contained in the word-choice "revolutionary" is encoded in all of the literary, cinematic, and civic interventions treated in our book, even when the content of the literary and filmic works presents structural migratory injustices. The "survivance"[13] strategies of the removed Native Americans and African slaves; the Africans and their families of contemporary times fleeing from war and environmental catastrophe, many in flimsy rafts; migrants moving underground in metropolises or adapting to EuroAmerican complexly transnational communities; Jewish women intellectuals, among many others, attempting to establish themselves elsewhere during the Third Reich; Turkish exiles seeking refuge in new media spaces; Hispanic and North African re-creation of fugitive belonging; understanding the othering and affiliations in films that influence global viewers—even more than the questionable trope of a welcoming host country, the "Mother of Exiles" is surely the aesthetic or engaged intervention itself.

NOTES

1. The influx of Asian migrants in the nineteenth century, culturally East to West, deserves mention, particularly the Chinese laborers, who have been the focus of recent research projects, notably the one at Stanford University, the results of which have been published in Chang and Fishkin, *The Chinese and the Iron Road* (2019). The first significant restriction by the US federal government on immigration was directed at Chinese migrants in 1882 (Miller 4; see also Künnemann and Mayer).

2. During the 1990s, a decade of intensive globalization and immigration to Europe, editors van Amersfoort and Doomernik developed an "intervention" approach to analyzing migration patterns, stressing regulatory policies for controlling immigration. "Intervention" in the sense of political measures to alleviate inequities is discussed in a publication by the University of Deusto in Bilbao/Spain in connection with the European network of excellence IMISCOE (International Migration, Social Integration and Cohesion in Europe) (Oñate et al., 2008). Our use of the term "intervention" connotes an active engagement with migration both civically and—on a meta-level—aesthetically.

3. "The New Colossus," Emma Lazarus, 1883:

Not like the brazen giant of Greek fame,
With conquering limbs astride from land to land;
Here at our sea-washed, sunset gates shall stand
A mighty woman with a torch, whose flame
Is the imprisoned lightning, and her name
MOTHER OF EXILES. From her beacon-hand
Glows world-wide welcome; her mild eyes command
The air-bridged harbor that twin cities frame.

"Keep, ancient lands, your storied pomp!" cries she
With silent lips. "Give me your tired, your poor,
Your huddled masses yearning to breathe free,
The wretched refuse of your teeming shore.
Send these, the homeless, tempest-tost to me,
I lift my lamp beside the golden door!"

4. The popularity of Larazus's poem as an encapsulation of the nation's supposed embrace of immigration and its willingness to serve as "an asylum for mankind," in Thomas Paine's memorable phrase (*Common Sense*, 1776), has been attacked in recent years by government officials who serve an administration bent on

undermining the poem's invitation to the "huddled masses," the "wretched refuse," and the "homeless" from the world's "teeming shore[s]" (see Fortin; Silow-Caroll; Simon).

5. For more historical context, see Berenson; Khan.

6. Olivier Suire Verley is compellingly characterized as an artist of "elsewhere" on a gallery website: https://www.addisonart.com/olivier-suire-verley/. Suire Verley's own website displays many further striking paintings of fugitive or nomadic groups on the move in landscapes of color and, paradoxically, watery aridity: http://www.suire-verley.com/galerie.aspx. We want to express our deep gratitude to him for granting us permission to use his marvelous "Voyageurs" as a cover image.

7. The German term in Charim's introduction is *Diasporisierung der Gesellschaft* (15). The experimental book edited by Charim and Borea is a collection of lectures at the Bruno Kreisky forum in Vienna, which included Homi K. Bhabha, Saskia Sassen, Gayatri Spivak, and Walter D. Mignolo. In contrast to this positive notion of diasporization, David Miller formulates a diasporic scenario considered to be fearful by many citizens of a receiving country: "As the size of the (unassimilated) diaspora grows, its pulling power increases, and the rate of immigration will tend to increase indefinitely if there are no effective controls" (3).

8. In addition to the Oxford "migration crises" handbook, among the many encyclopedic handbooks available two edited Routledge handbooks deserve special mention: Weinar et al., *The Routledge Handbook of the Politics of Migration in Europe* (2019); Triandafyllidou, *Routledge Handbook of Immigration and Refugee Studies* (2016). On related issues of immigration and democracy, see Song.

9. For a cross-section of diasporic family constellations, see Ducu, Nedelcu, and Telegdi-Csetri.

10. Three further promising publications in German were not yet available at the time of our manuscript preparation: Giessen and Rink; Oberprantacher; Kulaçatan and Behr.

11. Ballesteros's chapter "The European Family in the Face of Otherness: Family Metaphors and the Redemption of White Guilt" in *Immigration Cinema in the New Europe* (2015) offers insights into the role of film tropes in reflecting and breaking down borders between hosting and diasporic families.

12. Boucher and Gest create a taxonomy of national immigration models in *Crossroads: Comparative Immigration Regimes in a World of Demographic Change* (2018); of particular interest for economic matters is the way many traditional settler states have increasingly espoused a "market model" (1 and passim) that relies on temporary work permits and contingent residence, with little encouragement for naturalization.

13. "Survivance" is a felicitous term brought into circulation in Native American studies by Anishinaabe theorist and creative writer Gerald Vizenor; it can be understood as combining "survival" plus "endurance" and active "resistance" to hegemonic erasure, to colonialism and its legacy. "Survivance" characterizes Indigenous presence in actual and cultural life. The *locus classicus* is Vizenor's *Manifest Manners: Postindian Warriors of Survivance* (Wesleyan University Press, 1994; renamed *Manifest Manners: Narratives on Postindian Survivance* in the 1999 edition, University of Nebraska Press).

WORKS CITED

Abrego, Leisy J. *Sacrificing Families: Navigating Laws, Labor, and Love across Borders*. Stanford University Press, 2014.

Amersfoort, Hans van, and Jeroen Doomernik, editors. *International Migration: Processes and Interventions*. Het Spinhuis, 1998.

Ballesteros, Isolina. *Immigration Cinema in the New Europe*. Intellect, 2015.

Barber, Pauline Gardiner, and Winnie Lem, editors. *Migration, Temporality, and Capitalism: Entangled Mobilities across Global Spaces*. Palgrave Macmillan, 2018.

Berenson, Edward. *The Statue of Liberty: A Transatlantic Story*. Yale University Press, 2012.

Bhabha, Jacqueline. *Can We Solve the Migration Crisis?* Polity, 2018.

Boucher, Anna K., and Justin Gest. *Crossroads: Comparative Immigration Regimes in a World of Demographic Change*. Cambridge University Press, 2018.

Brockell, Gillian. "The Statue of Liberty Was Created to Celebrate Freed Slaves, Not Immigrants, Its New Museum Recounts." *Washington Post*, May 23, 2019, https://www.washingtonpost.com/history/2019/05/23/statue-liberty-was-created-celebrate-freed-slaves-not-immigrants/. Accessed Nov. 1, 2019.

Chang, Gordon H., and Shelley Fisher Fishkin. *The Chinese and the Iron Road: Building the Transcontinental Railroad*. Stanford University Press, 2019.

Charim, Isolde. "Einleitung." *Lebensmodell Diaspora: Über moderne Nomaden*, ed. Isolde Charim and Gertraud Auer Borea, transcript, pp. 11–16, 2012.

De Shalit, Avner. *Cities and Immigration: Political and Moral Dilemmas in the New Era of Migration*. Oxford University Press, 2018.

Ducu, Viorela, Mihaela Nedelcu, and Aron Telegdi-Csetri, editors. *Childhood and Parenting in Transnational Settings*. Palgrave Macmillan, 2018.

Ferguson, James Gordon. *Global Shadows: Africa in the Neoliberal World Order*. Duke University Press, 2006.

Fleming, Peter. *The Worst Is Yet to Come: A Post-Capitalist Survival Guide*. Repeater, 2019.

Fortin, Jacey. "'Huddled Masses' in Statue of Liberty Poem Are European, Trump Official Says." *New York Times*, Aug. 14, 2019, https://www.nytimes.com/2019/08/14/us/cuccinelli-statue-liberty-poem.html. Accessed Nov. 15, 2019.

Georgi, Fabian. *Managing Migration? Eine kritische Geschichte der Internationalen Organisation für Migration (IOM)*. Bertz + Fischer, 2019.

Giessen, Hans W., and Christian Rink. *Migration, Diversität und kulturelle Identitäten: Sozial- und kulturwissenschaftliche Perspektiven*. Metzler, forthcoming 2020.

Karim, Karim H., and Ahmed Al-Rawi, editors. *Diaspora and Media in Europe: Migration, Identity, and Integration*. Palgrave Macmillan, 2018.

Kaushal, Neeraj. *Blaming Immigrants: Nationalism and the Economics of Global Movement*. Columbia University Press, 2019.

Khan, Yasmin Sabina. *Enlightening the World: The Creation of the Statue of Liberty*. Cornell University Press, 2010.

Kulaçatan, Meltem, and Harry Harun Behr, editors. *Migration, Religion, Gender und Bildung: Beiträge zu einem erweiterten Verständnis von Intersektionalität*. transcript, forthcoming 2020.

Künnemann, Vanessa, and Ruth Mayer, editors. *Trans-Pacific Interactions: The United States and China, 1880–1950*. Palgrave Macmillan, 2009.

Löffler, Berthold. *Flucht nach Deutschland: Wie Migration Politik und Gesellschaft verändert*. Kohlhammer, forthcoming 2020.

Menjívar, Cecilia, Marie Ruiz, and Immanuel Ness, editors. *The Oxford Handbook of Migration Crises*. Oxford University Press, 2019.

Miller, David. *Strangers in Our Midst: The Political Philosophy of Immigration*. Harvard University Press, 2016.

Oberprantacher, Andreas. *"Illegale": Ein Grenzphänomen zwischen Flucht und Migration*. transcript, forthcoming 2020.

Oñate, Concepción Maiztegui, and Rosa Santibáñez Gruber, editors. *Immigration: Views and Reflections—Histories, Identities and Keys of Social Intervention*. University of Deusto, 2008.

Sager, Alex. *Toward a Cosmopolitan Ethics of Mobility: The Migrant's-Eye View of the World*. Palgrave Macmillan, 2018.

Silow-Carroll, Andrew. "Your Huddled What? White House Aide Stephen Miller Doesn't Think the Statue of Liberty Has Much to Do with Immigration." *Jewish Telegraphic Agency*, Aug. 2, 2017, https://www.jta.org/2017/08/02/culture/your-h uddled-what-white-house-aide-stephen-miller-doesnt-think-the-statue-of-liberty-h as-much-to-do-with-immigration. Accessed Nov. 15, 2019.

Simon, Ed. "What Stephen Miller Got Wrong about Emma Lazarus." *History News Network*, Aug. 3, 2017, https://historynewsnetwork.org/article/166604. Accessed Nov. 15, 2019.

Song, Sarah. *Immigration and Democracy*. Oxford University Press, 2019.

Staudt, Kathleen. *Border Politics in a Global Era: Comparative Perspectives*. Rowman & Littlefield, 2018.

Triandafyllidou, Anna, editor. *Routledge Handbook of Immigration and Refugee Studies*. Routledge, 2016.

Vlase, Ionela, and Bogdan Voicu, editors. *Gender, Family, and Adaptation of Migrants in Europe: A Life Course Perspective*. Palgrave Macmillan, 2018.

Weinar, Agnieszka, Saskia Bonjour, and Lyubov Zhyznomirska, editors. *The Routledge Handbook of the Politics of Migration in Europe*. Routledge, 2019.

Part I

LITERARY INTERVENTIONS

Chapter 1

Recuperating the Black Family in Graphic Narrative

Tom Feelings's **The Middle Passage** *and Kyle Baker's* **Nat Turner**

Daniel Stein

Attempts to memorialize the Middle Passage, the western route of the transatlantic trade that brought millions of Africans into a life of slavery on the American continent and caused the deaths of millions more on the voyage, appear sporadically throughout African American literature. Works like Robert Hayden's "Middle Passage" (1945), Amiri Baraka's *Slave Ship: A Historical Pageant* (1967), Charles Johnson's *Middle Passage* (1990), Kwame Dawes's "Requiem" (1996), James A. Emanuel's "Middle Passage Blues" (1999), and Lucille Clifton's "slaveships" (2000) strain to "render speakable what was formerly unspoken," as Toni Morrison observed in her famous Tanner lecture, delivered at the University of Michigan in 1988 ("Unspeakable" 132). In doing so, they seek to "transfigure the complexity and wealth of Afro-American culture into a language worthy of the culture" ("Unspeakable" 150). Yet as the doubly negated neologism in the title of Morrison's lecture—"Unspeakable Things Unspoken"—indicates, these authors confront the inevitable conundrum of representing a historical event whose magnitude calls into question the very capacity of literature to express the sense of loss that stands at the beginning of the African presence in the New World.[1]

A particularly painful and devastating part of this loss was the eradication of black families. Africans forced onto the slave ships and discharged to the shores of the Americas after a horrendous journey were reduced to the status of commodities. They could be sold at their owners' will, frequently and purposely without regard for family relations or tribal affiliations, and the women were often used as "breeders" to increase their owners' human property through forced reproduction. The traumatic effects of this epochal dehumanization, through which Africans became "black" (and thus denigrated as being racially inferior) and Europeans and Americans became "white" (and thus elevated to a status of racial superiority), continued long after slavery, as Morrison's novel *Beloved* (1987) illustrates.[2] Morrison's narrative centers on the ex-slave Sethe, a woman haunted by the ghostly return of her dead baby daughter, whom she had killed to save her from (re-)enslavement. Sethe wants to achieve a kind of "family relationship" (31) in the postbellum era that her experience as a slave, when she was raped and degraded by her owner's sons, her husband Halle going mad as he was watching the abuse, could never fully afford her. "Mother. Father. Didn't remember the one. Never saw the other" (258), Sethe's eventual lover and surrogate father to her children, Paul D., recalls about his life as a slave; "[t]he last of her children . . . she barely glanced at when he was born because it wasn't worth the trouble to try to learn features you would never see change into adulthood anyway" (163), Baby Suggs remembers. Struggling to address the historical magnitude of such lasting attacks on black families, writers like Morrison, Hayden, Baraka, Dawes, Emanuel, Clifton, and others creatively imagine the pain and anguish of the murdered, enslaved, and oppressed. They bear literary witness to the onslaught on the lives and minds of black folk while acknowledging that there is no escape from the pitfalls of representing the unspeakable: of turning historical and literary "absences [into] vital presences" and "implying a full descriptive apparatus (identity) to a presence-that-is-assumed-not-to-exist" (Morrison, "Unspeakable" 139, 145).

The pitfalls of representation might even be greater in the medium of graphic narrative, where stories unfold in sequences of panels and through the combination of images and words, which taxes them with complex histories of visual and verbal expression. Historically, graphic narratives, from caricatures and cartoons to comic strips and comic books, were largely complicit with the broader visual culture's racist ridicule and misrepresentation of black lives and culture (see Neary; Strömberg). Yet if African American literature can trace its roots to the slave narratives of the eighteenth and nineteenth centuries, the "coloring of America" in graphic narrative that Derek Parker Royal diagnosed in 2007 is a much more recent phenomenon. Given the still common association of graphic narration ("comics") with the funny and the hilarious, it is not surprising that the horrors of the Middle Passage rarely surface in this medium. While black history has been gaining traction as a subject matter since the 1990s—notably Ho Che Anderson's *King* (1993), Derek McCulloch and Shepherd Hendrix's *Stagger Lee* (2006), John Lewis, Andrew Aydin, and Nate Powell's *March* (2013, 2015, 2016), Damian Duffy and John Jennings's *Kindred* (2017), and Joel Christian Gill's *Strange Fruit: Uncelebrated Narratives from Black History* (2014, 2018)—only two graphic narratives have addressed the Middle Passage in detail: Tom Feelings's *The*

Middle Passage: White Ships/Black Cargo (1995), described as a "visual nar-rative" or series of "narrative paintings" in its peritexts, and Kyle Baker's *Nat Turner* (2008), advertised on the cover of the Abrams edition as a "graphic novel" about the slave rebellion that shook Southampton County, Virginia, in 1831. Both works picture the Middle Passage by completely (Feelings) or largely (Baker) excluding language and color from their revisionary images of black history. Rather than simply "drawing the unspeakable," as Consuela Francis maintained in her eponymous essay, they answer Morrison's call to unspeak unspeakable things by *undrawing* the unspeakable. They do so by graphically recuperating images of the black family and kinship affiliations as nodes in the African diaspora, veering back and forth between historical veri-similitude and visual hyperbole to negotiate legacies of racial representation.

Feelings and Baker face challenges peculiar to their chosen mode of visual expression. These challenges include the need to avoid the visual codes that continue to shape negative notions of racial difference while simultaneously acknowledging the pervasive politics of graphic representation.[3] They meet this challenge by emphasizing the violent actions of the slave traders and slaveholders as well as the counterviolence of the enslaved. Baker's account of Turner's rebellion, which left fifty-five slaveholders and their families dead and ended with Turner's public execution (which Baker covers at length), gloats in guts-and-gore scenarios of righteous black retaliation, but it also portrays the violence of the slaveholders that Thomas Ruffin Gray's *Confes-sions of Nat Turner* (1831), the white Southern lawyer's account of Turner's life and the rebellion composed on the basis of interviews conducted shortly before Turner's execution, had excised from his account of the events.[4] Feel-ings's tableaus depict the slaves variously as a dehumanized mass of bodies, both dead and alive, or as representative but unnamed black characters. Yet both creators contrast this violence with more harmonious, and occasionally sentimental, scenes of black family life, seeking to recreate a sense of black futurity and wholesomeness that survived slavery and continues into present imaginations of black life and culture.[5]

Considering Lisa Woolfork's work on Octavia Butler's *Kindred* (1979) and Charles Johnson's *Oxherding Tale* (1982), Michael A. Chaney discerns a difference between Eurocentric notions of traumatic memory as allusive and discursive and an African American sense of "a different kind of trauma, one tied to racial community" ("Slave" 280). Feelings's foreword to *The Middle Passage* underscores this difference by imagining a "race memory" that is shared, "consciously or unconsciously," by members of the African diaspora. Directing his remarks to a predominantly black readership, Feelings connects "those shackles that physically bound us together against our wills" in the past with the emergence of "spiritual links that willingly bind us together now and into the future." He proposes turning the Middle Passage into "a positive connecting line to all of us living inside or outside the continent of Africa." However we gauge this racially exclusive understanding of transhistorical diasporic affiliation, Feelings undoubtedly negotiates the discrepancy between the suffering of the individuals who survived the journey and the faceless and nameless mass of corpses on the bottom of the Atlantic Ocean. His foreword and his illustrations commemorate those who were "locked in the belly of each of these [slave] ships, chained together like animals throughout the long voyage from Africa toward unknown destinations, millions dying from the awful conditions in the bowels of the filthy slave galleys."[6]

The Middle Passage details a process of "unmaking" (Chaney, "Slave" 286) leading to a condition Hortense Spillers calls the "sameness of anonymous portrayal that adheres tenaciously across the division of gender" and inscribes "anonymity/anomie in various public documents of European-American mal(e)venture" (73). Feelings's and Baker's narratives foreground this unmaking by "grappl[ing] with transnational racial discourses that have historically marked and muted blackness as other" (Whitted 80). They interrogate this otherness by depicting the black body as a sign of spectacular erasure (Chaney, "Drawing" 176), filling page after page (in Feelings's case) with near-naked or naked black bodies as they are chained and beaten, lashed and whipped, tortured and terrorized, mutilated and killed by the pale, ghostlike whites who command control on the slave ship. By connecting "spectacle and spectatorship" (Whitted 80), both authors force moments of recognition by "trigger[ing] the readers' awareness of their own subject positions as observers" (81) and by "refus[ing them] the passivity of the spectator" (Chaney, "Slave" 284).

Early on, *The Middle Passage* displays a multilayered image of a white slave catcher shooting an African villager from behind (figure 1.1).[7] Due to the composition of the image, the shooter points his rifle not only at the villager, but also at the reader, who is positioned in the crosshairs and thus compelled to consider his or her own role in, and historical responsibility for, the transatlantic slave trade. This consideration hinges on the reader's racial affiliation, as readers identifying as "white" might be compelled to acknowledge their privileged racial position as descendants of the invaders, while readers identifying as "black" might imagine themselves in the role of the black villager, recognizing centuries of dispossession and murder as part of the historical conditions that still impact race relations across the globe.[8] I do not want to suggest an essentialist understanding of racial affiliation here, but I believe that this image invites us to think about our personal relation to the atrocities of Western imperialism and colonialism. The fact that the pained face of the black victim is placed at the lower left-hand corner of the image heightens this effect. It is as if he is about to stumble into our hands, fatally wounded by the bullet that may just as well have killed us. His eyes

Figure 1.1   A white slave catcher shooting an African villager from behind. From *The Middle Passage* by Tom Feelings. "Illustrations" from THE MIDDLE PASSAGE: WHITE SHIPS/BLACK CARGO; LIMITED EDITION by Tom Feelings, copyright © 1995 by Tom Feelings. Used by permission of Dial Books for Young Readers, an imprint of Penguin Young Readers Group, a division of Penguin Random House LLC. All rights reserved.

are closed and his mouth is agape in agony, preventing any overly romantic identification. The man's death is simultaneously interpersonal, since he is stumbling toward us, and anonymous, as he has no other discernable identity beyond being a victim of the slave trade.

The tension between mass anonymity and individual pain is emblematized by the diverging foci of Feelings's and Baker's narratives. Feelings emphasizes the scope of the Middle Passage and the dehumanization of slaves and enslavers alike through the title of his work. The main part, *The Middle Passage*, names the event, while the subtitle, *White Ships/Black Cargo*, evokes the inhumanity of the slave trade by reducing the slaves to the status of cargo and equating the merchants and helpers with the vessels of their trade. Baker, by contrast, centers his narrative on the slave rebel Nat Turner. He announces his concentration on the life and motivations of this historical figure through the title of his narrative—*Nat Turner*—whose brevity is telling because it refuses to evoke the moral framework imposed on Turner's experiences in Gray's *Confessions of Nat Turner*. Gray's title had marked the narrative as a religiously grounded as-told-to confession. Not only did Gray judge Turner according to the legal codes of the white antebellum South (a judgment Baker does not replicate). He also characterized the rebellion as a fight between "these barbarous villains" and his "fellow citizens" (258) and contrasted the

"fearful tragedy" and the "bravery" of one of the slaveholders with the "diabolical actors," "band of savages," and "remorseless murderers" involved in
"this dreadful conspiracy" (245, 263, 246, 245). He further contained Turner's life story within the classical Western mode of written autobiography,
which is at odds with the visuality of Baker's graphic narrative.

Feelings and Baker counter the attempted elimination of black communities through the Middle Passage and US chattel slavery by focusing
substantial parts of their stories on families. Nineteenth-century abolitionists
like Harriet Beecher Stowe had already subjected their readers to a process
of "sentimental wounding" (Marianne Noble's term) by depicting suffering
black slave families in novels like *Uncle Tom's Cabin* (1851/52). Moreover,
in her rememorization of Stowe's work in *Beloved*, Morrison sought to
overcome the historical erasure of black families that had troubled (popular)
representations of US history since Reconstruction (see Stein). New, however, are the medium-specific mechanisms through which Feelings and Baker
present the black family in a less sentimental, as well as less postmodernist,
mode that foregrounds the powers of visual rendition and absents (Feelings)
or separates (Baker) historically laden language from the graphic enunciation
of black counterhistory.

KYLE BAKER, *NAT TURNER*

Baker's *Nat Turner* was published about a decade after *The Middle Passage*,
and it borrowed from Feelings the conceit that the visual depiction of the
Middle Passage and the life in slavery that followed the voyage would largely
be devoid of language. Feelings had explained in his foreword:

> I should try to tell this story with as few words as possible, if any. Callous
> indifference or outright brutal characterizations of Africans are embedded in
> the language of the Western World. It is a language so infused with direct and
> indirect racism that it would be difficult, if not impossible, using this language
> in my book, to project anything black as positive.

We can read Feelings's shift from language to vision as a response to the
Enlightenment's privileging of writing over orality that Henry Louis Gates,
Jr., criticized in *The Signifying Monkey: A Theory of African-American Literary Criticism* (1988), even though the case could be made that Western visual
culture is equally infused with direct and indirect forms of racism. Baker's
Nat Turner foregrounds this tension by evoking the "Sambo" stereotype
of nineteenth-century blackface minstrelsy, depicting the characters who
betray Turner and his followers by informing the slaveholders of the looming

rebellion with bulging eyes, sheepish grins, and exaggerated gestures (Baker 130, 132, 136).[9] In addition, he presents one of these followers, Will, as "a hulking golem, a visual crystallization of the Big, Black Buck figure used to justify slavery" (Fisher 265), thus creating a graphic embodiment of Gray's pro-slavery semantics (murderers, savages, monsters). Yet he also includes a scene in which young Nat is reading the Bible and, when caught in the act by an overseer, flips the book upside down with an illiterate grin, utilizing the Sambo mask as a performative strategy through which the slave can resist the enslaver.

Baker rarely incorporates sound words and speech bubbles into the images, avoiding an overly comic-like feel of his "primarily imagistic" (Neary 171) narrative. He segregates selections of Gray's *Confessions of Nat Turner* outside of the panel frame. Qiana Whitted sees "a defiance of (black) pictures in a society dominated by the objectification of (white) words" (81), which is foregrounded in *Nat Turner* through the division of the narrative into Baker's "black" images and Gray's "white" words, the latter of which are not allowed to intrude upon the visual account. This becomes apparent in the contrast between the intimacy of the horrified look on Turner's mother's face as she is threatened with a razor by a slave trader and the detached account of this practice ("neatly shaved") from Captain Theodore Canot's memoir *Twenty Years of an African Slaver* (1854) cited below the image (Baker 36; cf. Bruno 936; J. Gray 188; Singer 200).

Baker takes the enigmatic character of Nat Turner as the starting point for his graphic revision of American history. Wondering in his preface to the book edition, "Who was this man who was important enough to be mentioned in *all* the history books, yet is never spoken about at length?" he reimagines his protagonist as a husband and father whose early childhood memories include his mother's report of an infanticide on board the slave ship that brought her to America.[10] In Baker's account, Turner's use of violence against the slaveholders is motivated by the separation of his family at a Southern slave auction. By devoting a quarter of his narrative to his mother's life in Africa and her voyage to America, he creates a teleological plot that moves from the African "home" to Turner's childhood "education" in the antebellum South and then toward "freedom" (the slave rebellion) and "triumph" (the lynching that turns him into a Christ-like figure of black rebellion, a counterimage to Stowe's Uncle Tom). This plot provides the backstory— and thus a rationale—for Turner's messianic violence.[11] Jonathan Gray calls the "home" section "early speculative pages [that] establish a genealogical continuity between events in Africa and those in the Americas that both the act of enslavement and the archive of slavery attempted to eradicate" (187). Moreover, proposing an "imaginative expansion" of the archive by depicting events that "have no counterpoint in Gray's text, . . . the story [these images] tell is not dependent on literacy for its legibility" (Neary 167). Showing Turner's mother's African origins emphasizes the diasporic affiliation of the slaves with their homelands, and it insinuates that America can never fully be home to the enslaved (cf. 187). While Turner's deeds appear as the efforts of a remarkable individual, they are presented as the direct result of the subjugation of black families and their lives as cargo below deck and as chattel on Southern plantations (cf. Francis 114).

The narrative begins with the disruption of life in an African village by black invaders intent on enslaving the villagers. Baker depicts the raid as an attack on the black family by complicit Africans. We see mothers grabbing their children to protect them from the aggressors, and we later witness Turner's future mother's attempted leap to death to evade capture in a sequence that rewrites David W. Griffith's Klan-inspired depiction of Flora's suicide in *Birth of a Nation* (1915) from an African American perspective.[12] Turner's mother emerges as a fierce fighter who does everything to resist the slave catchers but is ultimately overpowered. This places Turner, the rebel slave, in a line of black resistance and counterviolence and makes him a representative rather than aberrational figure. On a meta-level, banning written language from the "home" segment except for a few sound words "has the effect of linking the violence of colonial intrusion with the violence of white narrative control" (Neary 167), which Baker's narrative seeks to escape by visualizing a near-Edenic, precolonial life devoid of "white" discourse.

Significantly, the new life that emerges from the hold of the slave ship is birthed by a mother who dies after the delivery. The baby is picked up by two other slaves, one of whom cradles its head to protect it from harm and averts its eyes from the surrounding physical abuse. Chaney reads these slaves as "the equivalent of the nuclear African family during the Middle Passage" and finds "these visual cues of family" to be "an odd imposition . . . onto otherwise ungendered figures" ("Slave" 286). Recalling Spillers's point about the anonymity/anomie of the black subject, he suggests that "sameness is rendered, but it is also partly undone by the illustration" (286), as the scene "ascribes a normative heterosexual coupling to figures who may just as easily be read as same sex strangers" (286). We can read this sequence as a response to the destruction of the black family, since the absent family is replaced by a makeshift parental unit, albeit a traditionally gendered one, that chooses infanticide as a moral obligation. Upon recognizing the horrors that lie ahead, the surrogate father tries to throw the baby overboard and into the gaping mouth of a shark. Seeking to protect their cargo, a crewmember clasps the baby by the hand, stopping its fall toward death only to release it once the new father bites him in the arm. Baker's image arrests the baby's fall in mid-air, fixing its tiny body in a position that allegorizes the slave's precarious status as an eternally death-bound subject.[13]

Infanticide is a powerful topos in Baker's narrative. It marks the forestall-ing of a black futurity by ending the possibility of new black families.[14] Yet it also delivers the critical impetus for black rebellion. The scene of the baby thrown to the sharks has a discursive and visual afterlife, as it reappears two pages later in a speech balloon through which young Nat Turner relates the event to fellow slave children (figure 1.2). This visually mediated, cross-generational oral historiography connects the Middle Passage with American slavery and extends the story of the makeshift family's mercy killing into a mechanism for kinship affiliation and community-building as young Nat begins to rally his enslaved brethren in preparation for his role as a self-declared prophet. When Henry and Will, two members of Turner's posse, later kill the baby of Mr. and Mrs. Francis, the slave owners who are the first victims of the rebellion, we are spared the depiction of the final blow. But the killing emerges as the consequence of Turner's recollection of his own children being sold at the slave auction; images of the auction appear as inserts next to Turner's face, reiterating the separation of Turner's family as the event that motivates the rebellion. The baby's death is foreshadowed through its visual appearance in another speech balloon when one of Turner's accomplices realizes that they have forgotten to kill the child.

Baker's narrative is full of these visual echoes; an earlier scene in which Will grins at his owner's toddler culminates in the depiction of the boy's beheading through Will's merciless axe. Thus, Baker makes it difficult for his readers to root for the rebels, even though his depiction counters the many references in the *Confessions* to the poor families eradicated by Turner and his followers.[15] As Francis suggests, Baker offers "no euphemisms" and "forces the reader to look directly at what it would mean, what it would look like, to kill 55 men, women, and children" (134). In fact, Baker (re-)inserts the "retributive justice" (293) largely absent from the slave narrative, which can imagine such justice only from the perspective of Southampton's white population, as Gray's final comments on Turner's confession indicate, into the medium of graphic narrative. Here, the slave's exertion of retributive jus-tice, so common in superhero comics, is met with the extralegal violence of lynching as a means of protecting antebellum power relations.

Baker's emphasis on Turner as a family man and the narrative's return to scenes of child-killing revise Gray's *Confessions of Nat Turner*, which withholds the fact that Turner is married and has children.[16] Baker devotes ten pages to young Nat's love of his father and the boy's frantic attempt to save him from corporeal punishment. In the passage that follows the auction scene, he contrasts an image of the happy slave master and mistress as they tuck one of their children into bed and embrace their baby child, with a stick drawing on the floor of Turner's cabin (figure 1.3). This drawing marks the absence of his children and complicates Gray's neat distinction between the

**FROM
THE CONFESSIONS
OF NAT TURNER**

"It is here necessary to relate this circumstance—trifling as it may seem, it was the commencement of that belief which has grown with time, and even now, sir, in this dungeon, helpless and forsaken as I am, I cannot divest myself of it. Being at play with other children, when three or four years old, I was telling them something which my mother, overhearing, said it had happened before I was born—I stuck to my story, however, and related some things which went, in her opinion, to confirm it—others being called on were greatly astonished, knowing that these things had happened, and caused them to say in my hearing, I surely would be a prophet, as the Lord had shown me things that had happened before my birth."

Figure 1.2 Young Nat Turner relates an incident from the Middle Passage. From *Nat Turner* by Kyle Baker. Copyright © Kyle Baker 2008. Use by permission of Harry N. Abrams, Inc., New York. All rights reserved.

Figure 1.3 The white slaveowner family and the disruption of the black slave family.
From *Nat Turner* by Kyle Baker. Copyright © Kyle Baker 2008. Use by permission of Harry N. Abrams, Inc., New York. All rights reserved.

slaves as "diabolical actors" and the brave slaveholder and "his lovely and amiable wife" (245, 263). While the excessive violence of Baker's narrative can force readers out of their comfort zone, for instance by making them witness the cruel punishment of a slave who is whipped, has salt rubbed into his wounds, and gets his hands chopped off, these quieter moments utilize the affective wounding power of sentimental depiction. Baker achieves many of these effects through the specificities of graphic narrative, structuring his images and the passages he cites from Gray's *Confessions* into an "*ironic relationship*" (Francis 120) that contrasts an emotionless and detached written discourse with confrontational and disturbing images (cf. 114). We can connect the "dichotomy" and "disconnect" between images and words that Tim Bruno finds in *Nat Turner* (cf. 933, 934) with what Marc Singer labels the "friction between Baker's narrative and his source material" (200). Singer usefully notes that Baker either visualizes events that do not occur in Gray's *Confessions* (and are often also not documented anywhere else) and thereby creatively intervenes in the representation of Turner as figure of the (popular) historical imagination, or illustrates scenes from the *Confessions* in order "to rationalize his own contributions to the story" (201), rather than flat-out contradicting Gray's version of the story (203–4).

What's more, we can read the absence of color as a gesture toward the historicity of the material and the reduction of the world of slavery into a black, white, and gray life devoid of happiness. A more thorough analysis of the narrative, however, would have to address its status as a "mixed media adaptation" (Whitted 92) that remediates images from the historical archive and defamiliarizes them through Baker's "stylistic promiscuity" (Bruno 931). In the preface to the Abrams edition, Baker provocatively names "compelling graphics," "action and suspense," and "superhuman abilities" as his ingredients, and some critics have noted the visual reverberations between Baker's images and superhero comics, such as when character drawings recall Marvel's Incredible Hulk or when the graphic design evokes Frank Miller's silhouette style (figure 1.4).[17] Singer is especially critical of what he identifies as Baker's mixture of "fantasy, mythology, and pop-cultural cliché" (199) with "the paratextual conventions of historiography" (211), such as endnotes, photographic reproductions, and bibliographical references. This mixture, Singer suggests, cannot cover the "lapses, shortcuts, creative distortions, and outright errors" that turn the narrative into "a shoddy simulacrum of the past" (218), a form of "historical fiction of a particularly dishonest kind, one that freely invents and reshapes history while declaring its accuracy and objectivity" (216).[18]

Yet if Baker's goal is to illustrate the fallibility of the written (white) archive and insist on a black re-visioning, the bifurcation of his images and Gray's narrative makes sense both on formal and ideological levels. Jonathan Gray suggests that Baker "seeks to broaden the canon(s) in which it participates" (185), while Chaney argues that *Nat Turner* "bridge[s] chasms of history and memory, fact and inference" ("Slave" 279). The narrative does so, in part, by evoking centuries of writing about the slaves' attainment of literacy as a step toward freedom by opening with an image of a black reader holding a white book in his or her hands, completely enveloped in darkness. Baker ends the narrative with a young slave's retreating with Gray's *Confessions* into another completely blackened space—which can now be viewed as an incubator in which Turner's rebellion, though officially terminated through the lynching depicted a few pages earlier, may grow into new acts of resistance (cf. Neary 171).

TOM FEELINGS, *THE MIDDLE PASSAGE:*
WHITE SHIPS/BLACK CARGO

The Middle Passage shares a number of motifs as well as the focus on the black family with Baker's narrative. Like *Nat Turner*, the story begins with slave hunters raiding an African village. The hunters indiscriminately capture

Figure 1.4 Visual allusion to Frank Miller's silhouette style. From *Nat Turner* by Kyle Baker. Copyright © Kyle Baker 2008. Use by permission of Harry N. Abrams, Inc., New York. All rights reserved.

women, men, and children, but the illustrations repeatedly portray mothers holding babies and young children as victims of the raid. One illustration shows a man being shot in the back as he is running away from the attackers, leaving behind his wife and baby child.[19] The two double-page illustrations that follow present the villagers as they are driven by white slave hunters and their black helpers toward their ultimate destiny: the seashore, the slave ship, and, should they survive the ordeal, a life in American slavery. Feelings's depiction does not let us lose sight of the fact that the slave trade destroyed African families, whose members are tied up and prepared for the transatlantic journey. While the mother with the infant constitutes a recurring trope, two naked boys behind bars with chains around their necks, one of them wearing a foot shackle, foreground slavery's demand for black bodies regardless of their gender.

Slavery's attack on the black family—and on the future of black communities—is embodied by an iconic image of a family that presents the half-naked chained mother leaning forward and holding her head in pain, the father's disembodied face raised upwards with the eyes closed in resignation, and a baby hovering over his head between two spears pointed at its head and feet (figure 1.5). In the background, we see another chain of slaves and the notorious slave catchers, as well as, on another representational layer, the oversized heads of two Africans looking downward at the scene. This illustration collapses centuries of abuse into a transhistorical emblem that speaks to the past, present, and

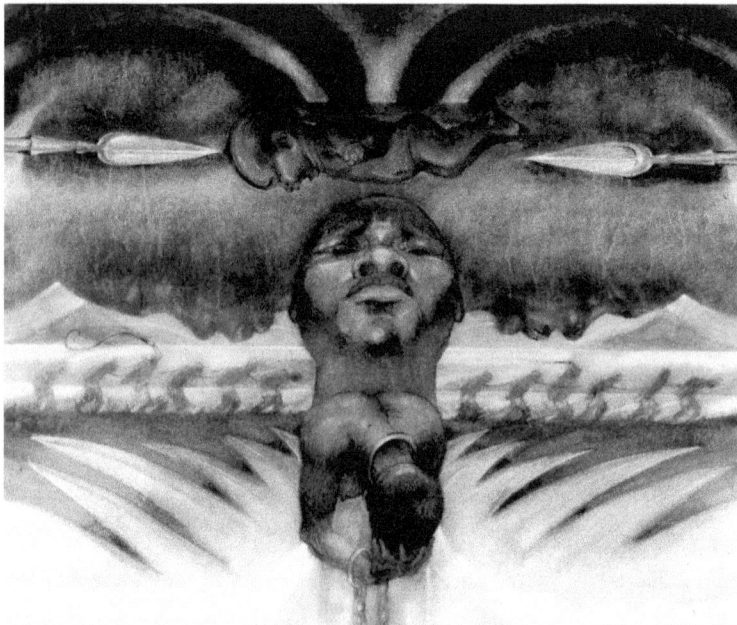

Figure 1.5   A transhistorical emblem of the black family in times of transatlantic slavery. From *The Middle Passage* by Tom Feelings. "Illustrations" from THE MIDDLE PASSAGE: WHITE SHIPS/BLACK CARGO; LIMITED EDITION by Tom Feelings, copyright © 1995 by Tom Feelings. Used by permission of Dial Books for Young Readers, an imprint of Penguin Young Readers Group, a division of Penguin Random House LLC. All rights reserved.

future of black suffering. Feelings chooses this type of condensed representation repeatedly, for instance when he shows a mother holding her infant child, her hands in chains and her torso superimposed with a drawing of the hold of a slave ship. This drawing is positioned between two images of an analogous visual structure: two faces screaming in pain as they carry the white slave ship forward, and a black figure in chains rushing through the sea covered by a historical drawing of a tight-packing slave ship. The two faces in the first image depict a man and a woman as a *pars pro toto* for the enslaved Africans, whose offspring, as shown in the second image, will either die or live a life of subjugation. The hold of the ship separates the baby from its mother's breasts and thus from the nourishment and sustenance necessary for physical and spiritual survival (figure 1.6). The third image subsumes the symbolic African family into the anonymous mass of Africans in the hold of the slave ship, connecting the practice of tight packing and the resulting misery (depicted very explicitly

Figure 1.6   The struggle for physical and spiritual survival. From *The Middle Passage* by Tom Feelings. "Illustrations" from THE MIDDLE PASSAGE: WHITE SHIPS/BLACK CARGO; LIMITED EDITION by Tom Feelings, copyright © 1995 by Tom Feelings. Used by permission of Dial Books for Young Readers, an imprint of Penguin Young Readers Group, a division of Penguin Random House LLC. All rights reserved.

throughout the book) with the loss of African identities on the voyage. That the illustration of the hold remediates an eighteenth-century sketch ("Stowage of the British Slave Ship 'Brooks' Under the Regulated Slave Trade Act of 1788") underscores Feelings's grappling with the archives of slavery that fail to convey the atrocities unleashed on generations of Africans and African Americans.[20] While we do not witness infanticide, we encounter scenes of suicide when some of the enslaved jump overboard, perishing amidst sharks and joining other corpses on the bottom of the Atlantic.[21]

Yet despite the barrage of horrifying images with which Feelings saddles his readers, not all is hopeless, not all is lost. Into a dark scene of human degradation and agony, he places a naked pregnant woman who seems oblivious to the carnage around her, placing her hand over her belly and feeling the new life growing inside her. This woman reappears as an inset image in the penultimate illustration of the narrative, which shows the slaves' arrival in America and the sale of the new black family to their prospective owners in the background. The pregnant woman thus memorializes the Middle Passage and instills in the narrative a sense of futurity despite slavery's erasure of black genealogies. "[I]nvisible things are not necessarily 'not-there,'" Morrison notes; "a void may be empty but not be a vacuum" ("Unspeakable" 136). The Middle Passage is not "a clean break between past and present, but a spatial continuum between Africa and the Americas, the ship's deck and the hold, the Great House and the slave quarters" (Diedrich, Gates, and Pedersen 8). Feelings evokes this continuum when he evokes the power of the slave family, a largely invisible and essentially unstable institution within the system of chattel slavery, in an image that turns historical absence into presence, the vacuum of the Middle Passage into a "spatial and temporal continuum" (Diedrich, Gates, and Pedersen 8), by featuring the survivors or descendants of the journey as they look toward the future with resilience and determination.

CONCLUDING THOUGHTS

The Middle Passage and the story of "the controversial, contested black icon" in *Nat Turner* each "represent . . . a site in which the very meaning of US blackness becomes contested and defined" (Bruno 925). Feelings's and Baker's "historiographic pedagogy" (Chaney, "Slave" 280) exposes the inability of the historical archive to preserve traces of black family life. The creators therefore transform this archive into stories of resilience and resistance, but they also return to a heteronormative notion of the family as the backbone of African American culture and life in the diaspora. If their narratives amend the historical record and insert new interpretive possibilities into the popular "image bank" (Chaney, "Drawing" 188) of transatlantic diasporic blackness, each of them develops a "fantasy that allows for the recuperation of a usable history of slavery for contemporary African Americans" (Chaney, "Slave" 283). This is not to say that they propose a "graphic black nationalism" (Peterson's phrase) but that they view "the historical record . . . as dynamic, dialogic units of communication available for recombination and interpretation" (Chaney, "Drawing" 199). They indeed "remember and perform insurrection" (Chaney, "Slave" 280), "baring and bearing" the burdens of history (Chaney, "Drawing" 187), creating a bulwark against the historical amnesia and denial that dominate contemporary American discourse. If Chaney is right to suggest that Baker provides us with "redemptive, reader-centered exercises of identification" ("Slave" 286) and that graphic narratives about black history revise "national iconography that requires from us small acts of recognition, decipherment, and transformation" ("Drawing" 198), then there is little doubt that these works urge us to consider our own entanglement in the conditions of the contemporary world, its history, and its future.

This leaves us with the question of how these narratives undraw the unspeakable. Referencing Naomi Mandel's *Against the Unspeakable: Complicity, the Holocaust, and Slavery in America* (2006), Singer proposes that "[t]he unspeakable doesn't simply describe acts of atrocity; it makes claims on how such atrocities should be represented while declaring the limits of representability itself" (229–30). Moving from Morrison's notion of unspeakability as a "prescribed absence" of African Americans from US history ("Unspeakable" 139) to an understanding of it as "a capacity to deny comprehension and to compel silence not in the name of avoiding the unspoken but, ostensibly, of respecting it" (Singer 230), Singer discerns a "willed deference" (233) to historical trauma according to which, in Jonathan Gray's words, "the magnitude of these atrocities can never truly be apprehended or appreciated—even as [artists] plumb these sites of trauma for narrative inspiration" (193). As a peculiar form of storytelling dependent on visually foregrounding the "crafting of histories and historiographies" (Chute, *Disaster* 2) through drawn, framed, and sequenced images whose "self-reflexive awareness of apparatus—drawing" (18) is on constant display, graphic narratives diverge from this deference, "assert[ing] the value of presence, however complex and contingent" (Chute, *Graphic* 2). In other words, narratives like *Middle Passage* and *Nat Turner* accept "the risk of representation" (Chute, *Disaster* 5) by "refus[ing] to follow the protocols of unspeakability, rendering trauma visible while recognizing the challenges it poses to representation" (Singer 230). These processes inform the double resonance of the term "recuperation" as it emerges in Feelings's and Baker's work: to accept the risk of representation by reconstructing a history that frustrates our capacity for capturing the past in words and images, and to heal historical wounds by reopening the pains of the past for contemporary consideration.

NOTES

1. On the "Middle Passage" in the "black imagination," see Diedrich et al. On "middle passages" in black women's writing, see Brown-Guillory.

2. Green defines "the Middle Passage as a site for, if not the origin for, both blackness (as a state of being) and white supremacy (a social myth)" (3).

3. For analysis of these politics, see Austin and Hamilton; Gateward and Jennings; Howard and Jackson II; Nama.

4. Gray's introductory statements abound with references to the horrific nature of Turner's and his followers' acts but remain silent about the cruelties of the antebellum slave system. He contrasts the rebels' "most atrocious and heart-rending deeds" with "the policy of our laws in restraint of this class [of violent slaves]" and appeals to "[e]ach particular [white] community . . . [to] look to its own safety" (246, 247).

5. For Francis, "it is precisely in . . . [the] hyperbolic imagery that Baker comes closest to recreating the sentimentality of nineteenth-century slave narratives" (122).

6. *The Middle Passage* is not paginated, which is why I cannot provide page numbers.

7. Other chained villagers appear in the background, being forced at gunpoint to walk toward the destination of the slave ship.

8. Reception studies could provide further insights. Rambsy II analyzes the reactions of black male college readers to Baker's *Nat Turner*. No such study exists for Feelings's *Middle Passage*.

9. On these minstrel echoes, cf. Kunka 178; Singer 209.

10. As Singer points out throughout his chapter on *Nat Turner*, Baker's claim about the lack of sustained analyses is disingenuous; it ignores historical scholarship (Oates; Stone; Greenberg) and neglects the controversy surrounding William Styron's 1967 novelization of Turner's life (titled, like Gray's nineteenth-century account, *The Confessions of Nat Turner*). See Clarke's *William Styron's Nat Turner* (1968).

11. Singer finds a problematic causality between the sentimental family scenes, their brutal disruption by the slaveholders, and Turner's retributive violence because it "remove[s the issue] from moral judgment" (229). On Baker's Turner as Christ-like and messianic, see Bruno; Whitted.

12. Singer accuses Baker of creating an ahistorical "cinematic spectacle" (195) that violates the principle of "historical fidelity" (195); that he misses the reference to *Birth of a Nation* indicates that he underestimates Baker's revision of popular representations of blackness.

13. Cf. Chaney's reading of this scene ("Slave" 287, 291–92); Green: "[I]t was there—in the Middle Passage—that forms of Black resistance to social death were born" (4).

14. Cf. Chaney: "the death of the slave child . . . comes to stand for a negated African American future" ("Slave" 295).

15. Cf. statements attributed to Turner such as "we were strong enough to murder the family" (254); "[t]he murder of this family . . . was the work of a moment" (255); "all the family were already murdered" (256); "[h]aving murdered Mrs. Waller and ten children" (257).

16. It remains unclear whether Gray chose not to include this information or whether Turner decided not to reveal it. Greenberg suggests that Turner may have "engaged in a kind of self-censorship" (11).

17. Cf. Chaney, "Slave" 281; Fisher 266.

18. Where Singer identifies the "visual and narrative vocabulary . . . from the fantasies of popular cinema" (192), criticizing Baker's Turner as "not just a heroic figure but as a victorious one" (188), Murray sees "a world where it is hard to find villains and heroes" (330). When Singer faults *Nat Turner* for proposing an "argument [that] is primarily dramatic rather than historical in nature" and interested in "novelty and spectacle" rather than in "historical fidelity" (195), he fails to connect Baker's version with Gray's already overly dramatic and spectacular presentation of the events: "It will be long remembered in the annals of our country, and many a mother as she presses her infant darling to her bosom, will shudder at the recollection of Nat Turner, and his band of ferocious miscreants" (247).

19. A few images later, we see the same woman herded together with others in front of huts set ablaze by the white captors. Cf. also a later illustration in which a family is torn apart: two women, perhaps mother and grandmother, trying to save a baby, a crying child, and a man restrained by the slavers.

20. The image is also reprinted in Baker's *Nat Turner*.

21. There is also resistance against the all-male white crew as the slaves are forced into the hold, including a man and woman who could be husband and wife, as well as women and children.

WORKS CITED

Austin, Allan W., and Patrick L. Hamilton, editors. *All New, All Different? A History of Race and the American Superhero*. University of Texas Press, 2019.

Baker, Kyle. *Nat Turner*. Abrams, 2008.

Brown-Guillory, Elizabeth, editor. *Middle Passages and the Healing Place of History: Migration and Identity in Black Women's Literature*. Ohio State University Press, 2006.

Bruno, Tim. "Nat Turner after 9/11: Kyle Baker's *Nat Turner*." *Journal of American Studies*, vol. 50, no. 4, 2016, pp. 923–51.

Chaney, Michael A. "Drawing on History in Recent African American Graphic Novels." *Coloring America: Multi-Ethnic Engagements with Graphic Narrative*, edited by Derek Parker Royal. Special issue of *MELUS*, vol. 32, no. 3, 2007, pp. 175–200.

———. "Slave Memory without Words in Kyle Baker's *Nat Turner*." *Callaloo*, vol. 32, no. 2, 2013, pp. 279–97.

Chute, Hillary L. *Disaster Drawn: Visual Witness, Comics, and Documentary Form*. Belknap/Harvard University Press, 2016.

———. *Graphic Women: Life Narrative and Contemporary Comics*. Columbia University Press, 2010.

Clarke, John Henrik, editor. *William Styron's Nat Turner: Ten Black Writers Respond*. Beacon, 1968.

Diedrich, Maria, Henry Louis Gates, and Carl Pedersen, editors. *Black Imagination and the Middle Passage*. Oxford University Press, 1999.

Feelings, Tom. *The Middle Passage: White Ships/Black Cargo*. Dial, 1995.

Fisher, Craig. "Provocation through Polyphony: Kyle Baker's *Nat Turner*." Gateward and Jennings, pp. 255–73.

Francis, Consuela. "Drawing the Unspeakable: Kyle Baker's Slave Narrative." *Comics and the U.S. South*, edited by Brannon Costello and Qiana J. Whitted, University Press of Mississippi, 2012, pp. 113–37.

Gates, Henry Louis, Jr. *The Signifying Monkey: A Theory of African-American Literary Criticism*. Oxford University Press, 1988.

Gateward, Frances, and John Jennings, editors. *The Blacker the Ink: Constructions of Black Identity in Comics and Sequential Art*. Rutgers University Press, 2015.

Gray, Jonathan W. "'Commence the Great Work': The Historical Archive and Unspeakable Violence in Kyle Baker's *Nat Turner*." *Afterimages of Slavery: Essays on Appearances in Recent American Films, Literature, Television and Other Media*, edited by Marlene D. Allen and Seretha D. Williams, McFarland, 2012, pp. 183–200.

Gray, Thomas R. *The Confessions of Nat Turner, the Leader of the Late Insurrections in Southampton, VA*. 1831. *Slave Narratives*, edited by William L. Andrews and Henry Louis Gates, Jr., Library of America, 2000, pp. 243–66.

Green, Tara T. *Reimagining the Middle Passage: Black Resistance in Literature, Television, and Song*. Ohio State University Press, 2018.

Greenberg, Kenneth S., editor. *Nat Turner: A Slave Rebellion in History and Memory*. Oxford University Press, 2003.

Howard, Sheena C., and Ronald L. Jackson II, editors. *Black Comics: Politics of Race and Representation*. Bloomsbury, 2013.

Kunka, Andrew J. "Intertextuality and the Historical Graphic Narrative: Kyle Baker's *Nat Turner* and the Styron Controversy." *College Literature*, vol. 38, no. 3, 2011, pp. 168–93.

Mandel, Naomi. *Against the Unspeakable: Complicity, the Holocaust, and Slavery in America*. University of Virginia Press, 2006.

Morrison, Toni. *Beloved*. Knopf, 1987.

———. "Unspeakable Things Unspoken: The Afro-American Presence in American Literature." *Michigan Quarterly Review,* vol. 28, no. 1, 1988, pp. 121–63.

Murray, William. "Reimagining Terror in the Graphic Novel: Kyle Baker's *Nat Turner* and the Cultural Imagination." *CEA Critic,* vol. 77, no. 3, 2015, pp. 229–38.

Nama, Adilifu. *Super Black: American Pop Culture and Black Superheroes*. University of Texas Press, 2011.

Neary, Janet. *Fugitive Testimony: On the Visual Logic of Slave Narratives*. Fordham University Press, 2017.

Noble, Marianne. *The Masochistic Pleasures of Sentimental Literature*. Princeton University Press, 2000.

Oates, Stephen B. *The Fires of Jubilee: Nat Turner's Fierce Rebellion*. 1975. HarperPerennial, 1990.

Peterson, James Braxton. "Graphic Black Nationalism: Visualizing Political Narratives in the Graphic Novel." *The Rise and Reason of Comics and Graphic Literature: Critical Essays on the Form*, edited by Joyce Goggin and Dan Hassler-Forest, McFarland, 2010, pp. 202–21.

Rambsy, Howard, II. "Reading Kyle Baker's *Nat Turner* with a Group of Collegiate Black Men." *Contemporary African American Literature: The Living Canon*, edited by Lovalerie King and Shirley Moody-Turner, Indiana University Press, 2013, pp. 285–301.

Royal, Derek Parker. "Introduction: Coloring America: Multi-Ethnic Engagements with Graphic Narrative." *Coloring America: Multi-Ethnic Engagements with Graphic Narrative*, edited by Derek Parker Royal. Special issue of *MELUS,* vol. 32, no. 3, 2007, pp. 7–22.

Singer, Marc. *Breaking the Frames: Populism and Prestige in Comics Studies.* University of Texas Press, 2018.

Spillers, Hortense. "Mama's Baby, Papa's Maybe: An American Grammar Book." *Diacritics*, vol. 17, no. 2, 1987, pp. 65–81.

Stein, Daniel. "Rememorizing *Uncle Tom's Cabin*: The Transformation of Race Melodrama in Toni Morrison's *Beloved*." *Melodrama! The Mode of Excess from Early America to Hollywood*, edited by Frank Kelleter, Barbara Krah, and Ruth Mayer, Winter, 2007, pp. 263–82.

Stone, Albert E. *The Return of Nat Turner: History, Literature, and Cultural Politics in Sixties America.* University of Georgia Press, 1992.

Strömberg, Fredrik. *Black Images in the Comics: A Visual History.* Fantagraphics, 2003.

Styron, William. *The Confessions of Nat Turner.* Vintage, 1967.

Whitted, Qiana. "'And the Negro Thinks in Hieroglyphics': Comics, Visual Metonymy, and the Spectacle of Blackness." *Journal of Graphic Novels and Comics*, vol. 5, no.1, 2014, pp. 79–100.

Chapter 2

Generational Doubling as Eth(n)ic Narrative Strategy

Annie Proulx's Barkskins *and* Yaa Gyasi's Homegoing

Cathy Covell Waegner

Jewish American Emma Lazarus's influential poem "The New Colossus" (1883) that personifies the Statue of Liberty, and thus America, as the "Mother of Exiles," a protective, kindly maternal figure, takes on ironic scope when considered in connection with two recent epic novels: Annie Proulx's *Barkskins* and Yaa Gyasi's *Homegoing* (both 2016). Proulx's work depicts the course of Indigenous genocide and the commercial destruction of the seemingly endless North American forests in the wake of European "exiles"—notably indentured servants and their descendants—settling the "New World," whereas Gyasi's presents the enslavement of Africans as big business, with its ensuing social racism that still troubles the United States. Both novels use generations of kinship to structure the vast material, indeed double generations with contrasting mixtures of ethnicity and wealth. Rather than referencing the classical cadences of Lazarus's sonnet, the two works draw on gothic conventions of dark family secrets, kinship ties "that both bind and oppress" (Andeweg and Zlosnik 1), transgression of many types, deviance from traditional norms, monstrous and evil machinations, haunted and incarcerating abodes, and the uncanny doubling in gothic tradition. Uncontrollable fires haunt the protagonists, particularly the matriarchs or patriarchs, as well as the land, in both books. Recalling that Janet Carsten, in *After Kinship* (2004), has emphasized kinship as a negotiated and experienced process, we see that the interweaving of the contrapuntal family lines, symbolized by the contrasting wooden tables in *Barkskins* and the totemic black-stone pendants in *Homegoing*, reflects the possibilities of cultural exchange and ethical choices to counter a measure of the horrors of hegemonic exploitation encoded in North American history.

Recent scholarship has emphasized the flexibility, functionality, and popularity of the gothic mode, the foundation of which is "transgression and power," as the editor of the recently published *Cambridge Companion to American Gothic* (2017), Jeffrey Andrew Weinstock, reiterates (cf. 2–6). The classic British Gothic as a full-blown genre that arose in the late eighteenth century segued into the "American Gothic,"[1] which saw the conversion of haunted European castles and abbeys into colonial mansions and labyrinthal forests. The dark sides of American colonizing history—near annihilation of Native Americans, horrors of slavery, expropriation of Mexican citizens and territory—gave rise to such multi-pertinent terms as "Frontier Gothic" and "Southern Gothic" with, as a new volume called *Undead Souths* shows, its "ghostly genealogies" and "overwhelming affect of terrifying spectacles and posttraumatic flashbacks" (Anderson et al. 3, 1).[2] The postmodern accent on philosophical haunting, particularly in Jacques Derrida's work, raises gothic-ity to a meta-level.[3] Horror along with vampires, witches, zombies assures best-selling in literature, film, television, graphic novels, and video games.[4] The two current works under consideration here draw on all of these applications of the gothic in what can possibly be viewed as a new mix: *the complex tropes of gothic kinship serve to expose the high cost in human suffering and eco-systemic destruction exacted by North America's rise to commercial power.*

Monika Elbert and Wendy Ryden's *Haunting Realities: Naturalist Gothic and American Realism* (2017) focuses on the seldom explicitly considered link between naturalism and the gothic, between deterministic realism and horror. When described in realistic detail, the devastating effects of an inexorable "Manifest Destiny" on Indigenous peoples and inhumane slave systems on captive Africans read like ultra-gothic novels. The slave systems cleave and terrify, for instance, making the enslaved and their descendants vulnerable: as a reviewer phrased it, "mothers and sons, husbands and wives, brothers and sisters—they all tend to lose each other in *Homegoing*. They're separated both by history—war, slavery, imprisonment—and the tragic stuff of individual life—abandonment, resentment, heroin" (Cha). In her penetrating study *Haunting Legacies: Violent Histories and Transgenerational Trauma* (2010), Gabriele Schwab argues that the unconscious transmission of the affect of shattering events and choking dominance from one generation to the next can debilitate the entwined "descendants of victims *and* perpetrators" (my emphasis), creating a gothic "crypt of silenced trauma"[5]; those descendants, who are in an affective "state of exile," must be "responsive to and take responsibility for the history they inherit," voicing narratives to process the seemingly "inassimilable" pain (4–26). Surely the two novels at hand aim to voice such narratives.

THE NOVELS: ENTANGLED FAMILIES AND
OVERLAPPING GOTHIC TROPES

Annie Proulx is a renowned octogenarian novelist originally from New England, who won the Pulitzer Prize with *The Shipping News* in 1994 and international praise for her pathbreaking short story sympathetically depicting homosexuality in a Western milieu, "Brokeback Mountain" (1997), award-winningly adapted for the screen in 2005. With its over 700 pages, *Barkskins* traces the vexed and intertwining family lines of two indentured servants in New France (present-day Canada), starting in the late seventeenth century. Charles Duquet, "a weakling from the Paris slums" (4), runs away from the laborious work and severe treatment, becoming a mercenary fur trader. René Sel, from a wood-chopping family in French forests, seems fit for the New World labor of clearing the land, but the narrative describes him as "other," with "stiff black hair" and "slanted eyes" (3) from his Hun ancestry. To further his business ventures, Charles plans his marriage to a bourgeois woman in Amsterdam like a military maneuver, whereas René is forced by his master to marry a Mi'kmaq woman. Rene's union produces beloved children, however; Charles must adopt—probably unofficially (cf. 547)—a plethora of orphan boys to establish his dynasty, although one son, Outger Duquet, is eventually born to him and his wife. Charles establishes his lumber company as "Duke & Sons" on the winner's side in British America rather than in New France; Rene's children are humble tree-fellers called "barkskins," disappropriated and beleaguered as "half-bloods" by both the French and later English settlers.

The major crossing of kinship lines lies in the legitimate marriage of Beatrix, Outger's daughter, to Rene's grandson Kuntaw. Other points of contact exist, such as various generations of Sel youths being employed by Duke & Sons as barkskins—but without either side having knowledge of family ties. Only the reader sees the connections. But by the end of the epic novel, private detective work reveals that the descendants of the adopted sons could be legally upended by the bloodline heirs to the Duke fortune, the economically disadvantaged Mi'kmaq-descended persons. Needless to say, the Duke lumber magnates try to destroy the evidence, burning the records in a criminal conflagration. One stolen copy still exists, however, and the implication of the narrative is that the Duke family's gothically dark secret will one day emerge to recompense the disowned Indigenes.

Homegoing is young Yaa Gyasi's first novel, well rewarded with major literary prizes. Gyasi was only two years old when her parents immigrated to the United States from Ghana, finally residing in Alabama, like Marjorie in her novel.[6] In *Homegoing*, two half-sisters arbitrarily suffer contrasting fates:

the haunting Fante matriarch figure Maame, enslaved by an Asante master in Africa, abandons her daughter Effia, the progeny of rape by the master, after Maame sets his village on fire; Maame returns to her Fante village and husband, bearing a second daughter, Esi, who is captured by African slavers and sold to the British, incarcerated in the filthy and dangerous dungeon of Cape Coast Castle before the agony of the Middle Passage and enslavement by a cruel master in the American South. Effia is "married" to the English governor of the Cape Coast slaving fort, unaware that her step-sister is being held in the Castle dungeon, although the sister-doubles both eventually know about the existence of each other. The entangling patterns of enslavement among the west African inimical ethnic groups and in the development of the lucrative Middle Passage slave trade have a nexus in the "glowing white" (298) Castle, one of forty such forts built by European commercial powers along the Gold Coast, which serves as a central "haunted house," a site for historical atrocities that go beyond even the cruelest scenes in traditional gothic novel settings.[7]

Effia's descendants on the Gold Coast do not develop in a smooth curve of success; the English commander's grandson James, for example, chooses to relinquish his slave-trading post and fortune, fleeing to a faraway village and living anonymously and in poverty with a woman he loves. Esi's descendants enslaved in America are finally officially freed with the Emancipation Proclamation but continue to endure maltreatment through imprisonment, discrimination, and economic disadvantage. The decisive reunion of the two family lines does not take place until the final chapter of the narrative, when Marjorie and Marcus meet, travel, and experience epiphanies on both sides of the Atlantic, in Alabama and in Ghana.

In the two novels, gothic tropes and rhetoric serve the purpose of underscoring the drastic, largely random, and certainly unjust ramifications of economic and socio-systemic power. The individual transgressions of the classical eighteenth and nineteenth-century gothic novels, the raping priests and incestuous siblings, are generally punished in those books as well as neutralized by the codex of Enlightenment and Victorian society. In the two novels at hand, it is the overarching transgressions of raw capitalism's commercial exploitation that are censured, with the personal transgressions often reflecting desperate acts to sabotage that system or at least to find viable loopholes, such as Maame's setting fire to her firstborn daughter's village or, in *Barkskins*, Kuntaw's desertion of his wife Malaan and child to seek his absent father and subsistence work. Focusing my discussion on the overlapping gothic tropes of (1) burdensome, often haunting kinship, (2) the so-called "deviant" sexuality, and (3) mysterious forms of doubling, I will attempt to demonstrate how the ethnic and the ethical are intertwined in the complex family stories of *Barkskins* and *Homegoing*.

MOTHERS OF EXILES AS HAUNTERS

Two of the more fully developed characters in *Barkskins* are the mirror-image matriarchs Beatrix Duquet and Lavinia Duke, two resourceful but thorny women whose strength and accomplishments can be viewed as haunting their future descendants in opposite ways—Beatrix through ghostlike absence and Lavinia through equally ghostlike presence. Beatrix is the well-educated daughter of Outger Duquet and an unnamed Passamaquoddy woman; Beatrix attempts to transculturally balance her double ethnicity, although she can only limitedly pass on this balance to her offspring. She chooses Kuntaw Sel as her legal husband, having two sons by him and then additionally adopting his three grandchildren from a previous relationship. The family lives in the European-style house on Penobscot Bay in present-day Maine, inherited from her father, already with a gothic touch in his day, the attic containing desiccated owls and a mysterious trunk with grotesquely hairy content (Charles Duquet's preposterous wig). This anomalous house is the site of the grand Duquet table, to be discussed more fully later, on which Beatrix teaches the children to read and write, and which she defiantly refuses to relinquish to Outger's adopted Duke brothers. The house and, by extension, Beatrix's family grow increasingly dilapidated, however; Beatrix finally succumbs to fatal stomach cancer, and her husband and most of the children scatter. Instead of the upward trend of the financially successful Dukes, Beatrix's Métis brood tends to be peripatetic, "like leaves that fall on moving water, to be carried where the stream takes them" (203). As timber workers they ironically contribute to the decimation of the forests and exile themselves from their Native culture, allowing the influence of alcohol "spirits" to dominate them rather than the transcultural "spirit" of the matriarch Beatrix.

The haughty and daunting Lavinia Duke has ambitiously entered the male world of entrepreneurship, bringing the timber company "Duke & Sons," now appropriately renamed "Duke Logging and Lumber," to the height of its commercial fortunes. When still unmarried and childless, her only unsolvable problem is that of the continuation of the company. Unaware so far that she has countless potential heirs via the Sel line, she reveals in narrated monologue her arrogant prejudice toward the immigrants clearing America's forests and presumably toward the barkskins in her employment:

> She had a swiftly dissolving thought of the human flotsam that came to cut trees, their lives nothing beyond a few sweaty years with an ax. Despite their winters in the forests they all seemed to produce large families. They had no worries about succession, nor about credit or character. (533)

Lavinia does at last marry the German forester Dieter Breitsprecher and produces a son. But the following generations are inadequate businessmen, unable to live up to the expectations of this powerful "reincarnation of Elizabeth I" (665) emanating beyond Lavinia's lifetime. The company is reduced to producing plywood. In gothic terms, Lavinia seems to function as a kind of matriarchal succubus, sapping the energy from her descendants, including those secret and rejected barkskin ones. In her will she specifies that "should a Canadian claimant come forth to seize a share of Duke-Breitsprecher assets that person should be resisted in every legal way" (634). Her energy-sucking and rejection has "trailed a black thread through the day" and through the generations, since—to apply an aphorism to the lumber-business magnate—she has self-defeatingly sawed off the family-tree branch on which she was sitting.

Matriarch Maame in *Homegoing* literally haunts her displaced and exiled descendants, particularly as the "firewoman" holding two children in Akua's dangerous nightmares. Nearly all of the chapters in this lyrical novel contain fire imagery, with Akua's story aflame with fire throughout. According to a local "fetish man," Maame's restless spirit wants to point out the evil in the family line caused by the African and EuroAfrican enslavers—but this spirit is herself to a decisive extent demonic, driving the unstable and sleepwalking Akua to set fire to her two little daughters and son. Nearly lynched by the inhabitants of her town Kumasi, Akua becomes a wise pariah, living on the very edge of the community; keeping night hours, she grows a wondrous garden and becomes, against all odds, a matriarchal figure herself, able to pass on a valuable sense of the family's African history to her granddaughter Marjorie living in Alabama. Akua utters a key insight that relates the domestic to the ethical: "'Evil begets evil. It grows. It transmutes, so that sometimes you cannot see that the evil in the world began as the evil in your home'" (242). Maame's enslavement and rape within an African compound are thus presented as an "ur-evil" precursory to the escalating international horrors of the slave trade. Guided by Akua's spirit, Marjorie in union with her distant cousin Marcus of the Esi family lineage are the homegoers who finally satisfy the ever-present firewoman Maame at the Cape Coast Castle, figuratively quenching her obsessive fire through their symbolic baptism in the ocean there.

TRANSGOTHIC: CHALLENGING HEGEMONIC SEX

A new book on the "transgothic" in literature and culture, edited by Jolene Zigarovich (2018), examines transgender or nonnormative sexual phenomena in the classical gothic, but extends the term "transgothic" to encompass the boundary-violation, fluidity, and flexibility of the genre, with paths leading to displacement and migration, and, on the whole more clearly positively, to mobility and social transformation. The first kinship relationship *Barkskins* presents in connection with "slant-eyed" patriarch René Sel is that with his beloved elder brother Achille; René sorely misses his Doppelgänger brother as he stamps though the gothically "dark and savage" forests of New France, wearing his brother's clothes (4). Achille's death in a dangerous job as a river logger in France is described in grotesquely erotic detail: "[Achille] had been powerful, immune to the water's chill, had worked until a log with a broken limb, sharpened and polished to a spear by the friction of its travels, had pierced his bladder, carrying him along like a gobbet of meat on a spit" (4). Achille and the incestuous homosexual relationship of the two brothers haunts René's marriage bed with the Mi'kmaq woman Mari:

> Not since he and Achille had intertwined and whispered and tried what they could think to try had he experienced the stunning excitement of another human body naked against his. Mari's elasticity, her hard muscles, her smell of bread, river eels and bitter plants made him wild. Mari was not Achille, but he thought of his brother as he proceeded. (50)

Not surprisingly, René names their first son Achille. The juxtaposition of death and forbidden or what Proulx calls "wild" eroticism within the framework of immigration, displacement, and kinship with Indigeneity fulfills the requirements of the "transgothic." Proulx's political incorrectness in presenting the Indigenous as sexually "exotic" is presumably intended, and it serves to mark the intensity of René's loyalty to his interethnic family—despised and cheated by the French community—and his sense of loss when Mari dies of an inexplicable illness.

The transgothic is also emphasized in the opposing generational strand, Charles Duquet's. One of his adopted sons, handsome Bernard, returns from travels to the Baltic and Scandinavian countries with a "great horsy wife" (141) named Birgit. Their unlikely domestic bliss in colonial Boston is enviable, and signs of her femininity abound:

> No one understood what had drawn him to Brigit. But their marriage, though childless, had lasted nearly thirty years. Birgit kept an orderly house and a rich table. She spent much time in the kitchen, not content to leave cookery to the [Pawnee] slaves. Despite hoopskirts she preferred to mix and singe and roast herself. . . . She had an especially sweet and gentle voice, the voice of an innocent girl, not the tough old matron she looked. (210, 214)

Bernard buys his wife a decidedly feminine "needlepoint flounce" on his last trip to Europe (246), before his death at sea from blood poisoning. Birgit mourns inconsolably. After her death, however, Birgit's well-kept secret of her biological sex is shockingly revealed when the clan women prepare her body for burial: "The thin and wasted body of an elderly man lay on the still sweat-damp sheet. It was Birgit, certainly it was Birgit, but Birgit was a man. Indubitably. The wispy hairs on the narrow chest and the male sexual organs, shrunken and withered but quite real, confounded them" (260). The discovery of Birgit's "darkly mysterious" (258) transgender affects the Duke family deeply, in that they avoid social interaction in Boston, fearing that the transgressive "skeleton in the closet" might emerge. The reader knows many other, graver secrets of guilt and passion involving the Duke clan that deserve censure: Bernard has carelessly caused a major forest fire by knocking out pipe ashes; Charles brutally buries alive an injured youth caught with lumber poachers; Charles's great-grandson James frames Posey's mentally ill husband for murder so that he (James) can marry her—although later repulsed by what he views as her masculine sexual aggression. The parameters of the narrative encourage the reader to assess Bernard's successful transgender marriage, though childless, as a commendable feat rather than a deviant slip.

The strict male–female sexual binary that goes hand in hand with heteronormative, patriarchal constructs and by extension with colonizing paradigms of possession of land and control of its original inhabitants is also challenged by incidents of sexual "deviancy" in *Homegoing*.[8] The erotic attraction between bi-racial Quey (the son of Effia and her English husband James Collins) and the Asante youth named Cudjo is discerned with abhorrence by James, who immediately banishes his son to school in England. Upon his return, Quey is forced to work with the slave traders and to marry the captured Fante princess Nana Yaa Yeboah. The result is a loveless, quarreling marriage of accusation and insult, deserving the labels of vicious and monstrous far more readily than Quey and Cudjo's relationship.

Hegemonic power to engender involuntary sex shapes the story of Willie Black, a dark-skinned female descendant of enslaved Esi with a unisex name, who marries her childhood lover, light-skinned Robert Clifton. When the couple and their son migrate to Harlem during the Jazz Age, Robert finds that he can secure economic stability by passing for white. However, forced by a white employer to have sex with Willie in a men's bathroom while the employer masturbates, Robert leaves his marriage out of shame and guilt, but not without a sense of relief, as he disappears in white Manhattan, implementing transgothic mobility. Oddly enough, Willie has anticipated the failure of her relationship with Robert through her "forward memories" (205),[9] which prepare her, seer-like, for traumatic developments and lend her strength in her struggle to support her drug-addicted son.

DOUBLING AND TRANSHISTORICAL GOTHIC

The omnipresent gothic-fictional doubling involving twinning of parallel siblings, incestuous pairs, or schizophrenic personality splits manifests itself in the two novels under discussion in all of those forms and mainly in the double family lines that zigzag across the Atlantic and, in *Barkskins*, as far as New Zealand. The repeated journeys abroad in different eras lend transnational and transhistorical components to the transgothic just discussed. The doubling of material objects deliberately plays a role in the transhistoricity and provides ethnic and ethical touchstones.

Tables, for instance, serve these purposes in *Barkskins*. Both of the indentured-servant progenitors René Sel and Charles Duquet create sturdy and individual tables as the centers of their family homes. René's much-used table in his and Mari's Native-style *wikuom* is appropriately transcultural: "Although Mi'kmaq sat on the ground to be in contact with the replenishing earth, there was a low, single-board table, the nails hammered into the legs from above" (154), scarred with "knife cuts"; son Theotiste later recalls that Mari always carefully wiped the table "with a piece of damp leather" (161). Befitting a rising lumber magnate, Charles' monumental but monstrous table has been "fashioned from a single slab of pine four feet in width" (140), "a single board from the largest pine Duquet had ever cut" (207). The narrative constantly contrasts these foundational tables with other tables that travel through the generations and continents: the delicate table brought to the Netherlands from China or the elaborate side table with a "secret drawer" fashioned by a sea captain and appropriated by the lumber empire heir James Duke on his way to Boston from Europe. These precious Duquet/Duke objects contrast starkly with the makeshift table in anthropological and ecological activist Sapatisia Sel's cottage in the narrative present (2013): "The only table in the room looked like it had been stolen from a provincial park" (696). The reader is certainly guided to prefer the Indigenes' pragmatic tables and the activities taking place on them to the upper-class tables reflecting the commercial success of the largely unscrupulous Duke clan.

The original matriarch Maame passes on twin pendants to her daughters, evoking both the disrupted mother–daughter relationship, "a piece of [Effia's] mother," as step-mother Baaba puts it (16), and the rich tangible heritage of the Gold Coast, the "black stone pendant . . . shimmer[ing] as though it had been coated in gold dust" (16). Effia's pendant is treasured and passed down through the many generations of daughters in Africa, but Esi's remains buried in the real and symbolic ordure of the Gold Coast dungeon. Not until Marjorie places her pendant around Marcus's neck in the trance-like final scene of the novel are the double family lines united materially and spiritually through the transnational cousins and lovers.[10] The pendants have their own doubles in the scars that re-emerge constantly in the flow of generations. Effia's countless scars from Baaba's beatings, Yaw's deforming facial scars from his mother's fire, the scars on the backs and shoulders of the defiant plantation slaves, especially Ness's, which are so horrifyingly visible that she is rejected irrevocably as a house slave despite her beauty and grace: "Ness's skin was no longer skin really, more like the ghost of her past made seeable, physical" (74). Scars and ethnic color make skin a significant trope in the novel; the physical scars marking the black body are an outward form of the emotional scars of familial and social violence.[11] The pendants worn next to the skin cannot cover these scars, but the agency of attitude can change the scars' function.[12] Ness does not "mind the reminder" (4), viewing the haunting by her scars as the "ghost of her past," a motivation for continued defiance and her engagement for the weaker slaves.[13] Reviewers have noted the influence of Toni Morrison's works on Gyasi; perhaps not since Toni Morrison's *Beloved* (1987) has the psychological and bodily scarring of slavery taken on such metaphorically ethic dimensions.[14]

COMPARING THE NARRATIVE STRATEGIES AND CRITIQUE

Gyasi presents only a cross-section of each character's life, like a sequence of short stories,[15] whereas Proulx compresses and interweaves entire biographies. The latter must thus imaginatively vary her many subjects' ends, most of them gruesome. As reviewer Ron Charles puts it in the *Washington Post*, "the primeval forests offer a rich variety of gothic ways to slice, impale and crush a man." Carol Margaret Davison, the editor of a recent volume on *The Gothic and Death* (2017), would no doubt approve of Proulx's reliance on death-focused biographies or what Davison calls "necropolitics," which stresses "intergenerational power dynamics between the (un)dead and the living" and the importance of how power is passed on when death occurs (2). Despite the functionality of the gothic tone, some readers find the accumulation of biographies tedious.[16] Proulx's novel has also been critiqued for its didactic tone, which tends to foreground her research, and the stilted dialogue, at times in "a cigar-store pidgin" (Vollmann), not overcoming "the awkwardness of mimicking 300 years of language evolution with complicating factors of dialects, accents and broken speech" (Quinn). I would be interested in hearing a First Nations or Native American response to the novel; perhaps the gothic lens leads Proulx to dwell somewhat too long on Mi'kmaq women being viewed as atrocity-committing witches (cf. 150), for instance, or the forests filled with stereotypical lurking "savages" silently pursuing white woodsmen and settlers (e.g. 14).

Gyasi's west African sequences have generally reaped more praise than her American ones, which have been criticized for relying on stereotypes such as the superhumanly strong John Henry-like mineworker: "It feels like these stereotypes are sometimes unquestioningly imported, rather than combatted, subverted, and complicated" (Simonian). For Anglo-American reviewers, the African chapters offer relatively new perspectives with what critics consider a fresh legendary touch: "The spell breaks as the narrative moves into the present and begins to be populated by familiar characters and themes" (Wilkerson). As with *Barkskins*, reviewers complain about the book being "overloaded" with "too vast an array of lives and emotional interiors" (Wilkerson). The novel has been viewed as piecemeal: "Too often . . . Gyasi struggles to make the linked-story form suit her epic enterprise," according to Laura Miller, but Isabel Wilkerson points out that the interrelating kinship lines are understandably less available to the American generations in the novel because of the "disruptions of slavery." This lack of coherence is paradoxically one of the main strengths of the novel, in Wilkerson's opinion: "The great, aching gift of the novel is that it offers, in its own way, the very thing that enslavement denied its descendants: the possibility of imagining the connection between the broken threads of their origins."[17]

As pointed out in my introduction, social anthropologist Janet Carsten presents kinship not merely as a given set of bloodlines, but as being "shaped by human engagement" (6), inextricably both cultural and personal, "an area of life in which people invest their emotions, their creative energy, and their new imaginings" (9). Indeed, the gothic filter encourages this process of constant re-orientation, if we follow Andeweg and Zlosnik's large although justifiable claim for gothic-influenced novels that "Gothic fiction is a key site where sociocultural figurations of the family are negotiated" (2). The two authors at hand do not give their allegiance to Emma Lazarus's "mighty woman with a torch," a statuesque mother who "glows world-wide welcome"[18] in America's master narrative. For them, the disruptions as well as choices experienced in the intertwining and doubled generations call for attention to the transgression and power of a more complex, vexed, but finally adjustable network of kinship between exiles and exploiters, between old and new homelands, among ethnic groups, between people and their environment.

NOTES

1. I capitalize "gothic" only in connection with a specified subgenre, such as American Gothic or Frontier Gothic.

2. "Ghostly genealogy" refers here to Choctaw funerary rites and generational haunting in LeAnne Howe's Native novels *Shell Shakers* (2001) and *Miko Kings* (2007); see Kirstin L. Squint's essay in *Undead Souths*, "Burying the (Un)Dead and Healing the Living: Choctaw Women's Power in Leanne Howe's Novels," 187–98. In a fascinating book titled *Gothic Imagination in Latin American Fiction and Film* (2019), Carmen A. Serrano demonstrates that one of the functions of Latin American Gothic is to express "conflicts with a colonial legacy" (7).

3. I discuss this meta-level elsewhere, illustrating the gothic rhetoric of Derrida's hauntology, Baudrillard's discourses on death and terror, Lyotard's and Žižek's thoughts on the sublime, and Kristeva's notion of the abject (see "Rampaging"). Maria Beville deals insightfully and in depth with postmodern theorists to establish her claim for a separate genre she calls "Gothic-postmodernism" in her monograph of the same title.

4. Lorna Piatti-Farnell and Donna Lee Brien trace intersections between the gothic, popular culture, and the new media, showing "re-elaborations and hybridities of genre" (6).

5. In a perceptive but as yet unpublished paper titled "Transgenerational Haunt-ing: Yaa Gyasi's *Homegoing*," Hanna Wallinger draws on Schwab's title and her postulate that "telling and witnessing are necessary for healing trauma" (Schwab 48) in Wallinger's analysis of the characters' damaging heritage of racial atrocities. I thank Hanna Wallinger for sharing her fine essay with me.

6. Gyasi herself points out this autobiographical trace in video interviews, for instance: https://www.youtube.com/watch?v=wheOsYCDezE. Accessed June 15, 2019.

7. *Homegoing* has been praised (e.g. by Ron Charles, review in *Washington Post*) for its differentiated attention to the enmity among the African ethnic groups and their complicity in the burgeoning transatlantic slave trade. The 2018 publica-tion of Zora Neale Hurston's 1931 manuscript titled *Barracoon: The Story of the Last "Black Cargo"* corroborates current interest in the long-lasting entanglement between enslavement among Africans and the lucrative European-propelled slave trade. Hurston interviewed "Cudjo Lewis," the last living human "cargo" shipped illegally as a nineteen-year-old to the United States at the late date of 1859 and pres-ents his harrowing story of war among African tribes and its aftermath in the Middle Passage, enslavement in Alabama, and post-Emancipation racism.

8. Annette Kolodny's study of the rape of the colonized land and its female inhabitants, *The Lay of the Land* (1975), is still pertinent.

9. Willie's "forward memories" are the mirror images of Toni Morrison's traumatically haunting "rememories" in gothic postmodern *Beloved*; see Waegner, "Rampaging," for reasons to call *Beloved* "gothic postmodern" (212–13). In the 2017 lecture collection, *The Origin of Others*, Morrison explicitly relates her experimental narrative device of a 'living dead' benchmark-character, the figure of Beloved, to the gothicity of slavery: "I inserted a speaking, thinking dead child whose impact—and appearance and disappearance—could operate as slavery's gothic damage" (83). Morrison also views the slavers' paradoxical slide into bestiality in order to maintain their racial superiority in terms of gothic villainy: "the sensibility of slave owners is gothic" (30). The title of Morrison's most recent publication, *Mouth Full of Blood: Essays, Speeches, Meditations* (2019) certainly conjures up gothic vampire imagery.

10. Two cousins of the youngest generation in *Barkskins* are also emotionally close, arousing Aunt Mary May's fear of incest: She says, "I just hope it don't get—funny" (688).

11. Anson Koch-Rein analyzes skin as a Gothic trope in "Gothic Gender in Skin Suits, or *The* (Transgender) *Skin I Live In*" (in Zigarovich 161–76).

12. Some reviewers have criticized the heavy-handedness of the pendant symbol: "Gyasi tries to achieve continuity by leaning hard on recurring symbols like the stone

pendant" (Miller, *The New Yorker*), but I question whether they have thought through its reverberations.

13. Laura Miller (*The New Yorker*) sees no opportunities for agency with Esi's African American descendants: Gyasi's "American characters, in particular, lead lives starved of self-directed narrative, their fates dictated by people, institutions, and historical forces over which they have no control." Miller is of course correct in pointing out the stultifying "dictation" by higher commercial and political forces, but Gyasi is at pains to show loopholes of agency—as well as guilt—on both sides of the ethnic line, particularly with her depictions of the African slavers.

14. The scars on Sethe's back are repeatedly described as a tree (e.g. *Beloved*, first mention 18–20 in Signet edition); Ness's are "shaped like a man hugging her from behind with his arms hanging around her neck" (74). In a *Stanford Magazine* interview Gyasi acknowledges Morrison's influence: "Even the stories I was writing at that [early] point [in my career] had mostly white protagonists," she says. "I don't think I really understood that there was a space for people who looked like me in the world of literature until I started reading Toni Morrison" (Scott).

15. Steph Cha, *Los Angeles Times*: "*Homegoing* is, in essence, a novel in short stories, so each chapter is forced to stand on its own, and inevitably, some chapters fare better than others."

16. Eileen Battersby is one of the critics who chastises Proulx for the plethora of biographies and the foregrounding of facts: "Proulx is in such a hurry to race through her research that the characters barely have time to drawn [*sic*] breath, reveal their various flaws, make enemies and then die, culled by an author with three centuries of human error to get through" (*Irish Times*).

17. Wilkerson is the acclaimed author of *The Warmth of Other Suns: The Epic Story of America's Great Migration* (2010).

18. The two phrasings are from her 1883 poem "The New Colossus." (The text of the sonnet is provided in the introduction to this volume, note 3.)

WORKS CITED

Anderson, Eric Gary, Taylor Hagood, and Daniel Cross Turner, editors. *Undead Souths: The Gothic and Beyond in Southern Literature and Culture*. Louisiana State University Press, 2015.

Andeweg, Agnes, and Sue Zlosnik, editors. *Gothic Kinship*. Manchester University Press, 2013.

Battersby, Eileen. "*Barkskins* by Annie Proulx: A Trite Caper of Eco-Calamity." *Irish Times*, June 25, 2016, https://www.irishtimes.com/culture/books/barkskins-by-a nnie-proulx-a-trite-caper-of-eco-calamity-1.2698095. Accessed June 15, 2018.

Beville, Maria. *Gothic-Postmodernism: Voicing the Terrors of Postmodernity*. Rodopi, 2009.

Carsten, Janet. *After Kinship*. Cambridge University Press, 2004.

Cha, Steph. "The Blazing Success of Yaa Gyasi's *Homegoing*." *Los Angeles Times*, June 10, 2016, http://www.latimes.com/books/jacketcopy/la-ca-jc-yaa-gyasi-2 0160523-snap-story.html. Accessed June 15, 2018.

Charles, Ron. "Annie Proulx's Long-Awaited, Spectacular New Novel." *Washington Post*, June 6, 2016, https://www.washingtonpost.com/entertainment/books/anni e-proulxs-long-awaited-spectacular-new-novel-barkskins/2016/06/06/75371af4-29ba-11e6-a3c4-0724e8e24f3f_story.html?utm_term=.c30211c59c55. Accessed June 15, 2018.

Davison, Carol Margaret, editor. *The Gothic and Death*. Manchester University Press, 2017.

Elbert, Monika, and Wendy Ryden, editors. *Haunting Realities: Naturalist Gothic and American Realism*. University of Alabama Press, 2017.

Gyasi, Yaa. *Homegoing: A Novel*. 2016. Vintage, 2017.

Kolodny, Annette. *The Lay of the Land: Metaphor as Experience and History in American Life and Letters*. University of North Carolina Press, 1975; re-issued as eBook 2017.

Miller, Laura. "Descendants: A Sprawling Tale of a Family Split between Africa and America." *New Yorker*, May 30, 2016, https://www.newyorker.com/magazine/2016/05/30/yaa-gyasis-homegoing. Accessed June 15, 2018.

Morrison, Toni. *Beloved*. 1987. Signet, 1991.

———. *Mouth Full of Blood: Essays, Speeches, Meditations*. Chatto & Windus, 2019.

———. *The Origin of Others* (Charles Eliot Norton Lectures, 2016). Harvard University Press, 2017.

Piatti-Farnell, Lorna, and Donna Lee Brien, editors. *New Directions in 21st-Century Gothic: The Gothic Compass*. Routledge, 2015.

Proulx, Annie. *Barkskins*. 4th Estate, 2016.

Quinn, Annalisa. "Annie Proulx's *Barkskins* Is Lovely, Dark, and Deep." *npr Book Reviews*, June 18, 2016, http://www.npr.org/2016/06/18/481427123/annie-prou lxs-barkskins-is-lovely-dark-and-deep. Accessed June 15, 2018.

Schwab, Gabriele. *Haunting Legacies: Violent Histories and Transgenerational Trauma*. Columbia University Press, 2010.

Scott, Sam. "The Story Behind *Homegoing*." *Stanford Magazine*, June 13, 2017, https://medium.com/stanford-magazine/the-story-behind-homegoing-f186672670c 8. Accessed June 15, 2018.

Serrano, Carmen A. *Gothic Imagination in Latin American Fiction and Film*. University of New Mexico Press, 2019.

Simonian, Kate Osana. "The Unbroken Line: Yaa Gyasi's *Homegoing*." *Kenyon Review*, vol. 40. no. 3, May/June 2018, https://www.kenyonreview.org/reviews/ homegoing-by-yaa-gyasi-738439/. Accessed June 15, 2018.

Tarr, Clayton Carlyle. *Gothic Stories within Stories: Frame Narratives and Realism in the Genre, 1790–1900*. McFarland, 2017.

Vollmann, William T. "*Barkskins* by Annie Proulx." *New York Times Book Review*, June 17, 2016, https://www.nytimes.com/2016/06/19/books/review/barkskins-by -annie-proulx.html. Accessed June 15, 2018.

Waegner, Cathy Covell. "Rampaging Red Demons and Lumpy Indian Burial Grounds: (Native) Gothic-Postmodernism in Stephen Graham Jones's *All the Beautiful Sinners* and *Growing Up Dead in Texas*." *The Fictions of Stephen*

Graham Jones: A Critical Companion, edited by Billy Stratton, University of New Mexico Press, 2016, pp. 194–217.

Weinstock, Jeffrey Andrew, "Introduction: The American Gothic." *The Cambridge Companion to American Gothic*, edited by Jeffrey Andrew Weinstock, Cambridge University Press, 2017, pp. 2–11.

Wilkerson, Isabel. "*Homegoing* by Yaa Gyasi." *New York Times*, June 6, 2018, https ://www.nytimes.com/2016/06/12/books/review/isabel-wilkerson-reviews-yaa-gya sis-homegoing.html. Accessed June 15, 2018.

Zigarovich, Jolene, editor. *TransGothic in Literature and Culture*. Routledge, 2018.

Chapter 3

"As Much the Invader as the Native"

Investigating Immigrant and Indigenous Family Ties in Wendy Rose's Itch Like Crazy

Ludmila Martanovschi

In *Itch Like Crazy* (2002), which was published by the University of Arizona Press as part of the Sun Tracks series exclusively dedicated to American Indian creative works since 1971, Wendy Rose reclaims episodes of family history, embarking on a journey of self-discovery that has personal and political significance. The volume centers on her European ancestors' migration to the United States and their exilic tribulations, while also affirming the need for reconciling this inheritance with her Indigenous affiliation. The very process of writing acquires therapeutic dimensions, as both the individual and ancestral traumatic experiences revisited are sifted through a Native propensity for healing, reconnecting, and continuing. By moving from time- and place-specific texts to considerations relevant for all America, Rose demonstrates that the genealogical endeavor in her volume has pertinence for a multiethnic and multicultural society that needs to confront and come to terms with its compositeness and complexity, especially since the twenty-first century will continue to complicate and challenge views on migration and transcultural affiliations.

Born in 1948, Wendy Rose (Hopi and Miwok) is often listed as a poet in studies dedicated to American Indian literature, but she is also an essayist, anthropologist, and autobiographer whose publishing career started in the early 1970s. The book-length analysis *The Heart as a Drum: Continuance and Resistance in American Indian Poetry* (1999) by Robin Riley Fast gives considerable attention to her verse and already captures the defining features of her early collection *Lost Copper* (1980): "Images of fragmentation are common, as are suggestions that language is problematical for one whose connections to community are ambiguous or broken" (56). But rather than insist on the poet's sense of disjointedness, other critics identify her capacity to draw from two separate traditions and focus on her militant stance as essential to her writing. In *Engaged Resistance: American Indian Art, Literature, and Film from Alcatraz to the NMAI* (2011), Dean Rader dedicates an entire chapter to contemporary poetry as "a site of aesthetic activism" and examines works by Louise Erdrich, Sherman Alexie, and Wendy Rose, explaining:

> Their inventive use of the lyric transforms both public and private discourses and allows them not only to counter establishments of identity but also to tell who they are, in their own words. These authors withstand cultural erasure by attacking those armaments designed to annihilate their ability to speak themselves into being; yet, through the lyric poem, they recoup the performative energies of the oral tradition, pulling from the best tradition of both Anglo and Native discourse. (115)

The insistence on self-definition, sovereignty, and orality becomes part of the decolonizing dimension of Rose's writing. Moreover, her searching for and struggling with her ethnic identity throughout her work is ultimately seen as a strength and a source of creativity. As disclosed in *Itch Like Crazy*, Rose's Indigenous ties are to Charles Loloma, a member of the Hopi tribe, about whom she declares: "the man who is most likely my father and whom I have always regarded as such" (Part 3: "Listen Here for the Voices"). Her literal connection to a tribal nation is not official since no documents can prove whether Loloma is indeed her biological father, her relatives' statements concerning his paternity are unreliable, and the Hopi tribe decides affiliation matrilineally, thus not granting her formal membership. Rose mentions her mother's Miwok ancestry in her accounts, but the specificities are unclear. Even so, what matters for the critical analysis of her creative production is that Rose explores her own Nativeness and models ways of relating to one's Indigeneity throughout her writing.

Predictably, the relationship between Rose's work and the autobiographical mode she embraces is multifaceted. In the contribution to the volume *I Tell You Now: Autobiographical Essays by Native American Writers* (1987), edited by Brian Swann and Arnold Krupat, she declares: "Everything I have ever written is fundamentally autobiographical, no matter what the topic or style" ("Neon" 253). Furthermore, she reflects on the ways in which she can relate to the various strands in her family's stories in order to produce the contribution requested by the editors as follows: "To uncover the memories, I have peeled back layers of scar tissue. I have invoked the ghosts and made them work for me" (261). Confronting one's wounds fearlessly and weaving the messages coming from her (ancestors') ghosts into a coherent narrative of the self are two important parts of the exercise she embarks upon not only for this essay, but in her poetry as well. As psychological studies often document, autobiographical accounts are intrinsically linked to identity construction, the process being in constant flux:

> Through examining autobiographical narratives, we gain access to individuals' construction of their own identity. What individuals choose to tell, what information they select to report, provides converging evidence of how individuals conceptualize their selves. But importantly, these narratives are not static entities; autobiographical narratives and self-identity are fluid and dynamic, changing both developmentally as well as situationally. (Fivush and Buckner 149)

These considerations preserve their validity in the case of creative writers who publish autobiographical texts, and even more so in the case of Wendy Rose, who is attuned to the multicultural and feminist debates of her time and particularly preoccupied with investigating her own identity through the lens of ethnicity and gender.

While valid for all of her poetry collections, the autobiographical nature of her writing is most evident in *Itch Like Crazy*, especially since this volume focuses on her understanding of kinship relations and the possibility of making peace with the contradictory drives in her ancestry once she has already reached (literary) maturity. Indeed, the urge to write about parents, grandparents, great-grandparents, and even more remote ancestors comes from a sense of disconnectedness acknowledged as part of her youth. More than once, Rose testifies to having been mistreated as a child and finally rejected by her family: "I am without relations. I have always swung back and forth between alienation and relatedness" ("Neon" 255). In an effort to bridge gaps, to stop feeling exiled and to overcome the sense of estrangement she has lived with all her life, in *Itch Like Crazy* she embarks on genealogical research, as she herself explains in an interview:

> Doing the genealogy work actually has really given me a family for the first time, because I never felt a part of my family and I don't know that my family ever saw me as part of them. I always grew up with the idea that I needed to find a family, I needed to find a place to fit in, and the genealogy has provided one way to do that. (Godfrey 74)

This poetic and autobiographical recreation of her familial network not only helps Rose develop her art, but it also gives her a sense of belonging and a sense of restoring herself back to wholeness.

This process further aligns Rose's endeavors with the project of decolonization, especially with the theoreticians who capitalize on connectedness not only with members of the same family, clan, or tribe, but also with the land and everything on and around it. In the essay "'Go Away, Water!': Kinship

Criticism and the Decolonization Imperative," Daniel Heath Justice advances pertinent considerations on community and kinship:

> Indigenous nationhood is more than simple political independence or the exercise of a distinctive cultural identity; it's also an understanding of a common social interdependence within the community, the tribal web of kinship rights and responsibilities that link the People, the land, and the cosmos together in an ongoing and dynamic system of mutually affecting relationships. (151)

The need for becoming aware of these kinship rights and responsibilities is sounded in Rose's *Itch Like Crazy* more than once. Reestablishing kinship to one's relatives and original place brings connectedness and healing, which is ultimately life-sustaining. And as Justice continues to insist in his recent book, *Why Indigenous Literatures Matter* (2018), kinship should be assumed and performed constantly: "The question of being and becoming a good relative itself presumes active and meaningful engagement—relatives are not just static roles or states of being, but lived relationships" (74). This type of engagement is not an easy or simple mission, as Rose shows when involved in communicating (poetically) with her relatives.

The first-person speaker in *Itch Like Crazy* discloses the paradoxical nature of her genealogical research: "the deeper I delve into the various family histories, the more I find that the people from whom I come were the perpetrators of those very acts that ignited my rage (and my art)" (Part 3: "Listen Here for the Voices"). While keenly aware of violent acts of colonization and misogyny in her family's and America's records, the rewriting that the poet proposes in order to depict her immigrant and Indigenous family ties and to reflect on the conviction that she is "as much the invader as the native" (*Itch* 81) is meant to lead to the identification of coping mechanisms, surpassing anger and overcoming trauma. When reviewing *Itch Like Crazy* for the *Studies in American Indian Literatures* journal, Margaret Dubin accurately states that the volume returns to some of Wendy Rose's most cherished themes: "her search for roots and belonging, the harsh realities of survival, the cruelty of colonialism" (87). The effort to trace and connect the various branches of the speaker's family tree(s), while also exposing and resisting colonization, is mirrored by the form chosen for the volume, in which several elements are interrelated. Just like other texts coming from multiethnic writers, *Itch Like Crazy* defies genre, which is often perceived as a European imposition; the volume contains two poetry sections to which a third one of prose and photography is added. In this final part of the book, the text is juxtaposed with family photos, which provide visual support, introducing the reader to the predecessors about whom Rose writes. Many autobiographies make use of photographs and for good reason: "Since photography appears to operate on a different plane than the verbal narrative, it would seem to offer life writing a unique way of authentication from a different perspective" (Ljungberg 251).[1] Photography is a two-dimensional medium that arrests the reader's/viewer's attention, photography's power of authentication, as Barthes famously established, exceeding its power of representation (quoted in Ljungberg 252). The fact that the pictures in *Itch Like Crazy* testify to the existence of all these absent relatives, even if unable to make them present, is more important than what they actually show about the subjects photographed.

In an interview that includes comments about the structure of the book, Rose complains that she had no control over the outcome, her initial intentions concerning the pictures having been different:

> when the book was being put together, my original idea was that the photographs, for example, and that the captions with the photographs, that these would be spread through the book as each person or each group of people appeared in the poems—that there would be their photographs there. (Godfrey 79)

The readers can only wonder now what the effect of the intended arrangement would have been. Given the finality of the printed volume, the readers either delay their engagement with the visual representation of the figures about whom they read or move back and forth, reconfiguring the original trajectory in an attempt to grasp all the data available for one individual before moving on to the next. Either way, active participation and engagement with the volume is required. It is also worth noting that the choice for visual content that complements the text is a recurrent practice among contemporary American Indian autobiographers, which, as Hertha Sweet Wong attests, is a recognizable part of a tradition that includes nineteenth-century Plains Indian pictography (148).[2] Thus, once again, Rose affirms her Native allegiance.

Another form of political protest as well as self-discovery in Rose's work is represented by her preoccupation with femininity and feminism. Rose displays her programmatic prioritizing of women's points of view. She is interested in revisiting their experiences and concerns, while giving voice to the formerly silenced members of her EuroAmerican family. As she does so, her decolonizing agenda appears in her approach to feminism, about which she says: "we Indians, or Chicanas, or Asian-Americans, or Black women have something to teach white feminists that can only be taught with some of us in leadership positions" (Hunter 81). In fact, Rose demonstrates that her perspective is different from the mainstream feminists' since it is informed by her knowledge and adoption of Hopi values: "When Hopi people talk about the power of women, it is meant as a spiritual, political, and social fact. Hopi women are the property owners, the decision-makers, the heads of the families" (Hunter 81). Reverence for and a sense of belonging to a Native culture that recognizes women's centrality empowers the writer to rewrite the family's history as *herstory*, insisting on the communication that needs to be established between generations, between herself and her grandmothers, both historical and mythical.

When choosing "These Bones" as the title for the first section in *Itch Like Crazy*, Rose opts for a recurrent image in her work, an early critic explaining that the bones "represent her most essential self, the most basic structure of her being both as a person and as a poet" (Wiget 31). Through this intertextual undertaking, readers are reminded of "I Expected My Skin and My Blood to Ripen," one of the emblematic texts in which she exposes the human pain and unethical dimension behind anthropological collecting. The epigraph to the poem quotes an art auction catalog that refers to the Wounded Knee Massacre and lists the prices of the items of clothing retrieved there, showing no awareness of the human suffering and loss identified with that place and moment in time. Trying to deconstruct such a discourse, often encountered in catalogs and museum exhibitions, as well as to expose it in all its horrific attempt at preserving scientific neutrality, Rose pays her respects to the departed by allowing a dead woman's voice to utter an account of her experience during and after the massacre: "I expected my skin / and my blood to ripen / not to be ripped from my bones" (*Bone* 18). Rose refers here to the fact that, because of the winter conditions at the time of the massacre, the removal of the clothing, which is also a form of theft, implied literally ripping off frozen human flesh from the bodies condemned to being buried naked and disfigured. The poet wants readers to realize that contemplating Indigenous garments and even human remains such as bones, exhibited in public places, equals taking part in colonizing and dehumanizing practices.[3] Moreover, in a gesture that anticipates the premise of *Itch Like Crazy*, she confesses: "Maybe what I'm saying is that the bones are alive. They are not dead remnants but rather they're alive" (Bruchac 262). In other words, Rose programmatically engages in conversing with her ancestors, thus making bones speak, a skill no longer reserved only for the living, in her poetic universe.

The section "These Bones" opens with a poetic text entitled "Imagine it like this.," testifying to the volume's thrust toward a pan-American dimension. It invites the reader to imagine the migratory movement of many generations across the sea: "They did not come all at once / but little by little over five hundred years" (Rose, *Itch* 3). The text speaks of the grandparents, great-grandparents, and other German, English, Irish, and Scottish ancestors, among whom Grandfather Webb, Margaret Castor, Joseph Bigler, Hugh Massey Barrett, and Andrew MacInnes receive special mention in the first section, as much as it speaks about the colonization of America at large. From the very beginning the poem identifies a special place that has tremendous power: "In the middle of the sea, there is a place / of ghosts and transformation" (3). This place makes the immigrants discard the burdens of what keeps them tied to the past and of what prevents them from returning to their homelands:

> They reached as far west as they could
> to touch that magic place in the center of the sea
> and mount the great curve beyond which
> they would never return.
> Right in the middle of the ocean they began to shed,
> ancestry and heritage
> dropping from their shoulders
> as termites drop their wings. (3)

Finding an external cause for the migrants' amnesia, as "the great curve" or "the magic place" determines them to part with their heritage, seems to excuse those who lose their connection to their homelands irredeemably. At the same time, amnesia seems to be a condition necessary for transplanting oneself to new soil successfully. The text suggests that only magic would have enabled the newcomers "to get it right" (4) in the New World. In reality it is impossible to leave behind personal and communal wounds that mark identity, and all this spiritual and psychological baggage continues to influence one's future even after migrating to another continent.

As the speaker investigates the stories of her EuroAmerican ancestors, she expresses understanding and empathy for their struggles, fears, and dreams, before and after crossing the Atlantic, as well as rage and anger at the way some of them related to the Native peoples they encountered at the end of their journey. The speaker takes it upon herself to address her elders from the place "where the living haunt the dead" (61), forcing certain necessary confrontations and imposing an ethical remembering of facts. One other possible interpretation can be advanced relying on Sheila Hassell Hughes's phrase "self-conception as a collaborative process" (39). Even if the critic does not refer to *Itch Like Crazy*, her clarifying the fact that throughout her work Rose engages a variety of readers without limiting herself to addressing just one ethnic group can be applied to the volume in question. Thus, the statements according to which Rose "opens the poetry to the possibility of multiple and shifting allegiances" and "opens the work of identity construction to collaboration across multiple lines of difference" (Hughes 40) testify to the writer's versatility and engagement with the identity politics of her age.

The whole volume seems to echo the question "Where are you, my grandmothers?" repeated several times in "1830 as I Remember It" (Rose, *Itch* 61–63). In numerous instances the speaker addresses each grandmother directly, relating to details she knows or imagines about their lives. Through

prayer, the speaker envisages an exchange between generations, relying on
the Hopi worldview that implies cross-death communication:

> For the Hopi all forms of prayer offering are understood to be prestations
> requiring reciprocity between the two realms. Prayer offerings in any form are
> operations of exchange. They are relational but, more important, they make
> obligatory and compensative requirements of the spirits of the other world.
> (Hieb 580)

Consequently, in "The Itch: Second Notice," the twenty-first-century
speaker entreats her predecessors to initiate her into the rituals of their respective communities: "Teach me what it means / to be in the circle," and she also
promises to share her experience in turn, "and I will teach you / how it feels /
to be on the outside of outside" (Rose, *Itch* 9). Admitting to her current isolation and marginalization translates into her quest for the opposite, for inclusion and acceptance. The very last lines of the poem appeal to the "Elders of
the World" to talk to the children and impart knowledge:

Tell them that if they give in
to the insatiable itch,
their roots will break open,
expose tender flesh
to blowing dust and searing heat,
may not set seed
in the crumbled dark earth
of other lands. (10–11)

Questioning the possibility of successfully uprooting oneself from one continent and growing roots in a new one subverts the image of the transplanted,
a metaphor often used to discuss the migration from Europe to America in
the twentieth century.[4] The fragility of the connections to the New World is
encapsulated in the image of the roots that suffer from the effects of unfamiliar soil type, wind, and drought. Verbs chosen from the semantic sphere of
destruction—break, expose, blow, sear, crumble—apply to natural elements
here, while concomitantly rendering a sense of threat to humans. Applying
an ecocritical interpretation, the reader should also notice that the images of
nature in crisis imply connections between colonization and environmental
calamity. The unsettling sense of displacement and suffering referenced in
these lines is associated with "the insatiable itch," the title image that is central to the volume.

When reflecting on the motivation behind writing the book in the opening
of its third section, Rose says: "I had to come to terms not only with the obvious historical facts of conquest and genocide, but with the personal fact of

being born into a family that could not keep its own secrets straight" (Part 3: "Listen Here for the Voices"). She further goes on to talk about her sense of being ethnically different and "mixed" while growing up, and hence singled out, only to conclude: "This condition is a part of the 'the itch' that is growing in intensity as young people find themselves feeling alone because they are 'multiracial,' when in fact the majority of Americans will be multiracial one day in the future" (Part 3: "Listen Here for the Voices"). Hence the itch stands for a spirit of revolt against the complacent present, a need for self-definition against impositions from the outside, an urgency to defy monolithic societal normativity. When asked about the connotations of her volume's title, Rose further elaborates that the term "is used to observe restlessness or lack of ease with whatever the circumstances are, whether that's a matter of being mixed-blood or whether that's a matter of being on the side of the coloniz-ers" (Godfrey 73). In managing to present the "cases" in her own family not as isolated and relevant only for the speaker working through them, but as emblematic for the colonization of America, Rose gives private matters a public dimension.[5] Her writing illustrates the conviction of much feminist writing, according to which the personal is political. And thus, she gives voice to the struggles of many multiethnic contemporaries.

Through her genealogical endeavor, the speaker embarks on rewriting American history as she discloses family secrets, such as the changing of a Scottish clan name. Delving deeper into historical records about her ances-tral Scottish roots, the great-great-granddaughter operates adjustments to the image she had constructed of Captain Andrew MacInnes. The heroic dimen-sion of the MacInnes freedom fighter and émigré to Canada, which she had read about, crumbles, and her actual ancestor is exposed as "the son of cattle thieves and outlaws / from another clan who changed their name / to avoid arrest" (Rose, *Itch* 47). Greed, stealth, oppression, and violence are the mark-ers of the story she has to confront, while dealing with the past:

You were one who bought other men
to work so you would grow rich
beyond measure; you stole them from their land,
their people, took their names, their languages,
turned them into blank slates upon which you would write
with the flick of your whip. (47)

By showing how unreliable a name is, since it can be easily appropriated by a person with a totally different biography than that of the person who originally bore it, Rose reflects on the relativity of historical truth and the evanescence of (auto)biographical reconstruction. More than choosing one of the two competing versions of her ancestor's life and setting the records straight, the speaker seems to be interested in exposing American history as a history of conflict and injustice.

At the same time, Rose embraces a Native view of history as circular rather than linear movement, and she blurs the distinction between past and future, between remembrance and premonition: "this is as much memory as prophecy" (42). In a text in which the young woman continues to address her ancestor, she envisages the ultimate ironic twist to the trajectory of Andrew's lineage as she prophesizes that his descendants "will go native, they will dance / to the rise and fall of summer, / surround winter's lodge / with their crackling song" (44). What is a prophecy for Captain Andrew MacInnes, if he had been able to listen to his twentieth-century descendant while alive, represents a memory for the poet, a recording of her own allegiance to Native culture and Native song and dance as forms of artistic expression that has already taken place.

Besides conversing with male ancestors, the speaker in the volume invests much more in interacting with the female members of her family. In her feminist enterprise of giving voice to the women from the past, Rose revisits the theme of motherhood and, more importantly, that of grieving for lost children:

He tells me—stop worrying so much. Don't cry
   for the babies buried in Ontario snow.
   Do not lie awake remembering
   that you held them for such a short time;
   we will have more. But, I tell him,
I would be more comfortable
   if summer did not run our sweat into streams
   deeper than his river, lonelier than the full moon
   of August and the smell of smoke, the sound
   of a thousand cicadas. (50)

The experience of migration is often shown to be unforgiving as it turns painful events, especially an infant's death, into unbearable landmarks in the new country. The female immigrants' sorrow, loneliness, and alienation are heightened. The rituals of mourning and commemorating the dead are subordinated to the urgency of continuing to work hard in order to survive. Even hope is too much to cling to.

Another feminist poem, "Women Like Me," is included in the second section of the collection entitled "This Heart," which can only lead the reader to expect more emotionally charged content. This time the speaker offers a self-definition by identifying with the American land and embodying the destruction engendered by colonizing practices: "I am broken / as much as any native ground, / my roots tap a thousand migrations" (81). The process of making the self whole again proves difficult, if not utterly impossible. The re-negotiation that the speaker alludes to in the following lines also points to the pain, contradiction, and fragmentariness that make up her present and cannot be easily dismissed or overcome:

Who should return across the sea
or the Bering Strait or the world before this one
or the Mother Ground? Who should go screaming
to some other planet, burn up or melt
in a distant sun? Who should be healed
and who hurt? Who should dry
under summer's white sky, who should shrivel
at the first sign of drought? Who should be remembered? (82)

These rhetorical questions problematize issues such as contested territories, competing histories, punishment vs. healing, remembering vs. obliterating the past. Most significantly, they are the poetic version of the itch that Rose equates with inquisitiveness, instability, and openness. If the Hopi believe in the people's emergence from four successive worlds that are situated underneath the earth (Courlander 24), hence the poetic reference to the Mother Ground, a return to the original place in the case of EuroAmericans would entail a reversed transatlantic journey, which is as impractical at this point in history as finding refuge on a planet or sun that does not sustain human life.

Exploring the possibility of embarking upon a visit to Europe, the speaker projects a journey to England, following in Pocahontas's footsteps. Rather than work with the image of the Indigenous "princess," who is often re-imagined and re-empowered by Native writers,[6] Rose chooses to have her own avatar take a seat at the queen's table. The text "Aborigine and Queen" is a notable addition to the body of work through which the empire is fighting back. It clearly mirrors the postcolonial and decolonizing impulses of the present moment in the history of world literature:

If I were to go to the Queen of England,
curtsy, and say, Hello there! I am your cousin
from the colonies, the part that you let go

till you started to dig beneath the moat,
then broadly smile from the center
of my round and brown face,

would she ask me to stay
for a spot of tea, sweet biscuits, nectarines? (14)

The cordial visit imagined would also include the queen showing her American visitor "the imperial war booty" and the imposing family portraits. An exchange would be involved as the guest would share "the turquoise secret of sky" and other Native items. However, the text ends with a full exposure of the reality that lies beyond the façade and the need for acknowledging the scars: "I come as both the colonial thrust / and the native wound" (15). It is this wound that lies at the center of Rose's vision for *Itch Like Crazy*, this awareness of the conflictual forces that converged on American soil.[7]

In trying to echo the Native circularity of Rose's work, the critical endeavor here aims at returning to the image of the bones, which reappears in "International Hour of Prayer for the Yellowstone Buffalo Herd," a poem included in the second section of *Itch Like Crazy*. While restating the need for prayer, the poem also points to the imperative of restoring ceremonial items and human remains to their original tribes. The poem comments on the hunting for saleable objects in Native graves and on the hunting of the buffalo, two activities that are destructively related. Once more, Rose speaks against exploitative approaches to Native cultures.[8] In her decolonizing efforts, she insists on the need to reverse the damage caused by decades of cultural genocide.

Like it was a hundred years ago
bounties are gathered from death;
trains, buses, cars, planes
carry the segmented body of the terrible worm
across the land and the screams of the hunted
split the sun awake. It is time to restore
the stolen beads and shards,
the bones and knives to every grave. (70)

The image of the grave as womb forces the reader to reconsider American Indian artifacts and their treatment all across the United States.[9] This time Rose does not just make bones speak, but she makes them dance vibrantly and beautifully:

And the graves are graves no longer but wombs;
the bounties burn their hands
and bones come flowing
from museum shelves
to dance in the rippling grass,
rebuilding lungs, starting hearts. (70)

As a matter of fact, the rising of the bones and their triumphant life dance is consistent with the Native belief in survival, healing, continuance, and the most adequate final image that the reader should associate with Rose's work.

Itch Like Crazy celebrates Rose's own and America's cultural hybridization[10] as she projects the commensality of the various ethnic groups traceable in her own and other Americans' ancestry. She invites to the table the Taino, Mohawk, Chukchansi, Hopi, Mandinka, Ibo, Pict, and Celt (44), giving all these ethnic identities equal status in the making of the nation. Elsewhere, she acknowledges the multiplicity of class affiliations that go into building a sense of Americanness and embraces the erasure of class distinction:

feudal lord or farmer,
tacksman or baron,
pauper or prince,
all of them tumble
together in my blood. (39)

The togetherness of divergent forces is the result of a personal and political action on which the poet had embarked from the very beginning. Thus, investigating her immigrant and Indigenous family ties, Rose assumes her own kinship responsibilities and makes others aware of their own. While programmatically militant in tone, her decolonizing and feminist text is also aesthetically valuable. How strongly Rose's approach to migration impacts others remains an issue for each of her readers to decide, based on their own affiliations and sensibilities.

NOTES

1. In "Rituals of Remembrance," Christina Ljungberg advances a detailed discussion of photography as a "unique vehicle for moving between past and present" (246), focusing on its functions in three novels.

2. Wong devotes the study quoted here, "Native American Visual Autobiography," to works by N. Scott Momaday and Leslie Marmon Silko.

3. When analyzing the viewers' involvement with colonization in this text, Robin Riley Fast ruminates:

Any reader who has, in museums or galleries, casually or studiously observed Native "artifacts" must be drawn into complicity by the juxtaposition of epigraph and poem: we have on some level benefited from some of the practices implied, for our aesthetics, or "appreciation," have been "enriched" by the collecting and cataloging of the objects on which we gaze. But each poem's body forces a recognition of the bodies and lives of Native peoples, and the horrors that made some of the artifacts "available" to collectors. (54)

4. George J. Sánchez's entry dedicated to the concept of ethnicity in *A Companion to American Thought* discusses John Bodnar's *The Transplanted: A History of Immigrants in Urban America* (1985), whose premise is that immigrants preserve

their culture, as one of the critiques offered to the history of the United States published by Oscar Handlin under the title of *The Uprooted* (1951).

5. Criticism about the volume has remarked this, Dubin's final pronouncement being:

> Despite her overwhelmingly personal subject matter, the poems are more than narcissistic confessionals; her sparsely populated lines leave room for larger meanings. In many ways, her story is our story, the story of anyone whose "mixed" ancestry includes the powerful and powerless and leaves us wondering where we stand. (90)

6. Among the many sources pertinent for this discussion, Paula Gunn Allen's *Pocahontas* (2004) stands out for its presentation of the American Indian perspective.

7. Elsewhere in the volume, Rose defines the meeting between these forces as "the loving and unloving clashes" between Europeans and Natives (Part 3: "Listen Here for the Voices").

8. The inappropriateness of desecrating Native burial grounds in the name of science is a concern that has been apparent from the earliest stages of Rose's career, as one of the first articles ever dedicated to her work addresses the issue in its opening paragraph. James R. Saucerman notices that Rose confronts the problem directly given her personal, tribal, and professional background (26).

9. The poetic endeavor here parallels Louise Erdrich's tackling of similar issues in her novel *The Painted Drum*.

10. Hybridization is the concept at the center of one of the most insightful critical essays written in connection to Rose's work to date (see Tongson-McCall).

WORKS CITED

Allen, Paula Gunn. *Pocahontas: Medicine Woman, Spy, Entrepreneur, Diplomat.* HarperCollins, 2004.

Bruchac, Joseph. "The Bones Are Alive: An Interview with Wendy Rose." *Survival This Way: Interviews with American Indian Poets.* University of Arizona Press, 1987, pp. 249–69.

Courlander, Harold. *The Fourth World of the Hopis: The Epic Story of the Hopi Indians as Preserved in Their Legends and Traditions.* University of New Mexico Press, 2000.

Dubin, Margaret. "*Itch Like Crazy* (Review)." *Studies in American Indian Literatures*, vol. 16, no. 1, 2004, pp. 87–90.

Fast, Robin Riley. *The Heart as a Drum: Continuance and Resistance in American Indian Poetry.* University of Michigan Press, 1999.

Fivush, Robyn, and Janine P. Buckner. "Creating Gender and Identity through Autobiographical Narratives." *Autobiographical Memory and the Construction of a Narrative Self: Developmental and Cultural Perspectives*, edited by Robyn Fivush and Catherine A. Haden, Lawrence Erlbaum, 2003, pp. 149–68.

Godfrey, Kathleen. "'A Blanket Woven of All These Different Threads': A Conversation with Wendy Rose." *Studies in American Indian Literatures*, vol. 21, no. 4, 2009, pp. 71–83.

Hieb, Louis. "Hopi World View." *Southwest*, edited by Alfonso Ortiz. Volume 9 of *Handbook of North American Indians*, edited by William C. Sturtevant. Smithsonian Institution, 1979, pp. 577–80.

Hughes, Sheila Hassell. "Unraveling Ethnicity: The Construction and Dissolution of Identity in Wendy Rose's Poetics." *Studies in American Indian Literatures*, vol. 16, no. 2, 2004, pp. 14–49.

Hunter, Carol. "A MELUS Interview: Wendy Rose." *MELUS*, vol. 10, no. 3, 1983, pp. 67–87.

Justice, Daniel Heath. "'Go Away, Water!': Kinship Criticism and the Decolonization Imperative." *Reasoning Together: The Native Critics Collection*, edited by Craig S. Womack, Daniel Heath Justice, and Christopher B. Teuton. University of Oklahoma Press, 2008, pp. 147–68.

———. *Why Indigenous Literatures Matter*. Wilfrid Laurier University Press, 2018.

Ljungberg, Christina. "Rituals of Remembrance: Photography and Autobiography in Postmodern Text." *The Seeming and the Seen: Essays in Modern Visual and Literary Culture*, edited by Beverly Maeder, Jürg Schwyter, Ilona Sigrist, and Boris Vejdovsky. Peter Lang, 2006, pp. 246–62.

Rader, Dean. *Engaged Resistance: American Indian Art, Literature, and Film from Alcatraz to the NMAI*. University of Texas Press, 2011.

Rose, Wendy. *Bone Dance*. University of Arizona Press, 1994.

———. *Itch Like Crazy*. University of Arizona Press, 2002.

———. "Neon Scars." *I Tell You Now: Autobiographical Essays by Native American Writers*, edited by Brian Swann and Arnold Krupat. University of Nebraska Press, 1987, pp. 252–61.

Sánchez, George J. "Ethnicity." *A Companion to American Thought*, edited by Richard Wightman Fox and James T. Kloppenberg. Blackwell, 1995, pp. 216–19.

Saucerman, James. "Wendy Rose: Searching through Shards, Creating Life." *Wicazo Sa Review*, vol. 5, no. 2, 1989, pp. 26–29.

Tongson-McCall, Karen. "The Nether World of Neither World: Hybridization in the Literature of Wendy Rose." *American Indian Culture and Research Journal*, vol. 20, no. 4, 1996, pp. 1–40.

Wiget, Andrew. "Blue Stones, Bones, and Troubled Silver: The Poetic Craft of Wendy Rose." *Studies in American Indian Literatures*, vol. 5, no. 2, 1993, pp. 29–33.

Wong, Hertha D. Sweet. "Native American Visual Autobiography: Figuring Place, Subjectivity, and History." *The Iowa Review*, vol. 30, no. 3, 2000, pp. 145–56.

Chapter 4

Mothers/Lovers of Exiles

Women Characters in Dinaw Mengestu's All Our Names

Patrycja Kurjatto-Renard

Emma Lazarus's sonnet "The New Colossus," written with the aim of raising money to build the pedestal of the Statue of Liberty and published in 1883, is frequently taken to mean that the greatness of the United States resides in its ethnic diversity. For instance, James Comey (former FBI director), Nancy Pelosi (House Minority Leader), and Madeleine Albright (former Secretary of State) all agree on this interpretation (cf. Hunter; Mettler). Consequently, the sonnet is often used to criticize anti-immigrant sentiment and legislation, as has been the case recently, during Donald Trump's presidency. Nonetheless, I agree with Walt Hunter that seeing this text as a celebration of America's diversity is somewhat restrictive. To my mind, what matters most is its ethical dimension. Indeed, the sonnet uses the image of America as the selfless bene-factor to reinforce the opposition between the Old and the New Worlds. The Mother of Exiles, representing the United States, is opposed to the statue of the Greek god Helios, standing for the Old Continent. Interestingly, the poem personifies the Statue of Liberty without doing the same for Helios's statue, a stylistic choice that highlights America's life-affirming values. Lazarus juxtaposes woman to man, modern to ancient, American to European, living to dead. Last but not least, she juxtaposes empathy to indifference.

What further complicates the sonnet's meaning is the historical context in which it was written. The 1880s was a period of the American working class' intense anxiety about losing jobs to an incoming labor force. In 1882, the Chinese Exclusion Act curbed Chinese immigration (cf. Dinnerstein et al., 210, 232), but this did not suffice to appease the white laborers worried about Chinese competition in agriculture. As a result, the white laborers resorted to violence in order to drive the Chinese out (cf. Takaki 200–201). Jewish immigrants from Eastern Europe came to the United States fleeing massive pogroms and often faced horrible living conditions in the New Land, working in sweatshops and sometimes perishing from fires in clothes manufactures, where many of them worked. Lazarus participated actively in the fight to improve the plight of this group of immigrants. Her sonnet was also penned in the period of massive development of European colonialism in Africa. In short, the context it was created in was one of rapid spread of colonialism, the rise of nationalism, and the development of measures directed against immigrants to the United States.[1]

In this chapter, I analyze Helen, arguably the fictitious equivalent of the Mother of Exiles in Ethiopian American novelist Dinaw Mengestu's *All Our Names* (2014). I propose a reading of this character based on its function in the novel and on some relevant intertexts. First of all, *All Our Names* is markedly different from Mengestu's previous novels because it is composed of interweaving male and female narratives—stories that appear gendered not only because of being told by a male and a female narrator, respectively, but also because of the apparent weight given to each gender's presence. Isaac's narrative is almost exclusively peopled with male characters. Helen's tale includes important male and female characters but focuses on the female point of view. It may thus be productive to read it in comparison with *The Beautiful Things That Heaven Bears* and *How to Read the Air*, Mengestu's previous novels, whose narrators are male. "The New Colossus" is an important intertext for *All Our Names*, so I will look at the way Mengestu comments on the Mother of Exiles. Finally, while Mengestu does not write traditional immigrant fiction, certain tropes from it do appear in his text, and discussing them may illuminate aspects of his novel. In particular, I will compare Mengestu's vision of cross-cultural relationship with its representations in Asian American novels.

Before I begin to discuss Helen, it is important to recall that contrary to Mengestu's previous novels, this one is not set around the time when it was written. Instead, it conjures up the beginning of the 1970s. The Vietnam War, the Civil Rights Movement, Women's Lib and second-wave feminism, as well as the "Cold War era of suburbanization, acquisitive individualism, coercive conformism, and *Leave It to Beaver* family idealism" (Lee 44), provide the sociohistorical context for the narrative. Moreover, as Mengestu said in an interview, Helen is "sort of a compilation of many women that I have met and known throughout my life. . . . I've never known a social worker exactly like Helen, but I have known many good women like her" (Neary). As the character who welcomes Isaac to American society, is Helen a Statue of Liberty-like, beckoning, mild-eyed, mighty woman, bearing the light of hope? The novel exposes her limitations, resulting from the structure of the racist and patriarchal society to which she belongs, from her own responses to that society, and from her psychological makeup. I will analyze Helen's functions as a character in the depicted world, where she is a relief worker, a daughter, and an unmarried woman uncomfortable with her own place in society. I will also discuss Helen's role as the source of one of the narrative voices in the novel. Last but not least, I will use various critical approaches because Mengestu's work calls for more than one theory to account for its innovative treatment of immigrant fiction.

THE RELIEF WORKER

Mengestu's Helen, the social worker from the Midwestern small town of Laurel who is given the task of welcoming and taking care of Isaac, freshly arrived from Africa on a student visa, can be seen as a modern, disenchanted version of Lazarus's Mother of Exiles. As a matter of fact, she draws the comparison herself when she says that at the moment of meeting Isaac, she "was convinced [she] had already spent all the good will [she] had for [her] country's poor, tired and dispossessed, whether they were black, white, old, fresh from prison, or just out of a shelter" (12). At that time, Helen had been a social worker for five years, and it appears that her initial enthusiasm had disappeared under the weight and the thrust of the sheer number of the dis-possessed she was supposed to help. At that point, Helen had arrived at the conclusion that her job was pointless and that she could actually change very little. She remembers being exhausted and feeling that instead of standing above the harbor, she was drowning in the water below: "I had lost too much of the heart and all the faith needed to stay afloat in a job where every human encounter felt like an anvil strung around my neck just when I thought I was nearing the shore" (12).

For us as readers, the image of drowning that Helen evokes is also the tragic fate of migrants trying to cross the sea and dying in shipwrecks, the number of which has increased so dramatically between 2009 and today. The most notorious of these shipwrecks is no doubt the 2013 Lampedusa disaster in which at least 300 migrants lost their lives, but numerous others have occurred on the crossing between Libya and Lampedusa, the crossing that Deborah Ball, writing for the *Wall Street Journal*, called "the deadliest migrant route in the world." The statistics of human loss are staggering: there were at least twenty-two shipwrecks between April and September 2015; the following year witnessed at least 4,500 migrant deaths in the Mediterranean Sea, a number that decreased in 2017 to under 3,000, still a large toll. It is as if, through empathetic association with the plight of the impoverished, Helen had turned into a boat woman in her own country. This transformation paves the way for her new mission of taking care of an actual immigrant from Africa.

Simultaneously, the shipwreck is a common theme in American and European literatures, both in popular narratives and in canonical works of fiction. Homer's character Ulysses suffers from shipwreck. If we limit ourselves to a few examples from American literature, we can mention Edgar Allan Poe's "MS Found in a Bottle" (1833), Henry Wadsworth Longfellow's "The Wreck of the Hesperus" (1842), Stephen Crane's "The Open Boat" (1897), Jack London's *The Sea-Wolf* (1904), and H. P. Lovecraft's "Dagon" (1917). There is a religious dimension to this tradition, as can be seen in Increase Mather's *Essays on the Recording of Illustrious Providences* (1682) or in Jonathan Dickinson's *God's Protecting Providence Man's Surest Help and Defense in Times of Greatest Difficulty and Imminent Danger* (1699). Literary shipwrecks may have a double meaning of evoking God's wrath or offering a promise of redemption. Furthermore, shipwrecks can offer a counterimage to colonial growth; "the tradition of shipwreck writing is a disruptive chapter in expansionist historiography, a narrative practice of representing disaster that (partially) establishes itself outside the official parameters of textual production and authority by which the workings and benefits of empire enter narrative representation" (Blackmore 28). Shipwreck is a violent disruption of status, in which the privileged subject is ejected from its subject position and loses the power to dominate the world. Besides, in many shipwreck narratives, the reader encounters tales of bestiality, as hunger and despair force the survivors to adopt behaviors they would never consider resorting to otherwise. Finally, the "shipwreck route is the road to nowhere" (Blackmore 33). Thus, when Helen uses the metaphor of drowning, she identifies both with the illegal immigrants from underdeveloped countries and with the characters firmly rooted in EuroAmerican cultural tradition. She hints at her despair when she feels she is "on the road to nowhere," and drowning reflects her loss of status as a privileged Western citizen whose job supposedly makes her able to deal with the other people's misfortune.

Later on in the narrative, Helen explains that over the years she has come to see herself as a caretaker, dispensing "bandages to bleeding souls and broken hearts" (Mengestu 74). For her, her profession has acquired the dimension of nursing. Nursing, taking care of the suffering, providing solace and assistance to the less fortunate, belong to the occupations classified in contemporary Western culture as typically feminine, and in this way, Helen may be said to correspond to the stereotype of the good woman. However, as we shall see, she does not feel comfortable in the role of mother/caregiver, and this is not only because of the psychological impact that dealing with the dispossessed has on her.

Helen's occupation and the fact that she meets Isaac through it link her not only to Lazarus's poem but also to the numerous works of fiction "whose protagonists go abroad, or who carry within them a sense of being abroad"

(Varvogli XIII). Typical characters of such narratives include aid workers and aspiring philanthropists. However, those characters are not always drawn sympathetically; in fact, their motivations and values are often questionable. Varvogli claims that in the contemporary American novel, the "typically American philanthropic impulse" is shown to be "an often misguided attempt to help the less fortunate" (75). For example, Russell Banks's *The Darling* features a "disorienting" (Varvogli 7) narrative in which confusion comes from the attitude of the narrator, Hannah, and from her "attitudes to gender and sex relations, her white liberal guilt and her attempt to reconcile her various roles as wife, mother, political activist and animal carer" (8). Philip Caputo's *Acts of Faith* also questions the sincerity and the motivations of relief workers, featuring an aid worker whose attitudes contrast with his vocation. As an aid worker involved in helping the dispossessed, Helen belongs to the long line of fictitious relief workers and nurses of the soul, but she repeatedly calls her motivations into question.

As Isaac's social worker and his lover, Helen is supposed to guide the young man in his transformation from a sojourner into an immigrant by showing him the model of correct behavior and teaching him the proper attitudes and cultural values of America (cf. Huang 124). However, Helen does not seem to be much more at ease in her own hometown than Isaac. In numerous situations, she starts something that she has no strength or stamina to control, for example when she suggests she and Isaac should have lunch in a diner that turns out not to welcome black patrons or when she hides in her car in front of the building where Isaac lives so as to learn who her lover is talking to, but ends up fearing discovery by that mysterious person. Helen does not appear to have many friends or other kin: she is almost as isolated as Isaac in spite of having spent her whole life in the same town. Even though she represents the resident mainstream society, she seems to be as estranged from it as Isaac is. While in some narratives dealing with migrants the reader meets the assumption that "racial discrimination [against a member of a non-white ethnic group] can be 'overcome' as long as one has a white friend/guide" (Huang 126), it is not so in Mengestu's narrative. In this sense, then, Helen fails in her role as the Mother of Exiles, which is not due to her lack of goodwill, but rather to her ambiguous status in the community and her ambivalent relationship to the gender roles that she is supposed to fulfill.

THE STORYTELLER

Helen is the narrator of roughly half of the novel, which consists in a series of short chapters told from her and Isaac's points of view. On the surface, this structure makes it look like a very popular and often criticized subgenre of the

Asian American novel, "the two-plot or multi-plot novel that connects culture clashes . . . to gender issues by juxtaposing the 'exotic' past of an earlier immigrant generation" and representations of the present life in America (Wagner 152). There are also obvious differences, since Mengestu's characters are the same age and are lovers, and since the depictions of American life are not sentimental. Besides, Asian American fiction of that subgenre tends to include large families and large family gatherings, while Mengestu's characters are isolated from their respective families. If I bring up this dissimilarity, it is because of the importance of two elements in Asian American two-plot subgenre fiction: the trope of food and the "pairing of domestic and exotic" (Wagner 155–56). Furthermore, Mengestu's novel features another favorite plot device known from Asian American fiction: the mother–daughter ongoing conflict, although the mother and the daughter in this text come from the dominant white ethnic group.

While Helen's chapters are set in America and deal largely with her relationship with Isaac, Isaac's chapters are set in Africa at an earlier date and deal with what happened to him prior to his arrival in the United States. As a reader, I progressively started having problems with the contents of Isaac's chapters, as it occurred to me that in spite of the lively pace of the story and of the insight they offered into the character's motivations, they remained somehow sketchy. Uganda as represented in the novel is "lawless and chaotic," which makes it similar to the symbolic or mythical Africa that appears in many Western narratives (Varvogli 5). In the diegesis, this sketchiness is justified because the narrator, Isaac, is a migrant from a neighboring country who has left behind his family, his village, and his country in order to strike out on his own and go to Uganda. The young man dreams about becoming a famous writer, and he claims that he has deliberately refused to call Kampala by its name and prefers using a more generic term: "capital." However, the image of Africa in his chapters is troublingly similar to the EuroAmerican representation of the continent, in which "the gap between imagination and reality remains a large one" (Varvogli 4). This does not mean that I wish to accuse Mengestu of profiting from the "'alterity industry' built on 'mechanics of exoticist representation/consumption'" (Wagner 158). However, I do think the awareness of the alterity industry is definitely present in the background. Isaac's narrative provides a vivid description of exotic atrocities. The question is: Who constitutes the avid audience at which those descriptions are targeted? To answer this question, it may be helpful to examine Mengestu's other novels.

In *How to Read the Air* (2010), Mengestu's second novel, Jonas imagines a number of lives. First, he tries to use what little he knows about his parents' past to reconstruct their early life in the United States, before he was born; then, he does much the same for a living, trying to write the accounts of immigrants' lives, which would appeal to immigration officers. Finally, he tells his students the story of his father's flight from Africa. Throughout the novel, he is constantly referring to the tales he spins, using the few facts in his possession to construct a fascinating story. My reading of *All Our Names* was increasingly influenced by the memory of the previous novel, until I arrived at the tentative conclusion that possibly Helen was inventing Isaac's tale.

In her narrative, Helen is constantly complaining about her lack of knowledge of Isaac's existence, both past and present. The questions she asks do not seem to receive satisfactory answers, and Isaac tends to disappear from time to time without any notice. As a social worker in charge of the case, she might expect and be expected to be well informed, but the file she receives has very little information in it: "There was no month or date of birth, only a year. His place of birth was listed only as Africa, with no country or city. The only solid fact was his name, Isaac Mabira, but even that was no longer substantial: any name could have filled that slot, and nothing would have changed" (98). The reader familiar with the novel knows how right she is: indeed, the name she has been given is not her lover's birth name, but the one he inherited along with the documents that enabled him to come to the United States, and it is a combination of his best friend's first name and the latter's lover's family name—according to Isaac's narrative.[2] Even when Helen jokingly tries to evoke the possibility of one day meeting his mother, he rejects the suggestion as if it were totally impossible.

There are a few possible ways of explaining this silence about his past on Isaac's part. For instance, it may result from Isaac's wish to be rid of his past and look forward to the future: "Migration can come to reference a 'geographical repression' of the past since it entails literally leaving behind a place where memories occurred, while entering a new land which is relatively empty of reminders of the past" (Einsiedel 24). However, I began to wonder if, given Mengestu's interest in storytelling and inventing lives, Helen may not be filling in the gaps in her knowledge of Isaac. If this is true, then Helen is Isaac's mother in the same way that Isaac #1 back in Kampala was his father: they take their turns filling in various empty places so as to create a wholly new character. Isaac and Helen build an "isolated reality" (21), which may also mean that it is isolated *from* reality. In fact, in Helen's narrative, her lover Isaac appears to have the same "mirage-like quality" that Bénédicte Ledent attributes to Judith (115), Sepha's love interest in Mengestu's first novel.

Judith's house is usually described as glowing with lights and illuminating the entire neighborhood. This element hints at its kinship with Lazarus's sonnet, representing the beacon projecting light over the troubled waters and showing the way to migrants. It also shows that the promise made in Lazarus's poem cannot be kept, as Judith's house represents gentrification. But in

All Our Names, Helen has no house of her own, and it is Isaac's apartment that is occasionally depicted as a source of light in the darkness of the street (cf. 114, 126). However, in his apartment lights are also described as insufficient: "while he was outside with me the lights in his living room, specifically the lamp next to the dining-room table—the one I had brought from my own house after he told me that his living room was too dark to read in at night—had been turned on" (Mengestu 114). The mood created by this sentence is one of mystery, as Helen does not know who may have lit the lamps. Comparing the two novels, the reader can observe a reversal of the situation: in *All Our Names*, the beacon is much dimmer and situated in an immigrant's dwelling. At the same time, it is significant that Helen, the Mother of Exiles, was the one who improved, so to speak, the light in Isaac's apartment by giving him a lamp by which to read.

First-person narration sometimes mirrors the character's problems with his or her identity construction. Evidently, Helen feels there is a discrepancy between her ideal identity (autonomous, adventurous, active, outspoken, honest) and the one society allows her to display (passive and dependent, full of secrets and lies). As the narrator of her own story, she tries to explain the discrepancy between the two. One of the techniques she uses to achieve this goal harks back to second-wave feminism and the women's liberation movement, which constitute part of the historical background of the novel. Helen consistently compares herself with her mother, presented as the stereotypical ideal woman.

THE MOTHER AND THE DAUGHTER

Reading the passages of the novel dealing with the relationship between Helen and her mother Audrey, the reader may be struck by their similarity to women's autobiographical and fictitious narratives of the 1980s and 1990s in their dealing with mother–daughter relationships. In those texts, "the mother appears as a problematic figure, towards whom the author experiences contradictory feelings of closeness and distance" (Gamble 279). However, in *All Our Names*, there is little reconstruction of the mother's story. Instead, the narrative is built around Helen's refusal to identify with the old and discredited model offered by Audrey's unsatisfactory personal life. The differences between Helen and Audrey are strongly emphasized, and they help to structure Helen's telling of her love relationship with Isaac.

Helen has a problematic relationship with her mother, Audrey. She keeps contrasting her own various decisions and characteristics with her mother's while at the same time depending on her mother's words to define herself. At the beginning of the novel, the reader learns that Helen is "a woman of a certain age," her mother's way of criticizing her daughter's status as an unmarried woman, which incidentally may be one of the ways the narrator uses to strike back at her mother's snobbery. It is as if Helen wanted to silence her mother, to exorcize her, in order to reassure her own survival, but without ever being able to reach this goal. After all, she keeps evoking the differences between herself and her mother, speaking of her desire to differentiate herself from Audrey, which signals her incapacity to free herself from the mother–daughter relationship in spite of not finding solace in it.

Unlike her mother, Helen speaks loudly, even screams, sometimes in public places, and yet keeps apologizing for raising her voice. Her mother, in contrast, is presented as a consistent whisperer careful about the impression she makes on others and therefore not willing to express her own opinions. It seems that by telling her story, Helen would like to eliminate or at least to repress the mother. In other words, her mother has to "die to narrative possibility" (Gilbert and Gubar 378). Helen's father, however, is deprived even of that small presence in the narrative: Helen does not even describe him clearly, claims to have lost touch with him many years before, and like her mother, her father is also presented as somebody who does not speak much. If "without language there is neither gender nor gender-oriented desire" (Wright 101), both Helen's parents are shown as asexual beings. This idea is confirmed by the passages in which Helen recollects lying in bed between her parents and feeling more alone than by herself in her own bedroom.

Contrary to her mother, Helen is a poor cook and housekeeper (cf. Mengestu 19), which in her own words stems from the desire to rebel against her mother's authority and example: "I ruined the domestic chores dear to her because they were the only things in her life she could control" (73). Helen's mother seems to consider housework as a means of expressing her femininity and her creativity, which constituted the basis of an ideal woman stereotype in the American 1950s (cf. Coontz 27). Helen also presents her mother as a person who is very emotional and who does not like driving, two elements associated with a stereotypical woman in Western society, representing the idea that women should be associated with feeling rather than with thinking, and nature rather than culture.

Furthermore, their physical appearance is totally different. Helen's hair is fair and rather short, while her mother's is "long and dark brown, almost black" (Mengestu 125). Helen's legs are said to be "slender," while her mother has thick calves and small feet. Helen also says that "she had small hands, with long, delicate fingers that I imagined could easily break. My palms were large, and so were my fingers—man's hands, a boy in grade school had called them" (125). These elements of description show that Helen wishes to highlight her mother's femininity and ladylike behavior, and at the same time present herself as masculine. Women's Liberation activists of the late 1960s and early 1970s would recognize the importance of this statement, since they strongly objected to the roles of "apolitical, unoffending, passive, delicate (but delighted by drudgery) *things*" (Morgan quoted in Gamble 31).

Helen does not desire to have children and claims never to have been in love before. She also combines educational level with maternity, saying, "I went to college; she was pregnant and married two years out of high school" (Mengestu 125). All these may be defense mechanisms, as Helen openly states that she is afraid of becoming like her mother. "She had an empty house that she tried her best to care for, and I had the lives of strangers that I was hopelessly trying to clean up after. I thought I would be fine as long as that was all we had in common" (76). Helen, like second-wave feminists, struggles hard (although in private) to get away from the fifties' ideal of femininity her mother represents.

Helen defines herself against the women she does not want to become because she lacks a positive role model. She refuses to be like her mother, and also like Rose, a widow living alone who has changed her name and whom she visits in her capacity as social worker. Neither does she want to resemble the young timid waitress who does not want to offend her but does not have the courage to stand up to her boss. Helen wants to be courageous and adventurous, to experience a real connection to others, but her wishes are often thwarted. In spite of all that, or maybe because of that, no sooner does she meet Isaac than she is overcome with dreams of spending her life with him. After seeking to escape the tyranny of the ideal woman paradigm, and of the cultural codes of romance, marriage, and motherhood, she is willing to embrace them. "Playing house was the last thing I would have done as a child—my mother did that for the two of us—but now that it was my turn I was surprised how much pleasure it brought me" (74). Helen seems to be influenced by gendered roles that so far she has not fulfilled. Until that moment, she has been a childless single woman postponing the act of moving out of the family home, whose rare attempts at housekeeping had always failed. After meeting Isaac, however, she wants to adopt a different model of behavior. At one moment she wishes to make a twelve-egg omelet in Isaac's kitchen, even though Isaac is not at home and she hates eggs, so surely nobody will eat the dish. She observes: "I had never cooked or eaten inside of Isaac's apartment, but I was suddenly determined to do so. I thought of it not as trying to leave my mark but, rather, as trying to leave an impression on the place, a fingerprint that couldn't be easily removed" (73). Although this passage of the novel shows Helen "playing house," it also reveals her fight against "the Anglo social and philosophical order of the world, which is characterized by 'an order of purity' in which 'mixed elements' are something 'impure' that should be wiped off" (Herrera 23). Indeed, Helen feels relieved because her cooking is messy and brings life to Isaac's perfectly clean apartment. The choice of the dish can be read in the light of psychoana-lytical theory, too: Omelet, a "shapeless mass of eggs," was used by Lacan to depict an early stage in an infant's development, before the infant begins to feel that while it is separate from the outside world, it is also complete and its desires are satisfied (Wright 100). If we keep this image in mind, we can see that, for Helen, making the omelet and tossing it into the trash bin insinuates gaining independence from her mother and from Isaac at once, while at the same time bringing her a satisfactory sense of wholeness.

While there are few descriptions of meals and food in the novel, they are all revealing. The food evoked is bland and generic: an omelet, fried chicken, mashed potatoes. There are no references to exotic dishes, even if Isaac men-tions at one point that he finds it difficult to shop in America as the produce seems different. Moreover, there is a degree of discomfort and embarrassment present at mealtime. In *Reading Asian American Literature: From Necessity to Extravagance* (1993), Sau-ling Wong analyses the importance and diver-sity of food-related metaphors in Asian American writing (cf. 18–76); food and meals are associated with "personal and cultural self-affirmation" (Otano 217). The lack of knowledge of the sign language that eating and drinking constitute is commonly used as a device to show the dysfunctionality of families, the lack of cultural knowledge, as well as various stains on charac-ters' personalities that will preclude harmonious relationships between them. Tamara Wagner writes about family dinners in the Asian American two-plot subgenre of immigrant fiction: "Instead of engendering any commonality, ethnic identity, cross cultural exchange, or even longing for lost homelands, family meals are the site of exclusion, repulsion, and humiliation" (168). They are also struggles for power.

In contrast with Asian American immigrant novels in which scenes of humiliating meals abound, Mengestu avoids exoticizing the food but retains the element of shame, embarrassment, and psychological suffering character-istic of cross-cultural meal scenes in novels by Amy Tan and Maxine Hong Kingston. The most blatant example is the lunch at the diner, mentioned ear-lier. Helen has often eaten there, first with her father, and then on her own. Going to the diner is intended to be a statement, a way of making her love affair with Isaac official, because eating together belongs to the codes of dat-ing in America. Although she does not remember ever seeing black people inside, she is determined to have her way. Their entrance is not spectacular, contrary to what Helen had imagined, and nobody seems to be paying them any attention at first. However, they are soon asked if they wish to take their food away, and when Isaac declines the offer, his Denver omelet arrives a long time before Helen's food is served. While his dish is served on a "stack of thin paper plates barely large enough to hold the food" with a plastic fork and knife placed on top, Helen's order is on the standard china plate with regular silverware. Even though Isaac is the one being discriminated against, the narrative dwells upon his strength and Helen's embarrassment. It is Isaac who insists on not leaving, as Helen desires, but on staying and finishing the food. "With every bite I was reminded that we were no longer, if ever, on the same side" (38).

Contrary to the trauma subgenre of the migrant novel, Isaac's feelings in this scene are not dwelt upon. If anything, he is remarkably strong and reassures Helen, even though he is the butt of racism. Caren Irr claims Mengestu belongs to the group of writers who move beyond the trauma subgenre, substituting "transnational cultural exchanges" for "the romance of migrant psychology" (26). Of course, there is trauma in the depicted world, but no past secrets are unveiled, and in the trauma subgenre of the migrant novel, the diner scene would have been described through Isaac's eyes. Speaking about *How to Read the Air*, Irr notes that telling the story of a migrant is "a way to continue the enormously brave and dangerous act of walking away from horror and toward something new, an act associated in this novel with both of the narrator's parents, but especially the mother" (54). In *All Our Names*, it may be this walking away from past horrors that makes Isaac disregard humiliation at the diner.

The dinner Helen shares with Henry and Isaac is another moment of exclusion and humiliation, albeit to a lesser degree. First of all, Helen does not know how to react to Henry, Isaac's white mentor. Furthermore, although the dinner takes place in Isaac's apartment, all the food has been provided by Henry and cooked by his wife, who is not present:

> Henry brought everything to the dinner: the wineglasses on the table, the silver forks and knives, and the real cloth napkins that, in my mother's house, no occasion was special enough for. The chicken in the oven, he admitted, had been cooked by his wife that afternoon. (157)

The reasons behind her absence are not provided, but can be inferred. Henry lives in a different city, so his wife may have been reluctant to come so far, but it is possible that she did not wish to socialize with a black man and his white lover.

By retaining the psychological impact of humiliating meals and highlighting the struggles for power that are involved while not dwelling on the description of food, let alone introducing the reader to exotically sounding dish names, Mengestu manages to avoid tapping into the alterity industry. His novel does not use the meal scenes to sell exoticism to Western readers. Instead, these passages reinforce the impression of total isolation of characters from one another. Besides, they consistently present Helen as an unreliable food provider, which clashes with her role as the benevolent mother.

Mother is, after all, the archetypal food provider, distributing affection along with sustenance. Helen's mother, in contrast, is said to always prepare balanced and nutritious meals, even if the family meals tended to involve suffering for young Helen, since the meals during which Helen's father was absent and her mother refused to eat were another example of family power struggle over food.

Helen wants to believe in the possibility of a serious relationship with Isaac, even though it is clear that he will not be able to extend his visa. The text might depict her determination to help him get an extension of the visa, or to engage in other kinds of meaningful activity aimed at lengthening his stay. But this is not what happens: as it is, Helen admits she mostly avoided thinking about the deadline.

MOTHER OF EXILES AS BUILDER OF THE NEW WORLD? CLAIMING THE SPACE

In *Toward the Geopolitical Novel: U.S. Fiction in the Twenty-First Century* (2014), Caren Irr asks three questions about the ideological matrix of geopolitical fiction:

1. What kind of world do we inhabit now?
2. What does an ideal world look like?
3. How should we move from the actual to the ideal? (17)

In Irr's work, the responses to these questions are used to create a typology of novels along the lines of what political methods are suggested in various works to achieve the desired state. I would like to use them here much more modestly to question Helen's political commitment. We have seen that initially she was an optimist, truly believing that the world can be changed. The actual world did not appear satisfactory, and the ideal world would have less (or no) suffering, no loneliness, and much empathy. However, by the time she begins narrating her story, she has problems with moving from the actual to the ideal. Isaac is different from the other charges that she has because he is the first foreigner and the first African. This gives her new hope, or maybe the desire to be hopeful. In any case, she decides to improve the world she lives in by challenging racism. This motivates her to take Isaac to public places, such as shops, streets, a university library, a post office, and the diner. Helen feels the need to conquer spaces that are forbidden to interracial couples, but her motivation is not limited to the fight for civil rights. She also wishes to conquer the space that separates her from Isaac and to claim space for herself.

From the very beginning, Helen tells us that as a child she was annoyed with the idea of discretion and decorum as the ultimate measure of an appropriate existence. The first space-claiming she undertook was reading aloud in the backyard, where she could fill the space with her voice. This strategy partly backfired, for Helen found her voice and a place to speak her mind, but she was alone there. When she realizes that Isaac, about whom she cares, grows distant from her, she decides to fight back and to "find other things to do" (32) in addition to buying food. At this point, she realizes that in her part of the United States, the Midwest, people

> were exactly what geography had made us: middle of the road, never bitterly segregated, but with lines dividing black from white all over town, whether in neighborhoods, churches, schools, or parks. We lived semi-peacefully apart, like a married couple in separate wings of a large house. (33)

Then Helen proceeds to draw a list of "conquered" places in town, in other words, the sites where she went with Isaac regularly and where other patrons could have seen them exchanging signs of affection. By and large, she is confident they have claimed the right to be in spaces less directly related to romantic love codes, such as various shops (where married couples tend to go, but not lovers), but they are not successful in claims made with regard to the spaces associated with romance, such as restaurants.

The most important space to claim, though, remains the home. In a radio interview Mengestu indicates the ramifications of losing this claim:

> We often think that the immigrant story is unique to people who have left their homes. But for me it has increasingly become a story of people who have lost something essential to who they are and have to reinvent themselves and decide who they are in the wake of that loss. How do they find someone to love again? How do they find another home? How is this tied to the experience of violence? How does it reshape our sense of identity and how do we come to terms with it? (Paulick)

The idea of home is related to homeland, hometown, and one's proper home.

The place where Helen lives, Laurel, a Midwestern university town, has no real-life counterpart to my knowledge. There are several towns of that name in the United States, but only one has a university, and it is situated in Maryland. This imaginary town is placed in what Frederick Jackson Turner called the "region mediating between New England and the south and the East and the West" (23). For Turner, writing a century ago, this was a region ideal for creating a modern society offering the freedom to choose one's own destiny. For Isaac and for Helen, however, this freedom is quite limited, of which Helen is well aware: "The distance between what we had and what we wanted was too obvious if we dreamed closer to home" (1). Helen repeatedly refers to some codes permitting the transformation of old-world immigrants into Americans, such as romantic love and melting pot, hoping to create a symbolic kinship with Isaac. However, the final scene of the novel raises the readers' doubts about a felicitous outcome of their relationship.[3]

When answering a journalist's question about his choice to tell an immigrant story in his first novel, Mengestu pointed out the difficulty of forging a home out of memory, forgetting, and imagination:

> The thing that we're really trying to pursue and that's much actually harder to obtain, but absolutely necessary to make life meaningful, is that sense of home, and figuring out how do you actually go about recreating it now. What are the things that you need to both give up and the things you need to be able to forget and create, to actually make that transition possible? (Cole)

A typical immigrant narrative is organized around arrival and occupation, while an exilic narrative focuses on departure and loss of home space (cf. Cesare 120–21). In both cases, home is a stable and desirable place, whether it be situated in the past or in the future. In *All Our Names*, however, it is almost as if Helen were homeless: she lives with her mother while also sleeping at Isaac's apartment; she has been telling her mother for years that she wants to move out, but even at the end of the narrative, it is not at all certain she will. What is more, her mother's house is clearly not a haven of peace. It is described as too big for two persons, too grandiose, and it makes Helen remember unpleasant childhood scenes. This house epitomizes the time when Helen was growing up, the fifties, "a decade in which international politics became studiously ignored through an extensive focus on 'the home'" (Lee 52). Isaac's apartment, which Helen helped him decorate, is not a safe haven either: it can be invaded by Henry, a mysterious benefactor or enemy— Helen cannot decide which of the two is true—and it is the place from which Isaac disappears without notice. For Irr, this usage of the home is typical of neoliberal allegory, while the national allegory presented home as a site of reconciliation (cf. 118). However, there are numerous older narratives (especially penned by minority writers in the United States) that feature home as anything but a site of reconciliation.

Home is also linked to founding a family. "Capitalizing on the domestic narrative of home as a place of comfort and family values, [the national narrative of home ownership] deliberately confuses home ownership with home-making, so that the home one buys seems to confer automatically domestic comforts" (Lee 50). In Mengestu's novel, it appears that Helen is playing with the idea of home acquisition: she helps decorate Isaac's abode, and they shop together for furniture, as if they were a married couple—but for Helen, this is just the thing that annoys her. The "romantic notions of the home as a secure space or sign of a loving relationship" (Lee 52) do not apply to either Helen's mother's house or the apartment she half shares with Isaac. Helen's efforts to seduce Isaac and make him stay with her remain extremely ambiguous. As the narrator, Helen persuades us that her hesitation about founding a family may be related to her awkward relationship to her mother in particular and to gender roles in general. During the nineteenth century, "the home was constructed as the locus of love, emotion and empathy, and the burdens of nurturing and caring for others were placed on the shoulders of women"; doing housework and taking care of one's children came to be seen as "women's 'sacred' duty" (McDowell 75), and this perception remained valid until late into the twentieth century and has not quite disappeared. Helen's mother conforms to this vision of womanhood and domesticity, which does not bring her satisfaction. Helen's mother's house is perfect, and above all, perfectly clean; this is yet another element Helen rebels against, saying at one point that life is dirty, so if a person wants to live, they must allow themselves to be dirty.

In fact, both houses in which Helen dwells but cannot quite claim have two points in common: they reveal few signs of life, and they are only reluctantly sites of real relationships. And yet, "the house is the site of lived relationships, especially those of kinship and sexuality, and is a key link in the relationship between material culture and sociality: a concrete marker of social position and status" (McDowell 92). And as Carsten and Hugh-Jones mention, "the house is an extension of a person; . . . it serves as much to reveal and display as it does to hide and protect" (2). But the houses Helen tries to inhabit do more to hide than to display anything about their inhabitants. In the end, Helen appears to struggle to make a connection with the house, if not with the person who inhabits it, and fails. Even when she dirties Isaac's kitchen she cleans it up at least partly, as if ashamed of her own impulse to claim it as her home.

While Helen's representation of the United States is "couched in a domestic, familial, and gendered framework" (Lee 3), her narrative tends to open up to transnational concerns, rather than local ones, thanks to the juxtaposition with Isaac's chapters, which are not set in the distant past and which broaden the scope of the narrative. At the same time, the United States is not presented as a utopian society or an exceptional nation. In fact, some images draw the reader's attention to its striking similarity with Uganda through the evocation of violence. Thus, both in Laurel and in Kampala, tear gas is used against student demonstrators on campus. Within the universe of the novel, there appears to be less violence in the United States than in Uganda, but there is frustration on both sides of the Atlantic. As Mengestu said in an interview,

One of the things I have found working as journalist—and specifically covering conflicts and trying to meet men who, at some point in time, are or were in the process of becoming their own sort of revolutionary-like figures—I often found that there was a total randomness to it, a randomness not only to how they came into power, but to their causes and their sort of logic of why they began the violence. You know, violence kind of unfolded without a logical necessity behind it. You know, there was an expression of frustration and I think when you don't have any other means to express that frustration, violence quickly becomes the form. (Neary)

When Emma Lazarus was writing her most famous poem, she had become a poet committed to a cause: facilitating the integration of Jews arriving from Russia because of massive pogroms. The poem expresses the wish to establish the authority of the United States as the beacon of freedom, which has proven to be a long-lasting image. It also establishes a sharp ethical contrast between the Old and the New Worlds. Helen, a tentative Mother of Exiles active some eighty years after Lazarus wrote her poem, lacks the confidence attributed by Lazarus to her illustrious literary model. Unsure about her motivations and about the ways to achieve her goals, Helen embodies good will but lacks stamina and conviction to act. Besides, she is strikingly isolated, which makes her struggle for any cause even more difficult. In her own account, Helen appears to be an inefficient dreamer, closing her eyes to reality, perhaps even imagining the past of the migrant she is supposed to help. Her love for him does not motivate her to actively promote his cause. She may be hindered by the gendered code of passivity, by a long-lasting experience of not being able to fight against the current, or by a combination of other factors. She has no understanding of Isaac's life and no idea how to act in order to keep him by her side. She feels helpless whenever he disappears. Bound by her own constraints, trapped in the place and situation that she has not chosen and that she apparently lacks the strength to leave behind, Helen may provide some relief but is unable to offer lasting help.

In the interview with Lynn Neary, Mengestu claims that *All Our Names* is a book about love that "saves his characters and redeems them." I may be a pessimist, but this did not seem to be the obvious conclusion when I closed the novel—at least if we think about the feeling between Helen and Isaac. The kind of love that may offer a measure of redemption is the first Isaac's love for his friend, which helps the second Isaac survive—so we are led to believe, as he probably would have been killed if he had stayed in Uganda. As for Helen, she drives Isaac to Chicago and leaves him there, with vague intentions of returning and starting a life with him. In spite of her criticism of her mother's ideals of marriage and domesticity, this ending sounds like failure, as Helen does not present it as gaining independence but rather as one more sign of her own helplessness. Somehow, empathy and love are not enough when they are confronted with the reality of migrant existence.

NOTES

1. "'The New Colossus' stands at the intersection of US immigration policy and European colonialism, well before the physical Statue of Liberty was dedicated. The liberal sentiments of Lazarus's sonnet cannot be separated from these developments in geopolitics and capitalism" (Hunter).

2. Isaac's part of the novel deals mostly with his friendship with Isaac #1, a revolutionary who encounters a wealthy man, Mabira, and joins him in the preparation and execution of the coup d'état Mabira is planning. However, they are overcome after initial victories. These chapters all bear the heading "Isaac," which may be read as the narrator's name since, in parallel, Helen's chapters bear her name as the heading. However, at the time when this story is supposed to take place, Isaac #2 is not yet called by that name. Moreover, at the end of the novel, Isaac #2 says that his story was written for him by the original Isaac, who made a very good job of it. Those elements introduce some doubts about the identity of the narrator of those chapters. Besides, the beginning of Isaac #2's narrative casts a doubt on his reliability by labeling him and his best friend Isaac #1"liars and frauds" (Mengestu 7).

3. Cf. Sollors: "contribute to the construction of new forms of symbolic kinship among people who are not blood relatives" (283).

WORKS CITED

Aichih Wehbe Herrera, M. "Smashed to Pieces: Portrait(s) of the Self(ves) in *The Mixquiahuala Letters.*" *Masculinities, Femininities and the Power of Hybrid in U.S. Narratives: Essays on Gender Borders*, edited by Nieves Pascual, Laura Alonso-Gallo, and Francisco Collado-Rodríguez, Winter, 2007, pp. 21–30.

Ball, Deborah. "Hundreds of Migrants Believed Dead in Shipwreck Off Libya." *Wall Street Journal*, Apr. 19, 2015, https://www.wsj.com/articles/about-700-believ ed-dead-in-shipwreck-off-libya-says-unhcr-1429432174. Accessed Aug. 15, 2019.

Blackmore, Josiah. *Manifest Perdition: Shipwreck Narrative and the Disruption of Empire*. University of Minnesota Press, 2002.

Carsten, Janet, and Stephen Hugh-Jones, editors. *About the House: Lévi-Strauss and Beyond*. Cambridge University Press, 1995.

Cesare, Nicole. "'How Did I End Up Here?': Dynamic Cartography in Dinaw Mengestu's *The Beautiful Things That Heaven Bears.*" *Ariel: A Review of International English Literature*, vol. 64, no. 3, 2015, pp. 113–36.

Cole, Laura J. "An Interview with Dinaw Mengestu." *University of Central Florida Today*, Jan. 20, 2018, https://today.ucf.edu/interview-dinaw-mengestu/. Accessed Aug. 15, 2019.

Coontz, Stephanie. *The Way We Never Were: American Families and the Nostalgia Trap*. Basic, 2000.

Dinnerstein, Leonard, Roger L. Nichols, and David M. Reimers. *Natives and Strangers: A Multicultural History of Americans*. Oxford University Press, 1996.

Einsiedel, Doris. "Colonial Recall in Motion in *Desirable Daughters* and *The Namesake*." *Moving Migration: Narrative Transformations in Asian American Literature*, edited by Johanna C. Kardux and Doris Einsiedel, Lit, 2010, pp. 19–43.

Friedman, May, and Silvia Schultermandl, editors. *Growing up Transnational: Identity and Kinship in a Global Era*. University Press of Toronto, 2011.

Gamble, Sarah, editor. *The Icon Critical Dictionary of Feminism and Postfeminism*. Iconbooks, 1999.

Gilbert, Sandra M., and Susan Gubar. *No Man's Land: The Place of the Woman Writer in the Twentieth Century. Volume 3: Letters from the Front*. Yale University Press, 1994.

Huang, Su-ching. "The Americanization/Westernization of Jackie Chan: *Shanghai Noon* as Model Minority Discourse." *Moving Migration: Narrative Transformations in Asian American Literature*, edited by Johanna C. Kardux and Doris Einsiedel, Lit, 2010, pp. 117–38.

Hunter, Walt. "The Story Behind the Poem on the Statue of Liberty." *The Atlantic*, Jan. 16, 2018, https://www.theatlantic.com/entertainment/archive/2018/01/the-story-behind-the-poem-on-the-statue-of-liberty/550553/. Accessed Aug. 15, 2019.

Irr, Caren. *Toward the Geopolitical Novel: U.S. Fiction in the Twenty-First Century*. Columbia University Press, 2014.

Ledent, Bénédicte. "Reconfiguring the African Diaspora in Dinaw Mengestu's *The Beautiful Things That Heaven Bears*." *Research in African Literatures*, vol. 45, no. 4, 2015, pp. 107–18.

Lee, Rachel C. The *Americas of Asian American Literature: Gendered Fictions of Nation and Transnation*. Princeton University Press, 1999.

McDowell, Linda. *Gender, Identity and Place: Understanding Feminist Geographies*. University of Minnesota Press, 1999.

Mengestu, Dinaw. *All Our Names*. Sceptre, 2014.

Mettler, Katie. "'Give Me Your Tired, Your Poor': The Story of Poet and Refugee Advocate Emma Lazarus." *Washington Post*, Feb. 1, 2017, https://www.washingtonpost.com/news/morning-mix/wp/2017/02/01/give-us-your-tired-your-poor-the-story-of-poet-and-refugee-advocate-emma-lazarus/?noredirect=on&utm_term=.225796dd24cc. Accessed Aug. 15, 2019.

Neary, Lynn. "From Uganda to the Midwest, *All Our Names* Draws Portraits of Love." *NPR*, Mar. 8, 2014, https://www.npr.org/2014/03/08/287317671/from-uganda-to-the-midwest-all-our-names-draws-portraits-of-love. Accessed Aug. 15, 2019.

Otano, Alicia. "Rituals of Mothering: Food and Intercultural Identity in Gus Lee's *China Boy*." *Asian American Literature in the International Context: Readings on Fiction, Poetry, and Performance*, edited by Rocio G. Davis and Sämi Ludwig, Lit, 2002, pp. 215–26.

Paulick, Jane. "Dinaw Mengestu: 'Immigrant Is a Very Political Term.'" *Deutsche Welle*, Sep. 15, 2014, http://www.dw.com/en/dinaw-mengestu-immigrant-is-a-very-political-term/a-17921813. Accessed Aug. 15, 2019.

Sollors, Werner. "Beyond Ethnicity: Patterns of Consent and Descent in American Culture." *American Studies Today: An Introduction to Methods and Perspectives,* edited by Amritjit Singh et al., Creative, 1995, pp. 279–95.

Takaki, Ronald. *A Different Mirror: A History of Multicultural America.* Back Bay, 1993.

Turner, Frederick Jackson. *The Frontier in American History.* Holt, Rinehart and Winston, 1962.

Varvogli, Aliki. *Travel and Dislocation in Contemporary American Fiction.* Routledge, 2012.

Wagner, Tamara Silvia. "Realigning and Reassigning Cultural Values: Occidentalist Stereotyping and Representations of the Multiethnic Family in Asian American Women Writers." *Asian American Literary Studies,* edited by Guiyou Huang, Edinburgh University Press, 2005, pp. 152–75.

Wong, Sau-ling Cynthia. *Reading Asian American Literature: From Necessity to Extravagance.* Princeton University Press, 1993.

Wright, Elizabeth. *Psychoanalytic Criticism: A Reappraisal.* Routledge, 1998.

Chapter 5

The Securitized Migrant

Migrant Mobility and Kindred Alliances in Post-9/11 New York Novels

Isabella Karlsson

According to American philosopher Thomas Nail, the migrant is the key political figure of the twenty-first century, as our societies will be increasingly characterized by constant migratory flows. Although the United States has always been a "nation of immigrants," migration continues to play an important role for the country in the twenty-first century. Today, rising numbers of people are forced to leave their homelands for religious, political, environmental, or other reasons—frequently due to the global networks in which US international politics co-authors the migrant's fate. The topic of migration is also central to the politics of the so-called world literary narratives, including three contemporary novels that focus on migrants moving through the urban space of New York, namely Joseph O'Neill's *Netherland* (2008), Teju Cole's *Open City* (2011), and Atticus Lish's *Preparation for the Next Life* (2014).

In this chapter, I argue that a shift of attention from the migrant as traumatized figure to the migrant as politicized figure and potential source of threat is discernible in this corpus of novels that focus on the experience of immigrants. Written in the aftermath of the 9/11 terror attacks, the novels portray how New York has turned into an increasingly securitized and monitored space. In addition, the protagonists' various encounters with state authorities reveal that migrants commonly are regarded as a threat to national security. In this respect, the novels also allude to recent nonfictional developments that stigmatize and block the migrant from moving freely. Published before the Trump presidency, the novels thus reveal that the stigmatization of migrants is not a new development in the United States. However, I maintain that the protagonists' movements through the cityscape also create a counternarrative, which opposes the popular right-wing view of the migrant as threat to the "homeland." In the novels, kindred alliances between migrants and direct forms of engagement with urban space via joint walks, runs, or other sporting activities such as cricket open up spaces for intercultural encounters and show that, despite increasing surveillance, New York is still a vibrant and hybrid living space where different cultures interact.

Like the novels' protagonists, the authors have been migrants themselves and are arguably able to offer an "outside" view on the United States. Joseph O'Neill has an Irish American background, Teju Cole is an African American who grew up in Nigeria, and Atticus Lish is an American novelist who lived as an expatriate in provincial China and taught English there. All three novels are written from the migrant's point of view. *Netherland* is told from the first-person narrative perspective of Hans, a Dutch financial analyst who moves from London to New York City with his family. After his wife and son have returned to London because Rachel feels insecure in post-9/11 NYC, Hans joins the Staten Island Cricket Club and befriends Chuck Ramkissoon, an immigrant from Trinidad. Together with Chuck, he explores not only New York's cricket culture but also the city's various mixed communities. Told in retrospective, the novel makes known from the beginning that Chuck has been found murdered in a river and that Hans has returned to live in London, reunited with his family.

Like *Netherland*, *Open City* is narrated from a first-person perspective. In this novel, the reader follows the paths and trails of Julius, a doctor who emigrated from Nigeria and who seeks relief from his stressful and rigid workday by walking through the streets of NYC. Movement through New York's urban space is also the major focus of *Preparation for the Next Life*, which portrays the odd relationship between Zou Lei, an illegal immigrant from Uighur, a region in Northwest China, and Skinner, a traumatized and depressed ex-soldier who served three tours of duty in Iraq. Narrated from a third-person perspective, the novel shows that while Skinner sinks deeper and deeper into his post-war depression, Zou Lei works hard to survive in the metropolis. Together, they traverse the city on foot. Hence, all three novels share a strong focus on mobility and, due to their transnational focus, they can be classified as world novels.

Influenced by the real-world phenomena of increasing migration and the rise of global commerce, the genre of world novels aims to "make global conditions newly legible to American readers," as literary scholar Caren Irr points out in "Toward the World Novel" (660). She argues that "we can understand the world novel as arriving when the genres of the nation stretch to incorporate politically charged elements of the global scene" (661). Commonly offering the perspective of immigrants to the United States, many world novels present an outside view on the country by portraying "a collision of 'worlds' that throws the institutional and political specificities of the US into sharp relief" (663). The novels I discuss in this chapter are set in post-9/11 New York City and feature protagonists who immigrated to the United States and, in two instances, jointly explore the urban space of New York by walking, running, or driving. Thus, these characters are representative of a mobility that takes place both on a global scale in the form of immigration to the United States and on a local scale in the form of movement through the streets of NYC. Besides walking, moving through the city by car or in trains shows that New York has become increasingly securitized and reveals how mobility creates kindred alliances in a paranoid environment.

While globalization continues to be on the rise, heated media discussions about migration and the security of Western nations demonstrate conflicting opinions on migration and emphasize the need to rethink the role of the migrant. Two days after Donald Trump signed an Executive Order in January 2017 curbing immigration rights from travelers from seven Muslim countries for ninety days, he underscored his will to reinforce border controls via Twitter: "Our country needs strong borders and extreme vetting, NOW. Look what is happening all over Europe and, indeed, the world—a horrible mess!" (@realDonaldTrump, Jan. 29, 2017). According to the British newspaper *The Telegraph*, which refers to the order as "Muslim-majority immigration ban," the Executive Order affects people traveling to the United States from "Iran, Iraq, Libya, Somalia, Syria, Sudan and Yemen" (Sherlock). As news agencies from all over the world reported, the commencement of the order resulted in chaos and protests at several major US airports. However, Trump's immigrant ban and his tweet clearly reveal that his policy is focused not only on the reinforcement of borders but also on the control of migration flows. Thus, the Trump order makes the migrant the center of debate when national anxieties and identity politics are negotiated.

Although the discrimination against migrants is not a recent development in the United States, the novels examined in this chapter as well as Trump's politics suggest that the stigmatization of migrants has intensified since 9/11. The three novels address the fact that immigration to the United States became more difficult after the events of September 11 and that the situation for migrants living in America has been changing. While Trump's views were articulated quite recently, Nicholas De Genova makes clear that they are not new. He argues that political and rhetorical strategies turned the United States into a "National Security State" after 9/11. According to this scholar, certain rhetorical expressions such as referring to the United States as "homeland" were applied by government authorities to evoke nostalgia and justify the "War on Terror" as well as increased security measures. The "rhetoric of 'homeland,'" he explains, "has long been a hallmark of diasporic nostalgia and desire, and in effect discursively re-figures US citizens as ineffably alienated from their own 'native' entitlement to the comfort of unproblematic belonging" (423). De Genova quotes Amy Kaplan, who argues that the homeland discourse is about "breaking down the boundaries between inside and outside, about seeing the homeland in a state of constant emergency from threats within and without," with the consequence of "generat[ing] forms of radical insecurity" (quoted in De Genova 423). While politicians seem to narrate their own fictions of migration, counternarratives such as *Netherland*, *Preparation for the Next Life*, and *Open City* are highly topical since they offer an antithesis to depictions of migrants as threats to the nation.

By portraying migrant figures as multifaceted characters who do not fit the government's security profile but who actively engage with their urban environment, the novels oppose stereotypical categorizations of migrants as mere threats against national security and reveal New York as a place where love and friendship between migrants and locals is possible. In doing so, the novels emphasize how these characters deviate from patterns that are encouraged in the policing of metropolitan areas by stop and frisk programs or racial profiling. Although the novels arrive at this conclusion differently, all of them show that migrant fiction no longer revolves merely around issues of cultural difference and multiculturalism but rather that migrant mobility is perceived from a political perspective. Consequently, the novels demonstrate a shift from identity politics to security politics, and thus their narrative drive feeds on the shared assumption that the migrant is a potential source of threat. In different ways, the migrant protagonists struggle with the arbitrariness of the state apparatus. Irr points out that world novels commonly combine a global and a local perspective and are characterized by their "detailed descriptions of ordinary, dedicated people wrestling with the problems of the new millennium" (*Geopolitical* 3). Consequently, this kind of fiction "reveals some key features of contemporary political experience" (3). Even though Irr acknowledges that "any literary work may be said to be political at an unconscious level," politics are at the center of attention in geopolitical novels,[1] which means that usually "politically charged characters, settings, conflicts, and styles of narration comprise the foreground of the narrative as well as the background of the geopolitical novel" (3). In short, world novels intertwine global and local, political and social issues.

In the beginning of *Preparation for the Next Life*, protagonist Zou Lei experiences the harsh and inscrutable conditions for illegal immigrants in detention facilities after she is caught, arrested, and held without the opportunity for legal advice: "No one had told her what she had been charged with or on what basis she was being held. When she tried to ask what was going to happen to her, a deputy ordered her to move away and return to her side of the room" (11). The other inmates of the detention camp reveal to her that "no one knows what will happen to you," and they further inform her that "they can do anything they want, because of your status" (13). Furthermore, *Preparation for the Next Life* frequently alludes to the fact that Arabs or Muslims in particular have turned into targets for the brutality of security officials. At one point, a Guyanese Muslim tells Zou Lei that his uncle, who even possessed a green card, had been arrested by the police although he showed them his legal papers (cf. 177). In prison, "the guards went after anyone who was Asian Muslim, Trini, black, brown, whatever—anything like Arab," and as he further tells Zou Lei, "they'd come in with dogs at midnight, tear up the cell, and tear up your legal papers" (177). He informs Zou Lei that, after some time in prison, his uncle was deported to Guyana; currently "he can't get back to the States," and the only chance, according to the lawyer, is "try and wait until George Bush is gone" (117). Hence, Arab immigrants are portrayed as being especially prone to random seizures after 9/11, and their chances of being allowed to stay in the United States are very low.

Open City develops a similar view. At one point in the novel, Julius reflects on a trip to a detention facility together with his then-girlfriend's church group "The Welcomers." The detention facility is run by "Wackenhut, a private firm, under the jurisdiction of the Department of Homeland Security" and is a highly securitized area (62). At the facility, Julius talks to Saidu, a refugee from war in Liberia who has been forced to stay in the detention camp for over two years (cf. 64–65). Similar to Zou Lei's situation in the detention camp, Saidu also suffers from the capriciousness of the state apparatus: "They have just finished my case, and we made an appeal, but it was rejected. Now they are sending me back, but there is no date, just this waiting and waiting" (64). Furthermore, Saidu reveals to his listener that his lawyer sees little hope in his case and that he "might have had a chance before 9/11" (69). Zou Lei and Saidu had emigrated to America in hope of a better life, and both experience the power the state apparatus exercises over them. In addition to these experiences, the novel also highlights the dubious legality of privatized security forces after 9/11. Thus, both *Open City* and *Preparation for the Next Life* allude to the fact that 9/11 increased the (privatized) warehousing of migrants and portray how the government constrains immigrants in their mobility.

Netherland also offers an outside perspective on governmental institutions and repeatedly demonstrates the migrant's subjection to the whims of local authorities. When Hans decides to buy a car in the United States he is forced to revalidate his driver's license as it is impossible to "trade [his] British licence (itself derived from a Dutch one) for an American one: such an exchange was for some unexplainable reason only feasible during the first thirty days of an alien's permanent residence in the United States" (O'Neill 82). However, due to a minor spelling mistake on Hans's green card, the supervisor refuses to issue his learning permit and forces him to apply for a new green card (cf. 87–88). Hans finds himself in a "state of fuming helpless-ness" given the vagaries of the Department of Motor Vehicles (DMV) and the administrative hurdles he has to overcome (88). *Netherland* repeatedly refers to the restriction of migrant mobility as well as to the arbitrary rules and regulations of governmental institutions. When Hans visits the "Bureau of Citizenship and Immigration Services" to obtain a new green card, he observes that "within the jurisdiction of the federal building a negative dance was the rage, one which prohibited all blamelessly instinctive movement" (153). Thus, during that morning, Hans observed a man being "removed from the building for looking out the windows, another for leaning against the heating units, another for taking a telephone call" (153). This situation dem-onstrates the migrant's subjection to the rigid rules of the immigration bureau and reveals that the people in the building are tightly monitored. Hence, the incident at the DMV and Hans's observations show the encounter between migrants and the state and imply that government institutions commonly block the migrant's mobility.

Interestingly, not even Hans, who has a higher social status than Julius and Zou Lei, is immune to the government's arbitrariness. What is more, the scene also shows the ways in which government authorities exert disciplinary power over the migrants and thus forge a notion of desired vs. deviant behav-ior. Deviancy here is marked by the migrants' perceived loitering, distracted-ness, and disruptiveness. All of this shows the travesty of a notion of "respect toward the state" on a micro-level: the government institution serves as a micro-representation of the state, the authorities are readers of the migrant's behavior, and the migrant is an applicant who is not on equal terms with the employees of the agency. But he or she can be read as a "tolerated subject" as long as (s)he does not attract attention by consciously using or disrupting any of the vicinity's interior objects or workflows. Moreover, the migrant is only tolerated when (s)he is invisible and detainable at the authority's will. This correlates with Irr's observation that world literature portraying foreigners in America "often reveal[s] a more direct approach to institutional authority" and quite often "[is] concerned with narrating responses to 9/11" ("World" 668).

Arguably, these novels suggest that 9/11 triggered the securitization of both global and local mobility via surveillance of, for instance, public means of transportation and public spaces. In *Preparation for the Next Life* the penetration of public spaces by security officials becomes drastically obvious when Tesha, an Afghan shop owner, tells Zou Lei how the local residents found out after a while that a plain building in the heart of Queens had been transformed into a top-secret prison by Homeland Security (cf. Lish 319). A Muslim immigrant, a gas station owner who had been living in the United States for a long time and who was, according to Tesha, "a nice guy" (319), disappeared all of a sudden after 9/11. The immigrant's family was desperate to find him while he, during the whole time, was in their immediate vicinity. As Tesha reveals to Zou Lei,

> It's Homeland Security. Happen right here. The family put up pictures and everything. It kill them. All their face are falling down. You know where he is? The whole time he is right here in Queens. Nobody can see and he is right there, right there in Queensboro Plaza. They got a building it looks like the post office. By the time, they know about it, they put him in another jail in Texas. Five years. When the family say, okay, let's go to court—you think he's done something—No. We going to keep him. No, we will send him to the Middle East. (319)

The arbitrary seizure of an innocent Muslim immigrant without any explanation to his family demonstrates Homeland Security's brutal and inhumane modus operandi after 9/11. In addition to the apparently random detention of (Muslim) immigrants, the passage reveals the transformation of public spaces into secured areas, where immigrants are detained and exposed to secret interrogations. However, the novels portray New York as a city that is heavily monitored but simultaneously as a space that still allows for migrant mobility.

In all three novels, walking is portrayed as having a therapeutic effect. In *Open City*, walking serves as stress relief from Julius's work as a therapist. Walking not only forms an existential part of Julius's daily routines but also liberates him from professional strictures: While his "work was a regimen of perfection and competence, . . . the streets served as a welcome opposite to all that" (7). He appreciates the "aimless progress" (7) and the freedom his walks offer him: "Every decision—where to turn left, how long to remain lost in thought in front of an abandoned building, whether to watch the sun set over New Jersey, or to lope in the shadows on the East Side looking across to Queens—was inconsequential, and was for that reason a reminder of freedom" (7). Hence, Julius drifts along with the flow of the city and thus experiences a sense of liberation despite the fact that the city is characterized by increased security measures. Julius's aimless strolls resemble Skinner's and Zou Lei's walks and runs, which also have no specific destiny and constitute a form of therapy.

Walks and runs through NYC are an essential part of Skinner and Zou Lei's relationship. Usually, their movement is characterized by its arbitrariness, which means "there was no plan, they just walked" (Lish 118). The novel repeatedly demonstrates how walking creates a bond between them: "They fell into a rhythm, going for miles," and when, at one occasion, they reach a point from which they can look down upon NYC, they feel like "they were at the center of a wheel" (118). However, they do not only walk the city together, but they also appropriate urban space for their workouts. As Cathleen Schine argues, "they both find freedom in the pursuit of physical health and strength" because "controlling their bodies is the only control they have left." Zou Lei does not have many freedoms in the United States due to her status as an illegal immigrant. At one point, the narrator informs us that "above all, she wanted to do something she could control" and "reject every solution that involved going through a government office" (Lish 345). Since her mobility is the only thing Zou Lei can regulate, "she wished she could reduce everything to the simple physical test of running away" (345). Skinner, because of his PTSD, is also restricted in what he can and cannot do. Thus, he lives on the money he received from the army and spends most of his days in a dark basement room he rents from an Irish immigrant family. By walking the city, however, the characters create a sense of momentary freedom far away from their troubles with the authorities. Instead, "they travel through neighborhoods and boroughs as if they were rugged unsettled territories, deserts, mountains, steppes," as Schine notes. While mobility was connected to danger and death in Iraq, it is connected to freedom and hope in the United States. According to Skinner, in Iraq, "you went outside the wire, and each time, either you died or you did not" (Lish 207). In New York, however, mobility is linked to hope for a better life for Skinner and Zou Lei. Furthermore, especially in Zou Lei's case, mobility is linked to freedom: as long as she can move, she is free and has not been detained by the state authorities.

In *Netherland*, walking is not only a form of exploring the city for Hans but also a way of coping with the loss of his mother:

> After my mother's death I began taking long walks to Chinatown and Seward Park and the old Seaport area, pushing baby Jake in his stroller. On summery Pearl or Ludlow or Mott I'd find respite from our apartment and its transformation into a kind of parental coalmine, and walk and walk until I reached a state of fancifulness, of indeterminately hopeful receptiveness, which seemed to me an end in itself and as good as it got. These walks were, I guess, a mild form of somnambulism—the product of a coalminer's exhaustion and automatism. (122)

Comparable to Julius, Skinner, and Zou Lei, walking represents for Hans a form of freedom and a diversion from the constraints of everyday life. For him walking also establishes a mental connection with his mother. Hans explains that "the fantasy did not consist of imagining her physically at [his] side but imagining her at a long distance," and, as he further acknowledges, "in this [he] was abetted by the streets of New York City, which abet desire even in its strangest patterns" (122–23). Consequently, in the novels walking is depicted as a way to cope with stressful situations. Thus, the protagonists create a personal space in the urban environment of NYC and by their movements reveal the multifaceted character of the city.

However, not only walking the city plays a crucial role for demonstrating migrant mobility, but also a new form of flânerie,[2] namely traversing the city by various means of transportation. According to literary scholar Nora Pleßke, "the motorised flâneur is the epitome of urban vigilance and best equipped to absorb, filter, and extract meaning from the multifariousness of the city in flux" (295). In the novels, two kinds of mobilized flânerie are represented, namely movement in the car and in subways/trains. Mobilized flânerie exposes the fact that the further out the protagonists move, the "darker" New York becomes. On her way to a factory in the Bronx where she hopes to find a job, Zou Lei remarks that "it was a long ride and she had to transfer twice to get to the Bronx" (Lish 339). While she moves further and further out of the city center, "the white people got off and the blacks and Spanish got on and stayed on," and thus "the train filled, got dark with dark people" (339). Hence, the train ride appears as a metaphorical ride through New York's social layers—the further out she moves, the more hybrid New York becomes. At the same time, train or subway rides are commonly shown to be penetrated by security officials. In one instance, Zou Lei is on the subway, and as "they went underground in Manhattan, the white people got off, and the subway headed into Brooklyn." As she observes further, "a policeman put his head out on the platform at every stop" (384). Zou Lei, who gets off at the last stop, notices how "the cops switched trains" (384). Hence, the novel depicts encapsulated spaces of New York's subways/trains as being under constant surveillance. However, Zou Lei is determined to find a new job in order to earn more money and be able to help Skinner, despite the jeopardy: "this demanded that she ride the subway with the cops, but she felt that she could risk it" (120). This situation demonstrates how her attachment to Skinner triggers mobility and underscores Zou Lei's willingness to help him.

While mobilized flânerie takes place mostly in trains and subways in Lish's novel, *Netherland* features a different form of mobilized flânerie, namely movement by car. Hans, who has befriended a food critic by the name of Vinay, drives around with him to test "cheap, little-known restaurants" (64). During these tours in the car, Hans experiences the underbelly of New York and its manifold food trends brought to the city via immigrants. In addition to that, their mobility through the city reunites him with Chuck. Hans accompanies Vinay to one of his assignments to find out where New York's taxicab drivers eat. Vinay's boss hopes that the cab drivers, who are commonly immigrants, were "men hungering for a true taste of homeland and mother's cooking, men who would, in short, lead one to the so-called real thing" (68). Although Hans "could not help thinking it simple, this theory of reality" (68), he explores both foods and places he would probably never have known without Vinay. In the last restaurant, Hans bumps into Chuck again, whom he had only met briefly on the cricket field in the beginning of summer. Thus, mobility creates attachment; Hans's movements through the city expand his knowledge of NYC and give him insights into New York's many different facets. Mobilized movements play as crucial a role in the novels as walking through the city.

Despite their depiction of the United States as becoming an increasingly hostile environment for migrants, the novels also portray migrants as mobile people who do not allow themselves to be deterred by increasing security measurements. Instead, by actively engaging with their urban environment they are depicted as creating alliances both with the manifold urban spaces of the city and with other migrants. In *Netherland*, it is especially cricket in the city's parks that unveils not only New York's long history of this sport but also counters the depiction of migrants as threats by showing the peaceful encounter of highly diverse peoples. As Hans points out, before a match he and his fellow players "huddled with arms round one another's shoulders—nominally, three Hindus, three Christians, a Sikh and four Muslims" (12). In *Open City*, Julius's long walks repeatedly reveal New York as space that consists of many microcosms. In a remote area of Chinatown, for instance, "it felt like an entire world away, for here no tourists were to be found and almost no one, in fact, who was not originally from East Asia" (188). In *Preparation for the Next Life*, Zou Lei repeatedly risks being caught by the police while working as a street vendor in order to make more money and help Skinner with his post-war depression. Consequently, the novels portray migrants not as security threats but as human beings who engage with their urban surroundings and, in doing so, uncover New York's many (socio-)historical layers. While the novels show how mobility creates bonds and vice versa, they depict three very different outcomes of the migration process.

Whereas Hans returns to London and Zou Lei moves on to other destinations, Julius is the only one who decides to stay in New York. As he acknowledges, "remaining here in the city is the only choice that makes emotional sense to me" (Cole 248). Julius declines a lucrative job offer in the suburbs of New Jersey, but as he freely admits, "in the end it hadn't been a difficult choice" (248). His walks through the city establish a tie to NYC despite the occasional obstacles he faces because of his skin color and the increased surveillance of urban space. NYC also leaves an imprint on Hans, although he returns to London to reunite with his wife and son. According to him, "life carries a taint of aftermath" after his return (O'Neill 2). In order to describe how NYC affects his mind, he uses a metaphor of growing grass, which both hints at the palimpsest structure of the human brain and at how New York has cast a spell over him: "New York City insists on memory's repetitive mower—on the sort of purposeful post-mortem that has the effect . . . of cutting the grassy past to manageable proportions." The difficulty, however, is that "it keeps growing back, of course" (2). Hans's metaphor shows how the memories of New York haunt him even though he tries to keep them away. Thus, his movements through the city and the ties he established with Chuck and his cricket teammates create a feeling of belonging in Hans. In contrast to Julius and Hans, Zou Lei leaves NYC behind, both mentally and physically, and inherits the role of the perpetual migrant. Her dream was to live a life on the road together with Skinner, "traveling from city to city, selling what they bought and traded," and "she saw them wearing sheath knives and cowboy hats and riding horses in a sun-filled land outside the reach of the authorities" (Lish 123). Hence, Zou Lei is characterized by her nomadic spirit and her romantic vision of borderless freedom. After Skinner's suicide, there is nothing that holds her in NYC, and "so she kept going . . . in the nomadic way that was natural to her" (413). For Zou Lei, her only way to survive is to keep being mobile. It was Skinner who made New York an attractive place for her, but without him, the obstacles she faces as an illegal immigrant are too high to overcome.

All three novels reveal the hurdles their migrant protagonists face in the post-9/11 environment of New York. Simultaneously, their movements reveal the manifold cultural influences immigrants brought to the city and depict that migrants contribute significantly to New York's charm and vibrancy. The novels' portrayal of migrants counters the image of the "dangerous" immigrant that the Trump administration promotes, and thus the novels encourage a positive view of migrants and migrant mobility. As a recent *New York Times* article reveals, nonfictional counter-movements to Trump's strict immigration policy can be ascertained within the boundaries of New York. The acting district attorney of Brooklyn, Eric Gonzalez, recently introduced a new policy protecting immigrants from deportation for minor crimes, rankling the federal government with this decision (cf. Feuer). As the policy states, "naturalized citizens, lawful residents and undocumented immigrants, they are all integral to our local economy and vibrant culture." Thus, the district attorney is "stepping up at a moment when immigrants in New York are facing great concerns for their safety" (Feuer). The policy underscores the important contribution immigrants make to the hybrid character of New York and emphasizes that much of its global attractiveness is due to the influence of the millions of migrants who have set foot in the city since its founding.

NOTES

1. In *Toward the Geopolitical Novel*, Irr uses "world novel" and "geopolitical novel" as synonyms. She introduces the term "geopolitical novel," which suggests

the entanglement of global and local as well as political and social issues in world literature. In this chapter, however, I use the more common term "world novel."

2. A flâneur is someone who aimlessly strolls through the city and observes. As Walter Benjamin explains in his work on Charles Baudelaire, the flâneur "is as much at home among the facades of houses as a citizen is in his four walls" (37). Thus, the city becomes both the flâneur's living and lived space.

WORKS CITED

@realDonaldTrump. "Our Country Needs Strong Borders and Extreme Vetting, NOW. Look What Is Happening All Over Europe and, Indeed, the World—A Horrible Mess!" *Twitter*, Jan. 29, 2017, 2:08 p.m., twitter.com/realDonaldTrump/status/825692045532618753.

Benjamin, Walter. *Charles Baudelaire: A Lyric Poet in the Era of High Capitalism.* Translated by Harry Zohn. Verso, 1997.

Cole, Teju. *Open City*. Random House, 2011.

De Genova, Nicholas. "The Production of Culprits: From Deportability to Detainability in the Aftermath of 'Homeland Security.'" *Citizenship Studies*, vol. 11, no. 5, 2007, pp. 421–48.

Feuer, Alan. "Prosecutors in Brooklyn Aim to Limit Deportations." *New York Times*, Apr. 24, 2017, pp. A21.

Irr, Caren. *Toward the Geopolitical Novel: U.S. Fiction in the Twenty-First Century.* Columbia University Press, 2014.

———. "Toward the World Novel: Genre Shifts in Twenty-First-Century Expatriate Fiction." *American Literary History*, vol. 23, no. 3, 2011, pp. 660–79.

Lish, Atticus. *Preparation for the Next Life*. Oneworld, 2015.

Nail, Thomas. *The Figure of the Migrant*. Stanford University Press, 2015.

O'Neill, Joseph. *Netherland*. Fourth Estate, 2009.

Pleßke, Nora. *The Intelligible Metropolis: Urban Mentality in Contemporary London Novels*. transcript, 2014.

Schine, Cathleen. "A Beautiful, Mournful Novel." *New York Review of Books*. Feb. 5, 2015, https://www.nybooks.com/articles/2015/02/05/atticus-lish-beautiful-mournful-novel/. Accessed Aug. 15, 2019.

Sherlock, Ruth. "Donald Trump's Chaotic Muslim-Majority Immigration Ban: The Full Story." *The Telegraph*, Jan. 30, 2017, https://www.telegraph.co.uk/news/2017/01/29/donald-trumps-muslim-majority-immigration-ban-full-story/. Accessed Aug. 15, 2019.

Part II

FILMIC INTERVENTIONS

Chapter 6

Mother(less) Exiles

The New Woman's Absence from the Migration of the Expressionists to Hollywood

Michele Rozga

Imaginative spaces can exist even when physical and legal spaces are restricted by arbitrary border walls or attempted legal or economic negation. Artists who are also women have often waged the battles of culture within their imaginative work, testing the boundaries of the legal, economic, and cultural countries they have called home, even when that home has been inhospitable. In the film industry so important to the Weimar Republic at its earliest inception, only a very few of the subsequent artistic escapees to new homes in Hollywood were women in the role of creator rather than of muse. I began to wonder about what happened to early female Expressionist filmmakers and artists, and further, about which of their contributions and impulses had proved to migrate across the ocean to America.

In the parallel imaginative and chronological spaces of film in burgeoning Hollywood, meanwhile, there had been a time when there were so many women involved in all work within the film industry that their presence as makers and controllers of creative products was not something exceptional. Anthony Slide wrote in 1996 that "[d]uring the first three decades of its existence, the American film industry was in many ways, a woman's world" (vii). One representative of that world, Ida May Park, screenwriter and director at Universal Studios, penned a chapter on the job of film directing for a 1920 book entitled *Careers for Women*, published by the respected publishers at Houghton Mifflin (cf. Cooper xv).

In his 2010 volume *Universal Women*, on the specifics of Universal Studios' early elevation of professional women in the film industry, Mark Garrett Cooper depicts this particular film studio as fertile ground to study the subsequent erasure of women from most jobs of creative control in Hollywood. It was a place where "the Universal women flourished during the decade [1910s] that called 'Hollywood' into being" (xv), but it was also the studio that "effectively closed the door to women directors by 1920" (xv). Cooper suggests that the door was closed to the women pioneers (with Universal as a test case) only partially because of what historian Karen Mahar (according to Cooper) "argues persuasively" to be "the increasing influence of finance capital [and how it] played a central role in more clearly gendering the occupation" (xvii). Cooper discusses a network of factors he says were also creating a space for women to be shoved to the side in the film industry, focusing chiefly on the ways that "films constituted a nexus of interpretation that proved consequential for the gendered division of labor" (xxix). Cooper argues that film topics and portrayals of society were gendered, and that this led to a rush to create female subordination among film workers so that the topics of female films would remain in their approved orientation to society overall (cf. xxix). This argument is somewhat circular, but many art theorists maintain that most art is mimetic and imitative, and often only popular or even given an audience when it is in a naturalized or unquestioning orientation to social norms, even if at first appearing subversive.

Though Mahar's argument in *Women Filmmakers in Early Hollywood* (2006) is portrayed by Cooper as a strictly economic one, she has also written about another precursor to the gendering of the film industry. In an article published in 2001, Mahar writes: "As studios moved from the artistic and entrepreneurial stage, conducive to the perceived qualities of women, to the corporate stage, the needs of the industry were masculinized and women were excluded" (1). This idea points to a diminution: creative works produced by women are evaluated based on the relative status of the women who produce them, rather than based on the qualities or characteristics of the creative work itself. Mahar also reinforces this idea about Hollywood change when she indicates not just that film artistry itself, or creative control itself, was wrested from women between 1910 and 1925, but that "movies . . . emerged *not* [my emphasis] from the world of art or live entertainments, where women existed in positions of creative control, but rather from the masculine triad of science, technology, and profit" (5). In a sense, Mahar's work hints that the demotion of previously accepted artistry, in order to replace it with a new definition of a "triad" of moviemaking that seemed to no longer need female creativity, is really about defining creativity as a fixed trait that is gendered, rather than an action in which any person can engage.

It is interesting that early work by Anthony Slide had, even by 1996, resisted coming to any conclusions about all of the reasons why women were essentially removed from power in the film industry in Hollywood during and after the transition from the silent film era:

The question I am most asked, and to which I am unable adequately to respond, is why there were so many women active before the coming of sound and so few after. The answer, in part, lies obviously in the social conditions of the day. . . . Also, the industry was changing. In the 'teens, it was easy to make a transition from actress, screenwriter, or editor to director, but by the late 1920s [when the exiles from the Weimar Republic began arriving], departmentalization was taking place. . . . The advent of the guilds and unions, in the 1930s, further hampered the role of female directors. They [the unions] were male dominated and remained so through into [*sic*] the 1960s. (xi)

Though Cooper's work does flesh out some of Slide's identified factors for the male gendering of Hollywood, there is another triad of factors that Cooper mentions in passing that can be useful in framing the evidence for what happened to the creative women of the early movie industry in the Weimar Republic. He develops this second triad from his reading of the work of film historian Janet Staiger, whose argument, according to Cooper, while not explicit, suggests "the insight *that aesthetics, businesses* [*sic*] *practice, and individual creativity* encounter one another most concretely on the studio lot" (xxviii, my emphasis).

If the concrete idea of the studio lot can be made to stand in as a metaphor for the artistic country of film, where "aesthetics, business practice, and individual creativity" must reside together, then surely the women creators of Expressionist cinema were both migrants and exiles at the same time:

1. Economically, just as early modern gains for women in the Weimar Republic provided broader access to some civil service jobs and other work outside the home, the people of Berlin became acquainted with scarcity in the time between the wars.
2. Aesthetically, as German and American film cross-pollinated, German studios came under pressure, via the anxiety of influence, to use male-dominated Hollywood techniques for lighting and set design, such that "[o]nce again an American influence had worked to the detriment of the Expressionist movement" (Thompson 115).
3. Female individual creative vision became marginalized. If the vision itself is not at fault, then the relative power of the persons holding the vision might be at the root of its rejection.

Just as there were (in the early twentieth century) suspiciously narrow gains in respect for women in society overall, or even backlash because of women's suffrage and other social advancements, films became a potent mirror, but much less of a lamp. This respect gap—put together with the idea that film and photography were still new technologies in the 1920s and that women were not considered competent with such technologies—seems to have kept most women in the role of object relative to the camera or movie camera, rather than in the role of operator, director, or producer. Notable exceptions were directors such as Olga Wohlbruck in Germany and Hollywood studio head Lois Weber.

Though there have been several decades of an increasing female directorial presence in Hollywood (the first female Oscar winner for Best Picture was Kathryn Bigelow in 2010), the legacy of early art films created by women in the Weimar Republic is essentially lost to the wider discipline of film, and to Hollywood, and therefore does not influence the medium as it should. As Slide notes, "The major problem in any attempt to rediscover America's first female directors is that the films themselves are missing" (xi). The same problem occurs for early female Expressionist innovators like Wohlbruck or Lotte Reiniger.

The digital algorithms and media that discriminate, both accompanied by the bias that says that women are not technologically savvy, traverse a well-worn track carved out during the pre-digital analog era. Caroline Criado-Perez's *Invisible Women* (2019) studies not just the continued lack of women in media power positions, but the actual ways that new media forms are creating a type of renewed erasure of women, twenty-first-century style. Media and technology in the digital age have become new countries with age-old restrictions on border-crossing for women, creating a continued lack of inclusivity in actionable creative revisioning of human society.

In the brief passages I discuss here, Weimar-era poet Else Lasker-Schüler develops a creative relationship to the issues I have presented so far. The connection from poet to film I would like to trace is that women came over the ocean to America during the collapse of Weimar not primarily in their new roles as breadwinners or creators of their new cultural or creative agency, but in their old roles as muse, homemaker, and object. These visible sites of transfer are the movies, but the old gender roles were critiqued in literary form in Weimar before being formulated again via the new technologies of photography and film.

In Berlin, in 1921, the Expressionist writer Max Krell published an anthology titled *Die Entfaltung: Novellen an die Zeit,* which was a compilation of excerpts of modern fiction. In this anthology, the German Jewish Expressionist poet and writer Else Lasker-Schüler—who had to leave Berlin in 1932 as part of the intellectual and cultural exodus completed by 1939, of roughly 3,000 mostly male artists, writers, musicians, journalists, and other cultural figures who fled the rise of Hitler—published a short piece excerpted from her work entitled *Wenn Mein Herz Gesund Wär* (cf. Schrader and Schebera 258). In this piece, Lasker-Schüler uses a persona, the Prince of Thebes,[1] to show the dynamism of her time, and the ways that the Weimar Republic used its sensibility to view art politically, and to see politics as grounds for creative response. For most of the filmmakers, but also for the writers, architects, sculptors, theater people, and musicians of the Weimar Republic, Expressionism—the most dominant artistic force in that small and hopeful Republic—was not art for art's sake, but a propensity for using the mechanics of art and its aesthetic to change the social status quo.

Says Lasker-Schüler, as the prince of Thebes: "Es ist mir genauso als ob ich das grosse Los gewonnen hab und noch nicht ausbezahlt bin" (for me, it is just as if I had won the Lottery, but not yet been paid). She goes on to say, "Das Leben ist doch eigentlich ein Wendeltreppendrama, immer so rund herauf and wieder hinunter, immer um sich selbst wie bei den Sternen" (life is actually like a spiral staircase drama, always circular and round on the way down and on the way back up, but always around itself just as much as among the stars). And further: "Denn regieren ist auch eine Kunst, eine Eigenschaft, wie die Malerei, die Dichtkunst und die Musik" (Because governing is also an art, a power, like painting, poetry, and music) (gutenberg.org, my translation). In these three passages, Lasker-Schüler demonstrates a certain fluidity in how she expresses her art and her ideas about art. She speaks as a Prince, rather than as a Princess—she is an actress on the page, re-gendering herself, perhaps as a way to play with increasing her artistic agency while simultaneously strengthening her political and social power. She also expresses a sense of motion while staying in place, on the "spiral stair" that is a lack of escape from self but also the way to access the stars above. Finally, she shows us what it might have felt like to live in Weimar as a Jewish woman, free as possible for the moment, but always waiting for the lottery pay-off that never comes.

When German Expressionists like Lasker-Schüler wrote, they often were also developing a relationship to other art forms that were infused with the creativity of the Weimar Republic—sculpture, architecture, painting, and most importantly for this essay, photography and film. The scholar Eric Weitz notes that the Weimar Republic was awash in a "flood of images" and that because of that fact, both photography and film caused artists in all media to question these new media, but to also thereby question what constituted art itself (212). Of film, according to Weitz, people asked whether or not it was simply a "crass form of commercialism" (212). They wondered if film "capture[s] reality better than any other medium—painting, sculpture, the written word—or alter[s] the very forms of visual perception?" (212). Indeed, Weitz notes that up until World War I, even "watching movies still had a disreputable connotation, and the admission of attraction was something that deserved to be heard in confession, not in public" (226).

However, in Weimar, the cultural crosswinds that then lent a sheen of validation to films also seem mostly to have kept women from taking the helm of those films.[2] During many instances of cultural change, such as with Weimar, women seem to be let in when they are in proper alignment with male power, but artistic adjectives do not apply. Freedom to create a new image is what art does—but, if you have no ability to take advantage of new freedoms (of economics or of role-assignment), then you cannot have the resulting freedom required to create a new image for life via a new art form.

As with Sophie Scholl, beheaded by the Nazis on February 22, 1943, and memorialized in film in *Die Letzten Tage*, produced in Bavaria in 2005 (IMDb), female social and artistic creators of the slightly earlier period of Weimar were regularly "beheaded" by the very economics that were giving them renewed social hope. Inevitably and unwittingly, these women of Weimar therefore often loaned their economic power to the movement toward traditionalism that took the Weimar Republic out of the zone of change and into the zone of repressive values, authoritarian views on social progress and gender roles, and a refreshed hatred of creative arts within Nazi culture. The twisted nexus of advancement and repression that the Weimar period in German history has come to signify has been studied by a number of scholars. Some have shown that the burgeoning repression that took over Weimar also led to a lack of female presence in the creation of Hollywood films later. In other words, the Nazis tamped down artistic development in their own arenas, but they also tamped it down in places where their victims and refugees attempted to begin new lives.

The importance of artistic flight from Weimar is illustrated in *Gender and German Cinema*, edited by Sandra Frieden, Richard W. McCormick, Vibeke R. Petersen, and Laurie Melissa Vogelsang, when the introduction notes:

> it was during the Weimar Republic when the German cinema first became important internationally, gaining a reputation that was then squandered by the influence of the Nazis on the film industry during their "Third Reich." Politically and aesthetically, some of the most interesting German films had been made by artists who fled Germany after the Nazis came to power. (1–2)

Christine Haase also gestures to the power of liminality and change to create the circumstances for artistic incubation when she notes that "many of the developments in the emerging motion picture industry progressed simultaneously in the United States and Germany, but they also advanced through transnational cross-fertilization" (15–16).

However, Julia Knight underlines the nonetheless persistent artistic respect gap for Weimar women with a relevant statistic about the low participation of women as creative generators in Weimar cinema, in that "from the early days of silent cinema, women in Germany—despite the undoubted ability of many of them—had traditionally managed to make only occasional and usually highly limited contributions as directors" (2). Indeed, the names of the film directors who took refuge in Hollywood in the run-up to World War II are the names of men: Lang, Siodmak, Sirk, and Wilder. Missing from the list are women who engaged with cinema arts in a director's role, people like Olga Wohlbruck, who, according to Knight, likely has "the honour of being Germany's first woman director," for the 1913 movie *Ein Mädchen zu Verschenken* (2); or Hanna Henning; or Lotte Reiniger, who made animated movies using cut-out silhouettes she scissored herself.

Reiniger's work, specifically her 1922 movie *Aschenputtel* (Cinderella), shows the clever way she used the new medium of film, plus an implement of ancient technology, a pair of scissors, to demonstrate a female film direc-tor's take on the possibilities of this new cinematic medium. In the opening frames of this short film, spectators see the director's own hands in the act of cutting out the figure of Cinderella. Then, the hands of the created cut-out grasp the scissors, as if the character has immediately acquired the agency of self-determination, right after having been made. Reiniger is clearly playing with her new medium, sussing out the possibilities. In her work, handicraft and new technology come together in a refreshing way.

These tiny moments from Cinderella—a narrative inside a narrative—are important in terms of how art and society comingle for women creators, as relates to Weimar's seismic cultural changes and importance. For some women, perhaps many, art is often not made in the context of expressing power or belonging; rather, women often make art in order to construct their own selves out of the social fabric they have been assigned. In some ways, women must become internal émigrés in their own cultures in order to create or survive. Women, then, often have the double task, while working in art, of separating their silhouettes from the existing background light. In film, especially, a director's medium, the confluence of social norms and technol-ogy during the Weimar period became a force that perched women in film primarily in front of the lighted eye of the camera, not as makers, but as that which the male director had cut out and created. This ethos clearly dominates the medium, even today.

In the opening scene of the 1923 Expressionist film *Die Straße* (*The Street*), directed by Karl Grune, a woman putters about in a kitchen, then enters the parlor and sets the table with a white cloth and a place setting for one, while a man stretched out on a couch looks on. The woman leaves the room for a moment, and the man watches a play of shadow and light cross the ceiling, then walks to the window to observe the street scene creating the chiaroscuro busy-ness inside his home. The man and woman do not talk, and the man goes out into the street on an imaginative journey, in a fantasy scene framed by a white circular aperture in the center of the screen. First, that white opening morphs into the laughing face of a clown, then into the face of a heavily made-up woman who disappears in a blaze of fireworks just as soon as she appears. Another woman, who stands in the street at the corner of two brick walls, seems to watch the man lasciviously, then her face changes into a skull. The man returns to his real life, sharing rooms with his wife, uncommunicative, as if the street has both destroyed domestic life but also replaced all desire.

These short scenes show push and pull between revolutionary film techniques using light and shadow overlaid by a somewhat oppressive narrative of the so-called battle between the sexes; the Weimar woman was indeed torn between the home and the spectacle of the street. She was a woman who had new opportunity but who was also circumscribed by frustrating traditional views. Alice Ruhle-Gerstel, a contemporary German Jewish psychologist, observed that the Weimar Republic contained "the new women [who] were pioneers [but who also] never constituted a majority and did not succeed in changing most Germans' ideas about the role of women in society" (facing-history.org). Ruhle-Gerstel further noted that "before [the new woman] could evolve into a type and expand into an average, she once again ran up against barriers."

Part of the barrier being erected for women during Weimar was a problem that came from within the field of German Expressionism itself—this barrier, inside a zone of innovation, served to make all but a few women artists in various media invisible and immobile for reasons of race and ethnicity as well as gender. It can be said of German Expressionism that, "[though] in its nature, the movement was interested in the relationship between art and society, and encompassed a broad range of fields, including architecture, painting, and film," its nature did not admit inclusion of women (Darsa). Even though novelty was present in the Weimar Republic's art products, Sandra Frieden and her co-editors conclude that "[e]xperimentation . . . did not mean freedom from the control of studios, producers, and political interests that looked askance at any clear attempts to undermine the status quo" (2). As Frieden and her co-editors also note, "Misogyny is not unrelated to modern anti-Semitism, which often views the Jew as a feminized or lascivious 'Other'" (4). It is quite clear that the Weimar Republic's art and film were generally more boundary-pushing in form than they were in cultural inclusion or in revolutionary content.

Renate Bridenthal and her co-editors do write that, in spite of the thin nature of that revolution of form in art, "still, social observers of all political persuasions—from journalists and sociologists to government experts and political leaders—detected the emergence of a 'new woman' and a 'new family' in the 1920s [in Germany]." The new woman was seen as newly energizing to society, for "Weimar culture did produce a certain heady and intoxicating sense of freedom in the big cities, especially for some intellectual and professional women" (facinghistory.org). But the nature of that freedom seems to have been limited.

In *A Room of One's Own*, the 1929 Virginia Woolf essay, she famously describes her own sense that the freedom inherent in economic viability and the space that such economics can afford a person must be the precursors for women to be able to experience freedom and space to explore artistic methods. But economic power does not necessarily result in ideas from women suddenly being deemed credible or artistically viable, as the case of the Weimar Republic shows. To contemplate the relative lack of migration of female film artists from Weimar to Hollywood therefore is to contemplate only part of the picture that depicts female artists working in all media becoming trivialized via multiple social stressors such as economic anxiety, yearning for male authority figures, and a companion male tradition that excluded women who also did transformative art. Further, I propose that film and photography each had a disproportionate influence on what happened to women artists working in them or in other artistic realms. Most women seem to have been considered nontechnological beings, even as they became modern—Weimar contained a technological revolution owned by that moment's male cultural ethos. It was that ethos that drove film and photography, and it was that new technology that entrapped most of the female image in a heart of metal or glass, then shipped her off to perform in Hollywood films, disallowing her the agency to co-create with the New Man of Weimar on equal technological terms.

The authoritarian machine that then evolved and became the Third Reich opened up like the Trojan Horse and overran a vulnerable new modern age with the violence of World War II. In the early 1980s, Jeffrey Herf wrote a treatment of the intertwining of technology, culture, and politics that reached a pinnacle in the Third Reich. In *Reactionary Modernism* (1984), he writes that "although the confrontation between technology and culture did not begin in Weimar, it certainly came to a head in those years" (18). I have tried to show that the confrontation between technology and culture during the Weimar Republic left out marginalized groups as being affiliated with that which was not part of a new vision of the future except as dictated by a vision borrowed from the past.

A lack of female agency and voice continues to haunt the film industry in Germany and in the United States—as the art of film has grown, then risen ever higher from the burgeoning film studios of Berlin and Hollywood, the film industry has used its technological magic to ensconce women in mostly subservient roles, even when they are allowed to be the objects of longing. But the story is not as simple as making a decree that the rise of talkies left women without a voice as creators of film; that complicated knot of identity and media is a fraught one for women to this day.

Do the media that are technology-driven (digital photography, filmmaking, and the Internet) continue to depend heavily on a core series of diminished female archetypes? I would say yes—when I attended the fiftieth anniversary of the National Endowment for the Humanities, held in Charlottesville, Virginia, in September of 2016, the brilliant Internet tactician Jaron Lanier, who has been working in cyberspace since the 1970s, admitted in a live lecture session that biases against women, and against people of color, are built into the foundational architectures of the digital world. When he made this statement, Lanier hearkened back, in a troubling fashion, to the Weimar Republic's creations, dominated by technology that was wielded by the traditional, male, holders of power. As scholar Karl Leydecker ruefully notes in an afterword to an Ariadne Press edition of the dramatic writings of Expressionist Oskar Kokoschka, "The Expressionists dreamed of a radical, even violent, transformation of society. The embodiment of and at the same time the catalyst for, that transformation was to be an extraordinary male individual, whom they called the New Man" (245).

As German intellectuals discussed the specific connections between technology and culture, they tended, during the period before 1933, to add in a specific political angle. Notes Herf: "The confrontation between technological advance and the traditions of German nationalism was sharper in Weimar than at any time before or since in modern German history" (19). The reason this is true is that "the battle over *Technik* und culture took place against a background of military defeat, failed revolutions, successful counterrevolution, a divided Left, and an embittered and resentful Right" (19). In a recent American historical moment (August 2017) that also involved activities of "an embittered and resentful Right," in the town of Charlottesville—where Jaron Lanier had spoken of the stereotype-reproducing American battle between technology and culture a scant year before—a woman named Heather Heyer, who was counter-protesting a rally of Rightists who had assembled (via Internet connectivity and cyber-driven hate) to defend a famous statue of Confederate General Robert E. Lee, was killed by a speeding vehicle driven by a Far Right supporter. What remains indelibly in our cultural memory here in the United States is the film-like photo sequence documenting her murder, shown countless times in various media outlets such that the images play like a movie inside the minds of viewers.

Though previous commentators have warned the current age against making false analogies between the authoritarian contractions that followed Weimar and the current rise of twenty-first-century autocratic leaders, it is a worthwhile endeavor to use an argument by analogy to attempt to peer into the future for women, for artists, for migrants, and for society. As Beth Irwin Lewis noted in her book on the Weimar artist and intellectual George Grosz, it is good to consider the artistic thinkers' social obligation: "What is the responsibility of the artist-intellectual critic within a troubled democratic society?" (32). And, the follow-up question to that asks whether the thinkers can change attitudes and procedures: "How influential is the artist-intellectual upon the actual political or social workings of society?" (33). The answer to this is elusive, once again quite vulnerable in the face of current events. Lewis's book, interestingly enough, came out in 1971, about a year after the Kent State shooting of unarmed students protesting against the Vietnam War. During the time that Lewis was completing her book, people were, just as they are sometimes now, attempting to see the Weimar Republic as an analogy for potentially productive turmoil that must eventually lead to autocratic crackdowns. Art is a part of the turmoil now, too, but it remains to be seen whether or not it can play a role in turning back the repressiveness of our age.

What could a study of specifically female art in culture, as transferred via war and the media of film, out of the Weimar Republic and into Hollywood, tell us about our current times? For though it might be easy to say that female political and social power—as a form of resistance to autocracy if not merely a hashtag called #metoo—is making a comeback, what is much harder to trace is whether or not that political and social power can become synergistic or reciprocal with artistic power. In fact, for the women of the Weimar Republic, new-found economic power was almost antithetical to a companion growth spurt in expanded roles elsewhere, in the realms of art.

To close, I would like to introduce a female voice who is part of the new Hollywood—the slightly more inclusive Hollywood—but who also creates a connection to German cinema. A 2018 film version of the novel *A Wrinkle in Time* was directed for Disney by a highly successful African American woman named Ava duVernay, who explained in an interview that she was inspired in some of her artistic choices for the film by her love for the German movie *The Never-Ending Story*, which was filmed in Munich and released in 1984. In DuVernay's movie, an innocent girl fights a giant technological, mechanistic, malevolent intelligence, depicted by DuVernay not as a literal brain on a pedestal as happens in the original novel by Madeline L'Engle, but as a series of giant synapses that the young girl, Meg, must navigate in order to become free of the control of the evil intelligence she and her compatriots have been fighting. In a way, the characters of this book and movie are migrants—they travel the universe, planet by planet, fighting against evil with normal tools—and three witches. When Meg enters the synapses of the evil brain, she enters a space where she is not defined as a female character, as a person of color, or as a person without a homeland, but rather by her strength and willingness to engage in worthy battle.

The pull of the original novel, one of my favorites even now though it is a book for adolescents, is that Meg becomes herself not in spite of her lack of category, but because of her ability to create a new category. She is, to borrow from Herf but to reverse his phrase, "a republican without a republic." Meg is a person doing battle with technology, autocratic tendencies, and herself. She is, perhaps, a young, novelistic version of Hannah Arendt, stateless while waging her lonely fight, but more fully whole because of that statelessness, more able to be at home in the world. To backtrack a bit: in Herf's quoted formulation, Germans of the Weimar Republic created, wittingly or not, a "republic without republicans" (20). In other words, Germans of the Weimar Republic created a shell of art, perfection, technology, and architecture, so theory-based that it was a republic that was also inhospitable to human life or to its governance. To flip that cycle, to create republics that are worthy of the current crop of citizens fighting against oppression, is now, again, ever more urgent.

Which tools in art will prove they have the resilience to make work that is both culturally meaningful and yet totally useless to a continuation of the status quo? Each tool works sometimes and then has to be redesigned when it can no longer usefully shape the materials and ideas of the world. Women are still, as if by imposed default, by lack of financing, and by continued relatively weak representation in roles of creative oversight, mostly following the path of acting on film, stepping in front of the camera but not directing as much as they could.

Very recently, the American film actress Geena Davis and the American film producer Tom Donahue have been promoting and marketing their 2018 documentary *This Changes Everything*, an ironically titled discussion of the persistent dearth of female creative control in Hollywood. As Donahue indicated in an August 8, 2019, taped television interview with the reporter Christina Amanpour, the question remains, "Why don't things change?" ("Geena"). In the interview, Donahue also notes the well-known but startling fact that in almost 100 years of Academy Awards, only one has been awarded to a woman director, Kathryn Bigelow, for Best Director. In the spiral stair formulation of everything-churning-but-remaining-the-same as depicted by Lasker-Schüler, it seems that women in Hollywood are holding their lottery tickets but are still waiting to have that investment paid off in artistic respect and its subsequent power. More broadly, in film and photography, as well as new digital media, technology often continues to duplicate the male gaze, instead of subverting that gaze, and women continue to lag behind in terms of being culturally or commercially valued for using technology in their own ways to create an artistic vision for the world. The feedback loop closes up very tightly around issues of technology because even often-destructive new media are mostly viewed as inevitable to progress. Yet the continued mostly motherless world in German and American film still beckons to the exiled who seek to tear down the borders in art, and therefore create the parent(s) of a new and finally more humane and inclusive way of looking at society through the stories that it chooses to film, preserve, and honor.

NOTES

1. "'I was born in Thebes, Egypt although I came into the world in Elberfeld in the Rhineland.' This is how Else Lasker-Schüler characterized her background, indicating the separation between imagination and reality, artistic and bourgeois existence that marked her life. To speak for her, she created the persona of Jussuf, Prince of Thebes, her alter ego who appears in her writings and drawings and with whose name she often signed her letters. This figure has an important Jewish component. Her Egyptian Jussuf is in fact the biblical Joseph with whom Lasker-Schüler identified already as a child. He is Joseph the dreamer and poet, ridiculed by his brothers, betrayed and sold" (Bauschinger, jwa.org).

2. See also Bridenthal; Hans; Knight.

WORKS CITED

A Wrinkle in Time. Directed by Ava duVernay. Walt Disney Pictures, 2018.

Bauschinger, Sigrid. "Else Lasker-Schüler." *Jewish Women's Archive,* https://jwa.org /encyclopedia/article/lasker-schueler-else. Accessed Sep. 1, 2019.

Bridenthal, Renate, Atina Grossman, and Marion Kaplan, editors. *When Biology Became Destiny: Women in Weimar and Nazi Germany*. Monthly Review, 1984.

Cooper, Mark Garrett. *Universal Women*. University of Illinois Press, 2010.

Darsa, Alissa. *Arthouse: An Introduction to German Expressionist Films*, Dec. 26, 2013, https://news.artnet.com/market/art-house-an-introduction-to-german-exp ressionist-films-32845. Accessed Sep. 1, 2019.

Frieden, Sandra, et al. *Gender and German Cinema*. Berg, 1993.

"Geena Davis and Tom Donahue on *This Changes Everything*." *Amanpour and Company*. pbs.org/wnet/amanpour-and-company. Accessed original broadcast Aug. 8, 2019. Retrieved online Sep. 1, 2019.

Grune, Karl. "The Street," 1923. *YouTube*. Cinema History, Feb. 10, 2016, https://ww w.youtube.com/watch?v=eCd35pF_XeQ&t=519s. Accessed Sep. 1, 2019.

Haase, Christine. *When Heimat Meets Hollywood: German Filmmakers and America, 1985–2005*. Camden House, 2007.

Hans, Anjeana K. *Gender and the Uncanny in the Films of the Weimar Republic*. Wayne State University Press, 2014.

Herf, Jeffrey. *Reactionary Modernism: Technology, Culture, and Politics in Weimar and the Third Reich*. Cambridge University Press, 1984.

IMDb. *Sophie Scholl: The Final Days*, https://www.imdb.com/title/tt0426578/. Accessed Sep. 1, 2019.

Knight, Julia. *Women and the New German Cinema*. London: Verso, 1992.

Lasker-Schüler, Else. *Wenn Mein Herz Gesund Wär*. Transcribed by Jens Sadowski from Max Krell, *Die Entfaltung*. Project Gutenberg release date Dec. 19, 2010, http://www.gutenberg.org. Accessed May 2018.

Lewis, Beth Irwin. *George Grosz: Art and Politics in the Weimar Republic*. University of Wisconsin Press, 1971.

Leydecker, Karl. "Afterword." *Oskar Kokoschka: Plays and Poems*. Ariadne, 2001, pp. 245–50.

Mahar, Karen Ward. "True Womanhood in Hollywood: Gendered Business Strategies and the Rise and Fall of the Woman Filmmaker, 1896–1928." *Enterprise & Society*, vol. 2, no. 1, 2001, pp. 72–110.

Reiniger, Lotte. "Aschenputtel." Original producer Institut für Kulturforschung, 1922. *YouTube*, Jajeg, Sep. 29, 2011, https://www.youtube.com/watch?v=Kku 75vGDD_0&t=59s. Accessed Sep. 1, 2019.

Schrader, Bärbel, and Jürgen Schebera. *The "Golden" Twenties: Art and Literature in the Weimar Republic*. Yale University Press, 1990.

Slide, Anthony. *The Silent Feminists: America's First Women Directors*. Scarecrow, 1996.

Thompson, Kristin. *Herr Lubitsch Goes to Hollywood: German and American Film after World War I*. Amsterdam University Press, 2005.

Weitz, Eric D. *Weimar Germany: Promise and Tragedy*. Princeton University Press, 2013.

"Women in the Weimar Republic." *Holocaust and Human Behavior*, chapter 4, part 16. facinghistory.org. Accessed Sep. 1, 2019.

Chapter 7

Go West, Young Men

Teutonic Myths and American Westerns Blazed Path for the Acceptance of Nazism in Germany

Cathy M. Jackson

The global influence of the Old West is truly transnational, but in Germany it found a filmic and historical similitude. The American frontiersmen echoed the Teutonic myths of Siegfried, adapted for the screen in Fritz Lang's 1924 film epic *Die Nibelungen: Siegfried*. The savage Indians were symbolic of the suffering Germans underwent when Rome invaded their land, and the conquering of the American West embodied nascent dreams of German national destiny. The amalgamation of the New World West and the mythological/ historical characteristics of Germany's budding film industry of the early twentieth century suited the masculine orientation of a country whose leaders began to fixate on the emergence of a blonde-haired, blue-eyed theory of world domination.

This chapter describes how the western film genre forged and maintained a male gaze cast by white "fathers of exile," which emerged in German writers' nineteenth-century letters and novels situated in the American West. Those novels depicted women as dutiful helpmates, damsels in distress, or captivity-story characters waiting to be rescued by Germanic heroes. After nineteenth-century German literature set the stage for a country already under the influence of sociological theories of male dominance, films cemented the image in the cultural imagination. German author Karl May sold over 200 million copies of his nineteenth-century westerns and netted the adulation of his countrymen, including Adolf Hitler, who based Nazi policies on May's plots. Nazism found fertile soil in a land already teeming with sociological, mythological, cultural, and mass-mediated heroes appropriately cast in the male images of Old West characters. That link drives this chapter's research, which begins with the German emigrants who sought a largely fictional land created by image makers and letter writers.

The waves of emigrants who came to America in the latter nineteenth century followed the call of less-than-honest land promoters and earlier German emigrants: relatives, friends, countrymen, who wrote glowing letters of their success in their New World home places. Those were the white "fathers of exiles," German expatriates who yearned for freedom from inferiority complexes created by Old World classism but harbored the same classist, racist tendencies against people of color in the New World. Among the emotional baggage they carried across the Atlantic were the unrealistic impressions of German novelists, such as May, and of American authors James Fenimore Cooper and Owen Wister.

From the pens and fertile imaginations of authors of frontier-based novels, New York composer of the "Leatherstocking" tales James Fenimore Cooper, western writers of fiction Owen Wister and Zane Grey, and television and Hollywood scriptwriters, a Wild West emerged that has "influenced millions who have never read an honest history" (Paul ix). However, as the western evolved from novels to dime novels to film, it established a false history of the United States. Framed in the wide-open landscape of the West, the western symbolized a national myth that largely omitted the major role of frontier/ Western women and people of color. Formed in the crucible of Cooper's frontier stories, the western is a story of triumphant, white American men. Despite the absence of many who built this country, the western stands as a testament to America's resilience, its destiny, and its exceptionalism (Ashliman 139–40). Other nations have seen fit to adopt that false narrative and mold it to bolster their own particular *Geist* and the indomitability of their male progeny. Germany was no different.

From Old West researchers to critics, few doubt the resilience of the western myth and its ability to stress the contributions of white males to the establishment of American exceptionalism. Arthur Redding writes that the western continuously illustrates and updates "an imagined American masculinity . . . [that] persists, in large part, as high camp, consciously or less so, lamenting, lampooning, or satirizing the supposed decline in status and power of white American masculinity" (10–11). This piece of the myth resonated with European immigrant audiences, who in the early twentieth century avidly viewed the silent westerns and their cavalcade of inferior Indians, and saw themselves, foreigners, strangers in a new land, similar to the early frontier settlers, who faced the American wilderness, overpowered the lesser people, and helped forge a powerful nation. This western myth of European domination is akin to Hitler's ideas set forth in *Mein Kampf*, in which he expounded upon an Aryan, Germanic future free from substandard races. Hitler's vision of a Third Reich would celebrate the victory of superior beings over the "weaker in accordance with the eternal will that dominates this universe" (383).

Although German novelists sometimes depicted an American West that violated reality, German leaders saw the possibilities of using the frontier dramas for propaganda, military lessons, and criticism of an American capitalistic society overrun—so claimed those leaders—by Jews, the *Untermenschen*. Despite its sinister connotations in the homeland, frontier stories, dime novels, and western films captivated millions of Germans in a love affair beginning in the seventeenth century and extending to the present. The German imagination was only partially fueled by professionally produced fiction. German travel writers and the exaggerated letters of emigrants spawned wanderlust of those left in the Old World. This latter group had the greatest personal influence. The missives from relatives and friends were also evidence of "the psychological needs of the emigrants. All harbored an unconscious fear that they had been exiled from the homelands and must justify their move: many suffered from the compelling urge to appear better than those left behind" (Billington 69–70).

Another group of American West promoters were guidebook authors, journalists of emigration newspapers, employees of steamship ventures and land-grant railroads, land speculators, and agents of companies determined to turn a profit from immigration. As Ray Allen Billington writes, many of these groups were "bent on fattening their own incomes whatever the cost in human dignity" (59). However, it is the propagandization of the American western by Adolf Hitler and the Nazis in Germany pre-World War II that provide the crux of this chapter. Use of the frontier story/western as a propaganda tool was easy; the die was cast by American authors and historians long before Hitler was born.

Frederick Jackson Turner's most influential essay, "The Significance of the Frontier in American History," first presented in 1893, mirrored the absence of any people of color and the minor role of women in silent westerns. As Wilbur R. Jacobs noted, Turner's frontier theory "set forth a popular, patriotic self-image beloved by generations of Americans. When Turner described our traits of individualism, inventiveness, and our exuberance for freedom that grew from the 'conditions of frontier life,' he rang a historical freedom bell that has not stopped pealing" (11). Over 100 years after Turner launched his then-earth-shattering frontier thesis, scholars still argue and research the West (cf. Emmons 437–39) to determine whether it is a region (cf. Malone 97), a process (cf. Worster 19–24, 28), the birthplace of American exceptionalism (cf. Wrobel viii), a garden (cf. Baritz 618–39), or a "living space" (Stegner 6–8). The Old West is defined as the entire region west of the 98th meridian, the line of diminishing rainfall, which runs from the eastern Dakotas on the north through central Texas to the south. The large area has, in addition to certain shared geographic and climatological factors, a common history. Turner presented it as a history replete with panoramic vistas, victorious battles against ferocious animals and savage, inferior Indians, and peopled by white settlers, frontiersmen, and cowboys conquering the wilderness. He ignored the plight, history, and achievements of other ethnicities, who, too, settled in the Old West (cf. Chan et al. 1–2).

Less than a decade after Turner delivered his frontier thesis, the West and the cowboy became first an American, then an international romantic fixation. According to Richard Slotkin, the frontier myth with its exclusionary tenets romanticized the "White male adventurer as the hero of national destiny" (655). Turner, like Wister, author of *The Virginian: A Horseman of the Plains* (1902), the first best-selling western novel, mourned the "vanished past . . . [with] the ending of the open range . . . and the passing of the romantic figure of the cowboy" (Cawelti 76). Subsequently, beginning with Edwin Porter's 1903 *The Great Train Robbery* through and well beyond the dawn of the sound age in 1929, minorities and women remained almost invisible in the Hollywood western. Turner's 1893 essay and his other pieces collected in *The Frontier in American History* are a major starting point for the establishment of the mythical image of the Old West and ultimately Hollywood's interpretations of that region's history and culture.

Turner is responsible for infusing the word "frontier" into the minds of historians and the world for generations to come. Until his death in 1932, Turner reiterated his hypothesis that the settling of the frontier served to forever separate Americans from their European roots. In Turner's writings, as Americans pushed inward from the Atlantic Coast, they forged a culture and civilization that shed Old World mannerisms and genteel ways to survive the wilderness, but once the savage land was conquered what remained was a purebred white American man clad in the buckskins of rugged individualism, democracy, and nationalism (cf. 290–310): the genesis for Hollywood's cowboy.

For Susan Kollin the earliest film definition for a western meant a variety of genres set in a particular region. Later, after the film industry located to Hollywood, California, circa 1908, the term developed to encompass any film catering to audiences who liked stories set in the West. She wrote:

> The "Americanness" of the genre was further strengthened by other developments. With ready-made sets in which to feature their stories, a landscape that lent itself to a particular storyline, and a large body of trained actors and extras who could play the "cowboy," "the Indian," or "the outlaw," the Western became associated with an American national setting and site of production. (8)

The western became another story of imperialism that appealed to Americans and Europeans: the colonized and the colonizer. Before "western was a noun . . . , it was an adjective," Slotkin claims, describing "part of a larger constellation of the adventure narrative that took place in various geographies across the globe" (149). These stories became guideposts luring Europeans to the frontier wilderness to seek solace and escape from their humdrum lives.

The widespread absence of non-whites, other than American Indians, from early westerns was not an oversight. Although blacks were among the first to settle in the West, helped to found Los Angeles, discovered major passes through the Sierra Nevada Mountains, established trading posts, ate the dust of trail drives, broke the law and kept the law, they had no place in the Hollywood western. One-third of 35,000 cowboys who rode the cattle trails during that industry's zenith (1866–1895) were Negroes and Mexicans (cf. Porter 159). Yet the myth of the Hollywood cowboy, beginning with nineteenth-century dime novels, told the story of white men. In a *Harper's* article entitled "The Evolution of the Cow Puncher" (Sep. 1895), Wister argued that American cowboys were descended from the Anglo-Saxon race and went west to test their courage. Wister wrote that American cowboys "came in shoals—Saxon boys of plucked courage (none but the plucky could survive) from South and North, from town and country" (quoted in Durham and Jones 222). The white supremacist overtones of the early western novels and, later, movies gave citizens and immigrants white male heroes who mirrored this country's patriotic blend of American exceptionalism (cf. White 620–22).

Turner preached a unifying theme of nationalism and a romantic dream of a frontier that forged a nation and spawned a glorious fate, Manifest Destiny. Not surprisingly, in the three decades after Turner declared the frontier closed in 1890, historians of the Old West reflected a profound sense of nostalgia, fueled by a feeling of loss. Reginald Horsman observed in *Race and Manifest Destiny* (1981) that Manifest Destiny was the belief Americans would own this country from ocean to ocean, and political leaders who embraced the expansionistic dream embedded it in a racist philosophy rooted in European scientific thought. Senator Thomas Hart Benton in 1846 applauded "the arrival of the 'van of the Caucasian race' at the Pacific Ocean as one of the greatest events in the history of the world" (quoted in Horsman 91). Generations of Americans and moviegoers worldwide were indoctrinated by an Old West saga devoid of non-whites and the essential, often-civilizing role of women. It was the historical influences, the closing of the frontier, the encroachment of industrialization and large influxes of immigrants, as much as their upbringings, that engendered in historians desires to, perhaps unwittingly, help enfold the nation's western regions into an ahistorical mix of myth and fable that has clouded modern conceptions of frontier history.

Often labeled a Progressive historian, Turner in his fifty-three-page the-sis set the stage for legions of researchers, journalists, fiction writers, and moviemakers, who believed the West spawned men of incredible courage, selflessness, and commitment to a higher cause. While researchers have yet to fully explore and define the connection between Turner's thesis to the racism embedded in the literary or filmic genre, the works of Ray Allen Billington, a major Turnerian disciple, might help establish a tenuous link not only for a domestic admiration for westerns, but a European fascination as well.

In *Land of Savagery, Land of Promise*, Billington used Turner's argument that the frontier was not static and its westward movement offered "European image-makers—travellers, promoters, and novelists—a challenging oppor-tunity" (Billington 29). Each of the frontiers created its own larger-than-life heroes, whose exploits titillated the minds and senses of readers worldwide. Of the literary mythmakers who capitalized on such American drama, nov-elists, who followed in the footsteps of the earlier German immigrant letter writers, ranked the highest. Their soaring imaginations created a school of writing that bore the largest responsibility for the transmission of misinforma-tion about the frontier to Europeans across the continent. European westerns won several of their authors, especially Karl May, a niche in the literary pan-theons of their homelands as they created a lasting image of the frontier as a land of lawlessness and savagery, but beauty and freedom from poverty and governmental edicts (cf. Billington 30).

Nineteenth-century Americans rationalized that the Turner thesis appeared to explain a great deal about the events occurring in their lifetimes. It cel-ebrated the passing of a glorious age in the nation's past and reflected a sense of foreboding and pessimism about the future. The West's wild and free land might be gone, but not the frontier myth, which thrived. For the nascent film industry, fiction writers, artists, and others, the West of the imagination was in its full-blown glory. The greatest impetus for worldwide diffusion of the mythic West, especially in Europe, was William Cody's Buffalo Bill Wild West Show during its late nineteenth-century tours. The show, which made Cody an international celebrity, "also enshrined a particular interpretation of Western—indeed of American—history and culture" (Kasson 65).

However, Cody and his colleagues worried their debut in London would be crude by European standards. The staging of a more sophisticated Wild West historical narrative for the London exhibition was the work of Steele MacKaye, a celebrated presence in the American theatrical world. MacKaye's production *The Drama of Civilization* was touted for its realistic portrayal of Native Americans and noted for setting a pattern for the western film genre (cf. Kasson 72–74). Cody's show and its conquering of the Western frontier was a tribute to Anglo-Saxonism, the mainstay thesis of the Aryan nation's Teutonic mythology. "By 1887, enthusiasm for such notions had reached near-hysterical proportions. Theories about the common Germanic origins of British and Anglo-American culture and institutions dominated historical writing . . . on both sides of the Atlantic" (Warren 1142). The authors of *Race, Gender, Class and Media* (2014) contend: "America has a history of over two centuries of racial superiority attitudes that privilege the white-dominant cultural group and subjugate those without white skin" (Bramlett-Solomon and Carstarphen 37). The authors also note, "movies . . . offer a rich cultural tapestry against which we can observe reflections of our own ideologies about power and privilege. Regardless of the genre . . . movies often project our fears and fantasies about the social tensions we experience" (267).

Although frontier literature and westerns helped to establish a pattern for racist theories in Germany, the origins of the Nazi version of the theory of the master race lay in nineteenth-century racial theories of many Europeans, including Count Joseph Arthur de Gobineau, who argued that cultures degenerated when distinct races mixed. As this school of race theories asserted, Southern European and Eastern European peoples were racially mixed with non-European Moors from across the Mediterranean Sea, while Northern Europeans and Western Europeans remained pure. Furthermore, Nordic peoples had developed innate toughness and determination due to the harsh, challenging climate in which they evolved; the racial ideal of these theorists was the tall, blond, and light-eyed Nordic individual. The postulated superiority of these people was said to make them born leaders, or a "master race." Other authors included the British racial theorist Houston Stewart Chamberlain, who felt the white race and Germanic peoples were superior to others. Nazism also was heavily influenced by the work of Francis Galton, who coined the term "eugenics" and was the founder of the Social Darwinist movement. Holocaust studies note the influential role Galton played in formulating racial anti-Semitism and the policies of the Third Reich (cf. Wrobel 10). Race in late-nineteenth-century Europe was not about color; instead it detailed the totality of who was superior and who was not. The conquering of the American frontier, the slaughtering of Native Americans symbolized European fears of societal decay, and the slow death and strangling of their superiority or a "weakening of the Anglo-Saxon race" (Warren 1127).

Cody's Wild West show's "very hybridity—rooted in the most clichéd melodramas and the most grandiose political rhetoric, claiming authenticity and mobilizing show-business glitz—made it powerfully persuasive. Its idea of personal heroism, which sprang from . . . belief in the triumph of European civilization in the struggle with savagery, which derived from an amalgam of popular science and imperialist ideology," was familiar to both Americans and Europeans at the high tide of empire-building (Kasson 65–66). America's Wild West was another example of an uncivilized world brought under the control of a white, enlightened authority. No wonder it became synonymous with "America" for millions of people at home and abroad.

Cody and his lively show of how white Americans whipped inferior Native Americans and achieved a powerful industrial country invigorated European nationalism. If Americans could do it, they, too, would prevail. However, the show also instilled fear; with the once-English colony, the child now outdoing the parent. The English delight in the show veiled a fear of reverse colonization depicted by "racially empowered" American warriors. Cody intentionally wanted his show to portray a historical vision of the white race conquering everything in its path. Lurking beneath Cody's vision were innate fears that perhaps one day the conquered would become the conqueror, that the next racial frontier war would not be won by the English, who were being eviscerated by a declining royal class, floundering industrial and political might, a weakened birth rate, and a feeling the world no longer saw them as a power. Louis S. Warren's essay emphasized that both Americans and Europeans shared the same apprehensions of a fading Anglo-Saxon culture and heritage (cf. 1127–29).

In *Land of Savagery, Land of Promise*, Billington wrote that Cody's Wild West Show, dime novels, travel writing, and letters from emigrants gave Germans much of their initial knowledge about America. But, in his account, nineteenth-century fiction writers were the most prolific creators of European misperceptions about the American frontier as "a land of savagery and ignorance" (30). Setting the stage for the wholesale myth of the frontier was Cooper's *Leatherstocking Tales*, which was published in England and France in 1823 and appeared in Germany in 1824. The next year, there were additional German editions of the tales as Cooper gained fame for later frontier classics such as *The Last of the Mohicans* (1826) (cf. Billington 30). Cooper was a hit in Germany; thirty publishers issued his books to feed the growing hordes of readers attracted by the tales of Natty Bumppo. Billington noted that Cooper became a favorite because his novels reminded Germans of their Teutonic myths and the legends of brave men from Germany's dim but never distant past. Cooper's savages were real for Europeans, and they assumed his frontier landscape was accurately drawn. He inspired European novelists to mirror his works. "Westerns became the standard literary fare of Britishers, Germans, Scandinavians, Frenchmen, Spaniards, even Hungarians and Poles, for a century to come" (31–32).

American frontiersmen echoed German heroes of myths and legends, which were prominent among the Weimar German films observing the mythological approach. The popularity of the western and its characters fit the folk heroes who fought and won battles over evil (cf. Billington 32). Natty Bumppo was Siegfried and Barbarossa, who triumphed for the glory of Germany. Nineteenth-century Romanticism also stimulated the desire for mythological heroes cast in the mode of American hunters, trappers, and Indians. Romanticism, with its emphasis on emotions and intuition over rational thought, elevated the past into prominence. The movement drove Germans to search for their national identity, their history, and the ideal of nationalism. It also fit Indians into their world view as symbols of a distant past, a people with a lost heritage. Indian imagery drove the process of nation-formation and nationalism in Germany and informed Nazi beliefs and methods. Germans invented traditions to incorporate the Indian mystique into "models of peoplehood," which supported "nationalist attempts to define a German creation myth, a sacred history, a national character, a sacred geography, and religion" (Usbeck 10).

It is ironic that an ideology—Nazism—immersed in decreeing its country's superiority over all people of color would embrace Native Americans. According to Frank Usbeck, it was not implausible, because Native Americans represented the superiority of the German race to defeat inferior foes (cf. 142). Indians were losing their wars against white Americans. Their culture was declining, but Germany's was ascending. Yet, Nazi leaders considered American Indians their comrades battling the same enemies. Indian imagery, their Native garb, and their battles to keep their homelands were used by the Nazis to stoke the loyalties of Germans, inculcate a national pride, and unite them in a shared hatred for the professedly despicable capitalism emanating from Allied countries. Like Karl May's Winnetou, Germans were adorned with nobility when compared to the villains from without. This fictitious, idealized, thoroughly Germanized Indian and his conquests over a treacherous half breed, a "murderous Mormon missionary," and a "villainous Yankee" helped Otto von Bismarck and the Hohenzollerns initiate a movement to enhance Germany's nationalistic fervor in the late nineteenth century (Cracroft 257).

Hitler and Nazi leaders were well prepared to use Indians as propaganda. Decades of reading explorer tales and frontier-themed novels by American and German writers, seeing Wild West shows and exhibitions drove the pre-Nazi fascination with Indian imagery. Germany's emerging nationalism incorporated both its own Teutonic tribal history and the unrealistic history of America's Native tribes into an ideology that wove Romantic thought and Indian imagery into a propagandist tale. For example, as Germany grew into a military power, there arose a militancy steeped in the Romantic tradition of using myth about Germanic heritage to evoke a reality in which Germans and Native Americans were brother warriors fighting capitalism and the hated Americans (cf. Usbeck 45). Usbeck holds: "If Indian imagery served to develop a German national identity, it naturally had to be a useful device for the Nazis to convey national pride to the populace" (46–47). German history and traditions, as well as the nation's ethnic origins, grew in importance. Such thinking, like Romanticism, was a rebellion against an industrialized, complicated period, and a leap back to a simple, primitive life. A journey to the past and a longing for the uncivilized lives of American Indians was escapism and regret for missed opportunities to establish colonies in America (cf. 10).

Germany, unlike other European countries, did not control any major swath of the New World. However, during the nineteenth century, German immigration to America increased more than tenfold (cf. King 29). As specified by a Library of Congress website on German immigration, from 1830 until World War I, almost 90 percent of all German emigrants chose the United States as their new homes. Once established, their letters home were laden with praises for the opportunities to be found in the New World. The letters were published in German publications and created "chain migrations." By the end of the nineteenth century, more than five million Germans, weary of continuous setbacks in their native country, traveled to what seemed a beacon of hope. Their decision to leave Germany became easier as emigration constraints were loosened and transportation across the Atlantic Ocean was enhanced by steamships (cf. Congress).

According to Billington, until the 1880s nearly 20 million immigrants, with most of them bound for the West, came to this country for its fertile land, bountiful game, and the excitement of fighting savages in the wilderness (cf. 59). Throughout the nineteenth century, the frontier was viewed not only as a retreating area of free land, but as the "Garden of the World" where a bountiful nature washed all newcomers of evil and transmuted them into models of republican virtue, all endowed with a lofty morality that matched their physical strength. This agrarian myth was basic to America's national folklore.

Images in the westerns served four needs for Germans. First, the West and America were prime destinations for German immigrants who sought to become property-owners and men of substance in the land of milk and honey and gold-laden hills. They eagerly sought the information about the United States and believed western literature gave them that knowledge. Second, westerns were a safety valve for Europeans stuck in long, industrialized workdays in factories. Third, westerns reminded Europeans of an idealistic, primitive culture where virtues, truth, and honor triumphed over evil. Overly indulgent and "civilized" Europeans saw themselves as they once were but would never be again. In Germany, the western represented a world where men could remake themselves and their country, which had suffered from defeat by Napoleon's forces and bitter infighting among the royal families. Fourth, the frontier answered the psychological need for heroes to win the day over savages and beasts of prey. However, German novelists always peopled the frontier with their own kinsmen. "German heroes never abandoned their mother tongue, were adept at locating Indians skilled in their language, clung doggedly to a rigid code of Teutonic morals, and dreamed always of returning to the Fatherland" (Billington 32–35).

As Lutz P. Koepnick outlines in "Unsettling America: German Westerns and Modernity," American westerns arrived in the 1920s' Weimar Republic, which projected an uneasiness with technology and changing times, wrestled with confused definitions of *Heimat* and the disruption caused by the late nineteenth-century petty bourgeoisie's angst over capitalism and a strengthening bureaucracy. "Portraits of bucolic homeland settings and idealized images of the American West became focal catalysts of fantasy production, offering imaginary redemption from cultural discontent . . . helping to release the disenfranchised urbanite from the iron cage of modern routinization" (7).

For Germans, westerns were more than just fantasy, adventures, and escapist literature; the genre was a guide to a better life in America. The lure of America was the impetus for the rise of Karl May, Germany's most noted novelist of frontier/western stories. For May, the American West was a chance for spiritual redemption. His fiction told of German heroes conquering the land without killing savages but transforming them into men worthy of Teutonic grace and God's mercy. According to Koepnick, Weimar officials used May's writing as a transformative tool to build the "imperialist projects of Wilhelminian Germany" (8). Koepnick argues:

> As his texts traversed fictional geographies, envisioned new social orders from scratch, and relocated traditional meanings, especially the rhetoric of Christianity, to exotic settings, May played a pivotal role in the proliferation of the cultural vocabulary necessary for imperial rule, the hierarchization of different cultures, the aligning of narrative and spatial practices, and the jargon of unquestioned authority and domination. (8)

German authorities viewed May's novels as the country's belated and futile quest for colonies in the New World after other European countries had conquered the best parts (cf. Farry 8). After World War I, westerns helped Germany to return to its ideological motivations of the past. As Germans flocked to see westerns, they did not realize the strategies of government officials, who altered the storylines and language of the American western to construct a national identity for Germany, to advocate for Christianity in a wild land. In Hollywood productions, the American West is a land filled with lonely men, who decry institutionalized law and order and Christianity but find solace in saloons and in the arms of fallen doves and red-eye whiskey. In German westerns, these plot devices are corrupted; the cowboy fights for social stability, fights against capitalistic corruption and villains. He becomes a superhero, an *Übermensch*: May's Old Shatterhand, Old Firehand, Old

Fellow. In America's Old West, the cowboy/outlaw hero rides off into the sunset. In Germany's American West, he fights for community and stays to populate it and bring racial purity to the frontier (cf. Koepnick 8–11).

Under Nazism, the western changed again. Klaus Mann controversially wrote, some say without sufficient proof, that May was the "Führer's cowboy mentor" (Farry 8). McDonough and other writers declare May to have been Hitler's favorite author (cf. 4). Hitler adored May's works as a child and ordered distribution of thousands of May's novels to his troops as a guide for military strategy and courage, especially when the Soviets began to rise as victors against the Nazi invasion (cf. Gilbert 6). May's novels, which featured only one noteworthy woman, Nscho-tschi, the Anglo-Saxon-looking sister of the Anglo-Saxon-looking Winnetou, chief of the Apaches and May's subject for four volumes, provided a formula for Hitler's vision for Germany. A woman had one combined task: to procreate and take care of her husband, the children, and the hearth. Men like Old Shatterhand and Old Firehand were the models for the golden-haired, blue-eyed men who would populate the Third Reich. Yet, there was a caveat; when Nscho-tschi desired to marry Shatterhand, her fate ended in death. There would be no mixing of heathens and Aryans in May's novels. However, there are significant differences in May's works and Hitler's appropriations of his fiction. May was a pacifist. His characters do not kill unless necessary to protect loved ones or destroy villains. They are devout Christians always seeking to convert the savages. Alan Gilbert remarks how American westerns influenced German writers, such as Clara Viebig, whose early twentieth-century novels described Poles as "blacks" and "vampires," inferior to the superior "blond Aryans." In the German imagination, the extermination of American Indians and blacks became their racist reason for conquest of lesser Europeans (cf. Gilbert 5–6).

As early as 1940, Mann decried the effects of May's influence on Hitler, of Hitler and many young German boys having viewed May's novels as exciting, romantic adventures that fired their imaginations for decades. Old Shatterhand, a fictitious version of Siegfried, declared himself "great" and "marvellous" on page after page (Mann 392, emphasis in the original). What Hitler

> admired in Old Shatterhand, was his mixture of brutality and hypocrisy: he could quote the Bible with the greatest ease while toying with murder; he carried out the worst atrocities with a clear conscience; for he took it for granted that his enemies were "of an inferior race" and hardly human. (393)

May's westerns and his characterization of Shatterhand as a true friend to the Negroes and Indians were used by German nationalists to vilify the imperialistic Americans who stole the Indians' homeland like the Romans who had invaded Germany. May's Negroes, epitomized by the continuous appearances of Negro Bob in his novels, were bumbling simpletons, exemplifying Germans' ideas of Southern Negroes. But Negro Bob was always the recipient of Shatterhand's sympathy and kind-hearted emotions (cf. Cracroft 254).

Yet Hitler, the future *Führer* and instigator of the mass murder of millions of Jews and other Europeans, drew inspiration from May's Old Shatterhand. Hitler "could see no reason why Old Shatterhand's [Christian] convictions and tactics should not work if applied to national and international politics" (Mann 393). Germany became the bloody site for Hitler's experiment to spread the inventive, literary genocide of May and Old Shatterhand, who was not only his hero, but a role model for thousands of German boys and adults. Shatterhand became a literary hero because he embraced his Germanness; May's novels encoded nationality as the most important weapon in his warbag against frontier dangers. With his Germanness in place, Shatterhand "demonstrates the superiority of German virtues and skills over those of the Yankees"; this Germanophilia explains Hitler's lifelong, heroic fascination with May and Shatterhand (Ashliman 140–41).

The emergence of heroes "is greatest in periods of social crisis, when established ways of life, rules and laws are undermined, ruling elites discredited, and traditions rejected. Then the only acceptable source of authority must be sought outside the existing order," according to Piotr Sztompka in *The Sociology of Social Change* (270). Nazi ideology and cultural policy mixed heroic, folk-mythical notions of blood, soil, honor, loyalty, service, sacrifice, struggle, labor, and destiny. These same elements were prevalent in May's westerns and heightened the appeal of that genre to Europe. Additionally, Americans massacring Native Americans gave Nazis an opportunity to claim the "moral high ground" (Usbeck 154).

Amid their rapidly changing and, in their view, rapidly declining society, many of Germany's citizens and their "fathers of exiles" embraced and clung to a frontier theory that was part of a new wind blowing across Germany, a harbinger of death and destruction: Nazism. Hitler, from young boy to fanatic *Führer,* embraced the racist casting of characters embodied in May's novels. His vision for a Germany free from the encumbrance of lesser beings mirrored Old Shatterhand's discombobulated quest to always stand taller, be better, and more godlike than America's Indians. Despite May's peaceful, Christian beliefs imbued in his western characters, Hitler was not torn by thoughts that Christianity could not coexist with genocide. He envisioned a by-any-means-necessary rebirth of the glorious Germanic history, a recapturing of its scientific beliefs in the racial inferiorities of the Other, a world illustrated by Teutonic myths of racial purity. In the end, May, America's Old West historians, and German emigrants gave Hitler the ingredients to go forth into the dark decade of the Third Reich, the "final solution" for millions of Europeans.

WORKS CITED

Ashliman, D. L. "The Novel of Western Adventure in Nineteenth-Century Germany." *Western American Literature*, vol. 3, no. 2, 1968, pp. 133–45.

Baritz, Loren. "The Idea of the West." *American Historical Review*, vol. 66, no. 3, 1961, pp. 618–40.

Billington, Ray Allen. *Land of Savagery, Land of Promise: The European Image of the American Frontier in the Nineteenth Century.* Norton, 1981.

Bramlett-Solomon, Sharon, and Meta G. Carstarphen. *Race, Gender, Class and Media: Studying Mass Communication and Multiculturalism.* 2012. Kendall Hunt, 2014.

Cawelti, John G. *The Six-Gun Mystique Sequel.* Bowling Green University Popular Press, 1999.

Chan, Sucheng, Douglas Henry Daniels, Mario T. García, and Terry P. Wilson. *Peoples of Color in the American West.* D.C. Heath, 1994.

Cracroft, Richard H. "The American West of Karl May." *American Quarterly*, vol. 19, no. 2, 1967, pp. 249–58.

Durham, Philip, and Everett L. Jones. *The Negro Cowboys.* 1965. University of Nebraska Press, 1983.

Emmons, David M. "Constructed Province: History and the Making of the American West." *Western Historical Quarterly*, vol. 25, no. 4, 1994, pp. 437–59.

Farry, Oliver. "The European Western: Popular Culture for the Late Imperial Age." *Westerns … All'Italiana!.* Apr. 21, 2017. http://westernsallitaliana.blogspot.com/2017/04/the-european-western-popular-culture.htlm. Accessed Sep. 1, 2019.

Gilbert, Alan. "The Cowboy Novels that Inspired Hitler." *Daily Beast.* Aug. 21, 2016. https://www.thedailybeast.com/the-cowboy-novels-that-inspired-hitler. Accessed Sep. 1, 2019.

Hitler, Adolf. *Mein Kampf.* Houghton Mifflin, 1943.

Horsman, Reginald. *Race and Manifest Destiny: The Origins of American Racial Anglo-Saxonism.* Harvard University Press, 1981.

Jacobs, Wilbur R. *On Turner's Trail: 100 Years of Writing Western History.* University of Kansas Press, 1994.

Kasson, Joy S. *Buffalo Bill's Wild West: Celebrity, Memory, and Popular History.* Hill and Wang, 2000.

King, Lisa Michelle. "Revisiting Winnetou: The Karl May Museum, Cultural Appropriation, and Indigenous Self-Representation." *Studies in American Indian Literatures*, vol. 28, no. 2, 2016, pp. 25–55.

Koepnick, Lutz P. "Unsettling America: German Westerns and Modernity." *Modernism/Modernity*, vol. 2, no 3, Sep. 1995, pp. 1–22.

Kollin, Susan. "'Remember, you're the good guy': Hidalgo, American Identity, and Histories of the Western." *American Studies*, vol. 51, nos. 1/2, 2010, pp. 5–25.

Library of Congress. "Immigration," n.d. http://loc.gov. Accessed Sep. 1, 2019.

Malone, Michael P. "The 'New Western History': An Assessment." *Trails: Toward a New Western History*, edited by Patricia Nelson Limerick et al., University Press of Kansas, 1991, pp. 97–102.

Mann, Klaus. "Karl May: Hitler's Literary Mentor." *The Kenyon Review*, vol. 2, no. 4, 1940, pp. 391–400.

McDonough, Frank. *Hitler and Nazi Germany*. 1999. Cambridge University Press, 2007.

Paul, Rodman W. Foreword. *Historians and the American West*, edited by Michael P. Malone. University of Nebraska Press, 1983, pp. vii–x.

Porter, Kenneth. "African Americans in the Cattle Industry, 1860s–1880s." *Peoples of Color in the American West*, edited by Sucheng Chan et al., D.C. Heath, 1994, pp. 158–67.

Redding, Arthur. "'Built Ford Tough': The 'Sincerity' of John Ford and the Persistence of the American Western." *The New Western: Critical Essays on the Genre Since 9/11*, edited by Scott F. Stoddart, McFarland, 2016, pp. 10–18.

Slotkin, Richard. *Gunfighter Nation: The Myth of the Frontier in Twentieth-Century America*. HarperPerennial, 1993.

Stegner, Wallace. *The American West as Living Space*. University of Michigan Press, 1987.

Sztompka, Piotr. *The Sociology of Social Change*. Blackwell, 1993.

Turner, Frederick Jackson. *The Frontier in American History*. 1920. Dover, 1996.

Usbeck, Frank. *Fellow Tribesmen: The Image of Native Americans, National Identity, and Nazi Ideology in Germany*, Berghahn, 2015.

Warren, Louis S. "Buffalo Bill Meets Dracula: William F. Cody, Bram Stoker, and the Frontiers of Racial Decay." *The American Historical Review*, vol. 107, no. 4, 2002, pp. 1124–57.

White, Richard. *"It's Your Misfortune and None of My Own": A New History of the American West*. University of Oklahoma Press, 1991.

Worster, Donald. *Under Western Skies: Nature and History in the American West*. Oxford University Press, 1987.

Wrobel, David M. "Global West, American Frontier." *Pacific Historical Review*, vol. 78, no. 1, 2009, pp. 1–26.

———. *The End of American Exceptionalism: Frontier Anxiety from the Old West to the New Deal*. University of Kansas Press, 1993.

Chapter 8

"What Pain It Was to Drown"

Quotidian Meets Tragic in Gianfranco Rosi's Fire at Sea

Page R. Laws

Lord, Lord! methought, what pain it was to drown!
What dreadful noise of waters in mine ears!
What ugly sights of death within mine eyes!
Methought I saw a thousand fearful wrecks;
Ten thousand men that fishes gnaw'd upon;

Richard III, 1.iv.21–25

When the sea gives up its dead come Judgment Day, look to see many thousands—mothers, fathers, and children—rising from the waters around Lampedusa, Italy's tiny island that has long served as a target for African and Middle-Eastern migrants desperate to reach Europe. Italy has shared an unsought spotlight with Greece and Turkey for horrific scenes of bloated bodies—famously little Alan Kurdi—washed ashore on beaches, or being sorted by rescuers from among those still barely living on overladen floating tombs, the human smugglers' boats.

The irony of Clarence's famous dream in Shakespeare's *Richard III* (source of my title) is that Clarence is stabbed and then drowned in a malmsey-butt, not the sea (as his vivid dream of drowning had foretold). One of a myriad ironies in Gianfranco Rosi's Golden Bear-winning 2016 immigration documentary *Fire at Sea* (*Fuoccoamare*) is that the title can refer not only to a gruesome 2013 fire aboard a migrants' ship that drowned 345 people half a mile off the beach of Lampedusa (cf. Kushner 201) but also to an inexplicably sprightly (even Felliniesque) tune of the same name ("Fuoccoamare") supposedly inspired by the burning of an Italian ship in World War II. This song is requested of a disc jockey on Lampedusa by the young protagonist Samuele's grandmother as she putters around her modest but attractive kitchen in the film. She, her ailing husband, Samuele, and his fisherman father all reside in middle-class comfort on Lampedusa. As Alberto Zambendetti writes in his essay "Unmoored Visions: Gianfranco Rosi's *Fire at Sea*," it is precisely the unspoken contrast between a life of safety and the migrants' lives of utmost suffering and peril that forms the—again unspoken—"third narrative" of Rosi's remarkable documentary, which focuses on the boy Samuele, trying to grow up in a place of both serenity and horror, and the town's deeply concerned Dr. Bartolo, Lampedusa's own "Father of Exiles," welcoming the new arrivals—some dangerously ill—while still caring for most of the island's natives.

Rosi's film, which like all great visual narratives shouts out for articulation of its unspoken metaphors, embodies the cost of the world's migrant crisis for those on *all* sides, as effectively as it may ever be stated. Chinese dissident artist Ai Weiwei's feature-length epic-scale migration film *Human Flow* (2017)—a small part of which also deals with Mediterranean migrants' drownings—will also be discussed as an example of participatory (Weiwei) vs. observational (Rosi) documentary typology. Weiwei now works out of Cambridge, UK, and, needless to say, both his and Rosi's films speak to the migration crisis in Germany, Austria, the whole of the EU, and beyond.

The issue of EU or even just Italian immigration ripples with swirling currents, countercurrents, and topic undertow. One might dive into filmographies of other immigration-themed films,[1] or one might survey other texts of the Afrodiaspora in Italy and elsewhere.[2] Other related visual art forms such as the Porta d'Europa by Mimmo Paladino (Ramsay 209) enrich Lampedusa, mainland Italy, and even Mediterranean sea beds, for example, Jason deCaires Taylor's underwater sculpture of a boat with thirteen passengers entitled *Raft of Lampedusa* and situated off the Spanish coast (cf. Kushner 204).[3] Scholars of geography, sociology (including criminal justice), and cultural studies beckon one to take the plunge, as do those famously strong swimmers who study film and postcolonial theory.[4] In this paper, I paddle in shallower, safer waters, attempting a close reading of scenes from Rosi's remarkable film and considering its reception (not universally positive). But the harrowing history of Lampedusa, including the statistics on drownings and deaths, must serve all as a launching point for any approach.

LAMPEDUSA—THEATRUM MUNDI

Luciano Baracco is one of many Italian scholars[5] to have studied Lampedusa, going back to 1630 when the Tomasi family was declared "Princes of Lampedusa" but eventually sold their birthright to Naples (in 1860), making the 20 square kilometers of now mostly barren rock Sicilian/Italian (444). The island was used as a penal colony both in the nineteenth and the twentieth centuries (under Mussolini), with the barrenness seen today possibly intentional deforestation. In the 1880s, sponge fishing became a valuable source of income. Rosi's film, in fact, includes several scenes of a silent, somewhat portly diver in a wetsuit, climbing gingerly down steep cliffs to reach dangerous-looking, restless waters where he plunges in, always without explanation. Rosi's camera follows him below the surface, even once during a night dive. Viewers eventually surmise he is seeking sponges or urchins—creatures he gathers into underwater crates, evidently for later retrieval. The viewer comes to almost dread this solitary diver's appearances, coupled as they are with high-risk behaviors that could easily lead to his very real watery death. In Lampedusa's economic history, bluefish surpassed sponges as the sought-after target species, peaking in the 1970s (cf. Baracco 444). Today, Lampedusa's roughly 6,000 citizens are still either fishermen or part of the migrant-processing "industry," which includes policemen, NGO workers, Coast Guard and Naval personnel, health workers, and detention center workers, many of whom are seen in Rosi's film. The irony is that the latter are often masked and wearing white protective suits and, with the exception of Dr. Bartolo, have no contact with the native Lampedusans. As critics have noted, Dr. Bartolo is the only human bridge between indigenous Lampedusans, the migrant rescuers/processers, and the migrants themselves, each of whom places his or her hand into Dr. Bartolo's as he gently checks for signs of infectious diseases around their nails. Dr. Bartolo then gives each person an apologetic, even welcoming pat on the shoulder or back.

Writing in *ACME: The International E-Journal of Critical Geographies*, Paolo Cuttitta—sounding as much like a theater impresario as a geographer—explains little Lampedusa's center stage position in the European and world imagination of the migrant crisis by using a compelling metaphor of dramatization and theatricality. Lampedusa has come to represent not only a border but "borderness" itself (Cuttitta 196). Because of its appalling death rates and the large numbers of migrants who have landed there, Lampedusa can be said to "perform" the world crisis. Cuttitta even divides the crisis (and Lampedusa's response) into five "acts": The First Act, Cuttitta calls "Toughness," the Second Act "Humaneness" (207), the Third Act "Emergency I" (208), The Fourth Act "Zero Immigration," and the Fifth Act "Emergency II" (210). The acts reflect Italian (and EU) politicians' shifting policies to control Lampedusa's attractiveness to migrants (what Cuttitta calls its "pull"). Right-wing politicians such as Silvio Berlusconi (father of "Zero Immigration") and Mario Borghezio (212) were happier with "push" policies—sometimes physically repelling migrants at sea or forcibly returning them to African ports. Tony Kushner, the American playwright, not surprisingly picks up Cuttitta's conceit of Lampedusa as a play. In his article about the island comparing the ongoing migrant crisis to both the Holocaust and (by implication) the Nakba, he points out that the migrants are sometimes forced to "perform" their own stories. Some consciously use their own children as "actors" to increase pathos and help them win asylum. Kushner's piece appears in *Mobile Culture Studies: The Journal*, another publication whose title alone indicates the broadly interdisciplinary interest in the subject of families and immigration.

Luca Ciabarri, also writing in *ACME*, speaks of the "intellectual construction" of migration routes (247). There is a word in Arabic, *tahrib*, which means "contraband and illegal cross-border activities" but also connotes "danger, challenge and freedom" (258). Even with the relatively large numbers who have crossed from Africa to Italy over time (and even with the unknowably large numbers of those who have tried and drowned), only 13 percent of Italy's "irregular immigration" has come via Lampedusa, far from the "uncontrollable invasion" right-wing politicians imply, often using metaphors of "swarming," with its connotation of insects, or flooding, with its implicit threat of drowning. The island has attracted dubious celebrities such as Marine Le Pen of the *Front National*, members of Austria's *Freiheitspartei*, Netherlands' *Pim Fortuyn* (cf. Dawson 166), and those of the British National Party (cf. Baracco 446). It also drew a widely covered visit of support from Pope Francis (2013), who spoke out against the "globalization of indifference" (Baracco 446). Needless to say, the "Acts" entitled Emergency I and II resulted from especially egregious incidents such as the May 2015 drowning of 772 out of 800 migrants on a boat that went down (Kushner 207). Differently named military operations, coordinated by the European agency FRONTEX established in 2004 (cf. Balkan 119; Ponaznesi 157), have also been part of the push–pull drama (cf. Baracco 446). Operation *Mare Nostrum* (2013) seemed to create pull by rescuing so many; therefore, it was replaced by *Operation Triton* (2014), which tried to repel more arrivals. During the filming of *Fire at Sea,* a more benign, liberal policy of rescue was in force, one more in keeping with the native Lampedusans' traditional magnanimity to "anyone or thing that comes from the sea" (cited by Rosi and others).

GIANFRANCO ROSI—TH' [UN]OBSERVED OF ALL OBSERVERS (CF. *HAMLET* III.I.154)

Fire at Sea is an example of "migrant cinema" (Ponzanesi and Berger 111), the very mention of which plunges one into a whirlpool of competing terms and definitions. Nikhil Sathe usefully collects similar terminology: "transnational cinema" (Elizabeth Ezra and Terry Rowden), cinema of "double occupancy" (Thomas Elsaesser), "cinema at the periphery" (Dina Iordanova), and "accented cinema" (Hamid Naficy) (Sathe 40). Sathe also includes "migrant and diasporic cinema" (Daniela Berghahn and Claudia Sternberg). Under these *roughly* synonymous headings, migrant cinemas can then be subdivided (cf. Ponzanesi and Berger 111) into three categories: films made by exiles, films made by members of a diaspora (longer-term residents of another country but still passionate about the fate of their people's homeland), and cinema made by "ethnic" and "identity" filmmakers. Rosi, though Italian and therefore consanguine with the Lampedusans, would seem to fit into the last category, an "ethnic or identity" filmmaker, when it comes to the migrants of Lampedusa. Indeed most of the negative press about the film has focused on Rosi's failure to lift individual migrants into the same prominence he grants his two "starring" Sicilian Lampedusans: Dr. Bartolo and the most memorable character: twelve-year-old Samuele. What Rosi does have in common with other creators of "migrant cinema" is the following list: "multilingualism, non-places and hapticness, . . . interstitial modes of production and alternative distribution channels" (Ponzanesi and Berger 112). Sandra Ponzanesi, in a separate solo article, explains that the "interstitial mode of production" often involves "multisource funding" from several countries (true for *Fire at Sea*). Rosi uses Sicilian dialect in his film, losing some audience-members—even Italians—unfamiliar with Sicilian, but gaining in authenticity. Ponzanesi praises the film as "showing the border of Europe and proposing its unravelment" (165).

Within the category of migrant cinema, *Fire at Sea* is, of course, a documentary, a subgenre with its own politicized, highly theorized typologies. Domitilla Olivieri surveys the six modes of documentary-making that Bill Nichols has proposed: "poetic, expository, participatory, observational, reflexive, performative" (quoted in Olivieri 137). She then goes on to cite characteristics of the "observational" that seem to make it the most applicable category for *Fire at Sea*. First Olivieri cites Anna Grimshaw and Amanda Ravetz's definition of observational cinema:

> [This cinema features] long shots and extended sequences, long takes, deep focus photography and synchronous sound. It has been defined as maintaining a respect for the spatial and temporal integrity of events, as being suggestive rather than declarative, with the emphasis being on shooting rather than editing, and on scenes rather than shots. (quoted in Olivieri 137–38)

This mode of "attending to the world" (quoted in Olivieri 138) has been related to "sensory ethnography" work done at the Sensory Ethnography lab at Harvard University. Olivieri continues its characterization saying "the focus [is] on ordinary people and the uneventful, the attention to issues of alterity and intercultural encounters, and a political engagement" (139). Olivieri also uses the evocative term "slow cinema," and the word I had already selected for my title: "quotidian." All these descriptions of observational documentary apply perfectly to *Fire at Sea*. The shock of the film—made manifest in its final gruesome shots of corpses found below deck on a human-trafficking boat—is the way horror coexists so quietly and *just* out of sight of the quotidian on Lampedusa. Its very *raison-d'être* is to teach its viewers to grasp that paradox. We become more aware of what T. M. Trinh calls the "space in-between" or what Homi Bhabha might call "third space" (quoted in Olivieri 143). Olivieri continues with two insights from Elizabeth Cowie: "We do not 'see for ourselves,' but in documentary it is 'ourselves seeing through another's eye, for we adopt as our own the look of the camera that has gone before us and that has selected and organized the space and the seen'" (quoted in Olivieri 144). Olivieri bases her observations about Rosi on the director's best-known film before *Fire at Sea*, titled *Sacro GRA* (GRA= Grande Raccordo Anulare), a documentary on the mixed community of people who live around the "ring" highway encircling Rome. *Sacro GRA* won the 2013 Golden Lion at the seventieth Venice International Film Festival (cf. 136), presaging the Golden Bear its successor *Fire at Sea* would win in Berlin in 2016 (leonine or ursine, golden is good).

Rosi, who studied film at New York University, would seem to be much at ease in the observational mode. Alberto Zambenedetti's Liner Notes for the DVD mention Rosi's earlier films: *El Sicario, Room 164* (2010) about a Mexican drug trafficker stuck in a room; the aforementioned *Sacro GRA*; *Below Sea Level* (2008) about the denizens of the California desert who live 120 feet below sea level; and *Boatman* (1993), shot from a rowboat on the Ganges River following the adventures of European exiles out of their element. What they all have in common is what Zambenedetti calls Rosi's "eth-nographic gaze . . . on the marginalized and the forgotten" (8). When asked during a Q&A at the New York Film Festival about his authorial position in his work, Rosi answered with theoretical correctness: "I'm not invisible at all. . . . No I'm there. The camera's there and changes things" ("Fire at Sea"). And yet Dr. Bartolo, in a Liner Notes interview, marvels aloud about Rosi's ability to make his filming unobtrusive: "He never let us feel the burden of the camera" (Zambenedetti 2). Shooting with a small camera and no crew, Rosi became a quiet, intermittent member of the Lampedusan community during a period of almost two years, discovering his narrative as he went and meeting his protagonist Samuele when the boy was playing with his (now trademark) slingshot. At the same NYFF Q&A, Rosi recalled Samuele's saying, "I hate this island because everyone's a fisherman. . . . I hate the sea. My soul is the soul of the hunter, not the fisherman." Rosi knew he'd met a "little boy with an old man head [*sic*]." What other twelve-year-old goes around say-ing things such as "in life you need passion"? Samuele, whom Rosi calls his "magic kid . . . at a magic age," became Rosi's protagonist and structuring (coming-of-age) principle/principal for the film ("Fire at Sea"). This decision, again, has not been universally lauded. Says Federica Mazzara in a special issue of *Crossings: Journal of Migration and Culture*, "Rosi's film limits itself to drag the viewer to compassion and pity . . . failing to encourage a more sophisticated understanding of the issue of migration" (130). Indeed, we never see Samuele with a migrant in the same frame (something others have pointed out repeatedly).

CINEMATIC CONCEITS IN *FIRE AT SEA*: NO MAN [OR BOY] IS AN ISLAND

Rosi begins his film with stark onscreen statistics: in the last 20 years 400,000 migrants have landed on Lampedusa, with an estimated 15,000 others dying in the attempt. And yet, our first encounter with Lampedusans is with a solitary little indigene, his face partially wrapped in a scarf against the cold wind, utterly preoccupied with somewhat clumsily climbing a tree. The boy, our Samuele, eventually succeeds, and hacks down a Y-shaped fork of wood.

We have been introduced to our slingshot-toting hero, the David of Lampedusa, who will spend the rest of the film fighting not Goliath, but instead seasickness (what greater embarrassment to an islander!?), homework, and some ill-defined malaise that gives him shortness of breath (later diagnosed as anxiety by our ubiquitous Dr. Bartolo). Samuele will also be diagnosed as having a "lazy eye," a childhood malady that results in one eye lagging behind the other in strength of movement and vision. This malady becomes, for the thoughtful viewer (and certainly for the film's critics), a kind of metaphor—even a conceit—for the migration crisis worldwide, a situation that Americans, Europeans, and the First Worlders in general are figuratively too "lazy" to focus upon properly. The correction of lazy eye consists in wearing a patch on the "good" eye (sacrificing one's superior vision assets) in order to strengthen the weaker eye. It's a painful process, particularly at first. Samuele loses his heretofore excellent aim as a slingshot shooter. (Slingshot shooters shoot with one eye shut anyway.) But eventually the therapy will work for him, improving his vision overall.

Returning to Rosi's chronology, however, from the initial cutting of the slingshot branch, we move with a direct cut (Rosi's way), to synchronous voice-overs (the speakers are out of frame) and shots of an electronic tracking screen in some maritime facility. It is night and one voice is frantic: "Please, we beg you!" The frantic voice is asking for help for a ship in distress. The radio dispatcher answering is maddeningly repetitive, "Your position, your position." Neither is a native speaker of English, and both disembodied voices are dead tired. The dispatcher cannot seem to get the information he needs. He seems all-too-familiar with these calls for help. He is not blasé, but he is frustrated. The scene shifts to a spotlight on the sea, a symbol of absolute futility. Water covers three-fourths of the planet. The spotlight illuminates a circle perhaps 30 feet in diameter. How can such a search method ever succeed?

In the following scenes, another "radio man"—Lampedusa's DJ—sings along with the song he is broadcasting, something rather old-fashioned and, one assumes, in Sicilian. In an old, time-honored editing trick, we next see the person *hearing* the DJ's voice. It's a pleasant-looking woman in a dress, cooking contentedly in a small, well-appointed kitchen. A newscaster's voice then comes on to report that 250 people have been shipwrecked 60 kilometers off Lampedusa. Thirty-four bodies have been recovered so far; 206 have been rescued. "Poor souls" says our cook to herself. She is sincere in her thoughts of condolence, but the striking contrast between her comfortable situation and the deadly, chaotic situation at sea is implicit.

We next hear a mosquito-like whine and see a weakly powered motor scooter outdoors on one of Lampedusa's rare roadways. It carries two boys, playfully weaving the vehicle back and forth. It is our tree-climber Samuele and some friend. Then Samuele and the same friend are working on some project in an island house's doorway. They are cutting rubber—a closer shot reveals rubber gloves—on the top of a barrel and then fastening the strips to Y-shaped handles: slingshots, of course. Samuele (still nameless to us) seems firmly in charge, dispensing advice to Boy 2 on things tangible and intangible. He discusses the best wood to use for slingshots: pine is his favorite. The other boy suggests olive wood. Samuele grants him that his idea has virtue, but he by no means relinquishes his position of superior knowledge. He finishes his weapon of choice; they discuss aiming technique. Samuele declares his new sling shot to be perfect; then, just as firmly, he says it's a little bit "hinky" (or the Sicilian equivalent thereof). Our scene ends with Samuele's decidedly precocious pontification, "To break this handle it would take the hand of God." It strikes us as the bravado of the insecure.

In the next scene—as always, just a cut without transition—we are with the two boys hunting birds at night, an important moment in Samuele's characterization. Rosi returns to another night hunt at the end of his film (figure 8.1). For now, the boys shoot at their prey, mostly, we guess, without success. And, just as suddenly, we are back at the maritime station with another call for help and the same exasperated radio rescue dispatcher. This time a woman's voice gives the desperate plea. The dispatcher tells her to calm down and, later, to save her battery, and that he will get back with her. Another helicopter launches from a rescue ship at sea. We watch it on an electronic monitor. The film is filled with such computer screens: land screens, seaborne screens, ultrasound screens. But the screens do not seem to be helping very much.

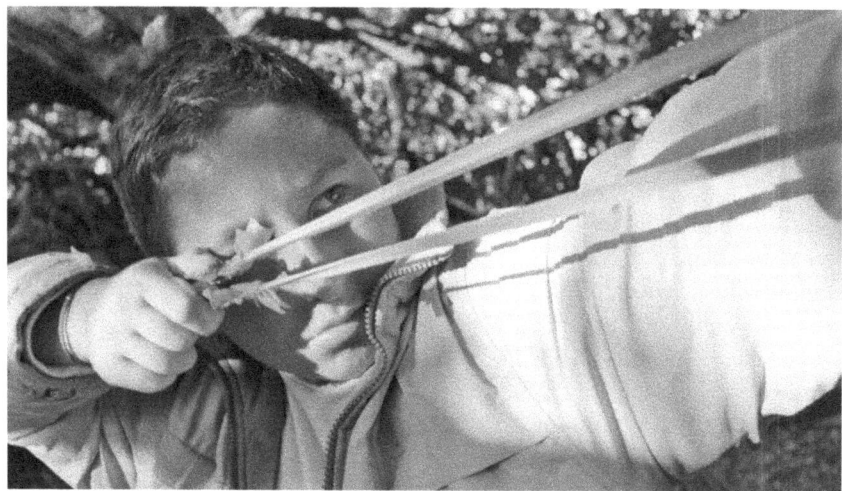

Figure 8.1 Samuele hunts birds with his slingshot, until, at film's end, he shows mercy on a helpless one (*Fire at Sea*, 2016, screenshot).

And now we are finally with the passengers, the migrants, though we cannot be sure whether they were the ones who were calling for help or others. Men in white hazmat suits are gently handling people, helping them from boat to boat, trying to match up family members. "There should be 13 women, eight boys and six girls." Then come some migrant men, some, we are told, with scabies. "There's just one with chickenpox," reports one of the rescuers by phone. "He'll be the last to board." We get super close-ups of men under shiny foil and clear plastic sheets, huddling for warmth. We cannot hear their words. They tolerate the super close-ups. One looks defiant, but too tired to verbalize it. We follow, still in the same boat, as Rosi himself must have been, with this same group of migrants as they approach the small port of Lampedusa.

Then we are suddenly on a different boat, during the daytime, and Samuele is asking his father about personal photographs stuck to the pilothouse's walls. The older man patiently answers Samuele's oddly urgent questions. (The boy is acting what Americans would call "hyper.") But the man remains patient. He speaks of living aboard for six or seven months on extended fishing trips. "It was a hard life. It wasn't a nice life," he says. Samuele seems both fascinated and repelled by his father's simple answers.

We are then back with Samuele's friend, this time alone on the scooter and clearly teasing Samuele with *his* superior status. Back and forth he rides, despite Samuele's calls for him to stop. We are back in the DJ's studio for a few moments; then with the two boys outside again, throwing rocks. The peculiar diver in his wetsuit walks across the horizon in back of them. We see him climbing down rocks to the water.

There is a cut to Dr. Bartolo doing an ultrasound on a migrant lady carrying twins. He struggles to communicate with her, mentioning in Sicilian that a "cultural mediator" is on the way. But he is also careful to keep her calm and comfortable. He talks to himself and to her, trying to figure out the gender of the babies in her womb. "We'll follow the spine," he announces with some confidence. The doctor switches to third person to say how scarce the amniotic fluid is because the mother has suffered so at sea. But he is pleased to see the babies are breathing well after such trauma.

From the babies in utero, we switch again to our two boys, Samuele and Matthias, cutting into thick, large cactus leaves with knives. (An American viewer immediately thinks of Halloween and carving pumpkins). Like the bird hunt, the boys' actions are mischievous and somewhat destructive. The boys fire their slingshots at the cactus "faces" they have created. They then add some firecrackers for increased destruction. The cacti don't stand much chance of survival. But then, toward the end, we see the boys inexplicably trying to tape the shattered cactus leaves back together, a marvelous metaphor for good intentions too long delayed to be of any earthly use. The analogy with Lampedusa and the world's migrant situation should be clear. There is a cut to night again, and another boatload of black faces, some wrapped in foil blankets. This is the scene where Dr. Bartolo examines the incoming migrants' hands, patting each one as he or she is dismissed. The people are counted: 59, 60, 61. They are loaded onto a bus marked "Misericordie" (a metaphorical name if ever there was one), and they peer outside, dazed. The processing continues in another building. They are directed into lines. The policemen remark that there's a stench of diesel fuel on many men: "They're drenched in diesel. If I flick my lighter, I'll go up in flames." Along they shuffle, a never-ending parade for processors. A woman doesn't want to show any hair in her ID photo. She's convinced to show a little (perhaps so that ID inspectors can check her hair color).

We are suddenly back with the diver, collecting something. There's an underwater cave and another crate, both mysterious and threatening. Then we are with an older woman (Samuele's grandmother), and Samuele reads his homework. There's thunder, and the woman speaks of the days she would take bread to his grandfather to eat on the boat. She speaks briefly of the thunder's sound reminding her of World War II barrages. "Like fire at sea?" Samuele asks (perhaps aware the film will be entitled that). "The sea turned red," she confirms.

We cut abruptly to a new day with crashing surf and two gray military ships in the distance, evidently on patrol for boats of migrants. The boys pretend to "shoot" at them, using their arms as rifles and "cocking" them between shots. The effect—clearly Samuele's invention—is strikingly real-istic. Matthias tires of the game first, saying, "Enough. You killed em all." One thinks of the countless American films—from westerns to *Star Wars*—that undoubtedly inspired such violent play. Planes fly over and there are more pretend shots.

The wild weather keeps the fishermen in port, so Auntie Maria (Samuele's grandmother) calls her nephew the DJ and requests "Fuoccoamare" in honor of her fisherman son, Nello. The sprightly song ensues (in the station and the kitchen). We'll later hear it at an impromptu street dance for Lampedusans.

The scene when Samuele learns about his "lazy eye" is next, followed by a night shot of a distant lighthouse. One wonders how many will see the light, intended to guide them to safety, especially in bad weather. On shore, those migrants lucky enough to have made it to land chant prayers in a makeshift mosque. They are dark male figures in a dark room. The sounds, to American ears now trained to fear all things Islamic, sound vaguely alien and threatening.

We cut to a young African migrant doing a lively performance about the harrowing journey of his group. It is part rap and part spoken word. "200 pas-sengers died!" he sing/shouts. Then he uses a different number—90—saying that 30 were rescued, but 60 died. He summarizes his point: "It is risky in life not to take a risk because life itself is a risk." The purpose of the young man's chant and whether or not he is telling his own story or someone else's are somewhat unclear. Still we have met an individual—a "spokesman" fig-ure for at least the Nigerian contingent. Does he tell such a tale because he has suffered or perhaps because people expect him to have suffered? Is he strengthening his case for asylum? Is he a noble testifier or ignoble manipula-tor? We have only his performance to judge him.

Cut to Samuele on a boat, not well. He throws up over the rail. We see squid have been caught on the boat. Then we cut to a scene of squid being slurped in the family kitchen, along with pasta. Samuele, now healthy because on land, slurps gleefully. His grandmother and father glance his way indulgently. No one bothers to correct the boy's table manners. One surmises that there are few enough sources of pleasure for Lampedusa's boys. Slurp-ing, at age twelve, will be tolerated.

Samuele discusses his seasickness with his family; they reassure him that he can get over it. (What he can do besides fishing is quite unclear.) Samuele senses there is more to this than they think. He goes to the floating dock for motion-practice, but he is a "sailor who's fallen from grace with the sea." How will he follow his family's calling?

We then get the scene when Dr. Bartolo explains the "class" system on migrant boats, a situation of greed on the part of smugglers and desperation on the part of travelers that is regularly killing hundreds. Says Bartolo, "It's

Figure 8.2   Dr. Bartolo discusses the need to help in Rosi's *Fire At Sea* (2016, screenshot).

the duty of every human being to help these people" (figure 8.2). This expository scene—it's another monitor screen on camera—is a metadiscourse clearly from the speaker's heart.

To balance Bartolo's sad soliloquy, Rosi gives us a look at the joyous humanity of the migrants, engaged in a makeshift soccer game at their detention center. There's no net, but great passion. Somalia, Sudan, Syria—men shout out their countries of origin, trying to organize "national" teams. The irony is that men so desperate to escape their home countries that they risk and sometimes lose their lives are the same men who still seem eager to claim allegiance to their homelands. Syria is the winner. Given the crisis there, perhaps more (and better) players ended up competing.

Samuele is, at first, pretty miserable in his new eye-patch glasses. But he demonstrates pluck in coping. The mysterious diver departs his home and then walks the cliffs to his nighttime rendezvous with possible death. Samuele struggles in his school classroom. We cannot be sure whether it is his eyesight or a simple lack of preparation. The teacher is displeased.

In the next scene an older friend is trying to teach him rowing. Samuele does poorly and drifts dangerously and uncontrollably over toward the military boats tied in the harbor. Samuele's friend berates him and rescues him, finding it easier to row them both home than deal with Samuele's ineptitude. We suspect it may be fear that defeats Samuele whenever it comes to waterborne activities.

Samuele discusses his "malaise" with Dr. Bartolo, the scene mentioned before. Bartolo's diagnosis is, "You're a little bit tense." Is it hypochondria or something "serious"? All the viewers know is that the boy seems unreasonably and inappropriately anxious about something.

Rosi, by his editing choice, suggests why. We see another boat full of migrants, one young man wearing a Lakers shirt. Bodies—barely moving—are pulled from the migrants' boat into the rescuers' skiff. Forty have died below decks. We see the final scene of Lampedusa's helplessness. Medical workers stand by as corpses are brought in bags to the modern ship. But the boat, apparently empty from the look of her deck (with the exception of two Hazmat-suited workers) is not empty. It is full of corpses below. Samuele may not be physically present, but something in him seems to know.

The remainder of the film gives us final glimpses of our protagonists. Samuele is hunting alone at night. He locates a chirping, but dazed-looking bird. We then cut to Aunt Maria (Grandmother) who makes a bed, smoothing it carefully, lovingly. A shrine to the Virgin Mary stands screen right. Maria kisses her husband (or son's) military photo, with Rossini's *Mosè in Egitto* (identified by Zambenedetti 10) playing in the background. Moses was, we do recall, a migrant and a leader of migrants. We cut back again to Samuele. Instead of killing the dazed bird, he strokes its feathers. But he still pretends he's shooting. Final black out.

From a focus on *one* conflicted twelve-year-old Lampedusan, living on a six-square-mile island amidst a sea of troubles and a crowd of suffering strangers just out of sight (either drowned or in a detention center), we move briefly, for the sake of comparison and contrast to Ai Weiwei's 2017 documentary *Human Flow*, inspired by similar altruism but executed on a contrastingly vast, epic scale. Weiwei covers 23 countries with 200 crew members. (Rosi was his own crew, though he did get help with editing.)

AI WEIWEI'S *HUMAN FLOW*: BEING THERE

Ai Weiwei, the most famous Chinese dissident artist of our era, is himself, of course, an immigrant who fled his homeland to escape repression and become a cosmopolitan, having recently moved from Berlin to Cambridge, UK. This is by no means his first work about the world migrant crisis. The online press kit for *Human Flow* lists other works of art on the large scale that Weiwei often favors (building-wrapping) plus some performance art. They include a 200-foot inflatable boat with 258 refugee figures; his wrapping of the *Berliner Konzerthaus* in 3,000 orange life vests (resembling images like figure 8.3); his covering of some of his own public sculpture with the familiar thermal blankets Rosi also shows us in *Fire at Sea*; Weiwei's recreating the now-iconic photo of the Syrian toddler Alan Kurdi with his own middle-aged body in place of the child's, a work that prompted some strong negative

Figure 8.3 Discarded life vests raise questions about the fate of those who wore them (*Human Flow*, 2017, screenshot).

reactions (cf. Ramsay 219); an eight-mile "Walk of Compassion" in London; and a work entitled "Good Fences Make Good Neighbors" (the title possibly intended as ironic?).

Human Flow was inspired by an incident on the Greek island of Lesbos where Weiwei, his son, and his girlfriend themselves witnessed a landing of exhausted migrants on the very beach where they were vacationing. Kathleen Miles quotes Weiwei as saying, "I saw people wet, falling down, and nobody was helping them" (36). Weiwei decided to help by *joining* the "human flow" in twenty-three countries where he saw it occurring. A believer in "participatory" documentary-making ("the script is writing you," he tells Miles in her interview), Weiwei lets himself be seen onscreen, consoling with, joking with, and sojourning with migrants on several continents, including the United States, at the Mexican border.

Reactions to Weiwei's film have been mixed—praise for his good intentions and what Catherine Russell, writing in *Cineaste*, calls his "high production values . . . making everything and everyone appear incredibly beautiful" (21). Russell notes that the film has twelve credited cinematographers (!). But he continues, "while empathetic, [Weiwei] often provides an almost clownish counterpart to their [the migrants'] desperate plights" (21). Critic David Yearsley calls *Human Flow* a powerful *Gesamtkunstwerk* but adds that he is using the term a bit facetiously.

Weiwei begins his film with an overhead (drone) shot of a crowded boat of migrants moving through blue waters. The only difference in this boat and the ones Rosi shoots is the relative absence of such overhead angles (no drone budget) in Rosi. Weiwei ends his film with a shot of used, empty life jackets stacked by the thousands in some warehouse. We immediately think of photos from the Holocaust—mountains of hair shorn from Jewish heads or gold teeth plucked from dead mouths. How many of the life jackets were taken off drowning victims or washed ashore with no further explanation?

Early in *Human Flow*, Weiwei sets his pattern. Statistics about migration are written over the screen, as are lines of poetry, many by African, Middle-Eastern, or Asian writers. We begin in Iraq where, we are told, 277,000 people live in the refugee camp we are seeing. We are told that 268,000 Iraqis have been killed since the US invasion. We meet Syrians, then move on to Lesbos, where in 2015 and 2016 "more than a million refugees" arrived. But then comes another, larger number: 65 million "forcibly displaced from their homes" worldwide. We hear Angela Merkel's brave exhortation to her countrymen *Wir schaffen das!* (We'll DO this!—my translation—quoted by Gerd Gemünden). She believes that Germany can open itself to a healing of its history *and* the present by welcoming the wretched. But fewer hearts answered than expected.

Weiwei cuts to Bangladesh, where a half million Rohingyas have fled their oppressors in Myanmar. He visits among them and we see they are not being universally welcomed by the Bangladeshis. The poetic epigraph for this section reads, "One cannot escape one's evil deed—Buddhist scripture." Just as suddenly we are back in Europe, in Northern Greece, walking down a road with crowds of people wearing coats, carrying bags, wearing backpacks. They "wear" and carry children, too, sinking in exhaustion by the roadside, then rising to walk again. The moving human chain is often shot from behind, from the position of another walker: Weiwei is there. There is a fence with razor wire. We are shown tents by train tracks and an opening of some kind, not much wider than a kitchen door. It is a heavily guarded crossing on the Greek-Macedonian border near a railway station. We are told "a million people walked through this gate." How is this possible—such a narrow opening, such a slim chance?

Now we and Weiwei join 2 million Palestinian refugees in Jordan. But wait. Now we are in Southern Italy with African refugees (those whom Rosi followed). There are the same silver and gold shiny thin "blankets." Then we are in Greece. There's a charging place for phones. Dozens of phones have gathered around it like camels drinking at some oasis pond. The mix of smart phone technology and Stone Age living accommodations just does not "work"—either aesthetically or rationally. Weiwei pretends to swap passports with another migrant. It gets a big but nervous laugh. Now we are in Turkey, where a deal has been struck. The Turks will keep refugees the EU sends back. As a recompense, Turks will receive 6 billion euros and visas for their own citizens' free travel to the EU. Ai Weiwei gets and gives haircuts in a camp. A screen epigraph reads, "A year is more than it is / And less." It comes from Adonis, a Syrian poet. Ai Weiwei includes more overhead (drone or helicopter) shots, making the people on the ground look like ants in a swarm. There is talk of IDs and drownings and also graves in the dirt. Weiwei visits Lebanon and the seemingly permanently displaced Palestinians in Gaza and the West Bank. He visits Kenya and "the world's largest refugee camp complex," where Somalians, Eritreans, and South Sudanese gather. There are brief talks with officials, such as a man in a tie from the UN High Commission on Refugees. We talk about climate change. Weiwei works with some goats. There is a dust storm, and we are in Pakistan and Afghanistan. But soon thereafter we are in Kenya, where a father and son drag a tree cut down for fuel across a barren landscape. There are busses in Pakistan for Afghans on the move.

But now we are in some hangars at Tempelhof—site of the Berlin Air Lift and Kennedy's *Ich bin ein Berliner!* Now Tempelhof houses refugees who are certainly better off than many we have seen but who still suffer from an apparent mix of stultifying boredom and wild uncertainty about their future. And now we are in the infamous Calais "Jungle" camp, the one French authorities eventually demolished, trying to disperse the thousands seeking a way into the UK and stymied by the same thing that gratefully slowed down Hitler: the English Channel. But no, we are in Iraq, and Mosul is being retaken from ISIS.

Weiwei cites another Syrian poet, Nizar Qabbani, with an onscreen epigraph:

the Secret of our Tragedy:
Our shouts are louder than
our voices,
Our swords are longer than we are.

Weiwei shifts to an overcrowded boat, looking much like the one at the beginning of his film. We are told 720–730 people are on board. One wonders why the count is not more certain, given the size of the boat.

Weiwei leaves his visit to the Mexican border too late in his film. It is damning—implicitly damning, but quite damning—of Trump's anti-immigrant stance and his pernicious presidential stoking of nativist hatred for the

Other. And then we see the warehouse and the mountain of used life jackets. It looks so much like those mountains of spectacles and suitcases, now memorialized in Holocaust museums.

The image of an impossibly overcrowded boat, its passengers more likely destined for drowning than a better life, is indelible. Rosi knew it, and Weiwei knew it. They share a central metaphor, of human migration being as natural and justified (and unstoppable) as the flow of the planet's waters. Thinking of this conceit, one might also recall the medieval motif of the *Narrenschiff*—the Ship of Fools. Humanity is all in the same boat; it is just that some of us practice brotherhood while others toss their shipmates overboard. And, as always, those in steerage—even on the *Titanic*—or crushed to asphyxiation in the hold of a smuggler's boat get the worst of it.

CONCLUSION: *THE ORIGIN OF OTHERS* AND THE "RIGHT TO HAVE RIGHTS"

In her recently published Charles Eliot Norton Lectures at Harvard University, the late Toni Morrison turned her attention to borders, globalization, and, as always, human nature. She suspects that it is the way foreigners unexpectedly remind us of ourselves that we find most perturbing about them: "For the stranger is not foreign, she is random; not alien but remembered; and it is the randomness of the encounter with our already known—although unacknowledged—selves that summons a ripple of alarm" (38). Morrison later speaks of borders as "the porous places, the vulnerable points where the concept of home is seen as being menaced by foreigners" (94), an understanding supported by Verena Berger and David Winkler's suggestion that migrants not only transgress the borders, they "also carry borderlines into the societies into which they move" (160). Morrison further notes that globalization "understands itself as historically progressive" but that it has "larger connotations . . . less innocent, encompassing as they do, the demonization of embargoed states" (96–97), as nation states may soon collapse "under the weight of transnational economics, capital and labor." Meanwhile, as Robert Stam and Ella Shohat put it, America revels in its exceptionalism (473) and "latter-day expressions of narcissistic nationalism" (480).

Writing in the journal *Mediterranean Politics*, back in 2007, Paola Monzini describes the paradox of globalization as "goods move; people are stymied" (my summary of her argument, 163). And as people are stymied by oceans, walls, fences, they shift their routes of escape, often to paths that are longer, more dangerous, or simply fatal. Ashley Dawson and Patrizia Palumbo conclude, "In Fortress Europe, then, mobility is for the privileged" (183). We are thrown back, again, to the Holocaust, the era that produced Hannah Arendt and informs the essay mentioned earlier by Tony Kushner. Arendt wrote, in

1951, about "the right to have rights," something so many are still so willing to deny, even to those on the very point of destruction. As both of our documentarians do, Julia Khrebtan-Hörhager turns to an image of vast open waters to explain the threat and hope immigrants face worldwide: "[T]he symbolism of the open sea, which might become an anonymous grave or turn into the reservoir of life-changing possibilities for the travelers metaphorically reflects the actual immigrant situation in the Mediterranean" (96). One can extend the metaphor (even to desert-crossings), and add the phrase "and worldwide." But to a coastal dweller, poor Clarence's fearful dream remains ever uppermost in my mind: "Lord, Lord! methought, what pain it was to drown!"

NOTES

1. Films about immigration from the late twentieth and early twenty-first centuries are too numerous to list here, but survey articles by Ardizzoni, Berger and Winkler, Caponetto, Olivieri, Ponzanesi and Berger; Ponzanesi, Russell, and Zagarrio help one dip a toe into the subject. An "Immigration filmography for educators" in *Radical Teacher* (2009) helps with American immigration films earlier in this millennium.

2. The special thirtieth anniversary issue of *Callaloo* (2007) looks at twentieth-century attitudes toward immigrants and early-twenty-first-century migration literature.

3. Maya Ramsay's "Reframing the Debate: The Art of Lampedusa" discusses the Archive of Migrant Memories (Dagmawi Yimer), Askavusa, a collective that gathers up discarded or washed-up immigrant belongings, creating performance art or artworks *trouvé(s)* on Lampedusa and elsewhere. Tony Kushner discusses Anders Lustgarten's play *Lampedusa* (2015) and other visual artworks; Federica Mazzara discusses Valentine Zagaria's play *Miraculi* and supports cultural and artistic capacities for promoting migrant voices.

4. Salvatore Coluccello and Simon Massey's "Out of Africa: The Human Trade between Libya and Lampedusa" explains the shifting, highly flexible networks of human smugglers centered not (as myth would have it) in Sicily, but in Northern Africa. Paola Monzini also looks at smugglers' business practices, ships, and organizations. Luca Ciabarri offers just that: a fresh interdisciplinary approach combining geography and cultural studies.

5. Judging from the authors' names (a questionable procedure!), at least fifteen Italian scholars or members of the Italian diaspora were consulted in the by-no-means-exhaustive research done for this chapter.

WORKS CITED

Ardizzoni, Michela. "Narratives of Change, Images for Change: Contemporary Social Documentaries in Italy." *Journal of Italian Cinema and Media Studies*, vol. 1, no. 3, 2013, pp. 311–26.

Balkan, Osman. "Disorder at the Border." *Studies in Ethnicity and Nationalism*, vol. 16, no. 1, 2016, pp. 118–20.

Baracco, Luciano. "Reimagining Europe's Borderlands: The Social and Cultural Impact of Undocumented Migrants on Lampedusa." *Italian Studies*, vol. 70, no. 4, 2015, pp. 444–48.

Berger, Verena, and Daniel Winkler. "Mediterranean Perspectives: Early Spanish and Italian Contributions to the Cinema of Irregular Migration (Giordana, Marra, Soler, Uribe)." *Cinémas*, vol. 22, nos. 2–3, 2012, pp. 159–77.

Caponetto, Rosettta Guiliani, "Another Country in My Eyes: Italian Cinema on African Immigration." *Metamorphoses*, vol. 14, nos. 1–2, 2006, pp. 294–301.

Ciabarri, Luca. "Dynamics and Representations of Migration Corridors: The Rise and Fall of the Libya-Lampedusa Route and Forms of Mobility from the Horn of Africa (2000–2009)." *ACME*, vol. 13, no. 2, 2014, pp. 246–62, http://www.acme-journal. org/volume13-2.html. Accessed May 15, 2019.

Coluccello, Salvatore, and Simon Massey. "Out of Africa: The Human Trade between Libya and Lampedusa." *Trends in Organized Crime*, vol. 10, no. 4, 2007, pp. 77–90.

Cuttitta, Paolo. "'Borderizing' the Island: Setting and Narratives of the Lampedusa 'Border Play.'" *ACME*, vol. 13. no. 2, 2014, pp. 196–219, https://www.acme-jou rnal.org/index.php/acme/article/view/1004. Accessed May 15, 2019.

Dawson, Ashley, and Patrizia Palumbo. "Hannibal's Children: Immigration and Antiracist Youth Subcultures in Contemporary Italy." *Cultural Critique*, no. 59, 2005, pp. 165–86.

Dittmar, Linda. "Immigration Filmography for Educators." *Radical Teacher*, no. 84, 2009, pp. 61–67.

"Fire at Sea." Q & A (with Gianfranco Rosi). Film at Lincoln Center. 54th New York Film Festival. Sep. 30–Oct. 16, https://www.youtube.com/watch?v=8O6eQBjD WDM. Accessed May 15, 2019.

Gemünden, Gerd. "Over the Fence, Across the Water: The 66th Berlin Film Festival." *Film Criticism*, vol. 40, no. 3, 2016, https://quod.lib.umich.edu/f/fc/13761232.0040 .307/--over-the-fence-across-the-water-the-66th-berlin-film?rgn=main;view=fullte xt. Accessed May 15, 2018.

Khrebtan-Hörhager, Julia. "*Italia—la terra promessa*? Lampedusa and the Immigrant Crisis of the European Union." *Journal of Multicultural Discourses*, vol. 10, no. 1, 2015, pp. 85–99.

Kushner, Tony. "Lampedusa and the Migrant Crisis: Ethics, Representation and History." *Mobile Culture Studies*, vol. 1, no. 2, 2016, pp. 59–92.

Laviosa, Flavia. "Modern Routes of Hope and Journeys of Faith in the Mediterranean: Apulia and Saint Nicholas of Bari." *Mediterranean Studies*, vol. 18, 2009, pp. 197–212.

Marmot, Michael. "Dignity in the Face of Suffering." *The Lancet*, vol. 388, no. 10039, July 2, 2016, pp. 22–23, https://www.thelancet.com/journals/lancet/article/ PIIS0140-6736(16)30942-4/fulltext. Accessed May 15, 2019.

Mazzara, Federica. "Editorial." *Lampedusa: Cultural and Artistic Spaces for Migrant Voices, Special Issue of Crossings: Journal of Migration & Culture*, vol. 7, no. 2,

2016, pp. 129–33, https://www.ingentaconnect.com/contentone/intellect/cjmc/2016/00000007/00000002/art00001?crawler=true&mimetype=application/pdf. Accessed Nov. 1, 2019.

Miles, Kathleen. "Nationality and Borders Are Barriers to Our Intelligence and Imagination." *New Perspectives Quarterly*, vol. 34, no. 4, 2017, pp. 35–39.

Monzini, Paola. "Sea-Border Crossings: The Organization of Irregular Migration to Italy." *Mediterranean Politics*, vol. 12, no. 2, 2007, pp. 163–84.

Morrison, Toni. *The Origin of Others*. Harvard University Press, 2017.

Olivieri, Domitilla. "Diasporic Proximities: Spaces of 'Home' in European Documentary." *Transnational Cinemas*, vol. 7, no. 2, 2016, pp. 135–50.

Palladino, Mariangela, and Iside Gjergi. "Open 'Hearing' in a Closed Sea." *Interventions*, vol. 18, no. 1, 2015, pp. 1–18.

Piazzo, Philippe. "Interview with Gianfranco Rosi." *Fire at Sea*. DVD. 2016. Universciné.

———. "Interview with Pietro Bartolo (médicin et directeur de l'hôpital de Lampedusa)." *Fire at Sea*. DVD. 2016. Universciné.

Ponzanesi, Sandra. "Of Shipwrecks and Weddings: Borders and Mobilities in Europe." *Transnational Cinemas*, vol. 7, no. 2, 2016, pp. 151–67.

———, and Verena Berger. "Introduction: Genres and Tropes in Postcolonial Cinema(s) in Europe." *Transnational Cinemas*, vol. 7, no. 2, 2016, pp. 111–17.

Ramsay, Maya. "Reframing the Debate: The Art of Lampedusa." *Crossings: Journal of Migration & Culture*, vol. 7, no. 2, 2016, pp. 209–25.

Rosi, Gianfranco. *Fuoccoamare* (*Fire at Sea*). Italian/Sicilian. Kino Lorber. DVD. 2016.

Russell, Catherine. "Migrant Cinema: Scenes of Displacement." *Cineaste*, vol. 43, no. 1, 2017, pp. 17–21.

Sathe, Nikhil. "Just in Time: Erwin Wagenhofer's Appropriation of the Classical Western Genre in *Black Brown White* (2011)." *Journal of Austrian Studies*, vol. 47, no. 4, 2014, pp. 39–64.

Stam, Robert, and Ella Shohat. "Transnationalizing Comparison: The Uses and Abuses of Cross-Cultural Analogy." *New Literary History*, vol. 40, no. 3, 2009, pp. 473–99.

Weiwei, Ai. *Human Flow*. DVD. 2016. Participant Media and Amazon Studios in Association with AC Films.

Yearsley, David. "Wrestling with Art: Ai Weiwei's *Human Flow*." *CounterPunch*, Nov. 3, 2017, www.counterpunch.org/2017/11/03. Accessed May 15, 2019.

Zagarrio, Vito. "Not Even in a Dream: Emigration and Immigration in New Italian Cinema." *Journal of Italian Cinema and Media Studies*, vol. 4, no. 3, 2016, pp. 421–38.

Zambenedetti, Alberto. "Unmoored Visions: Gianfranco Rosi's *Fire at Sea*." Liner Notes. DVD, 2016.

Chapter 9

Shifting Affiliations

Kinship Formation through Othering in the Marvel Cinematic Universe

Christopher Hansen

Departing from questions of existence in exile, this chapter focuses on kinship formation in popular culture, specifically on the ten-year movie franchise known as the Marvel Cinematic Universe (MCU). While, at first glance, there is no overt connection between notions of exile, kinship, and Othering in these superhero blockbusters, I will show that the MCU does, in fact, negotiate these paradigmatic concepts and addresses the status of the United States as an immigrant nation through narratives of shifting affiliations. A franchise as successful as the MCU can offer significant insights into debates about the changing face of the United States as an increasingly multicultural and multiethnic society. Applying postcolonial theories of Othering and subalternity, I argue that the MCU films adopt the idea of a universal migrant experience to manage the dynamic relationships among the extraordinary characters in the universe. In doing so, they speak to questions of shifting affiliations in US culture at large and create a literary figure representative of diverse migrant experiences: the Metamigrant.

Even with the rise of Comics Studies and more favorable views on popular culture, superhero films are still generally regarded as commercially driven rather than a social or artistic endeavor. Recently, Hollywood directors Martin Scorsese and Francis Ford Coppola disputed the artistic quality and cultural value of the MCU. Scorsese described the films as not being cinema, comparing them to theme parks (cf. Shoard); Coppola even called them repetitive and despicable (cf. Perez). However, it is exactly their popular nature, their ability to reach large audiences, and the need for internal consistency in ongoing serial narrative that affords this franchise with particular cultural value.

Considering the serial nature of superhero comics, Julian Chambliss identifies a central dialectic between constancy and change:

> The superhero comic is unique in its reliance on a shared narrative universe with continuity. While we can and do expected [*sic*] media to change, superhero comics are blessed or cursed with the need to relate events and people within the story to an audience that is changing. . . . The resulting structure creates strong reader loyalty, but it also requires the creators to fashion stories that must both relate internally according to logic and externally to a shifting audience. (150)

The constant oscillation between the retention of internal elements and the need to appeal to new audiences while retaining an existing fan base allows the superhero narrative to offer new perspectives enveloped in familiar ones. Superhero narrative "animates and ritualistically resolves basic cultural conflicts and contradictions" (Coogan 24); in the process, it can test new positions on these conflicts and contradictions, including on the social, political, and cultural implications of kinship and exile.

Superhero narratives always include extraordinary individuals. I will refer to these individuals as Metahumans, a concept common in superhero fandom and formally associated with the DC comics universe and its transmedial adaptations. Metahuman "refer[s] to anyone with extranormal powers, no matter the origins and including those not born with such power" (Burlingame). I am aware that the popular figure of the superhero (and villain) generally includes individuals with superpowers and those without, but since I focus on the different backgrounds and relationships among various characters in the MCU, I use the term Metahuman to classify characters considered extraordinary due to training, supernatural, or scientific means.

A notable aspect tying the superhero narratives of the MCU to US society is that all Metahumans have what Henk van Houtum and Ton van Naerssen describe as a "multiple-layered" background (132). Aside from belonging to the larger society, individual characters arrive in this society with other strong markers of identity. The most prominent example is the prototypical superhero Superman, who, coming from a different planet and growing up on earth, embodies the immigrant experience. However, the representation of this experience is more diverse in the superhero narrative, and even in the MCU.[1] Steve Rogers/Captain America and Bucky Barnes/The Winter Soldier, for instance, are natives of a version of World War II America who have been cast forward in time through cryogenics. Other characters were born as foreign nationals. Natasha Romanoff/Black Widow is of Russian descent; in the MCU version, Wanda Maximoff/Scarlet Witch originates from the fictional Eastern Europe nation Sokovia; T'Challa/Black Panther is a member of the royal family of the fictional African nation Wakanda. All of these characters retain ties to their backgrounds while operating within a US-based society of superheroes.

Moreover, several characters with an inhuman appearance come from foreign planets and therefore represent different species, such as the cast of *Guardians of Galaxy* (Gunn 2014). Groot is a plant-based lifeform with a limited capacity for speech. The result of experimentation, Rocket declares his existence a unique one in the cosmos. Gamora and Nebula are the adoptive children of Thanos, a native of the Jupiter Moon Titan, but they hail from different planets. As with the earth-based Metahumans, these characters display different aspects of their multilayered background when interacting within an Americanized idea of a multicultural cosmic society. These backgrounds place them in relation to a preconceived social group or culture and make them part of the larger social grouping of Metahumans. As such, they mirror the multicultural nature of the US society, where individuals often negotiate ancestral associations with a more general affiliation to the nation.

The complex of multiple identity-giving relations opens up questions of kinship and Othering, especially when different identities place characters on opposing sides of a conflict. Looking at the social complexes developed in the MCU and how they change when different backgrounds clash enables the identification of altering kinship relations. Such relations are only possible because the MCU has retained "different modes of serial narration" (Brinker 208) for more than ten years, when complex social relations were not only developed but have also changed gradually and significantly. Brinker explains:

> Like the comic book properties on which it is based, the MCU is organized in a number of separate subseries whose narratives all take place within a shared diegesis. Within this common "universe," events in one film or episode are continuous with others, producing lasting impact for succeeding installments, and characters . . . move easily from one subseries to another. (208)

Continuous serial narration inevitably alters the state of characters and their relationships through accumulating events and the continued addition of new material (cf. Mittell 253). Combining this with the potential alteration created by the ability to "move easily from one subseries to another" (Brinker 208) offers a complex representation of affiliations among individuals and groups as well as in their relationship toward society at large.

The MCU's Infinity Saga encompasses twenty-three films divided into three phases. The first phase marks the emergence of Metahumans, the second phase shows the escalation of their number and the subsequent consequences, and the third phase develops an internal dynamic within the larger culture/group. In the first phase, the Metahumans are treated as extraordinary individuals.[2] Their extraordinary status is measured vis-à-vis their individual context and their representation in the narrative. Tony Stark is introduced as an uncanny genius with the ability to create technology beyond normal human capacity; Bruce Banner is set apart through the monster inside of him; and Thor is doubly elevated, receiving special recognition as the heir to the throne of Asgard as well as being an unusual and capable individual in human society. Despite their hero status, each of these Metahumans is evaluated as a threat by government entities. Refusing to give up his technology to governmental oversight makes Tony Stark a political opponent to the US government. Thor is locked up, questioned as a potential foreign agent, and in *The Avengers* (Whedon 2012) singled out as an overwhelming threat to the US military. Bruce Banner/the Hulk is a monster and/or a potential military weapon; either embodiment places the individual character in direct conflict with society. Independent of the specific characters, the government shows a generally hostile attitude toward all Metahumans.

In contrast, the wider population judges Metahumans by their individual actions, celebrating heroes and condemning villains. In the same scene in which the government attempts to appropriate Stark's technology, the public cheers his remark of "successfully privatizing world peace" (*Iron Man 2* 2010). Thor is accepted as a hero among the Asgardians at the end of his first film and generally described as a good person by the supporting characters on earth in *Thor* (Branagh 2011). Due to his monster status and the film's focus on personal relationships, the Hulk does not hold the same heroic position intradiegetically. At least, a positive judgment of his person is only inferred by the character's action in the movie's final conflict (*The Incredible Hulk*, Leterrier 2008), but the audience is not presented with any direct public adoration as in the case of Iron Man or Thor. However, a heroic view of all characters in the first phase cements itself at the end of *The Avengers*, in which the entire team is celebrated as heroes. At the end of the first phase, kinship among Metahumans arises from the judgment of their actions. Individuals serving the "public good" find themselves in a social relation with others of similar goals. Criminals do not form a similar social group but are considered as Other and stand in binary opposition to the heroes. While this perspective is gradually established across six films, it does not remain in place for long. The perception of Metahumans changes from the first to the third phase through alterations in the fictional society in the second phase,[3] namely the sudden increase in Metahuman characters and activity.

The existence of Metahumans is normalized in the second phase in the first release of *Iron Man 3* (Black 2013), where the main threat comes from genetically modified ex-soldiers. The notion continues with the appearance of Dark Elves in *Thor: The Dark World* (Taylor 2014) and Ultron's robot army in *Avengers: Age of Ultron* (Whedon 2015). This presence of groups of

Metahumans (in contrast to individuals) normalizes the existence of Metahumans in the world. The phase also leads to the launching of new Metahuman characters such as Bucky Barnes/The Winter Soldier and Sam Wilson/The Falcon in *Captain America: Winter Soldier* (Russo 2014). *Avengers: Age of Ultron* introduces Piotr Maximoff/Quicksilver, Wanda Maximoff/The Scarlet Witch, The Vision, and Ultron. Finally, *Ant-Man* (Reed 2015) introduces a new, retired version of the titular hero. Whereas in phase one, the world perceives Metahumans as extraordinary individual actors, their sheer increase in number in the second phase marks them as a potential ethnic group definable by a uniting characteristic.[4]

As soon as a certain number is surpassed, a group whose members were formerly defined by individual actions becomes defined along the lines of its smallest common denominator. Metahumans are marked as Other by their extraordinary nature, which includes anybody perceived to be fantastically divergent from the norm regardless of individual considerations. A person with a sickness that transforms him into a "monster" and a person with the skill to build extraordinary technology are suddenly lumped together for no other reason than their beyond-human capacity. The process depicted in the MCU finds its real-world parallel in ethnic groups such as Latinxs, who are often amassed in public discourse despite cultural and hereditary distinctions in their individual backgrounds as Cubans, Dominicans, Mexicans, or Puerto Ricans.[5] This leads to a first degree of Othering and establishes a Self-and-Other duality in the Beauvoir-Hegelian sense:

> Beauvoir's engagement with Hegelian philosophy . . . yields a notion of consciousness as dualistic and leads to the assertion that the action of consciousness itself constitutes a set of oppositional, conflictual social relations because the self, or the subject, defines himself in relation to others as objects. (Purvis 129)

The Self essentially defines itself in contradistinction to the Other. In the MCU, the Self describes the perceived larger society (humanity, US culture) as the illusion of a unified dominant and hegemonic culture, while the Metahuman community functions as the Other.[6] Here, the Self appears as a mixture of the "normal" population, which is generally shown in the background as unnamed characters with throwaway lines, and the governing body, represented by politicians and government officials.

The binary opposition of normative society as Self and Metahumans as Other is maintained despite the fact that the audience is constantly related to the Other, which it knows through the different movies as individuals with diverse backgrounds, in contrast to the intradiegetic public. The illusion of a hegemonic Self stems from an illusionary understanding of the Other. An Othered group comprises, according to Edward Said, a "body of ideas,

beliefs, clichés, or learning" about the people and culture associated with
it; "the distillation of essential ideas . . . into a separate and unchallenged
coherence" creates a "reference . . . sufficient to identify a specific body of
information" (205). The potential body of information created around Metahumans in the MCU's second phase focuses on their dangerous nature and
compounds the understanding of their inherent destructive power by presenting their experience as diasporic in nature and potentially hidden. Metahumans do not possess any unifying physical features that would mark them
overtly as Other. As Houtum and Naerssen explain, this increases the sense of
threat and displacement on either side: "Displacement as well as othering is
a two-way process. . . . The actual placement of strangers is often conceived
of as a threat to nationally cohesively ordered space and identity, since the
other is now inside" (130). In the MCU, the fear of an unseen threat appears
with the Metahuman terrorists in *Iron Man 3*. As formerly "normal" humans,
these new Metahumans have not been publicly outed and carry no permanent
physical marker of their abilities. They highlight a diasporic affiliation as they
formally hold no association to a previously established Metahuman group or
character and are displaced from their previous association with the American
military. The combination of their destructive power and their obscure nature
presents a threat to the public since they cause great destruction in a series of
self-combusting explosions as well as to the governmental structure because
they are able to kidnap the president.

The idea of Metahuman terrorists and the danger they might present to
the rest of society is cemented in *Captain America: Winter Soldier* and, to
a larger extent, in *Captain America: Civil War* (Russo 2016). In the former,
the Winter Soldier/Bucky Barnes attacks government installations and opera-
tives, posing a threat to the state and its institutions with the capability of
harming these institutions severely. Even more than the Metahuman terror-
ist from *Iron Man 3*, he is displaced as he has lost his association to Steve
Rogers and operates outside of his formative time as well as personal values.
Barnes's unmarked nature becomes clear in *Captain America: Civil War*,
which reveals that he has been able to stay hidden in "normal" society since
the conclusion of *Captain America: Winter Soldier*. In *Captain America:
Civil War*, the combination of Barnes's and other Metahumans' extraordinary aptitude and the ability to remain hidden mark them as threats to the
"nationally cohesively ordered space and identity" as they are individually
capable of resisting capture and bring about unexpected levels of destruction.[7] This enhancement of fear of the Other through its hidden presence
leads to the disregard of formerly accepted internal distinctions. The previous distinction between villains (Metahumans who use their extraordinary
status selfishly) and heroes (Metahumans who use their extraordinary status
selflessly) becomes less meaningful and is finally ignored, with ordinary

humans treating every member of the perceived group as equally dangerous. This depiction motivates audiences to look at the MCU in conjunction with, for instance, classification of military veterans of Muslim faith. Despite the government and media's high regard for military service, veterans of Muslim faith are frequently categorized as Other in public discourse.[8]

As mentioned above, the MCU represents general society or the Self mostly through government officials. In fact, hegemonic society reacts through governmental action, specifically the attempt to establish a system of oversight, which comes in the form of a UN resolution called the Sokovia Accords, a set of internationally ratified legal documents that regulate the deployment of enhanced individuals. Using government entities as representation of the Self extends the frame of interpretation. While I have viewed this from a migratory and multicultural perspective, the use of a government entity that passes laws can stand in for several issues concerning a range of different audiences. The regulation of Metahumans could be read as a comment on current controversial debates concerning the right to bear arms and the government's role in such regulation. Something similar could be said about governmental action regarding discrimination or the suppression of political movements. This interpretive fluidity allows audiences to engage with the issues in any way that suits their current personal beliefs.

A secondary effect of using the government as the main representative of the larger hegemonic culture is that it can circumvent the classic trio of cultural studies research. This does not mean that class, race, and gender cease to play a role, but raising the frame of interpretation onto a political level creates the illusion of a clear argumentative distinction of sides—those rationally supporting a law and those opposing it—and furthermore allows the inclusion of other aspects of distinctions in Othering processes. In the MCU, the governmental involvement in the determination of the Other and its place (and function) in society thus adds another layer of Othering to the already-Othered group of Metahumans. This Othering is akin to Gayatri Spivak's subalternity as it constructs a hierarchical relationship among the three groups, similar to her categorization of colonized Indian society. The previous assertions of Self and Other appear to remain in place, as the distinction has not disappeared, effectively reasserting the government (representing the larger society) as a determiner of various groups' positions and meanings and thus as a force of imperialism. The new binary opposition of pro and contra to the new law apparently supersedes previously formed relationships with the Othered group, creating two subsections that must redefine their relationship to the imperialistic force. In line with Spivak's description of the oppression of Indian women during colonization, every aspect that differentiates an individual or group as "more" Othered decreases the potential of direct influence on the leading determiner of cultural meaning. In the MCU, the pro-Accords group is only singularly marked as Metahumans, while the other group is doubly marked, once as Metahuman and secondly as anti-Accords or as criminal. These aspects produce a hierarchy similar to what Spivak calls a "dynamic stratification grid" (79), in which the government takes the dominant position, followed by the pro-Accords group as in-between, and the anti-Accords group as furthest removed from power.

This hierarchy is visualized through the interactions between Robert Downey Jr.'s Tony Stark/Iron Man (representative of the pro-Accords Othered group) and William Hurt's Senator Thaddeus "Thunderbolt" Ross (governmental representative) in *Captain America: Civil War*. In these interactions, Stark/Iron Man justifies his decision and actions toward Ross or supports the Senator's reasoning. In an argument between Steve Rogers/ Captain America and Stark, Iron Man calls for the limitation and registration of his Othered community in proportion to the larger society's sense of endangerment by the Metahumans, reasoning for the imprisonment of Elizabeth Olsen's Wanda Maximoff/Scarlet Witch and referring to her as a "Weapon of Mass Destruction." However, while Stark supports the hegemonic society, he remains an Other to the representative of that society, since Ross questions Stark's objectivity toward Rogers, his ability to engage and take him down. In this scene, he literally speaks down to him, despite Stark's superior intelligence. Still, corresponding to Spivak's subalternity, Rogers (representative of the anti-Accords Othered group) has no interaction with Ross after the first formal presentation of the Accords at Avengers HQ (at which the anti-Accords movement had not yet formed), and in that scene Ross also speaks down to him. After Rogers opposes the Accords, Ross only speaks about Captain America and the need to obtain, maybe even eliminate, him, but he never addresses him directly. As described by Spivak, Rogers and his associates are now doubly marked as Other to the hegemonic society: as Metahumans and as opponents of the laws that regulate them.

Despite this clear removal from power, the existence of a subaltern group might appear unreasonable as the regulation of Metahumans in the fictional world might seem rational. Specifically, arguments based on a need to regulate individuals as material threats due to the destructiveness of certain abilities can have the veneer of necessity. Like most narratives revolving around some form of enhanced humans, the MCU displays this notion through debates about the right to regulate people based on their capabilities. Such a process of rationalization recalls real-world arguments about a potential drain of resources as a reason to limit or stop immigration. Viewed sensibly, it is easy to assume that the different sides within the Othered group would form around the most convincing argument or at least around the side that offers the greatest benefit to the specific individual. However, the new binary opposition is not as rational and argument-based as the use of a law might imply. Instead, the additional division within the group, which does not automatically form around lines of gender, race, class, generation, or ability but around the Metahumans' position on a law, appears to form around the people who lead the different sides. In outlining the disorientation of newly arrived migrants, Houtum and Naerssen emphasize the importance of an identity "anchor":

> During the transition in status from temporary to permanent migrant a process of identity formation takes place with a strong spatial dimension. If anything, they wander in identification. The migrant arrives with an already multiple-layered identity, which most of the time is predominantly framed into one of being member of a nation-state or nation. It could well be that the migrant is not aware of the dominance of a national identity, but they will soon discover that, for the time being, it will be their only anchor in the unknown sea of the foreign environment that identifies them as a stranger, the other. (132)

In the context of the MCU's third phase, the need to adhere to predetermined associations and relations in the absence of a national or ethnic identification falls onto a person. The anchor in uncertain times falls on previous relationships and associations like friendships and existing kinships. The characters are more likely to choose their side within the internal binary and act more along the lines of their previous kinship relation than their intellectual position.

This notion becomes visible in the choices significant characters make in *Captain America: Civil War*. Most obvious are the Vision's and Colonel James "Rhodey" Rhodes's associations with Stark. While both provide reasons, the Vision citing statistics and Rhodes mentioning his commission in the Air Force and Ross's authority, they remain deeply linked to Stark. The Vision begins its existence as the artificial intelligence J.A.R.V.I.S., which is in charge of Stark's private computer system and serves as a supporting voice in his development of new technology. The relationship between J.A.R.V.I.S. and the Vision is also maintained through the retention of the actor Paul Bettany, who voices the artificial intelligence in all its incarnations and later plays the Vision. Keeping this previous stage in mind, the J.A.R.V.I.S. aspect of the character has been with Stark at least since the first Iron Man movie. Before *Avengers: Age of Ultron*, where J.A.R.V.I.S. becomes the Vision, the artificial intelligence even served as the onboard computer of Stark's Iron Man armor. He appears in every film that included Iron Man. The transformation to the Vision deepens the relationship between the two characters as the Vision's body was masterminded by Stark's other creation Ultron. Half of the four components directly linked to the Vision's creation, the body created by Ultron, the AI created by Stark, the lightning channeled by Thor in the moments of his creation, and the Mind Stone, are directly related back to Stark.

Something similar can be said about James Rhodes. The character is part of each of the *Iron Man* films (played by Terence Howard in the first *Iron Man* from 2008 and later by Don Cheadle), serving as Stark's liaison with the military. Rhodes even receives his own armor (the War Machine armor) indirectly from Stark (*Iron Man 2*). Even after he starts to appear outside of the *Iron Man* franchise in other films of the MCU, he is only seen in connection with Stark. He appears at the party in *Avengers: Age of Ultron* and in the film's final battle. As such, the character is directly related to Stark and presented as a friend throughout all appearances. The only instance in which the Vision and Rhodes appear without a direct relation to Stark is the presentation of a new Avengers Team at end of *Avengers: Age of Ultron*, where both are part of the new team's roster after Stark mentions his retirement. Despite officially being part of the Avengers, however, neither takes part in that team's mission at the beginning of *Captain America: Civil War*, the only Avengers' mission in which Stark does not fight as an Avenger. Following Houtum and Naerssen, these previous relationships indicate that these two characters would always side with Stark when confronted with a new situation in which they have to "wander in identification" because their relationship with Tony provides a dominant kinship in Metahuman society. This assertion also holds true for the relationships surrounding Rogers/Captain America, for example, concerning Sam Wilson/The Falcon and Barnes/The Winter Soldier.

As with the previous example of Stark and Rhodes, Barnes appears in every film of the Captain America franchise. *Captain America: The First Avenger* presents him as Rogers's childhood friend. He is seen in the sequences showing Rogers's life before he receives the super soldier formula; Barnes motivates Captain America to defy orders and stage a rescue operation past enemy lines. He disappears and is presumed dead at the end of the first film, but he reappears as the main physical threat in *Captain America: The Winter Soldier*. Brainwashed and enhanced, the character serves as the primary threat, but he is not defeated through physical superiority but rather through Rogers's appeal to Barnes's memory of their shared past and friendship. Their kinship is evoked as an explanation for overcoming the Othering processes of two larger cultural organizations, S.H.I.E.L.D. and Hydra. It also marks some of Rogers's actions between films. *Avengers: Age of Ultron* mentions in a conversation with Sam Wilson that they have been searching for Barnes ever since the end of *Captain America: Winter Soldier*, where Rogers stated that he planned to do so. This kinship reveals its full depth when Rogers places faith in his friend over photo evidence presented by the authorities and goes against the Avengers to prove the Winter Soldier's innocence. Their kinship provides a bond that overcomes mental programming and assures that they will take each other's side when confronting divisive situations.

While marginally less prominent in the Captain America films, a similar bond exists between Wilson/The Falcon and Rogers/Captain America. Wilson appears for the first time in the second *Captain America* film, and the two characters bond over their shared military experiences in a war zone and the loss of a partner. Later in the film, Wilson provides shelter and support to Rogers and Natasha Romanoff after S.H.I.E.L.D. has been compromised. After joining forces with Captain America, the character only appears with Rogers in the MCU films, with the exception of *Ant-Man*, where he specifically states that his loss against Ant-Man should not be mentioned to Rogers; he looks for Scott Lang/Ant-Man to recruit him for Captain America. Each appearance underscores their mission to find Bucky and their friendship to one another, providing an equally strong kinship relation.

All of these examples demonstrate the influence kinship can have on a person's stance toward an issue. They do not, however, provide the most interesting or even the most convincing case, as these superheroes set their relationships early on and never waver in their loyalty to those relationships in the face of the Sokovia Accords. Romanoff/Black Widow, on the other hand, struggles with her overall connection to both leading characters and with her intellectual position on the question of the Accords. Black Widow, played by Scarlett Johansson, is introduced in the second Iron Man film, where she serves as a S.H.I.E.L.D. operative spying on and later supporting Stark. Compared to Rhodes, the relationship is mostly professional as all interactions between the two characters are either based on her cover as an assistant, her mission as an agent, or her attempts to keep Stark from blowing her cover. An indication of her lack of kinship with Stark reappears in *The Avengers*, where she is not sent to recruit Stark to the team, acknowledging that "Stark trusts [her] as far as he can throw [her]." Black Widow later plays a prominent role in *Captain America: Winter Soldier*, where she and Rogers bond over the nature of their loyalties, their past, and their military service. The film also indicates that they have been on missions together since the end of *The Avengers*. This bond is deepened after S.H.I.E.L.D. is compromised, which forces them to work alone and without the support of a larger organization. The conception of a felt kinship is presented through Romanoff's constant offers to help Steve Rogers develop a social life outside of S.H.I.E.L.D. by giving him options for a date throughout the movie. This behavior indicates an interest and a level of familiarity beyond the professionalism displayed in interactions with Stark. Black Widow has known Stark longer than Rogers, but she relates more to the latter on several levels before the events of *Captain America: Civil War*.

Despite her kinship relation with Rogers, Black Widow decides to side with Iron Man, believing that some form of oversight is necessary to manage the power wielded by the Avengers. She chooses sides based on her intellectual perspective on the issue and remains loyal to that choice for the greater part of the film, directly advising Stark and convincing T'Challa/Black Panther to work with Stark instead of hunting Bucky on his own. The greatest moment of her loyalty to Stark comes in a battle between the two sides in which she fights on the pro-Accord side, whereas a dialog with her former partner Clint Barton/Hawkeye indicates that neither is truly fighting his or her hardest. Until this moment, it seems as if intellectual reasoning wins out over kinship concerning this character. However, at the end of this battle, Romanoff turns on the pro-registration side, firing on Black Panther to let Rogers and Barnes escape. No direct argument or rationale is given for her change of heart other than an acknowledgment that Rogers will not change his course of action. Her kinship relation to Captain America, which overrides any of her own previous rationales, can best explain her sudden shift in loyalty from the Sokovia Accords to Rogers.

The influence of a multilayered identity in this new internal binary suggests that, despite the gloss of rationality, the sides in a controversy are not chosen via factual argument. Instead, the events across the MCU indicate that such choices are made in consideration of kinship associations, overruling any sense of reasoning, which leads to an agreement with the other side. Here, the flexibility of the frame of interpretation has its greatest effect because it technically allows audiences to agree with the leading character they feel the greater kinship with and fill in the issue they would like the conflict to represent, adding a new facet to the idea of kinship. The focus on persons or personalities over factual-intellectual arguments meshes with a tendency in recent years to base decisions in the voting booth on politicians' performances (i.e., their ability to invoke a sense of kinship) rather than on particular policies, as Gabriel S. Lenz observes in his study *Follow the Leader?* (2012).[9] What is also representative of US society, and perhaps of every multicultural society, is that while all the different binaries remain in place, they cause rifts by creating subsets of Self/Other and subalterns, even within an Othered group. These rifts become marginal when the larger society is threatened by an outside force. In the MCU, this becomes clear as the third phase begins its final run with *Avengers: Infinity War* (Russo 2018). Thanos, a powerful alien, attacks earth to create a weapon that would allow him to eradicate half of the universe's population. Faced with this threat, previous separations are forgotten in the service of protecting the larger society.

Combining all of the aspects discussed, the MCU offers four central concepts concerning kinship and Othering. First, the separation from a hegemonic culture by Othering is based largely on singular overt features, disregarding multilayered or even more complex backgrounds. Second, in contrast to assumptions of the hegemonic culture, members of an Othered group do not automatically form kinship affiliations but struggle with internal binary oppositions usually along the line of association with the hegemonic culture and rebellion against it. This is represented early in the MCU by the dichotomy of hero and villain and later by the binary of pro- and anti-registration (the Accords) among the heroes. Third, the latter also indicates that direct interference by the hegemonic culture in the Othered group supersedes previous binary opposition (to a degree) and leads to a division along lines of self-reliance and submission to authority. Fourth, the MCU suggests that association with a position on a contested issue does not follow any intellectual or rational process of decision-making but is dominantly influenced by previous kinship associations, most clearly visible in the behavior of the Black Widow.

While these insights into the MCU's negotiation of the migrant experience are valuable, maybe the most interesting insight lies in the use of fantastical characters as stand-ins for a potentially universal experience of migration and kinship. In the MCU, the Metahuman community is predominantly white and male. However, relationships among Metahumans and with the hegemonic culture represent the experience of the Latinx and Muslim communities in the contemporary United States as well as the struggles of immigrants in the past. Superheroes thus emerge as Metamigrants: as fictional figures that encapsulate and embody universal elements of diverse migrant experiences. In *The New Mutants* (2016), Ramzi Fawaz highlights the potential for such fantastical figures in his work on the hidden queerness in superhero comics. Fawaz has, however, been rightfully criticized for his "celebration of fantasy as politically more viable than concrete political content" (Stein 3). Focused on this form of representation as equal to direct representation, he does not consider its potential as a stepping stone for more direct forms of representation. Current trends in superhero comics support this move toward greater diversity. Characters like Miles Morales/Spider-Man, an Afro-Latino from Brooklyn, and Kamala Khan, a Pakistani American Muslim from New Jersey, have added notable racial representation to the superhero roster. Similarly, the alteration to Bobby Drake/Iceman's sexual orientation and a stronger focus on the gender-fluid nature of characters with shapeshifting abilities such as Raven Darkholme/Mystique or the Xavin the Super-Skrull indicate a greater inclusiveness toward non-heteronormative representation.

In that sense, the depiction of MCU characters as Metamigrants might point toward a greater diversity of representation in the films' (and the entire universe's) future. The general reaction to films like *Black Panther* (Coogler 2018) and *Captain Marvel* (Boden, Fleck 2019) indicates such a trend. The current phase 4 lineup, which will introduce the first Asian American superhero of the franchise in *Shang-Shi and the Legend of the Ten Rings* (Cretton 2021) and is rumored to offer the first gender-bending version of an already established character in *Thor: Love and Thunder* (Waititi 2021), promises a more diverse collection of Metamigrants.

NOTES

1. Superman is regularly attached to the immigrant experience. See the recent *USA Today* article "Superman Is the 'Ultimate Immigrant,' May Have Been Eligible for DACA" (Raphael). See also Benton; Fingeroth; Lund.

2. The first phase includes *Iron Man, The Incredible Hulk, Iron Man 2, Thor, Captain America: The First Avenger, The Avengers*.

3. The second phase includes *Iron Man 3, Thor: The Dark World, Captain America: Winter Soldier, Guardians of the Galaxy, Avengers: Age of Ultron, Ant-Man*.

4. This fictional representation of stereotyping due to the sudden perception of a group is comparable to processes of mass immigration like the wave of German and Irish immigrants to the US in 1848. Vincent N. Parrillo describes how such notions derive from the "cultural homogeneity myth" tied to the perception of nations and their population. On mid-nineteenth-century immigration, see also LeMay.

5. The matter of the homogenization of the Latinx and Hispanic community in media representation is currently challenged in public discourse. Victoria M. Massie writes: "Despite the broad racial diversity that actually represent Latinx and Hispanic people, they are often represented as one homogeneous group instead of being recognized as being just as racially diverse as the population of the United States." On the representation of Latinx in popular culture, see also Aldama and Gonzáles; Aldama, *Latinx*; Aldama, *Your Brain*.

6. I follow Said's reading of Gramsci's definition of hegemony as a "certain cultural form predominat[ing] over others, just as certain ideas are more influential than others" (7).

7. In the climactic battle between the opposing sides, the Leipzig/Halle airport is apparently almost completely demolished.

8. Discussions concerning veterans of Muslim faith usually occur when the notion of Islamic terrorism is (justifiably or unjustifiably) invoked. Many recent newspaper and magazine articles elaborate on the relationship between the perception of military service and the perception of Muslims in American culture. See Gibbons-Neff; Phillips; Wright.

9. I stretch the connection between Lenz's definition of performance and the idea of affiliation and kinship. While Lenz includes "previous success in office and trustworthiness" (2) in performance, he focuses on the perception of these attributes. As there is a general assertion that humans attribute positive characteristic in others they feel a greater relation to (see Tsankova, Vanma, and Kappas), I believe the connection to kinship is plausible.

WORKS CITED

Aldama, Frederick Luis. *Latinx Superheroes in Mainstream Comics*. University of Arizona Press, 2017.

———. *Your Brain on Latino Comics: From Gus Arriola to Los Bros Hernandez*. University of Texas Press, 2009.

————, and Christopher Gonzáles. *Reel Latinxs: Representation in U.S. Film and TV*. University of Arizona Press, 2019.

Ant-Man. Directed by Peyton Reed; produced by Kevin Feige. Marvel Studios, 2015.

Avengers: Age of Ultron. Directed by Joss Whedon; produced by Kevin Feige. Marvel Studios, 2015.

Avengers: Infinity War. Directed by Anthony Russo and Joe Russo; produced by Kevin Feige. Marvel Studios, 2018.

Benton, Mike. *The Comic Book in America: An Illustrated History*. Taylor, 1989.

Brinker, Felix. "Transmedia Storytelling in the 'Marvel Cinematic Universe' and the Logics of Convergence-Era Popular Seriality." *Make Ours Marvel: Media Convergence and a Comics Universe*, edited by Matt Yockey. University of Texas Press, 2017, pp. 207–33.

Burlingame, Russ. "The Flash: What Are Metahumans?" *Comicbook.com*, Oct. 4, 2014, https://comicbook.com/2014/10/04/the-flash-what-are-metahumans-/. Accessed Nov. 7, 2019.

Captain America: Civil War. Directed by Anthony Russo and Joe Russo; produced by Kevin Feige. Marvel Studios, 2016.

Captain America: The First Avenger. Directed by Joe Johnston, produced by Kevin Feige. Marvel Studios, 2011.

Captain America: Winter Soldier. Directed by Anthony Russo and Joe Russo; produced by Kevin Feige. Marvel Studios, 2014.

Chambliss, Julian C. "Superhero Comics: Artifacts of the U.S. Experience." *Juniata Voices*, edited by David Hsiung, vol. 12, 2012, pp. 145–51.

Coogan, Peter. *Superhero: The Secret Origin of a Genre*. Monkeybrain, 2006.

Fawaz, Ramzi. *The New Mutants: Superheroes and the Radical Imagination of American Comics*. New York University Press, 2016.

Fingeroth, Danny. *Superman on the Couch: What Superheroes Really Tell Us About Ourselves and Our Society*. Continuum, 2004.

Gibbons-Neff, Thomas. "For Muslims in the U.S. Military, a Different U.S. Than the One They Swore to Defend." *Washington Post*, Dec. 9, 2015, https://www.washingtonpost.com/news/checkpoint/wp/2015/12/09/for-muslims-in-the-us-military-a-different-u-s-than-the-one-they-swore-to-defend/. Accessed Nov. 7, 2019.

Guardians of the Galaxy. Directed by James Gunn; produced by Kevin Feige. Marvel Studios, 2014.

Iron Man. Directed by Jon Favreau; produced by Avi Arad and Kevin Feige. Marvel Studios, 2008.

Iron Man 2. Directed by Joh Favreau; produced by Kevin Feige. Marvel Studios, 2010.

Iron Man 3. Directed by Shane Black; produced by Kevin Feige. Marvel Studios, 2013.

Jensen, Sune Qvotrup. "Othering, Identity Formation and Agency." *Qualitative Studies*, vol. 2, no. 2, 2011, pp. 63–78.

LeMay, Michael C. *Transforming America: Perspectives on U.S. Immigration*. Praeger, 2013.

Lenz, Gabriel S. *Follow the Leader? How Voters Respond to Politicians' Policies and Performance.* University of Chicago Press, 2012.

Lund, Martin. *Re-Constructing the Man of Steel: Superman 1938–1941, Jewish American History, and the Invention of the Jewish-Comics Connection.* Palgrave Macmillan, 2016.

Massie, Victoria M. "Latino and Hispanic Identities Aren't the Same. They're also not Racial Groups." *Vox*, Sep. 18, 2016, https://www.vox.com/2016/8/28/12658 908/latino-hispanic-race-ethnicity-explained. Accessed Nov. 7, 2019.

Mittell, Jason. "Strategies of Storytelling on Transmedia Television." *Storyworlds across Media: Toward a Media-Conscious Narratology*, edited by Marie-Laure Ryan and Jan-Noël Thon, University of Nebraska Press, 2014, pp. 253–77.

Parrillo, Vincent N. *Diversity in America.* Pine Forge, 2009.

Perez, Lexy. "Francis Ford Coppola Defends Scorsese Marvel Comments, Calls Film 'Despicable.'" *Hollywood Reporter*, Oct. 20, 2019, https://www.hollywoodrepo rter.com/heat-vision/francis-ford-coppola-defends-scorsese-calls-marvel-films-de spicable-1248929. Accessed Nov. 7, 2019.

Phillips, Dave. "Muslims in the Military: The Few, the Proud, the Welcome." *New York Times*, Aug. 2, 2016, https://www.nytimes.com/2016/08/03/us/muslims-us-m ilitary.html. Accessed Nov. 7, 2019.

Purvis, Jennifer. "Hegelian Dimensions of *The Second Sex*: A Feminist Consider-ation." *Bulletin de la Société Américaine de Philosophie de Langue Française*, vol. 13, no. 1, 2003, pp. 128–56.

Raphael, T. J. "Superman Is the 'Ultimate Immigrant,' May Have Been Eligible for DACA." *USA Today*, Sep. 21, 2017, https://eu.usatoday.com/story/news/world /2017/09/21/superman-ultimate-immigrant-may-have-been-eligible-daca/6885900 01/. Accessed Nov. 7, 2019.

Said, Edward W. *Orientalism: Western Conceptions of the Orient.* Vintage, 1979.

Shang-Shi and the Legend of the Ten Rings. Directed by Destin Daniel Cretton; pro-duced by Kevin Feige. Marvel Studios, scheduled for 2021.

Shoard, Catherine. "Martin Scorsese Says Marvel Movies Are 'Not Cinema.'" *Guardian*, Oct. 4, 2019, https://www.theguardian.com/film/2019/oct/04/martin-sco rsese-says-marvel-movies-are-not-cinema. Accessed Nov. 7, 2019.

Spivak, Gayatri Chakravorty. "Can the Subaltern Speak?" *Marxism and the Inter-pretation of Culture*, edited by Cary Nelson and Lawrence Grossberg. Macmillan, 1988, pp. 66–111.

Stein, Daniel. "Review of Ramzi Fawaz, *The New Mutants: Superheroes and the Radical Imagination of American Comics*." *American Literary History Online Review* XV, May 2018, https://academic.oup.com/DocumentLibrary/ALH/Onlin e%20Review%20Series%2015/15Daniel%20Stein.pdf.

The Avengers. Directed by Joss Whedon; produced by Kevin Feige. Marvel Studios, 2012.

The Incredible Hulk. Directed by Louis Leterrier; produced by Avi Arad, Gale Anne Hurd, and Kevin Feige. Marvel Studios, 2008.

Thor. Directed by Kenneth Branagh; produced by Kevin Feige. Marvel Studios, 2011.

Thor: The Dark World. Directed by Alan Taylor; produced by Kevin Feige. Marvel Studios, 2013.

Thor: Love and Thunder. Directed by Taika Waititi; produced by Kevin Feige. Marvel Studios, scheduled for 2021.

Tsankova, Elena, Eric J. Vanman, and Arvid Kappas. "Interaction of Stereotypical Trustworthiness, Facial Resemblance, and Group Membership in the Perception of Trustworthiness and Other Traits." *Journal of Trust Research*, vol. 8, no. 1, 2018, pp. 31–44.

Van Houtum, Henk, and Ton van Naerssen. "Bordering, Ordering and Othering." *Tijdschrift voor economische en sociale geografie/Journal of Economic and Social Geography*, vol. 93, no. 2, 2002, pp. 125–36.

Wright, Robin. "Humayun Khan Isn't the Only Muslim American Hero." *New Yorker*, Aug. 15, 2016, https://www.newyorker.com/news/news-desk/humayun-khan-isnt-the-only-muslimamerican-hero. Accessed Nov. 7, 2019.

Part III

CIVIC INTERVENTIONS

Chapter 10

"Son, I Am Not Coming Here Anymore"

Migrations, Loss, Separation, Trauma, and the Underground Railroad

Cassandra L. Newby-Alexander

Robert Irving, alias Sheridan Ford, regretted leaving his wife and three sons in 1855. Born in Portsmouth, Virginia, in 1827, Sheridan was married to Julia Ann Gregory, hiring out his time at the Portsmouth Naval Hospital and giving a portion of his earnings to his slaveholder, Elizabeth Brown. Like many men who escaped without their families, Sheridan got wind that his owner was going to sell him. In November 1854, he fled, hiding in the woods just beyond the borders of the small city of Portsmouth, eventually hoping to reach his wife and children. But Julia's owner was wise to this scheme and placed them in Hall's slave jail in Norfolk, far from the reach of Sheridan or anyone who might assist. For months, Sheridan tried to secure his family, but, fearing he would be captured, he boarded a steamship and eventually settled in New Bedford, Massachusetts, still hoping that one day he would secure his family's freedom (cf. Still 57–58).

Little did Sheridan know that the circumstances that triggered his escape would also prevent him from reaching his wife and children before they were sold away. By the summer of 1855, a yellow fever outbreak in nearby Hampton Roads had devastated the community, leaving many among the dead, including Julia's owner, General John Hodges. In the aftermath of his death, the family sold Julia and her children to a relative in Goldsboro, North Carolina, removing her from their friends and family who kept him abreast of events (cf. Still 29, 57–58; Newby-Alexander 127).

Eight years after his departure, Ford abandoned all hope of seeing his wife Julia again. He married fellow Portsmouth native Clarissa Davis, who escaped in 1854 and, like Ford, settled in New Bedford along with hundreds of others from Virginia. Following the end of the Civil War and two years after they married, Ford's friend, David Johnson, contacted and informed him that his wife Julia had returned to the city. While reconnecting with his first family eleven years after his escape, the circumstances of his and his former wife's current marital status thwarted them from reassembling as a family. During what would be Sheridan's final visit to Portsmouth, forty years after his escape in 1895, he gave his youngest son Frank a gold watch. Then he turned to him and with a mournful tone said, "Son, I am not coming here anymore; it makes me sick in my stomach when I look at the place and see how I had to go away from my wife and children. Here is a watch, take it, it is nothing common, and when I die a part of my property will be yours. You will get your share of it" ("Depositions"). Then, Sheridan turned to Julia, his first wife, reminding her that had he not been forced to leave, they would have celebrated their fiftieth wedding anniversary. Two years later, Sheridan died and was buried in New Bedford, surrounded by hundreds of freedom seekers in the place he called home (see "Depositions").

The story of Sheridan Ford exemplifies how freedom seekers negotiated pathways to hope and possible freedom independently and through a loosely organized method to escape called the Underground Railroad. Yet, true liberty was elusive. Those who had established strong family ties were always at risk of being sold on the auction block. These constant disruptions within enslaved family units because of sales to the Lower South prompted increased fugitive activity. For some, the desire for freedom, an impending sale because of an owner's death or economic hardship, or unbearable treatment from their masters provoked their escape. Proximity to the Atlantic seaboard, especially from Virginia's numerous ports and northern states as well as the porous river borders separating Virginia and Kentucky from Pennsylvania and Ohio facilitated the possibility of successful escapes. And despite how the Underground Railroad is defined as operating from 1830 until 1860, freedom seekers continued their flight throughout the Civil War, forcing changes in the dynamics of the war and of the nation to confront its most divisive, dehumanizing, and controversial institution.

Sheridan Ford's story highlights a number of the themes mentioned in Eric Foner's *Gateway to Freedom: The Hidden History of the Underground Railroad* (2015). Many men and women fled slavery, sometimes reluctantly, leaving spouses, children, parents, and siblings in the hope that freedom would allow them the opportunity to reunite in the near future. Often the decision to escape arose from events transpiring in the lives of slaveholders (debt, death, relocation), or of those who were enslaved (fear of sale, brutality, opportunity, family, or desire for freedom). In the end, however, family connections affected the enslaved person's decision to flee and their future course (cf. 152). Foner did not address how the waterways allowed the countless families who left from port areas along the eastern seaboard to migrate to freedom zones in the North and Canada. Uncovering these stories reveals that in powerful and sometimes incongruous ways, focusing on the lesser-known but more representative accounts of fugitives who escaped from the center of the southern Underground Railroad, the Norfolk harbor, provides a more typical account of freedom seekers. As recorded in the mid-1800s, hundreds successfully escaped aboard the numerous ships that plied the waterways; the James, Elizabeth, York, Nansemond, Susquehanna, Rappahannock, and Potomac Rivers provided pathways to freedom and liberty from slavery, the source of their trauma.

Sheridan Ford's story is typical of what Philadelphia Underground Railroad stationmaster William Still recorded in his encounters with freedom seekers who passed through his station. Out of the 242 people whom Still chronicled from the Hampton Roads region, which includes Norfolk, Portsmouth, Virginia Beach, Chesapeake, Suffolk, Hampton, Newport News, and Williamsburg, 120 men left their wives and families. Their reasons were often like Sheridan's in that they fled because sale to the Lower South was imminent. Many hoped to reconnect with their wives later while others expected to be shortly reunited. According to Still, some of these men left because their wives and families had been sold away, while others left with their wives joining them a short time later (or in some cases, the women left first). Furthermore, some of the men who escaped mentioned that their free black wives would later join them in the North or in Canada. Of those listed by William Still, only a small percentage were women who traveled alone. Children escaping with their parents made up only about 10 percent. What is interesting are the numbers of couples, sixty-seven (or 134 people), whom William Still described as successfully escaping bondage, although sadly some left without their children. The remaining fugitives may have been single, although some of the accounts were too brief to determine their marital status (cf. 54–58, 162–64, 210–13, 227–28, 230–31, 297, 557–61).

These figures are especially important in telling a larger story because Virginia had the largest population in the South and, until the early 1800s, the largest in the nation. And even as Virginia continued to export more enslaved people through the domestic slave trade than any other state and have the largest number escaping through the Underground Railroad, it continued to have the largest African American population in America through the beginning of the twentieth century. In Virginia, the struggle for black freedom began as laws were passed establishing slavery and denying to all blacks their basic human and political rights, including the right to protect themselves and their families. And yet, even as whites set up these artificial barriers to self-determination, blacks constructed rivers of resistance, as historian Vincent Harding so eloquently discussed in his book *There Is a River* (cf. xix, 27;

Hine et al. 118.). What is amazing is that these individuals escaped despite extreme and coordinated efforts by Virginia slaveowners, who used legislation, public and private funds, and the force of law to prevent their departures. But it should not be forgotten that despite the success of some of the escapes, the role of slavery, escape, and trauma influenced the lives and destinies of freedom seekers and their descendants.

The stories of freedom seekers highlight the under-investigated occurrences of the role of trauma on these individuals, who were not only harmed by slavery but also by its destabilizing effects on family and love. Indeed, the word trauma stems from ancient Greek meaning "wound." But this term refers to a psychological wound rather than a physical one. It references an "emotional shock" that is "so powerful that it breaches 'the mind's experience of time, self and the world' and eventually manifests itself in dreams and flashbacks" (Eyerman 41–42). Yet, no information survives that informs us as to whether freedom seekers who left and/or lost family when they fled experienced dreams or flashbacks. What we have are remnants of information suggesting pain suppressed to such an extent that some of their descendants were unaware of their stories and experiences. As a result, amnesia and repression were emotional reactions emanating from this trauma, thus allowing people to suspend their pain, shielding themselves and their progeny from their experiences (cf. Richards 248, 257–58).

"For some years before escaping," thirty-one-year-old Portsmouth native John Atkinson was "a prisoner of hope." Hiring out his time for $120 annually, Atkinson labored "to support his drunken and brutal master," twenty-six-year-old James Ray, a sailor who lived at the US Navy Yard in Gosport. Atkinson declared Ray to be "a worthless sot" with a character that was "too disgusting for record" (Still 297). Eventually, the horrors of his situation and his expectation of imminent sale on the auction block compelled Atkinson to leave, even though that meant abandoning his free black wife, Mary Atkins, without a word, fearing knowledge would implicate her in his escape (cf. Still 297). This sudden departure from his wife, parents, and friends must have been particularly painful for Atkinson even though it was prompted by his imminent sale to the Deep South by his owner. In the summer of 1854, he connected with one of the Underground Railroad's most adroit and active conductors in Virginia, Henry Lewey, alias "Bluebeard," who arranged with Underground Railroad conductor John Minkins, a steward aboard the *City of Richmond*, to hide him in a secret compartment for a two-day journey to Philadelphia. Shortly after arriving in Philadelphia, Atkinson was ferried to St. Catharines, a city in Ontario (Canada West) and home to numerous fugitives. Reunited with his brother and probably others whom he knew from the Norfolk-Portsmouth area, Atkinson soon found a job and a place to live (cf. Still 298–99).

Yet despite achieving freedom, Atkinson was unhappy because he had left so much behind, which included family and clothing. In fact, many freedom seekers wrote their contacts requesting that clothing be forwarded to them, presumably because most worked hard to procure even the smallest of items. In his September 4, 1855, letter to William Still, Atkinson writes,

> I now embrace this favorable opportunity of writing you a few lines to inform you that I am quite well and arrived here safe, and I hope that these few lines may find you and your family the same. I hope you will intercede for my clothes and as soon as they come please to send them to me, and if you have not time, get Dr. Lundy to look out for them, and when they come be very careful in sending them. I wish you would copy off this letter and give it to the Steward, and tell him to give it to Henry Lewy and tell him to give it to my wife.

In that same letter, Atkinson wrote, "Brother sends his love to you and all the family and he is overjoyed at seeing me arrive safe, he can hardly contain himself; also he wants to see his wife very much, and says when she comes he hopes you will send her on as soon as possible" (298).

In his last recorded letter to William Still, in October 1854, Atkinson, who had changed his name to John Atkins, asked that his letter be sent to Henry Lewey so that his wife Mary would receive it. In the letter, he expressed his enduring love for her and his relatives. He wanted Mary to pass on his love and thoughts to her mother and cousin and his mother and father. Atkinson also wanted his wife to write to him and reminded her "to be of good courage, that I love her better than ever. I would like her to come on as soon as she can, but for her to write and let me know when she is going to start. Affectionately Yours, John Atkins" (300). According to Still, it is unknown whether Atkinson ever reunited with his wife.

Norfolk native Henry Atkinson escaped after the death of his owner. His owner, who lived in London, placed in her will that upon her death she would free all of her slaves and give them her property. In the interim, Atkinson was hired out by his owner's agent, who sent him to work for a list of sundry men ranging from kind to hard-hearted. Some gave him money, clothing, and food for his services, while others did not. Some even allowed him to visit his wife. When Atkinson's owner died, instead of freeing him, the agent continued hiring him out and then attempted a bogus sale to fabricated relatives. It was at this point that Atkinson decided to make his escape. He said that "after studying upon it a long time," he made the difficult decision to leave his wife and children. With tearful eyes, Atkinson recalled that "it was like taking my heart's blood: but I could not help it—I expected to be taken away where I should never see her again," and so he made his way to Canada (Drew 79–83).

Clearly, the accounts of numerous Underground Railroad agents, missionaries, abolitionists, and sympathizers were central to outlining the stories of freedom seekers in the hope of uncovering more information about their lives and family members. Moreover, understanding the methods used in their escape and the people who assisted them are important components of the story. What is known about those who fled from the Hampton Roads region is that many were either secreted aboard vessels, sometimes unbeknownst to their captains and crews, or received aid from the captains, crews, or stewards of these vessels. William Still's book and newspaper accounts listed the *City of Richmond*, the *Jamestown*, the *Pennsylvania*, the *Augusta* steamships, and the *Kesiah* and the *Francis French* schooners as the primary vessels that operated on the local waterways, transporting runaways from Hampton Roads to points north (cf. Bordewich 256–57).

Assisting freedom seekers were conductors or agents, and the most active ones in Hampton Roads were Henry Lewey, Eliza Bain, John Minkins, and William Bagnall. Lewey was a Norfolk slave who used the *nom de guerre* "Bluebeard" to hide his identity until he escaped in 1856, when word circulated that he was a suspected Underground Railroad agent. Lewey's activities were not unusual because accounts mentioned other enslaved African American agents who hired out their own time, thus allowing them the mobility to carry out this type of work (cf. Still 560). Similarly, Eliza Bains, who was identified as an important agent by abolitionist Thomas Garret, was owned by the pastor of Portsmouth, Virginia's Colored Methodist Society Church George M. Bain. Reported to have helped a number of enslaved African Americans to escape aboard schooners traveling to Boston and New Bedford, Bains worked at the Crawford Hotel, where most mariners stayed while in port. In April 1897, Elizabeth Cooley, a fugitive from Hampton Roads who lived in Boston, told historian Wilbur Siebert about Bains's activities, including how Bains assisted her during the time she hid out for two years prior to fleeing aboard a ship to Boston (cf. Siebert 449).[1] Cooley said that Bains harbored fugitives in her home, explaining how "[o]nce when a party of slave-hunters came to her house to find runaways, she outwitted them by hiding the slaves between the rows in her garden and spreading sheets over them. When some of her fugitives had been put safely aboard for the North, her happiness, she went about singing 'It's all right, hallelujah, glory to God'" (Da Silva and Grover 109–10).

The only clue as to the existence of Eliza Bains was a notation in the 1855 *Richmond Daily Dispatch* of her death in September, the victim of the yellow fever epidemic that devastated the populations in Hampton Roads.[2] Although her death was a tremendous blow to the network, Henry Lewey continued working through 1856, when, according to his wife Rebecca, he was to secure passage and join her in Canada. One brief reference in a letter to Still from

Anthony and Albert Brown, brothers who escaped from Norfolk in 1855, reported that Lewey did indeed make his escape successfully. In a June 1856 letter, the Brown brothers noted that although it had been two weeks, Lewey had not yet arrived in Hamilton, Canada (cf. Still 293, 563). Unfortunately, not much is known about this agent otherwise known as Bluebeard. William Still recorded that "although a slave himself, [Lewey] was one of the most dexterous managers in the Underground Rail Road agency in Norfolk. No single chapter in this work could be more interesting than a chapter of his exploits in this respect" (563).

Although Still's accounts only referred to Minkins as a free black steward who was known by those escaping from Hampton Roads as an Underground Railroad agent, it is probable that he was the John Minkins who was listed in the 1850 US Census as an omnibus driver. This occupation would have familiarized him with passenger ships, mariners, taverns and hotels, and the city at large. Since Norfolk restricted omnibus driving as a white-only occupation in the early 1850s, Minkins would have needed another job. John, unlike his younger brothers, was old enough to have assumed the important and demanding job of steward. His was the only free black family in the nation with the name Minkins. Fugitive accounts between the corridors of Richmond/Petersburg and Norfolk/Portsmouth indicated that Minkins worked as a steward aboard the steamships *City of Richmond* and *Pennsylvania,* which operated between Virginia and Philadelphia in the 1850s.[3]

William D. Bagnall, however, was unusual. Few historical treatises have examined the role southern whites had in the operation of the Underground Railroad in the South. Bagnall was listed in the Norfolk city directory in 1850 as a Virginia Bank branch bookkeeper who lived on Catharine Street near First Baptist Church, the city's first Baptist church that would become a predominantly African American congregation by the 1850s. He was credited with assisting in the escapes of numerous slaves and passing correspondence between those who had escaped and enslaved family members still living in Hampton Roads. As a member of the Seamen's Friend Society and a manager of the Norfolk Humane Association for the Relief and Improvement of the Poor, Bagnall was in frequent contact with men working in the maritime industry. Ironically, he was also a slaveholder. Fugitive Clarissa Davis speculated that Bagnall may have been sympathetic because his wife was a slave. Although Bagnall was listed in the census as married to Elizabeth, a white woman, it is possible that the census taker, who typically assigned race based on observation alone, may have mistaken a very light-skinned African American as white.[4]

Those who fled by ship usually disembarked in Philadelphia and New Bedford. From there, Vigilance Committees provided train tickets to all those willing to begin a new life in Canada, via the New York, Hartford, and the

New Haven railroads. But fugitives who escaped to southeastern Pennsylvania were not all sent out of Philadelphia by the same route. Frequently, they were passed on to the New York Vigilant Committee, with whom the Philadelphia committee had close ties. At other times, they were sent northwestward, the final goal being entry into western Canada and the state of Ontario. Caution had to be used at all times, however, because of the Fugitive Slave Act and the very real possibility of imprisonment for anyone caught assisting fugitives. There were also fugitives who arrived in Pennsylvania without assistance from conductors by pretending to be white or free, by traveling on foot at night, or by hiding on ships that had sailed from the South. Once escapees were in the North, however, the importance of these Vigilance Committees became critical. Committees in Pennsylvania and Massachusetts forwarded fugitives to more northern states and Canada. Those who opted to remain in the United States were assisted in finding housing and jobs and creating new identities. Prior to 1850, many white abolitionists supposed that it was unethical to entice slaves from the South, believing that they should only assist once the fugitives made it to the North.

Historian Kathryn Grover noted in *The Fugitive's Gibraltar* (2001) that New Bedford merchants frequently traded in Virginia. Some of those merchants were Quakers with strong anti-slavery leanings, such as Weston Howland and John Parker, owners of the sloop *Regulator*. Principally transporting flour between Alexandria and New Bedford, the *Regulator* was associated with assisting runaways from Richmond to Washington, D.C. Similarly, the sloop *Mercury*, owned by Samuel Chadwick, reportedly transported fugitives along with goods between various urban ports in Virginia to New Bedford throughout the first half of the nineteenth century. Many of those who escaped to New Bedford, unlike to other northern cities, tended to remain under the guise of an alias. And because they were often arriving on schooners, a number of freedom seekers arrived with their families intact: an unusual occurrence for most fleeing slavery. So many engaged agents to take them to northern ports from Virginia that after 1850, Virginia-born residents would emerge as the majority.[5]

Despite the prominence of Canada, Philadelphia, and New Bedford as debarkation points, no area received more fugitive slaves than Boston. Even as early as the 1760s, Boston was a hub for runaway slaves, such as Crispus Attucks and Lewis Hayden, who typically arrived as stowaways aboard vessels, which transported people and goods between southern and northern ports. By the 1840s, Boston had become the primary destination for fugitives primarily because of its port activities and because of the black and white abolitionist communities that actively sought to thwart any efforts by slaveholders to retrieve their slaves. Needless to say, it was Boston that acted as the backdrop for national fugitive slave cases. These cases would, in turn, serve as pivotal junctures for the defense of and assault on slavery. Because most of the North had abolished slavery by state edict beginning with the late 1790s, the New England region in general had become a haven for fugitives seeking freedom.

Those who fled to Canada during the antebellum period, unlike their counterparts thirty years prior, initially sought only refuge from slavery rather than citizenship. Their goals were wedded more to definitions of liberty from slavery than liberty from oppression, marginalization, and racism. Writing from Toronto to William Still in 1854, John Hill, who was among the few freedom seekers who escaped from Petersburg with his family, stated: "I am in good health and good Spirits, and feeles rejoiced in the Lord for my liberty." Similarly, Jane Johnson, who escaped from her owner in Philadelphia with her two children, recounted that she "appealed to the sympathies of a person whom she ventured to trust, saying, 'I and my children are slaves, and we want liberty!'" (Still 49, 82). Interestingly, while many found some aspect of freedom, they did not find true liberty because prejudice, discrimination, and social marginalization kept them from the assurances of true civil rights integration or protection from family separations.

Border and national identities became an issue for freedom seekers as they moved to the northern states or Canada. Seeking relief from the stigma or confines of slavery, those who fled to the North or to Canada regarded themselves as American refugees, thus creating an identity that was at odds with their borders. Adjusting to this differing identity required resourcefulness and proactive efforts through the formation of numerous self-help organizations and institutions that protected their holdings and buttressed their communities. For those who fled to Canada, these refugees sought to protect themselves, their families, and their communities from the sometimes subtle yet always pervasive racial discrimination in Canada by building up their communities with schools, businesses, and support groups. As Reverend Samuel Ringgold Ward maintained, "Canadian Negro hate" was still very common (Frost and Tucker 8, 14).

Despite the challenges freedom seekers faced in the Canadian "promised land," the reality of freedom from slavery overrode those hardships, at least for a while. Captain Chapman, whose ship sailed between Lake Erie and Canada, remembered a situation in 1860, when fugitives aboard his ship asked if they were in Canada. When he responded in the affirmative, Chapman recalled, "They seemed to be transformed; a new light shone in their eyes, their tongues were loosed, they laughed and cried, prayed and sang praises, fell upon the ground and kissed it, hugged and kissed each other, crying, 'Bress de Lord! Oh! I'se free before I die'" (Siebert 196–97).

Abolitionist, journalist, and Boston educator Benjamin Drew traveled through Canada West in the 1850s, recording over 100 first-hand accounts in his book *The North-Side View of Slavery* (cf. 19–20, 27–28). According to Drew's accounts, fugitives referred to themselves as refugees. This attitude suggests an awareness that these individuals saw themselves as taking shelter from enslavement in Canada, thus articulating a clear national identity as Americans, similar to how transnational Afro-Liberians clung to American ideals and culture even while living in another society and culture. Drew's study of these black fugitives in Canada highlighted the social alienation faced by many, especially those in segregated towns or communities, and indicated how "blackness" shaped the communities that would be established by these individuals.

Unlike in Canada, freedom seekers who remained in the North faced a different type of "otherness": an emerging anti-black movement that forced many to find sanctuary in free black communities or in smaller cities and towns. Because the profitability of cotton production and its global trade fueled America's primary industries, the presence of fugitives threatened prosperity. Moreover, complaints about free blacks socializing with slaves or harboring runaways were common. Whites also complained that free blacks were instrumental in teaching slaves how to read and write. Many free blacks even married and did business with slaves. Free blacks were also accused of disseminating anti-slavery sentiment that dominated the pages of newly established abolitionist newspapers. Eventually, the message was clear to most freedom seekers that safety lay in northern states such as Massachusetts and New Hampshire that passed legislation ending slavery within their territories.[6]

Passage of the Fugitive Slave Act of 1850 triggered another movement within the African Diaspora that sent thousands of free and enslaved blacks seeking freedom and liberty in Canada and to the newly formed country of Liberia. While smaller in number than those coming from other states, many free blacks from Philadelphia and West Chester County, Pennsylvania, were propelled by a desire to escape the debilitating American anti-black environment and to create a powerful African nation. Unlike many of the white abolitionists who advocated black migration to Liberia, these intrepid émigrés were not interested in permanently abandoning America to its white majority.

Few in America today can understand the heartfelt cries of joy expressed by those who stepped on the shores of Canada or Liberia. These shouts and praises to God deafened the ears of all around, wafting across the waters and winds that blew from the north to the south. The true costs that African Americans paid to be free may never be assessed. What is clear is that the choices that freedom seekers made were not always simple and entailed considerable sacrifice. And at their core was the inexhaustible desire for love, family, and the ability to control their own lives.

The heart-wrenching accounts of separation, loss, and trauma are part of the real stories of the Underground Railroad. Their subsequent lives highlight how those freedom seekers risked everything for freedom, but not without a cruel cost. Countless husbands and wives, children, and parents never reconnected because of escapes and sales during America's long history of slavery. And even those who were able to keep their families intact or were able to reconnect years later, like Sheridan Ford, did so with considerable family complications. Perhaps this is why the nation witnessed the emergence of Negro Spirituals. According to anthropologist Dona Richards, emotions of "joy and sadness, rage and love, tranquility and anxiety" (278) are ever-present in spirituals, with these conflicting emotions expressed simultaneously. Indeed, the songs often served as a coping mechanism, allowing those singing the songs to transcend their "emotional and physical trauma" that emerged from loss and separation (Richards 267–68). Even the repetition of the lines in these spirituals served as a communal bonding technique for those who had shared experiences, especially of the pain of separation. "Sometimes I Feel Like a Motherless Child," "Swing Low, Sweet Chariot," "Rock My Soul in the Bosom of Abraham," and "Wade in the Water" are songs that serve as examples of loss or as a message to lead people to freedom. But in more ways, these songs disguised the trauma of the singer by focusing on the power of resilience.

Since their forced arrival on the North American continent, people of African descent have sought what the ideals embodied in the *Declaration of Independence* intoned to be the most precious rights of humanity: unalienable rights of freedom and liberty. And yet, liberty was the concept that seemingly was unachievable for Africans in America. The idea of freedom or liberty, according to historian Francois Furstenberg, was instilled into the American psyche through the *Declaration of Independence*. The revolutionary period "joined liberal, republican, and religious traditions to define freedom as autonomy"; in other words, human agency or the power of choice (1296). Yet this idea of freedom or liberty in America was described in relation to potential slavery for white Americans, as the threat existed that passivity could lead to slavery, both socially and politically. Revolutionary writers argued that whites could lose their freedom as had blacks if they failed to resist efforts to reduce their personal autonomy (Furstenberg 1300–301). White revolutionaries saw liberty and freedom, as David Brion Davis observed, as "the reward for righteous struggle" (257).

This rationalization for enslavement in the nation that promoted ideas of liberty and freedom comforted white society despite evidence to the contrary. Efforts to marginalize African American agency and resistance or label leaders as cowards notwithstanding, the reality was that freedom and liberty seekers made decisions that were not always easy or without considerable sacrifice in their quest to achieve what we today define as the American Dream. At their core was their desire for self-determination and the ability to protect and maintain family. The accounts that highlight their efforts to balance these competing desires shape our understanding of the true price many paid for freedom and liberty.

Examining the stories of freedom seekers who began their journeys as early as the seventeenth century after they forcibly arrived at Old Point Comfort in the Virginia colony and continuing through the Civil War provides insight into the compelling lives and misadventures of men, women, and children who escaped from bondage. And once they decided to leave, many lived boldly under an alias, choosing migration to northern locales or to Canada that provided relative safety from recapture. However, in that "Atlantic world . . . slavery was nearly ubiquitous and freedom was ambiguous" (Lindsay 11), and personal liberty, often transient, exacted a high toll. The choices that freedom seekers made were difficult and, based on many of their accounts, not without substantial cost to their families and to their existences. Yet these choices allowed them to define their lives rather than continue to allow others to limit their freedoms.

NOTES

1. See also *The Liberator*, Mar. 20, 1846, and *Boston Commonwealth*, Mar. 16, 1846; Ancestry.com. *1850 U.S. Federal Census Slave Schedule* [database online]. Provo, Utah: MyFamily.com, Inc., 2004. Original data: United States. *1850 United States Federal Census*. M432, 1009 rolls. National Archives and Records Administration, Washington D.C.; Stewart 33, 40–41, 44, 49.

2. "The Yellow Fever in Norfolk and Portsmouth, Virginia, 1855, as reported in the *Daily Dispatch*, Richmond, Virginia," http://www.usgwarchives.net/va/yellow-fe ver/yftoc.html. Accessed Aug. 28, 2019.

3. Ancestry.com. *1850 United States Federal Census* [database online]. Provo, Utah: MyFamily.com, Inc., 2005. Original data: United States. *1850 United States Federal Census, Norfolk, Norfolk (Independent City), Virginia*, M432, 1009 rolls. National Archives and Records Administration, Washington D.C.; Still, 47–48, 53, 55–56, 194; Bogger 61, 78–79.

4. Still 61; 1850 Norfolk, Norfolk (Independent City), VA Census Schedules, Ancestry.com. 1850 United States Federal Census [database online]. Provo, Utah: MyFamily.com, Inc., 2005. Original data: United States. 1850 United States Federal Census. M432, 1009 rolls. National Archives and Records Administration, Washington D.C.; *Southern Argus*, Jan. 5, 1852, 2; Elmwood and Cedar Grove Cemeteries, Database of Interments, Bureau of Cemeteries, Norfolk, VA, http://ftp.rootsweb.com/ pub/usgenweb/va/norfolkcity/cemeteries/elmcgcem-a-benn.txt. (Accessed July 10,

2006); William S. Forrest, *The Norfolk Directory for 1851–1852,* 44, 90, 96; "Died," *Southern Argus* Jan. 5, 1852, 2.

5. Grover argues that an analysis of the 1855 Massachusetts census reveals that the majority of people of color who claimed free states as their birthplace actually came from the South. William Ferguson was an example of a fugitive claiming birth in northern free states. Not until the late 1850s would Ferguson and his wife Nancy admit to their status as runaway slaves who had left Virginia in 1847 (cf. 57, 59, 85).

6. Cf. Bordewich 43–45; Goldin 33–36; Berlin 42–43; Wade 61.

WORKS CITED

Berlin, Ira. *Slaves without Masters: The Free Negro in the Antebellum South.* 1974. Vintage, 1976.

Bogger, Tommy L. *Free Blacks in Norfolk Virginia 1790–1860: The Darker Side of Freedom.* University of Virginia Press, 1997.

Bordewich, Fergus M. *Bound for Canaan: The Epic Story of the Underground Railroad, America's First Civil Rights Movement.* HarperCollins, 2005.

Da Silva, Janine V., and Kathryn Grover. "Historic Resource Study." Boston African American National Historic Site, 2002.

Davis, David Brion. *The Problem of Slavery in the Age of Revolution 1770–1823.* Oxford University Press, 1999.

Depositions of Julia Ann Brown, Oct. 5, 1899; David Johnson, Oct. 23, 1899; Mary Ann Hodges, Oct. 12, 1899, Leonard A. Ford, Oct. 10, 1899. Commonwealth of Massachusetts, Probate Court, Chelsea, Massachusetts, May 23, 1903, 758/276.

Drew, Benjamin. *A North-Side View of Slavery: The Refugee: Or the Narratives of Fugitive Slaves in Canada. Related by themselves, with an Account of the History and Condition of the Colored Population of Upper Canada.* John P. Jewett and Company, 1856.

Eyerman, Ron. "Social Theory and Trauma," *Acta Sociologica,* vol. 56, no. 1, 2013, pp. 41–53.

Foner, Eric. *Gateway to Freedom: The Hidden History of the Underground Railroad.* Norton, 2015.

Frost, Karolyn, and Veta Tucker, editors. *A Fluid Frontier: Slavery, Resistance, and the Underground Railroad in the Detroit River Borderland.* Wayne State University Press, 2016.

Furstenberg, Francois. "Beyond Freedom and Slavery: Autonomy, Virtue, and Resistance in Early American Political Discourse." *Journal of American History,* vol. 89, no. 4, 2003, pp. 1295–330.

Goldin, Claudia. *Urban Slavery in the American South, 1820–1860: A Quantitative History.* Univeristy of Chicago Press, 1976.

Grover, Kathryn. *The Fugitives Gibraltar: Escaping Slaves and Abolitionism in New Bedford, Massachusetts.* University of Massachusetts Press, 2001.

Harding, Vincent. *There Is a River: The Black Struggle for Freedom in America.* Vintage, 1983.

Hine, Darlene Clark, et al., editors. *African Americans: A Concise History*. 5th ed., vol. 1, Pearson, 2014.

Lindsay, Lisa A. *Atlantic Bonds: A Nineteenth Century Odyssey from America to Africa*. University of North Carolina Press, 2017.

Newby-Alexander, Cassandra L. "The Strange Case of Sheridan Ford and Clarissa Davis: The Underground Railroad in Portsmouth, Virginia." *Voices from within the Veil: African Americans and the Experience of Democracy*, edited by William H. Alexander, Cassandra L. Newby-Alexander and Charles H. Ford. Cambridge Scholars, 2008, pp. 113–39.

Richards, Dona. "Let the Circle Be Unbroken: The Implications of African-American Spirituality," *Présence Africaine*, vol. 117/118, nos. 1/2, 1981, pp. 247–92.

Siebert, Wilbur H. "The Underground Railroad in Massachusetts." *New England Quarterly*, vol. 9, no. 3, 1936, pp. 447–67.

Stewart, Charles. *The African Society Becomes Emanuel African Methodist Episcopal Church*. Guide Quality, 1944.

Still, William. *The Underground Railroad*. 1968. Ayer, 1992; originally published in Philadelphia by Porter and Coates, 1872.

Wade, Richard C. *Slavery in the Cities: The South 1820–1860*. Oxford University Press, 1964.

Chapter 11

Contested Affiliations

The Migration of US American War Resisters to Canada

Sarah J. Grünendahl

Camps and shelters bear witness to the fact that the process of seeking asylum in another country may turn out to be lengthy. Any such decision to leave the habitual place of living for another abroad comes at the risk of lasting uncertainty: asylum-seekers are left to wonder whether their refugee claims will eventually be recognized and residency, in turn, be granted. Menjívar refers to this situation as "liminal legality" (1008). It is liable to considerably curtail the individuals' means to build new lives in the country of refuge. Claimants are meanwhile trapped "betwixt and between" (Turner, *Ritual* 95). Their affiliation with their country of origin is diminished; at the same time, they do not as yet fully belong in their destination country.

In most research, legal constraints coincide with language and cultural barriers, all of which hamper claimants' integration into the host society. This chapter, however, analyzes potential repercussions of legal uncertainty, specifically regarding participation in society and the formation of place attachment, in the context of US American Afghanistan/Iraq War resisters' flight to Canada, a country similar in language and culture. The design of the study allows readers to observe the effects of legal uncertainty on refugee claimants' livelihoods, largely irrespective of other factors. The analysis shows that these contemporary war resisters encounter similar challenges in obtaining status and building new lives, and they also employ strategies comparable to those of other asylum-seekers to get by in their day-to-day lives.

Aspects on which the chapter sheds light include Afghanistan/Iraq War resisters' prolonged waiting for refugee status, their sense of "permanent temporariness" (A. J. Bailey et al. 139), and the concept of "deportability" (De Genova 439). Further, the chapter analyzes what these aforementioned factors mean for this cohort's involvement in Canadian society. Both the

example of Vietnam War resisters, who came to Canada some decades earlier, and the activism by local lobby groups on behalf of Afghanistan/Iraq
War resisters throw the current war resisters' experiences into relief.

My analysis begins with an overview of the circumstances under which
both Vietnam and Afghanistan/Iraq resisters came to Canada in the late 1960s
and early 2000s, respectively. The section thereafter is concerned with the
empirical study's methods and sampling. The section "Maneuvering Liminality: Afghanistan/Iraq War Resisters' Strategies to Negotiate Legal Uncertainty" discusses the findings from the Afghanistan/Iraq War resister study.
The next to last section "Mediating the Effects of Legal Uncertainty: Vietnam
War Resisters, Canadian Activists, and the Anti-Deportation Struggle" then
gives examples of how local activism can mediate the effects of legal uncertainty. The conclusion highlights the importance of a secure legal status for
participation in society.

HISTORICAL CONTEXT: US WAR
RESISTERS' MIGRATION TO CANADA

The flight of US American Vietnam and Afghanistan/Iraq War resisters to
Canada presents a peculiar case of war-induced forced migration. Members
of either cohort sought to escape not from a war-torn homeland but from
potential deployment to a combat zone. As for their destination, Canada's
geographic location as well as principally common language and culture held
the promise of unhampered and speedy integration—a favorable lot compared to that of many other forced migrants.

In the earlier instance, in the late 1960s and early 1970s, young men were
subject to the draft and therefore likely to serve in Vietnam. The prospect of
having to fight in a controversial war prompted the exodus of over 50,000
draft-eligible men to Canada (see Hagan; Jones, *Contending*). Generally,
Vietnam War resisters did not encounter many obstacles: provided an
immigrant accumulated sufficient points for a combination of given skills,
landed immigrant status, and thus the right to remain in Canada, was at
hand (see A. G. Green and D. A. Green). Prime Minister Pierre E. Trudeau's
alleged reference to Canada as a "refuge from militarism" often comes up
in this context (see Hagan; Kasinsky). In any case, a considerable number
of Vietnam War resisters is said to have remained in Canada, two amnesty
programs under Presidents Ford and Carter notwithstanding (see Maxwell).
What is more, without much ado, many, including this study's first group of
participants, have since taken out Canadian citizenship. Their case serves as
a foil against which to reflect on the current war resisters' situation.

Circumstances have meanwhile changed on both sides of the 49th parallel. As of July 1973, in the wake of the Vietnam War, the US Armed Forces

were transformed into an all-volunteer force (see B. L. Bailey, "Army"; B. L. Bailey, *America's Army;* Rostker). Accordingly, soldiers such as the ones due to be deployed to Afghanistan or Iraq, who make up the second sample group in this chapter, joined the military voluntarily; educational aspirations and upward social mobility are some of the key incentives for enlistment (see Kleykamp; Schake and Mattis). Regardless, an estimated 300[1] individuals refused service in the Afghanistan and Iraq wars and, from 2004[2] onward, followed the Vietnam War resisters to Canada. As was the case with their predecessors, their act of resistance was in refusing complicity in the war efforts. However, as opposed to the earlier cohort, contemporary resisters could not avail themselves of *landed immigrant status* in Canada, particularly because Canadian immigration policies have long since prioritized educational attainment and employability (see Ferrer et al.). Filing a refugee claim thus appeared to be one of the more feasible options, all the more if a deployment was imminent and they did not have ample time to prepare for departure. These claims were anything but successful—and what little hope had existed was quashed after 2010, when, as per *Operational Bulletin 202*, soldiers deemed deserters were marked criminally inadmissible (see Government of Canada). Though the pending refugee claims have afforded Afghanistan/Iraq War resisters an interim leave to remain in Canada, they have had to be ready for a deportation order at any time. This still holds for the premiership of Justin Trudeau—ironically, former Prime Minister Pierre E. Trudeau's son— who took office in late 2015. Asked by a war resister's spouse while still on the campaign trail, Trudeau stated that he was "supportive of the principle of allowing conscientious objectors to stay" and committed to "examining that case with full compassion and an openness to actually allowing him to stay" as well as, more broadly, to "restoring our sense of compassion and openness and a place that is a safe haven for people to come here and build their lives and their futures as invaluable and important parts of our community" (WarResistersCanada). However, as the end of the 42nd Canadian Parliament and of Trudeau's term in office approached in October 2019,[3] there had been no noticeable shift in policy; in fact, *Operational Bulletin 202* remained in effect. The media and lobby groups have largely fallen silent in recent years concerning both deportations and approval of refugee claims.

Before we proceed with the empirical study, it is worth noting that the two war resister generations' northbound migration is also peculiar in another regard. Though not always reflected in policy, the United States prides itself on being a land of opportunity for people fleeing from dire conditions, including oppression. The flight of Vietnam and Afghanistan/Iraq War resisters seems to turn the often-cited trope of the United States as a "mother of exiles" on its head. Quite to the contrary, here the United States, or rather its foreign policies, proved to be the root cause of Vietnam and Afghanistan/ Iraq War resisters' taking exile elsewhere. Over the centuries, their joint destination, Canada, often served as a refuge from the United States, as the exodus of Loyalists during the American Revolution or the flight of slaves by way of the Underground Railroad illustrates.[4] However, applied to the two generations of war resisters at the heart of this study, the protection and nourishment Canada as a "mother of exiles" afforded them appear anything but equitable. While the country allowed Vietnam War resisters to grow into fully-established Canadian citizens, members of the cohort of Afghanistan/ Iraq War resisters have largely continued in the role of neglected children.

METHODS AND SAMPLING

An exploratory study such as the one at hand suggests a qualitative approach. The empirical basis for the research project consists in problem-centered interviews with war resisters from both cohorts (Vietnam, Afghanistan/Iraq) and Canadian activists, conducted during Stephen Harper's last premiership (2011–2015). Local networks of supporters were the starting points; further respondents were recruited in a snowball fashion. The interviews with Canadian activists were largely concerned with their anti-deportation lobbying; in the case of the war resisters, interviews were based upon respondents' migration experiences, including their perceptions of carving out a new existence in Canada. Further, all three cohorts were asked to talk about any current and/ or previous civic engagement, especially against the backdrop of any ongoing anti-deportation activism.

In keeping with Grounded Theory tenets, which serve as the methodological framework for the study, the overall objective for the analysis was to glean a common theme from the groups' narratives. To this end, the interviews were coded; concepts were gradually clustered, collapsed into categories and, finally, narrowed down to separate core categories.[5] This chapter discusses solely the core category of the Afghanistan/Iraq War resister cohort; excerpts from the interviews with Vietnam War resisters and Canadian activists were clustered thematically for the purposes of this chapter.

MANEUVERING LIMINALITY: AFGHANISTAN/ IRAQ WAR RESISTERS' STRATEGIES TO NEGOTIATE LEGAL UNCERTAINTY

According to Eastmond, refugees' livelihoods are generally marked by "uncertainty and liminality, rather than progression and conclusion" (251). These were also the pervasive themes in the interviews with Afghanistan/Iraq War resisters[6]: Their narratives conveyed indecision and a sense of impasse as opposed to a restart in their country of refuge, Canada. The in-vivo codes[7] "being in limbo" and "life ha[ving] been put on hold" are direct evidence of livelihoods perceived as precarious. Particularly the former phrase's salience in the data made it the quintessential candidate for the core category.

To better conceptualize the Afghanistan/Iraq War resisters' accounts, this chapter draws on two scholars' theorizations. The first scholar is Arnold van Gennep: Afghanistan/Iraq War resisters' narratives of their migration to Canada suggest a tripartite process that is reminiscent of *rites of passage*. In keeping with this pattern, the resisters' flight breaks down into three stages: *separation* in the shape of desertion and flight to Canada; *transition* as the waiting period prior to the adjudication of their refugee claims; and potential, yet at the time of the interviews seemingly unlikely *incorporation,* should their refugee claims and thereby residency in Canada eventually be granted. The second scholar whose works inform the analysis is Victor Turner: building on van Gennep, he contributed considerably to the dissemination of the concept now known as *liminality* (see Turner, *Forest;* Turner, *Ritual*). Etymologically implying a threshold, the term directly corresponds to the *rites of passage*'s transitional stage and, likewise, situations of upheaval and incertitude as to the future course of events; additionally, it may also imply third-person dependency.[8]

Bearing said connotations in mind, the term *liminality* appeared a very fitting abstraction of the in-vivo code "being in limbo." In full, the core category is *maneuvering liminality*.[9] It alludes to the continuum of strategies Afghanistan/Iraq War resisters pursued to navigate this period of uncertainty and make their day-to-day lives bearable. In a nutshell, they needed to strike a balance between remaining aloof to spare themselves the disappointment, should they receive a deportation order, and establishing social and professional ties to demonstrate their willingness to integrate in Canada. Differently put, the challenge war resisters faced consisted in becoming involved in their Canadian communities without growing too invested, both emotionally and in terms of property.

Overall, the analysis of the interviews yielded six strategies on which respondents were drawing interchangeably and to varying degrees, depending on individual circumstances and needs. They range from *fighting off the (potential) return to the United States* as one extreme to *(re)establishing a fit in Canada* as the opposite extreme. In the first case, Afghanistan/Iraq War resisters appeared to be keeping a distance from Canadian society; the United States remained their key point of reference. In other words, they were predominantly concerned with (averting) the negative consequences they might have to suffer upon a return to the United States, most notably a court-martial or jail time. Under the circumstances, they did not find it appropriate to commit to Canada. In the second case, Afghanistan/Iraq War resisters relayed concerted and multifaceted attempts at making Canada their new home. With the objective of establishing a foothold, respondents seemed to follow a more proactive, forward-looking course of action; for instance, they were eager to establish meaningful social ties and adopt Canadian living patterns to better fit in. Hence, conversely, their focus was on Canada. The strategies in between these two poles cannot be lumped in exclusively with either end of the spectrum. Concretely, the six strategies are entitled (a) *cocooning: shutting out new surroundings,* (b) *keeping the status quo,* (c) *safeguarding an emotional balance,* (d) *restoring/maintaining normalcy,* (e) *getting one's bearings,* and (f) *Canadianizing.* We will now consider them in more detail.

Cocooning: Shutting Out New Surroundings

At this end of the spectrum, respondents still appeared rather absorbed in life in the United States.[10] According to one interviewee, for instance, the (war resister) spouse "follows the news there" rather than in Canada. Another respondent self-identified as an "armchair activist": as such, the person was continuously "trying to bring discussion on message boards" dealing with US politics, for example, the person was posting comments on "certain laws trying to be passed in America." Removed from actual events, they used technology for virtual interaction with fellow US Americans.

With the United States still serving as the point of reference, Canada was not considered on its merits, but simply remained the country that is "North of Washington, and it's North of New York," as one interviewee put it. At best, with the repercussions of a deportation to the United States in mind, Canada was a place of respite where war resisters composed themselves before suffering the legal consequences of their flight. In the words of one respondent, "that's part of my stay up in Canada, that's like the serious thing—that I feel like I need to maintain my fitness, my cardio, my ability to fight," so as to stand a chance against harassment in military prison. Life in Canada was thereby merely a distraction that needed to be shut out.

Another factor to be reckoned with in this context is symptoms of post-traumatic stress disorder. To the extent that interviewees had had exposure to combat, minimizing the number of contacts and interactions was partly a necessity. One individual relayed, "my senses are too stimulated. . . . So I like try to hang out by myself, I stay in the room." Another stated, "I just wanna be left alone inside the house." Within this limited space it is easier to establish a sense of control as there are fewer stimuli.

The courses of action just described can be thought of as cocooning. They are protective measures that allow respondents to get by. The downside of the self-confinement is, however, that it precludes any meaningful familiarization, let alone affiliation, with Canada.

Keeping the Status Quo

There are two dimensions to this category: one concerns legal measures, the other Afghanistan/Iraq War resisters' behavior. First, in legal terms, the resisters struggled on different institutional levels to secure the right to permanent residency; examples include the filing of claims and appeals of any unfavorable court decisions. This endeavor was generally perceived as an uphill battle. Said one interviewee: "There have been gains from courts of appeal. *Politically* it's been really really difficult to get the support that we need." Despite the odds, however, another respondent demonstrated great resolve to fight the case through to the end: "I'm pretty much in this, win or lose, but hopefully to win."

Second, regarding Afghanistan/Iraq War resisters' comportment, the analysis showed that respondents were careful not to draw attention to themselves in public. By all means avoiding upsetting the subtle balance, they were reluctant to engage in any civic activity. Knowing that being in the spotlight could put their status in jeopardy, one respondent explained: "It holds us back. Because you never know who's looking and how that would affect your own situation." As another person aptly described it, the strategy was therefore to "[keep] my profile low." Considering the precarious legal status, this respondent, as others in the study, refrained from exercising free speech and participating in society.

How conducive to civic engagement a secure status would be becomes apparent in another interviewee's statement: "If I knew I was safe here in Canada—like truly safe and I had residency and they couldn't deport us, I think I would be—we would both be much more involved in standing up, you know, for issues that we feel strongly about." Inasmuch as their own cause was concerned, however, study participants did in fact seek to increase their base of support through activism. The objective of their self-interested lobbying, according to one respondent, was to "get all these people [in their communities] to band together *with* you" and thereby render them advocates of the Afghanistan/Iraq War resisters' cause, that is, of their struggle to procure permission to remain in Canada, if only for the time being.

Safeguarding an Emotional Balance

This third strategy is closely related to the aforementioned (temporary) social withdrawal. It comprises other measures respondents took to find relief from legal uncertainty. For some it was helpful not to expose themselves to situations in which they would have to talk about their liminal status. One individual's comment in this vein was that "you just kind of want to take a *break* every once in a while, and just be a regular person *not* involved in an immigration struggle." In that case, this person would discontinue any such interactions until there was "enough of a heal." Other respondents, conversely, did seek out interlocutors to discuss their precarious status. To restore mental equilibrium, they sought the help of psychologists; as a result, an interviewee narrated, "there isn't that black hole of despair" anymore.

Another widespread approach among Afghanistan/Iraq War resisters to keeping their emotional balance was to avoid any sort of commitment. In the face of "liminal legality" (Menjívar) and "deportability" (De Genova), making long-term plans appeared futile, as the following statement illustrates: "I don't really see the point in doing a whole lot of planning in advance. Because, I mean, tomorrow I could get that little brown envelope in the mail." Earlier, this was referred to as "not becoming too invested" in Canada. This attitude concerned, quite literally, financial investments. Said one respondent, for instance: "Like the idea of getting a car: Should I buy a car in Canada? Is it worth it? Or maybe like putting a down-payment on a house. . . . I can't think about those long-term decisions cause always, in the back of my mind, I'm still kind of on uneven ground." The prospect of having to give up everything again precluded building a new life in Canada. In the same vein, emotional attachments, particularly in the shape of friendship with people in the community, proved hard to maintain.

With the length of their interim residency so unforeseeable, Afghanistan/ Iraq War resisters narrated how they tended to break up time into smaller units. With these it appeared easier to retain some sense of control over their situation and reduce stress associated with their precarious status. Asked about any plans for the future, one interviewee negated having a clear concept of what lay ahead. In the person's own words, "I just take it like a day at a time, just enjoy the time." Another respondent was equally reluctant to get their hopes up. The experience was "that expectations just kind of let you down in the long run. Try to just take it day by day."

Restoring/Maintaining Normalcy

The strategy of restoring/maintaining normalcy is intertwined with the previous approach. After all, normalcy, such as familiar routines, fosters a sense of control and thereby contributes to a person's emotional balance. However, this fourth strategy differs inasmuch as it is more change- and future-oriented and geared more to increasing the interaction with the social environment. That is to say, the focus here is on Afghanistan/Iraq War resisters' attempts to network and socialize rather than conduct their often solitary soul-searching. By making new friends and establishing ties to their milieu, respondents were rebuilding their support networks and lives. Consider this interviewee's account: "We've formed a circle of friends with [the neighbors] that I feel we've become very close in very short amount of time. And it's great—like to, you know, to know that there's people that I can reach out to and depend on if I need something." Another respondent also spoke of the importance of personal interactions, stressing how these helped with place-making in Canada. In the person's own words: "I have a lot of close personal relationships with the people who live around me you know. So in that respect it feels a lot like home to me."

Some respondents more than others in the sample were able to work in Canada. Employment had a structuring effect on life, for one thing; what is more, as interviewees reported, it fostered the exchange with co-workers, ideally even after working hours. In this respondent's case, workplace relations had evolved into friendships, occupying parts of the person's spare time. On account of the team being "a very close community, there's a lot of social events that go on among the staff and things like that. So we're not just co-workers, we're also friends." Such interactions provided social outlets because they helped to temporarily take one's mind off any distress.

The overall tenor of the interviews was that respondents were eager to live "normal" lives, to the extent that their "liminal legality" allowed. According to one person, everyday life was "surprisingly more normal than people think. I'm not on sure footing with my status in this country, and I also have a lot of obstacles. . . . But I still work, [my partner] still works. We still do things, for the most part, that a lot of other people do." The statement of another individual struck a similar chord. With regard to any spare time activities, the person said: "I just do normal junk. . . . I hang out with my friends and watch movies and—same stuff that pretty much everybody else does." So as to fit in with and diminish differences vis-à-vis average Canadians, the goal was to be "just another person living in [this city], who goes to work every day and, you know, comes home and does whatever boring crap you're gonna do that evening," as one respondent phrased it.

Getting One's Bearings

Implicit in the title of this fifth strategy is that events have (temporarily) upset an equilibrium and plans for the future have been called into question. This requires the individuals to define their new normal and determine who they are in relation to the new social environment. The phrase "getting one's bearings" also alludes to the—increasingly successful—acclimatization process. Overall, Afghanistan/Iraq War resisters thought their stay in Canada to be fraught with anxiety; yet there was also the notion of new beginnings. Despite the uncertainty, one respondent stated, "at least we knew here in Canada, you know, there's a chance to start over and a chance to continue. . . . There was hope for the future!"

Starting over, however, generally also meant that respondents had to rebuild their lives from the base up, without substantial assets to speak of. A telling turn of phrase invoked by a few interviewees was "being back to square one." One concluded the account of the journey across the border as follows: "I started out in Canada with, in essence, no money and a backpack with clothes." Earning a living, if at all psychologically possible, also hinged on personal ties and/or a sound employment history—a resource possibly lost in the migration process. A respondent described the job hunt in the following terms: "You're starting from nothing. You're going and someone—you don't know the person. All you have are your skills and your ability to sell yourself."

Generally, leaving the United States Armed Forces and thus a military career exacted a professional (re)orientation: Despite looking into a series of occupational fields, one interviewee stated, "I haven't found anything that I really like, I think is my niche yet." Apart from laying the economic foundation for their livelihoods in Canada, Afghanistan/Iraq War resisters' acclimatization entailed a parallel soul-searching process concerning a new life concept overall. Trying out various activities and mingling with different groups, one respondent was still in the process of "find[ing] out where I, like—where I fit in to everything." In a similar vein as the previous strategy, getting one's bearings entails respondents' proactive and deliberate attempts to shape a way of life in Canada. They seemed to be gradually recovering a more coherent sense of self. As one individual aptly put it: "Ever since I came to Canada—since day one, it was like a healing process."

Canadianizing

This final strategy addresses Afghanistan/Iraq War resisters' targeted efforts to conform to Canada as a whole. It encompasses the adoption of Canadian beliefs. Consider, for instance, the trope of Canada as a "refuge from militarism," a term supposedly coined by former Prime Minister Pierre E. Trudeau in reference to the influx of Vietnam War resisters.[11] Respondents repeatedly used the phrase, both literally and metaphorically, as one respondent's statement illustrates: to them, Canada represented a "safe harbor for those seeking refuge." War resisters in fact saw their migration to Canada in the tradition of other US Americans who came as early as the nineteenth century. The reasoning of one interviewee was: "Canada was a safe haven for people on the Underground Railroad, and they helped lots of draft dodgers or war resisters during Vietnam." Another stated:

> Canada, I mean, sort of has a history of sooner or later opening their arms
> to people like me. I mean if you—you can go as far back as the American

Revolutionary War and see sort of that pattern in Canadian history. . . . And you can move forward in history and see other examples—the Underground Railroad is often brought up. . . . You know, and again Canada opened its arms to people that were fleeing the—essentially, the politics of the United States. Vietnam—it happened again. And we're hoping that the situation with the Iraq War will turn out the same way. You know, it's—the history is there.

A second, somewhat related, topos invoked by respondents was that of Canada as a "peaceable kingdom." Juxtaposing Canada with the United States, one person's impression was that the former was "a peacekeeping nation." Another interviewee equally perceived Canada as a country of pacifism and, in addition, commented positively on its multiculturalism, a policy often touted by Canadians. In the individual's words, Canada "is actually quite diverse. . . . You see people of different races and ethnicities. . . . So, like there is much more diversity and acceptance and pacifism."

Canada's official bilingualism, that is, the coexistence of English and French as official languages, reflects the country's appreciation of diversity. While it is possible to master everyday conversations speaking just one of the two languages, proficiency in both may in fact prove to be an asset. One interviewee, who happened to be a parent, promoted the child(ren)'s French language skills through enrollment in French immersion classes. The incentive was the following: "I think it could give [our offspring] such a better head-start in life to be bilingual." This approach may not be different from that of other average (Canadian) parents. However, in the same vein, it can be deemed a token of a person's willingness to integrate and build a new life in a given country of refuge, in this case Canada.

MEDIATING THE EFFECTS OF LEGAL UNCERTAINTY: VIETNAM WAR RESISTERS, CANADIAN ACTIVISTS, AND THE ANTI-DEPORTATION STRUGGLE

As the preceding discussion has shown, Afghanistan/Iraq War resisters interviewed in this chapter have begun to network and establish social ties in Canada, though to varying degrees. They have rebuilt (parts of a) base of support to compensate for the loss of social capital incurred by their forced migration. Both the former generation of Vietnam War resisters, meanwhile fully settled, and Canadian activists have been pivotal in helping this contemporary cohort of war resisters establish a foothold. Across the interviews conducted with these two groups, three types of activities could be identified through which they were trying to mediate the effects of Afghanistan/Iraq War resisters' legal uncertainty, if need be, preempt their deportation, and ultimately secure residency. These activities can be clustered as follows: (a) *providing for an infrastructure*, (b) *broadening the base of support through events*, and (c) *lobbying at the political level*. Statements from these interviews shed light on the mediators' respective activities.

Providing for an Infrastructure

As excerpts from the interviews with Afghanistan/Iraq War resisters in the preceding section illustrated, upon leaving their lives behind and crossing the border into Canada, they had to start from scratch. Generally, they were able to bring with them only the bare necessities. Accordingly, getting set up again was a task very high up on the agenda of both Afghanistan/Iraq War resisters and their supporters.[12] Many of these initial efforts concerned shelter, as activist Cassie[13] narrated. In her local group of supporters, the early stages were marked by "trying to find households that would volunteer to take people in when they first arrived until they could get on their feet and find, like, their own housing." In Vietnam War resister Valentin's experience, their activities equally revolved around "housing and helping people to find employment." Similarly, activist Courtney's account revealed that her group would help with "work permits, legal fees, clothing, pots, pans, . . . mattresses, all kinds of things, so that people coming up could have some things." Finally, to help Afghanistan/Iraq War resisters get established in Canada, supporters also tried to get monetary donations, in addition to the everyday objects just mentioned, so as to compensate for (temporary) unemployment, pay for legal counsel, or help with an exceptional, but much-needed purchase. To this end, Veronica related, they had "had a fundraiser recently to help raise funds" for an Afghanistan/Iraq War resister's special medical needs.

Broadening the Base of Support through Events

Fundraising, to a large extent, revolves around convincing people to donate money for what a given party deems a worthy cause. Apart from amassing a financial base, it is also a matter of building momentum for the issue at stake. In either case, it is indispensable to reach out to communities, spread the word, and raise awareness about the Afghanistan/Iraq War resisters' struggle to remain in Canada. The means by which this can be accomplished are manifold, as the following accounts illustrate. According to Vincent, he and his fellow supporters garnered support for Afghanistan/Iraq War resisters by "ha[ving] *concerts* and *movie showings* and *dinners*. And we've had border events at [a border crossing] where Americans come over." Valentin spoke of another strategy, "tabling," to broaden the base of support within society at large: "You know, we'll set up a table by a church or in the different ridings [i.e., electoral districts] and stuff like that, and just—*chatting* with people and the majority of people are saying: Yeah! They support it or will sign a petition or whatever." To this list of activities and places supporters used as platforms for their lobbying, Cynthia added, it "could be anything from, like, going to a farmers' market on Saturday morning, and doing *leafletting* to, like, speaking engagements. Have a war resister come out and do a public *talk*." These events were deemed effective inasmuch as they fostered an exchange of ideas, involved people's thoughts directly in the matter, and, above all, put a face to the issue.

Lobbying at the Political Level

A very important long-term point in winning public support was to effect changes in legislation that would allow Afghanistan/Iraq War resisters to remain in Canada permanently. To this end, supporters also geared their measures toward moving politicians to take up the issue, thus making it *their* concern. By "tabling" in ridings deemed pivotal in the outcome of an election, supporters were trying to swing votes, above all where the Conservative Party, known to hold an antagonistic view, was considered strong. According to Cassie, she and her fellow supporters would "collect a lot of signatures, . . . so to try to just remind Conservative MPs that [their] constituents also support this issue." Conversely, some supporters sought to convince other parties to bring their political weight to bear. Vincent, for instance, narrated how the local group of supporters had "had meetings with opposition parties, the Bloc Québécois, NDP, Liberals" to win them as proponents and, at best, initiators of legislation. Finally, supporters also employed a sort of guerilla lobbying, as Cynthia's statement demonstrates: with the support of the general public, they would organize "a *huge* call-in. We're gonna *call* the Prime Minister's office, the Immigration Minister's office and your local MP and we're gonna like *flood* them with calls."

CONCLUSION: PROMOTING INVOLVEMENT

The case of Afghanistan/Iraq War resisters in Canada shows that although the post-migration adjustments both in terms of language and culture were small in comparison to most other forced migrants, they encountered very similar challenges in their country of refuge, owing to the asylum process. Their "liminal legality" and "deportability" severely limited their orientation toward the future. Not knowing when, if at all, their legal uncertainty would end and whether they would be allowed to remain in Canada after all, they could not begin to conceive new lifeways, nor form new affiliations. This also impacted the present inasmuch as, meanwhile, Afghanistan/Iraq War resisters deemed it too risky to fully participate in society for fear of jeopardizing their precarious status.

This chapter discussed six strategies on which Afghanistan/Iraq War resisters were drawing to navigate this difficult time in their lives, aptly subsumed in the core category of *maneuvering liminality*. The two extremes in between which these strategies oscillated were *fighting off the (potential) return to the United States* and *(re)establishing a fit in Canada*. Whereas in the former case individuals lived largely in withdrawal from society, the latter case included individuals who were deliberately and proactively socializing with community members. The new social networks included Vietnam War resisters, who shared Afghanistan/Iraq War resisters' experience of war-induced flight to Canada, as well as Canadian activists, who had taken on this issue as part of an antiwar movement. Together they had been helping the contemporary cohort of war resisters with the transition. First and foremost, they had taken various measures to mediate the effects of legal uncertainty and ultimately resolve the issue of Afghanistan/Iraq War resisters' pending status.

The chapter introduced three ways in which supporters went about this task: particularly in the beginning of Afghanistan/Iraq War resisters' stay in Canada, activities evolved around providing an infrastructure. As time progressed, they hosted a variety of events to increase the number of proponents across Canada furthering the Afghanistan/Iraq War resisters' cause. Finally, supporters addressed their activism at the political level directly.

At the time of the interviews none of the activities had secured Afghanistan/Iraq War resisters' right to remain in Canada. As a result, they expressed that they were generally reluctant to become involved in civil society as well as to form new affiliations to their country of refuge—an approach they share with many other forced migrants in similar contexts. However, inasmuch as these early stages set the tone for refugee claimants' societal participation going forward, immigration policy would do well to foster their involvement from the very beginning rather than create a climate of self-effacement and aloofness.

NOTES

1. Given the lack of official records of the number of Afghanistan/Iraq Wars resisters in Canada, the estimate is based on a House of Commons debate. According to NDP Member of Parliament Libby Davies, there were approximately 300 war resisters in Canada as of September 27, 2010 (cf. Canadian Parliament 4392).

2. An early documented case is that of Jeremy Hinzman, who filed for refugee status in Canada on the grounds of a conscientious objection to the Iraq War in January 2004 (Immigration and Refugee Board of Canada).

3. Trudeau was narrowly re-elected in October 2019 but his Liberal Party lost its majority in Parliament.

4. A special issue of *Études Canadiennes/Canadian Studies* sheds light on various instances in which Canada became a refuge for US Americans (Association Française d'Études Canadiennes).

5. In Grounded Theory, the term "category" denotes an aggregate of codes and concepts; the "core category" is a term under which the most salient concept(s) in the data can be subsumed (see Creswell and Poth; Charmaz).

6. The author gratefully acknowledges fellowship support from the University of Victoria's Centre for Global Studies, which facilitated her research.

7. In Grounded Theory terminology, an "in-vivo code" is a verbatim expression that derives directly from a respondent's narrative (see Corbin and Strauss; Charmaz).

8. Gazit discusses in a recent article how van Gennep and Turner's theorizations mesh with one another (cf. 269–70); moreover, she reviews how contemporary scholars have applied these concepts to the field of migration studies and thereby carried the earlier academics' theories forward.

9. The other stages of the migration process are beyond the scope of this chapter. Thus, suffice it to say that, within the *rites of passage* pattern, the categories corresponding to the stages of separation and incorporation are called *losing fit* and *getting status*, respectively.

10. With a sample as small as the one at hand, the respondents' protection of privacy is paramount. Therefore, the author withholds the interviewees' identities, to the extent that they do not even go by pseudonyms. Members of this contemporary cohort will unanimously be referred to as Afghanistan/Iraq War resisters, respondents, etc. to obscure, inter alia, theater of war and gender; to that end, the author furthermore uses the singular "they" instead of gender-specific pronouns.

11. For a thorough discussion of the trope of Canada as a "refuge from militarism" and its erroneous dissemination, see Jones, *Happenstance.*

12. The term "supporters" comprises Vietnam War resisters and Canadian(-born) activists.

13. All names stated in the following are aliases. The initials indicate the group to which they belong, that is, either Canadian activists ("C") or Vietnam War resisters ("V").

WORKS CITED

Association Française d'Études Canadiennes. "Le Canada, refuge américain?" *Études Canadiennes/Canadian Studies,* vol. 85, 2018, pp. 5–223. https://journals.open edition.org/eccs/1384. Accessed Aug. 15, 2019.

Bailey, Adrian J., et al. "(Re)producing Salvadoran Transnational Geographies." *Annals of the Association of American Geographers,* vol. 92, no. 1, 2002, pp. 125–44.

Bailey, Beth L. "The Army in the Marketplace: Recruiting an All-Volunteer Force." *The Journal of American History,* vol. 94, no. 1, 2007, pp. 47–74.

————. *America's Army: Making the All-Volunteer Force.* Harvard University Press, 2009.

Canadian Parliament. *House of Commons Debates: Official Report 40th Parliament, 3rd Session (Sep. 27, 2010)*, vol. 145, no. 71, 2010, pp. 4391–4458.

Charmaz, Kathy. *Constructing Grounded Theory.* 2nd ed., Sage, 2014.

Corbin, Juliet M., and Anselm L. Strauss. *Basics of Qualitative Research: Techniques and Procedures for Developing Grounded Theory.* 4th ed., Sage, 2015.

Creswell, John W., and Cheryl N. Poth. *Qualitative Inquiry and Research Design: Choosing among Five Approaches.* 4th ed., Sage, 2018.

De Genova, Nicholas P. "Migrant 'Illegality' and Deportability in Everyday Life." *Annual Review of Anthropology,* vol. 31, no. 1, 2002, pp. 419–47.

Eastmond, Marita. "Stories as Lived Experience: Narratives in Forced Migration Research." *Journal of Refugee Studies,* vol. 20, no. 2, 2007, pp. 248–64.

Ferrer, Ana M., et al. *New Directions in Immigration Policy: Canada's Evolving Approach to Immigration Selection.* Working Paper No. 107, Canadian Labour Market and Skills Researcher Network, 2012.

Gazit, Orit. "The Sociology of the Limit: Reformulating the Question of Migration through van Gennep." *Journal of Classical Sociology,* vol. 18, no. 4, 2018, pp. 266–82.

Government of Canada. *Operational Bulletin 202: Instruction to Immigration Officers in Canada on Processing Cases Involving Military Deserters*, 2010, modified Sep. 2, 2016, https://www.canada.ca/en/immigration-refugees-citizenship/corpora te/publications-manuals/operational-bulletins-manuals/bulletins-2010/202-modifie d-september-2-2016.html. Accessed Aug. 15, 2019.

Green, Alan G., and David A. Green. "The Economic Goals of Canada's Immigration Policy: Past and Present." *Canadian Public Policy/Analyse de Politiques,* vol. 25, no. 4, 1999, pp. 425–51.

Hagan, John. *Northern Passage: American Vietnam War Resisters in Canada.* Harvard University Press, 2001.

Immigration and Refugee Board of Canada. *Jeremy Hinzman (a.k.a. Jeremy Dean Hinzman), Nga Thi Nguyen, Liam Liem Nguyen Hinzman (a.k.a. Liam Liem Nguye Hinzman): Decisions TA4-01429, TA4-01430, TA4-01431.* 2005, https://irb-cis r.gc.ca/en/decisions/Pages/hinzmanDec.aspx. Accessed Aug. 15, 2019.

Jones, Joseph. *Contending Statistics: The Numbers for U.S. Vietnam War Resisters in Canada.* Quarter Sheaf, 2005.

————. *Happenstance and Misquotation: Canadian Immigration Policy, 1966–1974, the Arrival of U.S. Vietnam War Resisters, and the Views of Pierre Trudeau.* Quarter Sheaf, 2008.

Kasinsky, Renée G. *Refugees from Militarism: Draft-Age Americans in Canada.* Transaction, 1976.

Kleykamp, Meredith A. "College, Jobs, or the Military? Enlistment During a Time of War." *Social Science Quarterly,* vol. 87, no. 2, 2006, pp. 272–90.

Maxwell, Donald W. "'These Are the Things You Gain If You Make Our Country Your Country': U.S.–Vietnam War Draft Resisters and Military Deserters and the Meaning of Citizenship in North America in the 1970s." *Peace & Change,* vol. 40, no. 4, 2015, pp. 437–61.

Menjívar, Cecilia. "Liminal Legality: Salvadoran and Guatemalan Immigrants' Lives in the United States." *American Journal of Sociology,* vol. 111, no. 4, 2006, pp. 999–1037.

Rostker, Bernard. *I Want You! The Evolution of the All-Volunteer Force*, RAND, 2006.

Schake, Kori, and Jim Mattis. "A Great Divergence?" *Warriors and Citizens: American Views of Our Military,* edited by Jim Mattis and Kori Schake, Hoover Institution, 2016, pp. 1–20.

Turner, Victor W. *The Forest of Symbols: Aspects of Ndembu Ritual.* Cornell University Press,1967.

———. *The Ritual Process: Structure and Anti-Structure.* Aldine Transaction, 1969.

Van Gennep, Arnold. *The Rites of Passage.* 1909. Routledge and Paul, 1960.

WarResistersCanada. *Justin Trudeau's Response on U.S. Iraq War Resisters in Canada.* (Winnipeg, MB; July 4, 2015), 2015, https://www.youtube.com/watch?v=cponOdar4f4. Accessed Aug. 15, 2019.

Chapter 12

"No Asylum from the Germans"

Policies of Deterrence and the Early West German Refugee Movement

Andreas Kewes

There are two popular interpretations of recent German refugee policy, both of which work on the basis of unquestioned self-evidence.[1] The first interpretation assumes that the German chancellor Angela Merkel, as head of the federal government, initiated the acceptance of a large number of Syrian refugees in the late summer of 2015 in accordance with an *ethics of ultimate end* that is widely shared in Germany. Ethics of ultimate end means that the actor does not consider possible consequences of his or her action, but rather sees that action as unquestionably right in itself.[2] The second interpretation assumes that the Federal Republic of Germany advocated the suspension of Dublin III[3] deportations of Syrian refugees because of a German "folk narrative" born of an effort to make amends for the past.[4] Both interpretations assume a high level of consensus in Germany on normative questions of migration and asylum, suggesting that the need to help is self-evident to the majority—and has been since 1945. This hypothesis may seem plausible considering that the German constitution since 1949, the *Grundgesetz* (Basic Law), contains a fundamental right to political asylum that was formulated by the law's authors precisely in reference to the experience of World War II with the Holocaust and displaced persons. An examination of the entitlement to this fundamental right enables many refugees to stay in Germany at least temporarily and represents an additional protection alongside that of international refugee law, albeit one that is now rarely granted.[5]

One could counter these interpretations empirically by addressing the heterogeneous German "scene" of supporters for asylum-seekers (e.g. Schiffauer et al.) that is composed of very different groups. The German sociologist Albert Scherr cites a) assistance provided in specific cases, b) legal positivist positions, and c) advocates of a right to freedom of movement (cf. 396). We can also use the consensus hypothesis to ask whether liberal migration policies have always been part of the "folk narrative," how the migration movement in the Federal Republic of Germany actually came into being, and what its core demands were and still are today. These are the broad outlines of the present chapter, whose scope is restricted to forced migration to Germany. This focus is justified in light of the current national, European, and international debate on German refugee policy. The scope is also restricted in time: as an analysis of the German refugee movement overall would have to cover a considerable period, I focus on the late 1970s and early 1980s, a phase I consider to be constitutive for current debates and organizational contexts. I ask what normativity the activists in the refugee (protection) movement have articulated and why this position appeared self-evident to them.[6]

This chapter argues that organized support for refugees in the Federal Republic of Germany originated in the German civil liberties movement of the late 1970s and early 1980s against changes in West German law on aliens.[7] It is useful to reconstruct precisely this dispute over better migration policy, its actors, and their (protest) mobilization and institutionalization. I propose the following argument: a change in refugee numbers was rapidly noticeable following the first intake of refugees in the Federal Republic of Germany in the 1970s. This became a controversial political issue, resulting in the increasing decentralization of accommodation provision/asylum procedures. As the number of asylum-seekers increased, a right-wing populist discourse on bogus asylum-seekers, economic migrants, and asylum tourism developed.[8] This discourse went hand-in-hand with restrictions on the right to asylum; some voices spoke openly of a policy of deterrence (see Ausländerkomitee; Zepf). The reconstruction of both types of political framing is necessary if we are to show the context to which the action of the movement is articulated, for despite the policy of deterrence, a social movement in support of refugees also developed, as I explain at the end of the chapter. Using contemporary material, I demonstrate that the basis of this movement is the creation of intersubjective certainty on state wrongdoing toward refugees and migrants.

The forms of action taken by the refugee movements of the time focused very specifically on local issues and problems. Politicization thus did not happen through abstract demands or philosophical justifications but through clearly identifiable personal stories. I therefore seek to show empirically how the refugee protection movement in the Federal Republic of Germany resulted from a criticism of state provision for migrants rather than from abstract reference to the Nazi dictatorship.

THEORY, DATA, AND METHOD

The following remarks are an attempt to understand a long-standing dynamic in German asylum policy on the basis of the conflict between the political establishment and an emerging social movement. To the extent that the following pages describe not only the actions of actors in the movement, but also those of other civil society actors, and they also consider the challenging and challenged legislators, I follow a contentious politics approach (see McAdam et al.). This approach does not simply consider structural conditions for the emergence of protest, but it also makes us aware of mechanisms and processes in the development of certain policy fields and is currently being adopted both in social movement (e.g. in Ataç et al.) and in migration research (see Cinalli). The contentious politics approach takes account of the agency of both civil society and state actors. More specifically, I apply the idea of transgressive contention (cf. McAdam et al. 7–9): I am interested in how new actors take to the political stage, making innovative demands or using unconventional forms of mobilization. This theoretical setting is useful, as it does not limit the perspective to the microsocial perception of opportunities and strategic use of frames but also take into account the establishment and effect of interpretation patterns and frames at the macro level.

The data presented in this chapter are taken from a review of contemporary asylum law and research literature. I have evaluated the relevant key literature that was widely accepted within the social movement. As this chapter reconstructs certainties in the social movement, it has a slight imbalance in the literature used toward studies closely related to the movement. I supplement the published sources with archive material, for example publications by actors in the movement, items from private collections, and publicly accessible gray literature. To evaluate the material, I make use of discourse analysis from the field of the sociology of knowledge. A discourse analysis drawing on Keller (and indirectly also on Michel Foucault) uses different conceptual tools such as episteme and classification systems for the reconstruction of social practice. In this chapter, however, this reconstruction necessarily needs to be rough, but I believe that it can provide new insights in combination with the contentious politics approach.

THE QUESTION OF HOUSING

A subject that is now discussed relatively rarely is the changing German practice of housing for refugees in the 1970s. This is remarkable inasmuch as the decentralization of accommodation provision brought about lasting changes in the power structure and actors involved in German refugee policy.

A former gendarmerie barrack in Zirndorf, Franconia, was for a long time the nationwide holding center for refugees and also the site of the *Bundesamt für die Anerkennung ausländischer Flüchtlinge* (Federal Office for the Recognition of Foreign Refugees), the predecessor of today's *Bundesamt für Migration und Flüchtlinge* (Federal Office for Migration and Refugees). Refugees were housed in this center upon reaching the Federal Republic of Germany, ideally until the end of their asylum procedure. This meant that the local administrative court in the nearby small city of Ansbach was originally the only competent court for appeals against asylum decisions.

Looking back today at the way the question of housing was discussed at the time, what is particularly striking is how dramatic a picture was painted: the center was apparently already overcrowded in the early 1970s, and no further refugees were being admitted (cf. Spaich 43–4).[9] Local newspaper reports seemingly denounced untenable conditions, and there was talk of fear on the part of the local population and of civil defense organizations (cf. 44). Current reconstructions focus on the instrumental nature of these pictures, suggesting that the out-of-control accommodation situation in Zirndorf gave the impression that forced migration was an insurmountable social challenge that brought unrest and danger (cf. Poutrus 885). Politicians, it is argued, wanted such an impression inasmuch as there had already been discussions in the 1960s about expanding the center or opening an additional site (cf. 885).

In 1974, it was decided to send some asylum-seekers to other federal states before their applications had been processed. Dispersal of successful asylum-seekers among the federal states had already been implemented in previous years on the basis of a set allocation ratio (see Theis). One consequence of this policy was that, suddenly, most districts in the Federal Republic—the local social security providers—were now confronted with the need to cater to asylum-seekers. As a result, calls for a change in the asylum procedure were now coming not just from the federal state of Bavaria but from all parts of West Germany (cf. Münch, *Asylpolitik* 73). Bavaria had thus to some extent lost its "special institutional role" in refugee and asylum policy, which was organized on a federal basis (Poutrus 888).

If we now try to reconstruct the images and certainties on this subject that were being discussed by the German public, we notice one aspect that deviates significantly from the thesis of a German "folk narrative" or the ethics of ultimate end cited earlier, namely clear connotations in connection with the housing question: refugees are reviled as "pollution," and politicians want to keep their constituencies "clean" (Spaich 52). It would therefore appear that an image of the refugee was created at this time that had multiple negative connotations, and that this image seemed self-evident to conservative politicians and their voters. Refugees were held responsible for unrest and disruption; they were seen as a source of problems and therefore to be avoided. The example of accommodation illustrates how societal knowledge, a certainty, develops and spreads in sections of the population.

THE POLICY OF DETERRENCE

In addition to the decentralization of providing accommodations, asylum law was also tightened in a number of ways in the late 1970s and 1980s. The new measures targeted specifically the application procedure itself. One aim was to speed up asylum procedures, which were genuinely lengthy, taking more than six years when all legal remedies or appeals were implemented (cf. Münch, *Asylpolitik* 72). This created legal uncertainty about the right of the asylum-seekers to remain. However, this was not the only reason for speeding up the process. Pressure was also coming from the federal states and local authorities, which had to take in refugees but wanted to avoid integrating them into German life (cf. 73). The initial legal consequences of this pressure were the first and second acts accelerating the asylum procedure, the *Erstes Beschleunigungsgesetz* of 1978 and the *Zweites Beschleunigungsgesetz* of 1980. The first act abolished the right of appeal against administrative decisions in the appeal committees of the Federal Office but still allowed cases to be brought before the administrative court. Appeals against administrative court decisions before higher administrative courts were abolished for those cases in which the asylum application had been rejected as "manifestly unfounded." In accordance with the nationwide dispersal of asylum-seekers, the administrative court procedure was decentralized, and it became possible to launch proceedings before administrative courts other than the one in Ansbach. As the new legislation did not shorten asylum procedures but in fact placed a greater strain on the administrative courts, the Second Acceleration Act came into force on August 23, 1980. This act provided for the replacement of the three-person asylum committees at the Federal Office by individual decision-makers who were not answerable to the Federal Office.[10]

As an immediate measure to accompany the Second Acceleration Act (cf. Münch, *Asylpolitik* 83), a visa requirement was introduced for the main countries of origin in Asia and Africa in June 1980. This applied to Afghanistan, Ethiopia, Sri Lanka, India, Bangladesh, and Turkey. The federal government was quite aware that it was making entry into Germany impossible for those suffering political persecution, but it justified the move by stating that political refugees could not be granted unlimited access (cf. Klausmeier 58). The only way to circumvent this visa requirement was to enter Germany via East Berlin, as there was no visa requirement between East and West Berlin. The measure initially led to a drop in the number of asylum-seekers, but by making access to German territory more difficult, it also led to increased illegal entry (cf. 58).

As early as 1977, an administrative regulation authorized border officials to carry out a preliminary evaluation of asylum applications. They were to assess an applicant's chances of success and, if applicable, to deny entry on that basis (see Spaich). Churches, Amnesty International, immigrant associations, youth associations, and judges protested against this provision, which they saw as potentially undermining the right to asylum. The regulation was not declared unconstitutional by the Federal Constitutional Court and was repealed only in 1981 (cf. Poutrus 889). When the *Asylverfahrensgesetz* (Asylum Procedure Act) came into force in 1982, the idea was taken up once again. Different categories of asylum application were now to be identified, and these had different legal implications (cf. Münch, *Asylpolitik* 92). As all applications had to be submitted to the aliens' department in charge, it could, for example, classify repeat applications as irrelevant or manifestly unfounded. Furthermore, the Asylum Procedure Act regulated forced placement in asylum centers, the further curtailment of the right of appeal, and the use of single judges instead of a panel (cf. 93–94). Restrictions such as the two-year ban on working were also introduced by the Asylum Procedure Act (a one-year ban had been in place since 1980), as was the obligation to stay in the district of the aliens' department in charge.

Using the example of the tightening of asylum law, we can reconstruct three types of societal knowledge or constructions of reality via discourse theory. The first is the construct of the refugee as a potential fraudster and lawbreaker, whose asylum application is so obviously unfounded that this can be proven at the border or in any given office. By seeking to create an image of refugees as migrant workers in search of economic advancement rather than victims of political persecution, the contemporary federal government and the opposition led by the Christian Democratic Party undermined from the outset any support for those individuals as potential holders of legal rights. Second, by indicating that there was too great a strain on the Federal Office and administrative courts, the two Acceleration Acts broadened the picture that had already been painted in relation to accommodations: refugees were a strain on state order. This has remained an established topos to the present day.

A third construction of reality concerns the supposed motives for refugees' migration. Working on the basis of the image of asylum-seekers as migrants merely in search of a way out of their economic misery, restricting all economic incentives and any financial support such as welfare payments appears logical. This was the approach chosen by the federal government, which banned asylum-seekers from working and stipulated that social security was to be awarded primarily in the form of benefits in kind. As a result of these restrictions, the UNHCR (cf. Münch, *Asylpolitik* 99–100), nongovernmental organizations (cf. Hennig and Wießner 56–57), and academics (cf. Wipfler 68–82) acted as advocates for the refugees and took up the question of economic marginalization. In the process, these actors developed a conflicting set of images and topoi: in publications and at public events, pro-immigration groups and individuals shaped a narrative about refugees in which the latter appeared as poor, needy, and impoverished (e.g. Ausländerkomitee). Broken sanitary facilities and overcrowded rooms are just two of many widely reproduced images that must have fueled the impression that refugees were the Others of the West German affluent society.

CIVIL SOCIETY PERSPECTIVES

Almost all political parties in the Federal Republic of the late 1970s responded negatively to the rising numbers of refugees. The dominating public opinion was critical of further refugee movement to Germany. The image of the refugee as a burden and potential fraudster seemed to appear self-evident to large sections of the population and the political elite. Yet the era of stricter asylum laws and debates on abuse of the system was not shaped solely by illiberal migration policies. This period also saw the emergence of refugee policy and refugee social work structures (organizations, professional journals) that still exist in Germany today. On January 22, 1980, the documentation center *Zentrale Dokumentationsstelle der freien Wohlfahrtspflege für Flüchtlinge e.V.* was founded. In response to a decision by the federal government on the provision of advice and support, the welfare associations set up a service providing information on relevant legislative procedures and judgments and situations in countries of origin (see Bueren 1990).[11] This example shows how welfare associations were involved in the federal government's policy of deterrence, for the *Dokumentationsstelle* not only works/worked to provide legal support for refugees, but also helped and still helps today to legitimize a potentially exclusionary policy by providing advice and information to refugees (cf. Münch, *Asylpolitik* 193). Numerous local initiatives were also set up. Alongside the Amnesty International asylum teams, which saw support to those threatened by deportation and the fight for their right to remain in Germany as preventive human rights work, there were initially also countless local initiatives. Gray literature from the state of North Rhine-Westphalia from 1986 lists 25 asylum support groups in that state alone, many run by churches (see Asboe et al.). The year 1986 saw the establishment of *Pro Asyl* at a national level, which is still the main nongovernmental organization in this field in Germany today. The launch of *Pro Asyl* as a platform for exchange between different representatives of churches, trade unions, welfare associations, and human rights organizations happened largely on a top-down basis. However, *Pro Asyl* is now also an indispensable resource for many local initiatives.

We can therefore see that new actors and new identities emerged in the late 1970s and early 1980s. A failure to handle migration properly in West Germany on both the part of the state (and in particular the local aliens' departments) and—even if to a lesser degree—welfare associations was self-evident to these new actors. Such a development can also be understood on the basis of the contentious politics approach, which allows me to reconstruct a typical pattern I call organized indictment. This pattern was followed in civil society contexts between 1982 and 1984 at various places in the Federal Republic of Germany. There are similarities in the manner of its application in terms of orchestrated seriousness and references to local experiences in each case.

In November 1982, a delegation from the European Committee for the Defense of Refugees and Immigrants (C.E.D.R.I.)—an international non-governmental organization founded shortly before in Switzerland—traveled throughout the Federal Republic to assess the situation in asylum centers. Its concluding report documents its observations at three accommodation centers in southern Germany and seeks to interpret those observations in political terms. It links them to contemporary political debates in West Germany, on, for example, the tightening of asylum laws and a widely read publication by conservative intellectuals in a major German daily newspaper, the "Heidelberg Manifesto." The C.E.D.R.I. interprets both the right to asylum and the proffered interpretation by the intellectuals as an expression of a far-reaching hostility to immigration in West German society. To support this picture, the NGO quotes statements by politicians from center-right parties (CDU, CSU) that document negative attitudes to refugees (centers should simply be fenced-in barracks with guards; cf. C.E.D.R.I. 23). The report also features statements from refugees about paternalism and poor conditions in social welfare services (restrictions on provision of cash, cramped living quarters, inedible food; cf. 25–29), and describes staff at asylum centers who complain about refugees rather than being in any way committed to supporting them (cf. 29–38). In its conclusion, the C.E.D.R.I. finds that there is a policy of intimidation and reports that refugees are interned, with all the psychosomatic problems that this causes (cf. 51–52). The organization also accuses the federal government of violating Article 16 of the Basic Law and failing to respect the Geneva Refugee Convention in its asylum practice.[12]

It is not only the tone of the indictment that makes this document so remarkable, but also the situation itself: an international group visits the Federal Republic of Germany as if it were an unjust state and then proclaims its verdict—as if it were from a neutral outside perspective. Two otherwise separate and unrelated tribunals against local immigration policy in Hamburg (cf. Deutsch-Ausländisches Aktionsbündnis, *Massenausweisungen*) and Hanover (cf. Koordinierungsausschuss) are comparable in terms of the creation of the role of a spokesperson and the speech act of indictment. Here, too, we see the creation of a certainty about asylum policy intended to mobilize actors in the movement. Both tribunals arose out of civil society networks.[13] They were not part of the judiciary but rather constituted attempts at a trial *from below* to implement alternative interpretations and judgments. The two tribunals indicted the federal states in question for their immigration practices. Asylum law was only one point; others included work permits, residence rights, and the political participation of migrants. Through the tribunals, both networks revived a form of mobilization of the new social movements that had already been used in the 1970s against the Federal Republic (see März).

Tribunals on immigration policy in the 1980s called witnesses—sometimes accompanied or represented by lawyers—who described their problems with current immigration policy. At each of these events, which were publicly advertised and therefore well attended, a jury then pronounced a form of guilty verdict. The main argument was that the state was not acting in accordance with the law and was withholding fundamental rights from foreigners (such as the protection of the family, the right to work, the right to asylum, and the right to political participation). In Hamburg, for example, the tribunal outlined the case of Hüseyin Inci, who had first been granted refugee status and was then threatened with deportation to Turkey because of alleged involvement in a criminal offense there. The Turkish state had filed an extradition request that was being examined by the German authorities. Inci accused the Turkish state, at that point a military dictatorship, of criminalizing him in order to get him back. The German state and, in particular, German public prosecution services were accused of cooperating with the military. This case is important in light of the fact that the increase in asylum applications until 1980 was in large part due to people fleeing the military dictatorship in Turkey.[14] In Hanover, detention on the grounds of alleged illegal entry into the country, social security benefits for refugees, and the housing situation were also explored. This tribunal was also directed at the Lower Saxony district authorities, which had apparently instructed asylum-center managers to report any asylum-seekers who "scorned, through their inappropriate behavior, the right to hospitality granted to them" to the Federal Office in Zirndorf; this was to allow steps to be taken to terminate the asylum procedure in question. From the tribunal report, it is clear that those in charge of the tribunal considered these instructions constitutionally questionable on the grounds that they opened the door to arbitrary action, since refugees had to correspond to the moral beliefs or preconceptions of individual case workers or asylum-center managers (cf. Koordinierungsausschuss 35).

The civil society narrative thus emphasized an illiberal, aggressive state that took action against refugees and also cooperated with unjust systems. Criticisms of restrictions on residence, bans on work, and threats of deportation were presented as substantive, personalized through the witnesses, and more or less confirmed by the authorities.[15] These processes were designed to create and consolidate intersubjective certainty. Tribunals could therefore also be understood as moments of collective indignation, as well as moments of collective joy about the community in the movement and mutual reassurance with regard to one's own political position. The main subject of the indictment was not the situation of those who were outside the country's borders, but the way in which state agencies were dealing with migrants within those borders.

A hearing on the social and legal position of refugees in West Berlin was the third major civil society initiative alongside the human rights report and tribunals (see Hofmann). The event was initiated by two NGOs that are still active today (*Gesellschaft für bedrohte Völker* and *Flüchtlingsrat Berlin*).[16] The name of the event—hearing—is reminiscent of a parliamentary procedure. It was held in January 1984 and had no relation to other parliamentary activities. The event and its report were designed to provide a summary of individual measures and restrictions that, it was claimed, were creating an atmosphere in Berlin that left refugees in despair (cf. Hofmann 10). The hearing criticized deportations and custody pending deportation; the implementation of the law on aliens by the local aliens' departments and the Federal Office; social security provision for refugees, including the accommodations situation, benefits in kind, and the ban on work. Like the tribunals, this hearing was also followed by an international jury, which picked up on these points in its concluding statement and demanded improvements on the part of the Berlin authorities. Moreover, the jury reasoned, a key duty of all state agencies—and in particular the Berlin Senate—should be clearly and unequivocally to speak out against prejudices against foreigners (cf. 190). The jury's verdict thus went beyond the asylum question to touch on other discourses, for example, that on population and workforce development.

In terms of discourse analysis, these protests are significant because they collected and articulated a body of knowledge suggesting that fundamental rights were under threat in Germany.[17] Instead of presenting asylum-seekers as a danger or burden, they presented state action—especially the action of the federal states and the local aliens department—as a threat: regulations such as accommodations provision, social security benefits, and a ban on work had an extremely negative impact on the life of the individual.

Looking at the historical material, we can identify the following conviction on the part of the activists: a state that no longer respects its own constitution or international treaties appears in this reality to be the real problem, a problem in the face of which both subjective and fundamental humanitarian rights must be protected. Instead of looking at the asylum-seekers as applicants for a residence permit, the members of the protest movement portrayed them as human beings. The conviction that the (non-)migrant protesters and asylum-seekers all belong to the same species was explicitly mentioned with reference to human rights and human dignity. The image of the foreigner as some kind of brother or sister might have been due to the important role that church groups and members played in the establishment of the early movement. This legitimizes a practice of reaction, of obligatory objection to state immigration policy, which is the first step to taking a completely different approach to migration processes than that of local, state, or federal governments up until that point. However, often the result was not a radical rejection of the state, but an attempt to exert greater influence—whether through targeted lobbying, meetings with the authorities at a state level, or close networking at a municipal level.

As we have seen, asylum policy in the Federal Republic of Germany has long been controversial and remains so today. Skepticism toward practical state migration control and support, embodied in the work of local and regional authorities, has been identified here as a central, shared assumption in the refugee (protection) movement in the Federal Republic of Germany. That skepticism manifested itself primarily in the aforementioned forums and subsequently also in associations and through actors in refugee social work organizations focused on providing legal advice and practical assistance for refugees and on combating racism. Recently, the early German refugee movement and its most visible actor, the association *Pro Asyl*, have been criticized by younger activists for taking a positivist approach: for calling for a correct implementation of existing law instead of raising the political question of open borders (cf. Oulios 323–34). The recent immigration policy groups campaign in a more radical manner. The movement thus continues to develop, and it is becoming more diverse in its demands and goals and in the images of flight and migration that it disseminates.

Antagonistic systems of knowledge and certainties have developed since the 1970s in particular, with a perspective on flight that links refugees to danger, disorder, abuse of the law, and inadequate control, on the one hand, and a perspective that criticizes marginalization and unjust treatment, and commits to far-reaching solidarity with refugees, on the other. These two systems of knowledge constitute a fundamental dispute (and not one "folk narrative"!), which is repeatedly reinforced by the creation of intersubjective certainty.

NOTES

1. This paper is a shortened and revised version of Andreas Kewes, "The Production of Intersubjective Certainty in the Early West German Refugee Movement." *Proceedings of the 2018 ZiF Workshop "Studying Migration Policies at the Interface between Empirical Research and Normative Analysis,"* edited by M. Hoesch and L. Laube, ULB Münster (miami.uni-muenster.de), 2019, pp. 51–69. doi: 10.17879/95189440086.

2. The term *ethics of ultimate end* is the opposite of *ethics of responsibility* and comes from Max Weber's essay "Politics as a Vocation" (120).

3. Dublin III refers to the Dublin III Regulation. This European Union law that determines which EU member state is responsible for the examination of an application for asylum. It usually holds that member state responsible where asylum-seekers apply for asylum for the first time. Because of the main migration routes to Europe the southern EU member states are responsible more frequently than others, for example, Germany. But still there is the right of member states to make use of the so-called "sovereignty clause," which means that it voluntarily assumes responsibility for the processing of asylum applications for which it is not otherwise responsible.

4. This explanation for the German refugee policy in 2015 is given by Betts and Collier (cf. 83). The term "folk narrative" is used by Betts and Collier in the sense of a widely shared German self-understanding.

5. In 1993—during the Yugoslavian civil war—article 16 of the German constitution was changed. Since then, people cannot apply for asylum if they come from a safe country of origin, which has made it quite impossible for refugees from these countries to be granted asylum according to article 16a of the German Constitution.

6. Compared to the present situation in Germany, the refugee movement at that time was dominated by white, middle-class German activists with leftist political positions. Many current activists are, or have been, refugees to Germany themselves. Therefore, I differentiate between "refugee movement" and "refugee (protection) movement." To me, it seems obvious that a refugee movement as we witness it today would not be the same without the refugee (protection) movement of the 1970s and 1980s. It was this movement that institutionalized resources (such as money and organizational structures) that are still in use by the organizations that emerged afterwards.

7. I cannot explore here how the change in the fundamental right to asylum in the German Basic Law was prepared and implemented in 1993. Although this change in asylum law represents a black day for the refugee (protection) movement and fundamentally changed German asylum law, my observation, which I will not elaborate on further at this point, is that it did not change the relevant group of actors.

8. These terms were already being used in the late 1970s, not only "in the pub," but also in the German Bundestag. Cf. Simone Klausmeier's discourse theory and political science study (41–8).

9. The number of asylum-seekers had fallen from 11,664 (1969) to 5,289 in the early 1970s (1972). It then rose, first moderately and then more steeply to peak at 107,818 (1980). The numbers subsequently fell to 19,737 (1983) before rising again (cf. Zepf 57).

10. For an assessment of the regulations at that time, which included asylum decisions being taken at the border and decentralized administrative jurisdiction, see the critical response by Franz (797–98), who maintained that the preliminary examination of asylum applications by the border and aliens' departments had simply unnecessarily prolonged the procedure. Dispersing refugees and allowing them to enter the labor market before processing their applications was in his view also problematic, as such a system could be abused by job-seekers. Such a view was still taken by Münch (cf. "Asylpolitik" 79). From today's perspective, Poutrus (cf. 890) notes that the procedural changes did not prevent the exercise of asylum rights in general, but merely shifted the problems.

11. The service has been provided by the *Informationsverbund Asyl und Migration* since 1999; the information is published at www.asyl.net and in *Asylmagazin*.

12. The UNHCR reached similar findings, and this led to a crisis in relations between the Federal Republic of Germany and the UNHCR in the early 1980s (see Milzow).

13. The tribunal in Hamburg was organized by a group called *Deutsch-Ausländisches Aktionsbündnis* (German-Foreign Action Group). This group was composed of "mainly German, Turkish and Spanish initiatives, groups, associations, organizations and individuals" (Deutsch-Ausländisches Aktionsbündnis, *Wir klagen an* 4). The tribunal in Hanover was initiated by the *Ausländerkomitee Hannover* (Foreigners' Committee Hanover). Although this sounds as if it comprised immigrants, this group also had members with German nationality.

14. The best-known case is that of Turkish refugee Cemal Altun. Altun killed himself on August 30, 1983, by jumping from the sixth floor of a courtroom in Berlin Moabit, where his extradition to Turkey was being debated before the administrative court. The case subsequently received enormous attention (see Arendt-Rojahn).

15. McAdam et al. cite certification as a key mechanism in endorsing or supporting actors and their actions (cf. 121–23). Certification means that an external authority is needed to, for example, vindicate protesters and their concerns. Trade unionists, teachers, pastors, and academics, most of whom had no immigration experience, provided this certification in the tribunals in Hamburg and Hanover. Certification apparently came from people who were supposedly not affected by immigration policy, who were respected, and who were considered to have good judgment because of their social position.

16. The *Flüchtlingsrat Berlin* (Refugee Council Berlin) was neither founded by the state nor a church. In its beginning in 1981, it did not have any legal character. It was just a forum of people with "the concrete and daily experience of working with asylum seekers" in Berlin (Hofmann 19).

17. Also worth noting are the titles of the publications at that time, which similarly construct a threat scenario and therefore pursue a pattern of interpretation used within left-wing movements of the 1970s and 1980s: *No Asylum from the Germans: A Fundamental Freedom under Attack* (Kauffmann 1986), *Right of Asylum without Asylum Seekers* (Zepf) and *Are Mass Deportations Imminent?* (Deutsch-Ausländisches Aktionsbündnis), in my translations.

WORKS CITED

Arendt-Rojahn, Veronika. *Ausgeliefert: Cemal Altun und andere*. Rowohlt, 1983.

Asboe, Karin, Ingrid Just, and Hans-Martin Milk. *Flüchtlingshilfe: Asylarbeitskreise stellen sich vor*. 2nd ed., Diakonisches Werk der evangelischen Kirche im Rheinland, 1986.

Ataç, Ilker, Kim Rygiel, and Maurice Stierl, editors. *The Contentious Politics of Refugee and Migrant Protest and Solidarity Movements: Remaking Citizenship from the Margins*. Routledge, 2017.

Ausländerkomitee Berlin (West) e.V. *Gast oder Last? Berichte zur Lage der Asylbewerber*. EXpress Edition, 1981.

Betts, Alexander, and Paul Collier. *Refuge: Rethinking Refugee Policy in a Changing World*. Oxford University Press, 2017.

Bueren, Ilse. "Information und Dokumentation zu Flüchtlingsfragen: Die Zentrale Dokumentationsstelle der freien Wohlfahrtspflege für Flüchtlinge e.V. (ZDWF)." *Vierzig Jahre Asylgrundrecht—Verhältnis zur Genfer Flüchtlingskonvention: Viertes Expertengespräch für Asylrichter, 25.–27. September 1989 in Bonn*, edited by Wolfgang G. Beitz, Nomos, 1990, pp. 95–100.

C.E.D.R.I. *Asylrecht und Asylpraxis in der Bundesrepublik Deutschland: Bericht einer internationalen Delegation des Europäischen Komitees zur Verteidigung der Flüchtlinge und Gastarbeiter*. Basel, 1982.

Cinalli, Manlio. "Fields of Contentious Politics: Migration and Ethnic Relations." *Social Movement Studies in Europe: The State of the Art*, edited by Olivier Fillieule and Guya Accornero. Berghahn, 2016, pp. 86–99.

Deutsch-Ausländisches Aktionsbündnis. *Stehen Massenausweisungen bevor? Die geplanten Verschärfungen des Ausländergesetzes: Auswertung der Berichte der Bund-Länder-Kommission Ausländerpolitik*. Hamburg, 1983.

Deutsch-Ausländisches Aktionsbündnis. *Wir klagen an: Tribunal zur Hamburger Ausländerpolitik*. Archiv der Sozialen Bewegungen. Hamburg, BRD-04.143. Dokumentation, 1983.

Franz, Fritz. "Die Krise des Asylrechts—Wege zu ihrer Überwindung." *Handbuch des Asylrechts: Unter Einschluß des Rechts der Kontingentflüchtlinge*, vol. 2 *Verfahren, Rechtstellung und Reformen*, edited by Wolfgang G. Beitz and Michael Wollenschläger, Nomos, 1981, pp. 775–810.

Hennig, Claudius, and Siegfried Wießner, editors. *Lager und menschliche Würde: Die psychische und rechtliche Situation der Asylsuchenden im Sammellager Tübingen*. AS, 1982.

Hofmann, Tessa, editor. *Abgelehnt, ausgewiesen, ausgeliefert: Dokumentation zum Hearing über die soziale und rechtliche Lage der Asylbewerber in West-Berlin (20.–22.1.1984)*. Gesellschaft für bedrohte Völker, 1984.

Kauffmann, Heiko, editor. *Kein Asyl bei den Deutschen: Anschlag auf ein Grundrecht*. Rowohlt, 1986.

Keller, Reiner. *Diskursforschung: Eine Einführung für SozialwissenschaftlerInnen*. 4th ed., VS Verlag für Sozialwissenschaften, 2011.

Klausmeier, Simone. *Vom Asylbewerber zum "Scheinasylanten": Asylrecht und Asyl-politik in der Bundesrepublik seit 1973.* EXpress Edition, 1984.

Koordinierungsausschuss für das Tribunal. *Tribunal zur Ausländerpolitik in Nieder-sachsen.* Archiv der Sozialen Bewegungen Hamburg, BRD-04.143. Dokumenta-tion, Berichte, Analysen, 1984.

März, Michael. *Linker Protest nach dem Deutschen Herbst: Eine Geschichte des linken Spektrums im Schatten des "starken Staates," 1977–1979.* transcript, 2012.

McAdam, Doug, Sidney Tarrow, and Charles Tilly. *Dynamics of Contention.* Cam-bridge University Press, 2001.

Milzow, Katrin. "Anatomy of a Crisis: Relations between the United Nations High Commissioner for Refugees and the Federal Republic of Germany from the 1970s to the 1980s." *Refugee Survey Quarterly,* vol. 27, no. 1, 2008, pp. 74–88.

Münch, Ursula. *Asylpolitik in der Bundesrepublik Deutschland: Entwicklung und Alternativen.* Leske & Budrich, 1992.

———. "Asylpolitik in Deutschland: Akteure, Interessen, Strategien." *20 Jahre Asylkompromiss: Bilanz und Perspektiven,* edited by Stefan Luft and Peter Schi-many, transcript, 2014, pp. 69–86.

Oulios, Miltiadis. *Blackbox Abschiebung: Geschichten und Bilder von Leuten, die gerne geblieben wären.* Suhrkamp, 2013.

Poutrus, Patrice G. "Zuflucht im Nachkriegsdeutschland: Politik und Praxis der Flüchtlingsaufnahme in Bundesrepublik und DDR von den späten 1940er Jahren bis zur Grundgesetzänderung im vereinten Deutschland von 1993." *Handbuch Staat und Migration in Deutschland seit dem 17. Jahrhundert,* edited by Jochen Oltmer, de Gruyter Oldenbourg, 2016, pp. 853–93.

Scherr, Albert. "Across Borders? Flüchtlinge, soziale Bewegungen und Soziale Arbeit." *Soziale Passagen,* vol. 8, no. 2, 2016, pp. 395–403.

Schiffauer, Werner, Anne Eilert, and Marlene Rudloff. *So schaffen wir das—eine Zivilgesellschaft im Aufbruch: 90 wegweisende Projekte mit Geflüchteten.* tran-script, 2017.

Spaich, Herbert. "Demontage eines Grundrechts: Eine Dokumentation." *Asyl bei den Deutschen: Beiträge zu einem gefährdeten Grundrecht,* edited by Herbert Spaich. Rowohlt, 1982, pp. 40–75.

Theis, Horst. "Probleme bei der Verteilung ausländischer Flüchtlinge." *Zeitschrift für Ausländerrecht,* vol. 1, no. 1, 1981, pp. 29–32.

Weber, Max. "Politics as a Vocation." *From Max Weber: Essays in Sociology,* 7th ed., translated, edited and with an introduction by Hans H. Gerth and C. Wright Mills. Routledge & Kegan Paul, 1970, pp. 77–128.

Wipfler, Richard. *Asyl Konkret: Lageralltag als kritisches Lebensereignis.* EXpress Edition, 1986.

Zepf, Bernhard. *Asylrecht ohne "Asylanten"? Flüchtlingshilfe im Spannungsfeld von Weltflüchtlingsproblem und Abschreckungspolitik.* Verlag für interkulturelle Kom-munikation, 1986.

Chapter 13

Contesting Home, Nation, and Beyond

The Digital Space of New Migrants from Post-Gezi Turkey

Mine Gencel Bek

To the memory of Mehmet Fatih Traş, an academic for peace, who committed suicide after being dismissed from his job because of signing the peace petition and following his failed attempts to leave Turkey and migrate to France.

The increasing authoritarianism of Turkey after the 2013 protests in Istanbul's Gezi Park reached its peak following the emergency law declared after the failed military coup on July 15, 2016. The emergency law did not serve to quell so-called military coup organizers as was claimed but rather was used to legitimize suppression of all critical voices. President Tayyip Erdoğan's pressure of one-man rule, supported by his AKP ("Justice and Development Party") regime, has led to the compelled expatriation of many journalists, academics, and artists, who mostly were either dismissed from their jobs and/or faced threats of imprisonment. In addition, a plethora of young professionals do not see their future in Turkey and are leaving the country. This chapter focuses on how this emerging exile culture is mediated in digital space. I will discuss blogs, social media, TV channels, and websites in terms of how online space is being used in transnational settings, what is being contested, and how new affiliations are functionalized. Through analyzing and mapping this emerging culture, we can gain new insights into the heterogeneity of diasporic exile cultures as well as the ways in which dissent is sustained beyond borders.

CONCEPTUALIZING CHALLENGES TO HOME AND NATION IN THE DIGITAL ERA

The relationship between migrants, their diaspora experiences, and digital affordances has been widely discussed in research literature over the past decade. In the introduction to their volume *Diasporas in the New Media Age* (2010), Andoni Alonso and Pedro J. Oiarzabal offer an extensive list of studies that investigate how different migrant groups (Italian, Arab, Indian, Filippino, Haitian, Croatian, Chinese) use online and mobile technologies to communicate, interact, maintain their identity, and enhance political mobilization (cf. 5). Referring to Benedict Anderson's *Imagined Communities* (1991), which discusses the role of the media in constructing the nation as an imagined community and a shared territorial community of nationals by producing homogeneous discourses of identity and culture, Alonso and Oiarzabal argue that a postnational media is created by a new infosphere. National boundaries are transcended, and deterritorialized space or cyberspace is created in this infosphere:

> Thus, information and communication technologies that were once confined to producing national cultures no longer conform to these fixed territorial boundaries. . . . The Internet offers the ability for diasporas to exchange instant factual information regardless of geographical distance and time zones. Again time and space shift meanings; there are no constraints on synchronicity or locality. That is, the Internet offers the possibility to sustain and re-create diasporas as globally imagined communities. (8–9)

Digital diaspora is described by Michel Laguerre as the engagement of diaspora members or immigrant groups outside their homeland in activities related to information technology. Laguerre elaborates that digital diaspora

> uses IT connectivity to participate in virtual networks of contacts for a variety of political, economic, social, religious, and communicational purposes that, for the most part, may concern either the homeland, the host land, or both, including its own trajectory abroad. ("Digital Diaspora" 50)

In this definition, digital diaspora is more than virtual diaspora, with the "interweaving of the virtual and the real in the hybrid production of everyday life in an immigrant enclave" (51). Similarly, Alonso and Oiarzabl define digital diasporas

> as the distinct online networks that diasporic people use to re-create identities, share opportunities, spread their culture, influence homeland and host-land policy, or create debate about common-interest issues by means of electronic devices. Digital diasporas differ from virtual communities and nations because in digital diasporas there are strong ties with real nations before creating or re-creating the digital community. (11)

Another term that opened academic horizons and expanded the debate is Dana Diminescu's "connected migrants," which challenges home and nation-centric political and academic understandings. Karim H. Karim further argues that diasporas are cosmopolitan because of their transnational experiences and imaginaries. However, even in the major scholarly and media debates on multiculturalism this is not acknowledged; these debates tend to "seal" migrants within the borders of the countries to which they relocated, limiting them to a national context in relation to state policy (cf. 12–13). As Janroj Yılmaz Keleş elaborates in *Media, Diaspora and Conflict* (2015), in the digital age migrants can form multiple ties and social connectedness and participate in political and cultural developments in both their "homeland" or "nation" and their settlement country through virtual communities, discussing, creating forums, petitions, and campaigns and developing their transnational political activity and resistance to repression. He cites the virtual political activities of Sri Lankan Tamils, Kurds, Palestinians, Sikhs, and diasporic Iranians and Armenians as examples of this phenomenon (cf. 123–24). The intensity, impact, and range of these activities depend on the extent to which the respective diasporic group is involved in organized politics. Yet this is beyond the scope of this chapter, which will investigate the recent diverse diaspora from Turkey and its digital space.

The studies I have quoted challenge migration literature that follows the mainstream line of nation and home as research units. As Radha S. Hedge underlines in *Mediating Migration*, even though migration is "neither linear nor contained within the nation-state," studies of migration have historically been framed by the centrality of the nation (4). As far as I can see with my background in media and cultural studies, approaching migration as a complex transdisciplinary matter, including using the lens of media and cultural studies, has expanded earlier conceptions. The diaspora and diasporic use of the media do not work in only one direction but rather create dynamic networks among the affiliation groups linked to present and past, sending and receiving societies across national borders. For instance, one study reveals through an analysis of *DiasporaTürk* social media presentations (Gencel Bek and Prieto Blanco, forthcoming) that the Turkishness of early guest workers in Germany is re-mediated in the digital era. Michelle Timmermans' chapter in Karim's volume points out the double edge of the use of diasporic media, showing that diasporic communities, cultures, identities, or media can all be deterritorialized and reterritorialized (cf. 53). The concrete analysis of specific cases can illuminate which edge or edges are at issue, as Morley suggests in *Communications and Mobility* (2017). Before turning to specific cases, I outline a trajectory of migration to Europe from Turkey with a specific focus on new migrants.

MIGRATION FROM "NEW TURKEY"

Keleş categorizes the history of Kurdish and Turkish immigration to Germany into four distinct periods as labor migration, family re-union, refugee migration, and settlement of the second and third generations (cf. 78). One can add a fifth period: The fourfold migration process that started in the 1960s has entered a new phase, especially after Erdoğan's authoritarianism reached its peak in what he calls "new Turkey," in which he uses and forces the whole state apparatus to design and realize his vision of nationhood.

Sociologist Zafer Yılmaz, who himself was forced to flee from Erdoğan's regime, states in a book he published in Turkey and in Turkish in 2018 that the AKP maximizes the interaction of symbols with power politics in "new Turkey." What is dominant in Turkey's symbolic universe—nationalism, statism, Islamism—has been used by the AKP to develop a reactionary, paranoid politics on the basis of the dichotomy of we and they, friends and enemies, through a series of conspiracy theories and the ongoing production of the perception of threats and insecurity. Here the "real" inhabitants of the country are represented as Anatolia's religious, nationalist Sünni Turks (cf. 28–29). Following the extra emergency order in summer 2016 and the annihilation of civil rights in the absence of legal protection, as well as the loss of their employment for political reasons, countless citizens left Turkey legally or illegally. The group is diverse. It includes critical journalists, academics for peace, leftists, trade unionists, Kurdish and Alevi activists, and religious Fethullah "hizmet" community members (who are accused of plotting the military coup). Furthermore, young people fled who were actively involved in the Gezi uprising but lost their hope after the following developments, with the state wielding its extreme forms of violence and power on peaceful demonstrators (or through the "use" of ISIS bombers against peaceful civilians, as the following Suruç and Ankara massacres tragically confirmed). Even young professionals migrated who are not very political but pessimistic about their future in Turkey and want to work and live abroad and/or raise their children in a safer country.

At the end of their book *Leaving This Country* (*Bu Ülkeden Gitmek*) (2018), Gözde Kazaz and H. İlksen Mavituna include an interview with Bekir Ağırdır, coordinator of Konda, a public opinion research and consultancy company. Ağırdır emphasizes that this new migration phase is different from the earlier ones: "They do not only design their future and careers in a different country, but they experience an emotional rupture [kopuş in Turkish] from the future of Turkey" (114).[1] To understand the "new migration" phase, Kazaz and Mavituna interviewed twenty-seven people who decided to leave Turkey; most of them are highly educated, middle-class, and professionals. What is particularly interesting is that many participants wanted neither to label themselves as migrants nor their decision to leave as migration. Perhaps they did not want to carry the emotional burden of this wording. Or they might have wanted to differentiate themselves, the "newcomers," from earlier migrant workers (cf. 90).

The Women's Initiative of Solidarity *Pudupeha* in Berlin carried out research with these "newcomers" (the term the participants used to describe themselves) who came to Berlin after 2015 as a result of directly or indirectly being influenced by Turkey's state policies that are not in accordance with human rights and universal legal principles. According to a questionnaire filled out by 165 people and focus groups containing twenty-six participants during 2018, newcomers are mostly highly educated students or white-collar professionals such as academics, artists, journalists, and engineers. The majority of participants are from Istanbul. The motivations for coming to Germany are worries about the future, political reasons, the desire to live freely, and the need for security. Half of the participants planned their migration, while the other half was forced to leave quickly.

In the remainder of this chapter, I analyze this newcomer diaspora in terms of the digital space the participants use or mediate. Although different migrant groups choose different media to express themselves, mostly discussed in the research literature as consuming media, I look at how "polymedia" (Madinou and Miller) are being used to produce dissent against the autocracy and affinity with members of the diaspora and Turkey.

REPORTING ON TURKEY BEYOND THE BORDERS

Turkish media in Europe are not a new phenomenon: print media in the Turkish language have been available in Europe since the 1960s, transnational media in Turkish and Kurdish since the 1990s. There are the state-controlled nation-building television channel TRT, private commercial TV stations, Islamic nationalist TV, Alevi-oriented TV, left-oriented TV, and Kurdish transnational satellite TV (Keleş). What Kumru Berfin Emre Çetin calls "communicative ethnocide" against Kurdish and Alevi communities and the subsequent transnationalization attempts as a reaction to these policies also deserve to be mentioned here. Even though the origin of these attempts is not completely new, they have gained new shapes and formats in the age of online communication. Satellite TV has been a solution for both Kurdish (i.e., MED TV) and Alevi (Yol TV) communities. In fact, while the Turkish state used the diplomatic channels and obstructed TV channels by interfering with the reception of airwares in Turkey and by interfering beyond the borders, the communities managed to try again in other countries and develop other ways (cf. A. Hassanpour 1998 as quoted by Emre Çetin in the case of MED TV), including broadcasting online and employing technological infrastructure, as Yol TV recently did. We can add to these examples another new initiative, Jin TV (jin means "women" in Kurdish; "Jin, Jiyad, Azadi," that is Women, Life, and Freedom, has been a slogan of Kurdish and "Turkish" [non-nationalist] feminists and peace advocates). Jin TV can be considered ethnic television with its Kurdish focus, but it is also television made by and for women. It was established on International Women's Day, March 8, 2018; it is followed by 8,671 users on Facebook and has 1,728 subscribed users on YouTube.[2] It broadcasts in Kurdish, Turkish, and Arabic. Although the medium being used is not location-specific, the focus is. Content can be "location-oriented," in our cases, mostly Turkey, Kurdistan, or the Middle East.

Turkish news platforms abound in Europe, including *Artı Gerçek*, *Özgürüz*, *Ahval*, and *Boldmedya*. *Artı Gerçek* ("Plus Truth") was established in February 2017. Its Facebook page has 49,835 followers.[3] The language is exclusively Turkish. Its satellite TV, Artı TV, which broadcasts from Cologne, has 24,763 subscribed users.[4] In an interview I conducted during my visits to *Artı Gerçek* in 2017, the editor-in-chief Celal Başlangıç explained the reasons for this choice of venue. Cologne is geographically at the center of Europe, thus enabling easy and relatively economical travel for the experts and commentators to talk on live TV. The early infrastructure arising from the legacy of the existing ethnic Alevi and Kurdish media can be drawn on there. *Artı Gerçek* claims to broadcast without censorship and auto-censorship, advocating truth, democracy, and peace, presenting reliable news with objective language.[5] It declared that those using the language of racism, Islamism, and war will not find a place under its umbrella. News and comment are to be kept separate, but there will be commentary on and analysis of every news item.

Özgürüz ("We Are Free"), coordinated by the exiled journalist Can Dündar, whose journalism is criminalized in Turkey, has been supported by the *Correctiv*-investigative news organization since January 2017 and publishes in two languages, Turkish and German. *Özgürüz* Periscope TV is liked by 11,054,367 people. Facebook shows 80,076 followers. Fourteen thousand users are subscribed on YouTube.[6] Similar to *Artı Gerçek* (and *Ahval* below), *Özgürüz* focuses on liberal journalistic values as principles:

> We will not comment on the news. But we will interpret the news. We will question the meaning behind the news. . . . Most of our experts, our commentators from the world and Turkey, will interpret for us. We will mobilize a basic institution of journalism, which Turkey has lost, to make investigative journalism live. We will give you an opportunity to read from a broad perspective, with deep, comprehensive files. (http://siyasihaber4.org/can-dundarin-sitesi-alman yadan-yayina-basladi-ozguruz/amp)

But while *Artı Gerçek* includes some exiled scholars of peace as producers or commentators, for *Özgürüz* this remains a goal yet to be achieved.[7] In both cases, the issues of the Turkish and Kurdish diaspora in Germany are not as prominent in the news as the critique of AKP and Erdoğan (although in *Artı*

Gerçek, the Kurdish agenda is dominant). Addressing concerns of the Turkish migrants in Germany is another target for *Özgürüz*.[8]

Ahval (this Arabic word translates as "situation" or "event"), established in March 2018, has 103,100 followers on Twitter, 5,174 followers on Facebook, and 4,938 subscribers to the YouTube channel. The "mission statement" is similar to the principles of *Artı Gerçek* and *Özgürüz*. *Ahval* declares democracy, freedom of expression, truth, and editorial independence as its core values, as well as accuracy, fairness, impartiality, transparency, accountability, and diversity. Their mission statement further emphasizes sharing the facts and analyzing them rationally.[9] The editor-in-chief of *Ahval*, Yavuz Baydar, explains the funding of the platform, which creates content in English, Turkish, and Arabic, as Arabic capital that had been in the media business in London for a long time. At first, publication only in English was considered, then the project evolved into an international stage: "It is necessary to explain Turkey with all dimensions to the Arabic world, and thus it is better to publish in at least three key languages" (*Artı Gerçek*, Nov. 1, 2017).

The founders of *Boldmedya*, established in April 2018, describe themselves as exiled journalists. It seems that most of them have previously worked in media sympathetic to the Fethullah Gülen community (boldmedya.com). *Boldmedya* circulates the produced visual content on YouTube to 105,000 subscribed users.[10] Their principles emphasize universal journalism, human rights, and public interest. A total of 2,814 users follow the *Medyabold* Facebook page.[11] *Boldmedya* has 229,600 followers on Twitter.[12] *Bold* carries out journalism with the focus on injustices following the July 15, 2016, military coup, which was, they argue, a scenario staged by the AKP and Erdoğan, not a Gülenist attempt.

What are the challenges or openings these media bring, and what are the limitations? One can easily say that they manage to produce journalism on Turkey outside of Turkey, publishing articles which would be considered transgressive within Turkey. When writing, even very classical liberal news articles can be a reason for so-called "legal" punishments within Turkey, the recently established diasporic news platforms with their internationally visible dissent must be viewed as daring.

How different are their news production and publication compared to mainstream media organizations in Turkey? Currently, the journalists working for these media organizations do precarious labor. They receive very low salaries, work long hours, and have no social security, as the case of Hayko Bağdat, who was working at Özgürüz, revealed.[13] At any rate, the journalists working there have fragile positions; they are mostly not free to go back to Turkey because of the legal threats and do not enjoy secure conditions abroad either. Exploitation of labor also involves the editing and use of existing news from the critical "domestic" media in Turkey, such as *Duvar*,

Diken, Evrensel, or *Jinha,* sometimes without giving the source on the news platforms' websites. Labor exploitation is encouraged by globalization in general. According to Hedge:

> The global flow of and flexible forms of capital accumulation have led to an expansion of precarious forms of labor that include temporary, short-term, and sub-contracted jobs that typically fall outside of forms of state protection (for example, social welfare, insurance, or benefits). At the same time, globalization has also accelerated the increasing erosion of the welfare state, the rise of privatization, and the emphasis on the individual over the collective. (5)

Nonetheless, one should be surprised and question the employment practices of the media organizations at issue since they claim to defend democracy. There is a risk of foregrounding certain journalists as well, as we have seen in the case of Can Dündar. The organizations seldom manage to produce in-depth, investigative reports, being mostly preoccupied with short pieces of news and commentary, which they circulate on social media, especially *Artı Gerçek.* In a way, aiming for high hit and click numbers with "last minute" alarms makes them sensational and superficial. Critical coverage of the right-wing European discourses remains a potential future prospect. The news platforms' circulation of the critical news about Erdoğan's regime can be commended. But at the same time, they amplify his voice as well. Disseminating Erdoğan's declarations and using his image in the news so often unintentionally aggrandizes his power.

SELF-EXPRESSION, SOLIDARITY, AND EMPOWERMENT OF ACADEMICS IN EXILE

"Academics for Peace Germany,"[14] established in October 2017, is an organization of academics who were dismissed from Turkish universities because they had signed the peace petition. They use social media (Facebook and Twitter) to circulate the threats against academic freedom in Turkey to the international community of human rights organizations and civil rights defenders. They also try to build up solidarity among themselves and between the exiles and those academics for peace left in Turkey. The peace academics also raise their voices for others subjected to injustice. The group administratively was formed as an association in Germany, and most of the members are located in Berlin.

Making alliances beyond the citizens of the Turkish nation is the objective of the group called "Off-University," which emerged from Academics for Peace Germany in affiliation with German academics.[15] Off-University aims to create emancipatory forms of teaching and research in cooperation with academics who have been dismissed by anti-democratic regimes in other countries as well as Turkey. On the path to establishing an online university, an online conference on "tough questions about peace" was organized in 2017.[16] Off-University manages to organize online courses, at least for some of the dismissed scholars who are not permitted to give lectures abroad due to international travel ban and "legalized" passport restrictions, and cyberspace meetings for academics and students. The participating scholars are offered a honorarium through different German universities. It is an empowering move materially and symbolically for the academics who are being criminalized and victimized by their respective state governments.

GAK Gurbetteki Akademisyenler[17] (Academics in Gurbet) is a blog page of academics experiencing *gurbet*[18]). The symbol of the blog page is a black crow, and the acronym GAK is the crow's call, "caw" in English. The reference to the cawing of crows invites the blog's readers to assume that the contributions will be disturbing, sharp, and high in volume. But in fact they are not, except for an open collective letter called "Bok" (English: "shit"). It shrilly criticizes masculine power and domination, but most of the entries focus poetically or humorously on the inner world of the authors, their emotions about the enforced mobilization to which they are subjected. Almost every entry has a visual, a photograph, or an image. Music is permitted. The authors contribute anonymously by choosing and explaining a three-letter name. Even the chosen names and explanations show their expressiveness and creativity. Currently, there are fourteen entries for the names and thus fourteen authors. The blog is open to any academic or person connected to academia who is suffering from *gurbet* or feels alienated from his/her homeland and wants to write creatively about the sense of exile. This blog discourages "pure politics" articles and explains the reason for this as such:

> Each of us already has very serious channels for making and writing politics. This is a different place. There is love here, intrigue, tears, inner outpouring, hugging without emojis. There are snapshots, sections and emotions from our lives like a photonovel. (https://gak3harfliler.wordpress.com/hakkinda/)

A piece titled "'*Gurbet*,' '*Sıla*,' and Longing for the Lost and Gone" by Fer includes a link to a song, "Hasret" ("longing"), by a female singer, Sema Moritz.[19] It is an entry about the frustrating experience of being dismissed by decree and not being able to travel to Turkey. The experience of being a newcomer in exile (or perhaps in asylum) is compared with both the early and current life of so-called guest worker migrants and others. The risks of imprisonment, unemployment, and a lack of access to health service and other issues are listed. That is the sad experience of many dismissed public sector workers and criminalized critical intellectuals, academics, and peace advocates at the hands of the brutal regime of the AKP, which decivilized politics (see Gencel Bek 2020). This blog piece by Fer shows that even though the blog page is more about everyday life and emotions, in a broader perspective they are connected to the political economy. The piece continues more affectively:

> [L]onging for the country doesn't go away with the remote communication with the rest. The longing remembers the air, the smell, the passage of the seasons, the dynamics. The street has energy. The smell of pepper fries leaking from the kitchens. The sound of teaspoons from the balconies. Children chirping on the street, returning from the grocery store. . . . Especially the "dismissal thing" is a litmus paper. You have expectations and hope while maintaining a relationship with the barriers of time and space. Yet, no technological means can revive the relationships that end, or even if they do not end, become dry, rickety, lifeless, suspended, unfamiliar. Distance is distance in every sense. In this case, the feeling of longing is much layered and intensified. The hardest is to live the rest of your life knowing that this distance is not just physical and that you will never be as happy as you once were.

As this blog entry shows, the writings can be very subjective, emotional, and melancholic. In a way, this blog provides a safe space where academics experiencing *gurbet* can express themselves freely beyond the boundaries in every sense as they could not do in another platform.

YOUNG COSMOPOLITANS' NOMADIC SPATIALITY AND TEMPORALITY

This section provides two examples of a more nomadic digital diaspora: *Gurbet Veri Bankası* and *Kopuntu*. The first group, through blog and social media pages, brings together more young people and students, not all of whom are politically engaged, while the second group exists in virtual and nonvirtual levels, and has members from a broader age range who are more politically engaged. The common denominator of these two groups is their "cosmopolitan" sensibilities (see Christensen and Janson). In the first group, this is achieved through everyday encountering and intercultural comparison and dialogue; in the second, it is based on a group with more political, academic, or cultural engagements. Different from the group of journalists in my "Reporting on Turkey Beyond the Borders" section, the cosmopolitan bloggers are not only focused on what is happening at the moment in Turkey but are connected more to the international diaspora, and they are more future-oriented. Especially for the first group, *Gurbet Veri Bankası*, their cosmopolitan sensibility has increased through their travel, and their "mind-sets were transformed as a result of being receptive to cultural difference," as Leurs explains the parameter of cosmopolitan belongings of youth in London (43–44). In the second, *Kopuntu*, the cosmopolitan sensibilities seem more the result of political choices. At the same time, they try to communicate with other people from Turkey.

The words of the name of the blog page, *Gurbet Veri Bankası* (Gurbet Data Bank), show the hybrid character of the group. *Gurbet,* as has been explained earlier, is a sad word to express the "expat" experience, used mostly by early "guest" workers. It was often found in popular songs and poems in the 1960s migration phase. "Data" and "bank" imply the newness of being in the digital age as highly educated, highly skilled, professional, but precarious characters. The blog page[20] brings together the experiences of the Turks living abroad because the editor believes that these stories are valuable. The editor of Gurbet Data Bank adds: "If you want to have information on topics such as making a visa application, obtaining a residence permit, writing a reference letter, etc., unfortunately you have the wrong address." Gurbet Data Bank also had a Facebook page followed by 845 people when I started my research in 2018, but the page has been closed down.

Gurbet Veri Bankası starts with Ömer. He used to live in Amman and now is in Oslo. He explains the aim of the blog as follows: "Through shared stories we offer information for the others and also empower people, let them feel that they are not alone. Make our different experiences visible. As long as it is not hate speech, every idea is welcomed." The blog explains the choice of "Türkiyeli" (people of Turkey) rather than the Turks as such: first of all, they value the stories of different people rather than approaching people in an ethno-based sense. Second, the blog prefers stories from people abroad with a link to Turkey rather than those Turks who were born or grew up abroad. Finally, they also want to allocate space for the stories of "foreigners" who have lived in Turkey for a while and can express themselves in the Turkish language.[21] As far as I can see, this last point has not been realized yet.

From January to June 2019, the blog page had forty entries. Countries written from are mostly in the West, including the United States (eight), Germany (six), and the Netherlands (three). The participants' blog pieces include jokes and emojis as well as their photos. It is interesting that more affective words like *gurbet* and *sıla,* recalling early migrant workers, are used as well as the term *expat.* The graphics are mainly outside photos of people in a positive mood, enjoying their difference, identity, and freedom. The bloggers upload photos with friends from the country they live in. As in travel blogs, mainly selfies in cities, nature, happy moments or other daily-life views from the country of residence are shown. Participants are mostly university students

(MA or PhD-seeking), researchers, or white-collar workers. Even though for some, learning the language of the country of residence was the main reason to travel, on the whole, a different life in a different country was chosen. LGBT+ identities are visible. The initiator and moderator of the blog is gay. There is also an LGBT+ activist (Kenan from San Francisco). Many mention that they were active in the Gezi uprising, and some are still engaged in politics through social media. For many, the oppression after Gezi seems to be a major point in their decision to emigrate. There are some critical remarks about the country or the city they live in as well as longing for their friends, networks, and food in Turkey. However, in general, the narratives are based on comparisons that justify people's decisions to leave Turkey; good things in their life now vs. bad things in Turkey dominate the stories. Breathing, confidence, being an individual, happiness, freedom, being a world citizen, a calm and easy life without fighting and violence, and the uncertainty of the future in Turkey are the repeated themes.

"Turkey threw us down, spat, threw us out," says Erkan, who resides in Pittsburgh, and adds: "I do not want injustice or surrender to darkness." This tone sounds similar to the entries on the blog initiative *Kopuntu*. "Kopuntu" is explained on its website[22] as having two different meanings: the first is "diaspora" and the second "a torn piece." This chosen name shows the affective tone of the group. It is described as an interdisciplinary solidarity network among journalists, academics, writers, artists, students. Besides, it is open to "anyone else who claims to be generating ideas and correspondingly has been oppressed, silenced or excluded due to the politics that narrowed production and living space in Turkey." In addition to the website, *Kopuntu* has a Facebook page with 2,000 followers (July 2019). Their manifesto underlines real and organic togetherness regardless of the differences of their backgrounds and experiences. These statements evoke *Gurbetteki Akademisyenler* since being in exile may be a physical as well as psychological experience. In a way, this is another group that cannot be easily categorized as "migrants living abroad." Their identities are more complex:

> We are people who were forced or chose to leave our native soil, due to . . . the psychological and physical oppression of our wish to live together. Or maybe we are those people who did not, could not leave when given a chance. Or we are those people who wake up to an idea of leaving every day.

The following list of cities shows the wide range of political sensitivities. It includes those worried about Kurdish oppression, those protesting miners being killed in accidents, and those contesting environmental destruction, including the extermination of sea turtles: "We are individuals who have gone to Van, Reyhanlı, Soma, Kobani, Sur, Cizre, and Cerattepe, or wanted to be there instinctively." Like the *Gurbet Veri Bankası* participants, *Kopuntu* is open to and respectful of different sexual orientations.

Through *Kopuntu*'s monthly multimedia online magazine (kopuntu.org), different genres of writing, including academic articles, journalistic pieces, critiques, essays, and literary texts in Turkish, English, German, Italian, and Spanish are published. The members organize seminars, art, and multimedia exhibitions, concerts in Europe (so far in Italy, Germany, and Sweden), including talks, exhibitions, screenings, and live performances. *Kopuntu* does not only exist as a digital space but also creates physical spaces, as can be seen in the exhibitions and other public events. It challenges being restricted by the state "verbally, legally, politically, physically, and geographically."[23]

One of their public events was called "Confusion: Home and Hope." Realized in Milan in December 2017, it focused on the experiences of homelessness and constant displacement, and it asked: "Is it possible to create a new sort of diaspora among those who share the same emotions and experiences but not the same space, nationality, language, race or religion" in a search for home and hope and in a mental displacement that is homeless but not rootless? Their statement of "Solidarity, not Solitude!"[24] is more than a motto, as the latest call for a press release in Istanbul to stop deportations of unregistered migrants shows very well.[25]

Besides these, new initiatives targeting specific groups of exiles started to emerge in both physical and digital space. For example, *Puduhepa*, a women's initiative for solidarity in Berlin, was established there in 2018.[26] The Twitter page explains that the participants are women from Turkey who could not find living space in Turkey because of the limitations in their home country and came to Germany to try to start new lives. *Puduhepa* seeks to connect "early" and "new" migrant women. At the time of my writing, its digital space does not have very much content. Another new organization being established in Berlin has the name *Türkiyeli Kültür İnisiyatifi* (Culture Initiative from Turkey); it serves to guide artists on practical matters. However, they do not seem to have a digital space yet, and my questions to the organization to confirm that have remained unanswered.

MOBILITY AND TRANSFORMATION BEYOND THE BORDERS AND BOUNDARIES

This chapter shows that different groups from different ages, genders, and professions continue their lives, identities, and modes of dissent in another land. It contributes to the theoretical and empirical efforts that address and document the heterogeneity and complexity of migrant identity. I am not interested in breaking down this complexity into categories that fit the empirical evidence.[27] "Newcomers" from Turkey are not only migrants but humans with different identities, experiencing inequalities, suffering from or reacting to political agendas, and demonstrating sensitivities. Analyzing their complexity and multiplicity can disclose the migrants' questioning of home, nation, and nationhood and show multiple experiences within migration and mobilization.

A number of the new media participants cited in this chapter avoid using the terms "migration" or "migrant," preferring "mobility." This gives us further reason not to confine the realities within the category or categories of migration. David Morley distinguishes between "sedentarist" and "nomadic" as two contrasting "metaphysics" of mobility while suggesting that that binary has been superseded. It seems that even though the cited examples of exiles are nearer to the nomadic, that category does not "encapsulate" them, even though affective words like *gurbet* are used by these new migrants, similar to the previous migrant workers. These examples are definitely not near to the "sedentarists," whom Morley describes as traditional, conservative, praising authentically "rooted" culture, validating the authenticity and charm of the place of origin (59). They have a problem with that location and use mobility to rid themselves of the limitations of the nation-state they lived in. At the same time, they embrace those who could not move physically but feel alienated because of the same shared concerns. As Madly Simba Boumba states with reference to Stuart Hall's concept of cultural identity as a "dynamic process that involves constant transformation" (Boumba 168), diasporic identity "cannot be understood as an 'either/or' process but as a more inclusive 'and/and' process" (168).

The new migrants (mostly academics, journalists, and artists in exile) try to be visible and express themselves through digital spaces. They aim to connect, memorize, document, resist, and produce beyond the limits of time and space. It is difficult to guess to what extent the newly emerging diasporic culture can contribute to a post-Erdoğan period in the diaspora. The European diaspora, especially in Germany, currently has a strong pro-Erdoğan faction alongside the both old and new exile culture of leftists, Alevis, and Kurds. Besides, the emerging diasporic culture is not all necessarily collective. It can be individualistic, focusing on protecting a free lifestyle in some cases. However, even defending an emancipatory lifestyle has the potential to gain a collective character in the future. The new media platforms developed by academics, writers, and artists in exile have certainly managed to record what is happening and to contest and make dissent virtual and viral, easily dispersed and accessed. The alliances forged beyond home and the nation also have the potential to challenge authoritarian, right-wing populist, and neoliberal politics beyond Turkey, beyond home, and beyond any specific country or nation.

NOTES

1. All translations from Turkish or German texts into English are mine.
2. All the numbers in this chapter for social media followers were updated on July 23, 2019.
3. See https://www.facebook.com/artigercek/.
4. See https://www.youtube.com/channel/UCxVicskgBc8OD66iLKc7Uaw.
5. See https://www.artigercek.com/yolumuz-acik-olsun, Feb. 8, 2017.
6. See https://www.youtube.com/channel/UCacZabSZVnGGq5mVjA5Ccfg.
7. "The scholars who have been kicked out of their universities and have found themselves at the world universities will be an integral part of our team and will show us the 'big picture'" (http://siyasihaber4.org/can-dundarin-sitesi-almanyadan-yayi na-basladi-ozguruz/amp).
8. "We will be the voices of the Turks living in Germany, we will also air their problems and create a discussion ground for solutions. We made an agreement with the best of the German media. We will translate and publish the news and comments they write about Turkey for our readers. Thus, we will allow the Turkish readers to read different interpretations from Germany. Likewise, we will publish the news and comments from the Turkish press in German" (http://siyasihaber4.org/can-dundar in-sitesi-almanyadan-yayina-basladi-ozguruz/amp).
9. See https://ahvalnews.com/mission-statement.
10. See https://www.youtube.com/boldmedya.
11. See https://www.facebook.com/pg/MedyaBold/about/.
12. See https://twitter.com/boldmedya?lang=de.
13. Hayko Bağdat resigned and left *Özgürüz* after what happened to a colleague, who fainted at work. He criticized and narrated this event ironically, suggesting that neither the company they worked for was sensitive to the "workers" they exploited, nor was the German health system sensitive to a migrant patient in this accident (http s://odatv.com/amp/hayko-bagdat-ile-can-dundarin-yollari-ayrildi-1306171200.html).
14. See https://academicsforpeace-germany.org/.
15. See www.off-university.de.
16. See https://off-university.com/en-US/News/Detail/tough-questions-abou t-peace.
17. See https://gak3harfliler.wordpress.com/.
18. *Gurbet* means a foreign land or place; living far away from home, the birth place. This is quite different from less affective words such as abroad, foreign, or expat. *Gurbet* is found often in early folk songs and poems referring to those, espe- cially "guest workers," who live and in fact have to live far away from the homeland in a foreign country (cf. Gencel Bek and Blanco, forthcoming).
19. See https://gak3harfliler.wordpress.com/2018/03/20/gurbet-sila-ve-bitip-yi tene-hasret-fer/. "Sıla" means a place being left, home.
20. See https://gurbetveribankasi.blogspot.de/.
21. See https://yesilgazete.org/blog/2017/06/03/yurtdisinda-yasayan-turkiyelil erin-deneyimlerini-paylasma-noktasi-gurbet-veri-bankasi/.
22. See https://kopuntu.org/hakkimizda/.

23. See the videos at https://www.facebook.com/kopuntunetwork/videos/25683915
1515622/ and https://www.facebook.com/kopuntunetwork/videos/218432582022946/.

24. See https://kopuntu.org/2017/11/28/kopuntu-presents-confusion/.

25. See https://kopuntu.org/2019/07/30/call-for-a-press-release-in-istanbul-to-stop
-deportations-of-unregistered-migrants/.

26. Facebook and Twitter names are @puduhepaberlin, whereas on Instagram the
women's initiative can be found under @puduhepa.berlin.

27. For an example of developing typologies, cf. Hepp et al. (9–14). They develop
three types of appropriation of cultural identity and communicative connectivity as
origin-oriented, world-oriented, and ethno-oriented.

WORKS CITED

Alonso, Andoni, and Pedro J. Oiarzabal. "The Immigrant Worlds' Digital Harbors:
    An Introduction." *Diasporas in the New Media Age: Identity, Politics, and Com-
    munity*, edited by Andoni Alonso and Pedro J. Oiarzabal, University of Nevada
    Press, 2010, pp. 1–18.
Boumba, Madly Simba. "Participative Web 2.0 and Second Generation Congolese
    Youth in Brussels: Social Network Sites, Self-Expression, and Cultural Identity."
    Karim and Al-Rawi, pp. 175–83.
Christensen, Miyase, and André Jansson. *Cosmopolitanism and the Media: Cartog-
    raphies of Change*. Palgrave Macmillan, 2015.
Diminescu, Dana. "The Connected Migrant: An Epistemological Manifesto." *Social
    Science Information*, vol. 47, no. 4, 2008, pp. 565–79.
Emre Çetin, Kumru Berfin. "Communicative Ethnocide and Alevi Television in the
    Turkish Context." *Media, Culture and Society*, vol. 40, no. 7, 2018, pp. 1008–23.
Gencel Bek, Mine. "Collective Myths and Decivilizing Politics in Turkey." *Collec-
    tive Myths and Decivilizing Politics*, edited by Stefan Kramer and Peter Ludes, Lit,
    pp. 142–57, 2020.
———, and Prieto Blanco. "(Be)Longing through Visual Narrative: Mediation of
    (Dis)affect and Formation of Politics through Photographs and Narratives of Migra-
    tion at 'Diasporatürk.'" *International Journal of Cultural Studies*, forthcoming.
Hedge, Radha S. *Mediating Migration*. Polity, 2016.
Hepp, Andreas, Cigdem Bozdağ, and Laura Suna. "Mediatized Migrants: Media
    Cultures and Communicative Networking in the Diaspora." *Migrations, Diaspora,
    and Information Technology in Global Societies*, edited by Leopoldina Fortunati
    et al., Routledge, 2012. pp. 172–88.
Karim, Karim H. "Migration, Diaspora and Communication." Karim and Al-Rawi,
    pp. 1–23.
———, and Ahmed Al-Rawi, editors. *Diaspora and Media in Europe: Migration,
    Identity and Integration*. Palgrave Macmillan, 2018.
Kazaz, Gözde, and H. İlksen Mavituna. *Bu Ülkeden Gitmek*. Metropolis, 2018.
Keleş, Janroj Yılmaz. *Media, Diaspora and Conflict*. I.B. Tauris, 2015.

Laguerre, Michel S. *The Digital City: The American Metropolis and Information Technology*. Palgrave Macmillan, 2005.

———. "Digital Diaspora: Definition and Models." *Diasporas in the New Media Age: Identity, Politics, and Community*, edited by Andoni Alonso and Pedro J. Oiarzabal, University of Nevada Press, 2010, pp. 49–64.

Leurs, Koen. "Young Connected Migrants: Remaking Europe from Below through Encapsulation and Cosmopolitanisation." Karim and Al-Rawi, pp. 25–49.

Madianou, Mirca, and Daniel Miller. *Migration and New Media: Transnational Families and Polymedia*. Routledge, 2011.

Morley, David. *Communications and Mobility: The Migrant, the Mobile Phone, and the Container Box*. Wiley-Blackwell, 2017.

Timmermans, Michelle. "Media Use by Syrians in Sweden: Media Consumption, Identity, and Integration." Karim and Al-Rawi, pp. 51–70.

Yılmaz, Zafer. *Yeni Türkiye'nin Ruhu: Hınç, Tahakküm, Muhtaçlaştırma*. İletişim, 2018.

Chapter 14

Religion, Family, Community, Difference

Immigrant Millennials in Cologne, Germany

Aprilfaye T. Manalang

Germany has taken in a record number of Syrian as well as other refugees in the past several years, adding to the already large population of migrant-descended residents and citizens. The country is now among the major immigrant nations in the world, and, more than ever before, religious pluralism is part of its social reality. According to the Pew Research Center, while Muslims comprised 4.9 percent of Europe's population, they accounted for approximately 6.1 percent of the population in Germany (2017). Moreover, the Pew Research Center also notes that between mid-2010 and mid-2016, Germany accepted roughly 670,000 refugees, about 86 percent of whom are Muslims (2017). In 2018, the overall number of refugees (*Schutzsuchende*) living in Germany was 1,781,750 (see Landeszentrale).

With the makeup of Germany's population changing because of recent immigration, debates about the religion of immigrants and their ability to integrate into German society are at the center of public discourse, and they are becoming a more significant factor of social analysis as well. According to religious studies scholar Diana Eck, "even humanists, even secularists, even atheists have to rethink their worldviews in the context of a more complex religious reality" (*New Religious* 9). This chapter addresses the nexus of immigration and religion by presenting results from a two-year study conducted at Berufskolleg Ehrenfeld (BKE), a highly diverse vocational school in one of Germany's most diverse cities in one of the most diverse states.[1] Cologne, one of the largest cities in Germany, ranks fifth (34.2 percent) with respect to "people who themselves or who have at least one parent who were born without German citizenship" (see "Data Report"), while North Rhine-Westphalia is the German state with the largest number of inhabitants with a migratory background (*Migrationshintergrund*).[2] The chapter explores the range from religiosity to unbelief among migrant millennials as well as among millennials of migrant background (second and third generation). It examines specifically how integration impacts their family dynamics as they navigate life in one of the more secular countries in the world. Our aim is to shed light on the question of how Germany will handle its new religious diversity by providing a greater understanding of the religious views and dispositions of young immigrants. This transnational comparative framework takes a deep interest in two of the most industrialized countries in the world: United States and Germany. The research considers how millennials navigate these respective countries in contrasting social milieus: Germany, the largest immigrant-receiving nation in Europe; and the United States, one of the world's most ethnically and religiously diverse industrialized countries.[3]

Through extensive in-depth personal and focus-group interviews, the chapter seeks to answer the following question: How do the millennial immigrants at BKE negotiate family, community, and difference with regard to their host nation? Exploring the role of religion in these students' lives can offer clues about transnational family and kinship models. It can also illuminate reasons for the persistent educational inequality among immigrants and their attainment of high school/college degrees as well as clarify processes of educational, civic, and political integration.

MIGRANTS AND RELIGION: LITERATURE REVIEW

With respect to the United States, previous social scientific research has focused on religion and its prosocial effects on immigrants and communities of color at large.[4] For instance, sociologists of religion have taken a keen interest in the role of religion in American adolescents' lives. Christian Smith and Melinda Lundquist Denton, drawing from the National Study of Youth and Religion, develop a scholarly and public understanding of the spiritual and religious lives of American teenagers in their book *Soul Searching* (2005), which was the first to explore teenage religiosity on a national level. Researchers have found that religiously involved youth are more likely than nonreligious youth to volunteer and participate in community service (see Youniss and McLellan; Youniss and Yates). Religion helps youth develop analytical and interpersonal skills, known as developmental assets (see Wagener et al.). Other data seem to indicate that religiously involved teens are generally better off than nonreligious teens. For instance, Catholic, inner-city, and minority youth benefit, oftentimes greatly, from religious involvement when compared with nonreligious youth who attend nonparochial, public schools (see Schneider et al.). Overall, religious attendance positively correlates with informal prosocial activities like giving money, helping, and giving advice to family, friends, and neighbors; and on a civic level, attending public meetings, political engagement, volunteering, and charitable giving (see Lewis, MacGregor, and Putnam). While teenage religious involvement seems to produce positive developmental outcomes and encourage prosocial behavior, there is scarce research that considers how and in what capacity immigrants understand and frame the range of their religiosity, and subsequently, how religion impacts their respective host nations with respect to family, community, and difference.

In contrast, current burgeoning research on religion and religious affiliation with regard to migrants and the population in general explores the range from religiosity to unbelief. For instance, scholars have investigated notions of "believing without belonging" (see Davie; Smith et al.), with a special interest in millennials because, overall in the US population, there is a marked rise in religious disaffiliation: 20 percent of American adults are now categorized as religious "nones," or report having no formal religious ties. Moreover, one in three are millennial, or under thirty years old (see Funk and Smith). More than any other time in United States history, this generation is the largest group of young Americans who have formally disaffiliated from church. In contrast to the United States, in Germany, the overwhelming majority of Germans do not attend church. In fact, especially in the Eastern states, the trend of religious decline has persisted since the dissolution of the German Democratic Republic in 1989 (see Pollack and Rosta). Broadly speaking, according to the Association of Religion Data Archives, more than one-quarter of Germans report they are not religious, including atheists: 26.6 percent. Note that this is more than those affiliating as Protestants (21 percent), and nearly as many as those identifying as Catholics (30.2 percent) ("Germany"). Despite the 20 percent of the US population identifying as religious "nones," American adults, both unaffiliated and Christian, are significantly more religious than their European counterparts, according to the Pew Research Center's 2014 Landscape Study in the United States and a 2017 survey of Western Europeans. For example, only 9 percent of Germans pray daily, in contrast to two-thirds of Americans (68 percent) who engage in this ritual. Interestingly, immigrant millennials in Germany actively pray and report on the value of prayer, according to the findings in our study.

Research on the role that religion plays in conceptions of race/ethnicity has also garnered tremendous interest among scholars (see Frederick; McRoberts; Park), as has its significance for immigrant communities (see Cadge and Ecklund; Ebaugh and Chafetz; Galvez; Leal et al.; Manalang, "Religion"; Manalang, "Role"; Mora; Numrich and Kniss; Orsi; Stepick et al.; Yang and Ebaugh). Even though many social scientists have explored the complex relationship between religion and race/ethnicity, less is known about the children of immigrants and how the relationship impacts their lives in a Western European setting. This chapter addresses this blind spot.

Others have investigated the connections among religion, civic engagement, and politics (see Bakalian and Bozorgmehr; Ecklund and Park, "Asian"; Ecklund and Park, "Religious"; Gonzalez; Kurien; Manalang, "Religion"; Manalang, "Role"; Stepick et al.). For instance, research by Bakalian and Bozorgmehr illustrates that the events of 9/11 have caused aggressive societal and governmental responses against Muslim American and Middle Eastern communities in the United States. To redress this issue, Bakalian and Bozorgmehr report that several Muslim American organizations have formed to mediate between their constituents and the greater society. In Germany, this mediation has been channeled in part through the Deutsche Islam-Konferenz, an ongoing series of conferences initiated in 2006 by the then-federal minister of the interior Wolfgang Schäuble, whose purpose is to facilitate the integration of the Muslim population into mainstream German society and foster the dialogue between the German government and Muslim representatives.[5] Essentially, when targeted groups like Muslim immigrants experience backlash, they mobilize and engage in civil and political community-based movements that ideally lead to greater integration of out-groups or minorities (see Bakalian and Bozorgmehr). In the European context, the research on religion, civic engagement, and politics often focuses on the older generation of immigrants rather than the children of immigrants, or millennials. Few studies have directly engaged young immigrants in Germany using qualitative methods such as in-depth interviews.[6] Therefore, by speaking directly with students, our study offers new insights into the role that religion plays in the lives of immigrant millennials in Germany.

Overall, the United States is considered the most religious industrialized country in the world. More specifically, in *A New Religious America* (2001), Eck argues that the United States is the most religiously diverse country worldwide. Considering the social and demographic relevance that religion has in the United States, the departure from religion among millennials is a striking development. This finding, to some extent, also applies to millennials of color, though even less is known about them in the European context, in this case Germany. Globally, there is a huge lacuna in studies on unbelief among communities of color. This study addresses this gap in the literature. Since Germany is the second-most popular migration destination nation in the world after the United States (cf. Brown and James), we argue that it is important to explore the role of religion among immigrant millennials in Germany. This research is especially significant since, while immigrants tend to come from highly religious families, Germany is a country that is largely atheistic. For instance, sociologist Peter L. Berger has stated that Berlin, the capital and biggest city in Germany, is "the world capital of atheism" (195).

IN-DEPTH INTERVIEWS: METHODS AND FINDINGS

Our study investigates the role of religion and its influence on immigrant millennials' integration in BKE, where over 90 percent of students have an immigrant background. BKE is a vocational school with first-, second-, and third-generation immigrants from a range of nations. Because of this diversity, BKE is an excellent location in which to conduct this research. Students have emigrated from a remarkable range of countries, including Azerbaijan, Bosnia, the Congo, Ethiopia, Greece, India, Iraq, Italy, Jordan, Kazakhstan, Peru, Syria, and Turkey. Moreover, broadly speaking, it is also meaningful to research immigrant millennials in the school setting because this is the place where we will see the effects of new immigration the most. With respect to immigrants, Diana Eck states: "They're speaking many different languages and bringing to school with them many different religious backgrounds" (Abernathy).

In the summers of 2017 and 2018, we recruited students via the snowball sampling method[7] and conducted thirty-three in-depth interviews and five focus-group interviews on the following themes: Social Networks, Religion and Integration, Religion, Religion and Homosexuality, Religion and Apprenticeship. Students ranged in age from seventeen to twenty-three years. Thirteen interviewees reported that they were born outside Germany, while sixteen stated that they were born in Germany. The interviewees were immigrants or came from families who immigrated to Germany.

Half of all the immigrant millennials (fifteen) reported that they are personally religious; ten shared that they are not religious; eight labeled themselves "spiritual." Two-thirds of immigrant millennials reported that they come from "religious homes." Five said that they come from spiritual homes, and seven reported that they did not come from religious homes. Less than half of the immigrant millennials interviewed attend services regularly (thirteen). About half do not attend church or mosque regularly (fifteen), though nearly all millennials in this study attend services occasionally due to familial, cultural, or social ties with friends. The remaining (two) told us that they want to attend services but that there was no church or mosque available in their vicinity or conflicts in their work schedule prevented attendance.

PRORELIGION VIEWS AND
COMMUNITY CONNECTIONS

Two main themes emerged across our interviews with the German immigrant millennials: (1) whether or not they attend services regularly, German immigrant millennials largely report proreligion views, and (2) with respect to community, religion plays a vital role in connecting these millennials with their families and friends. We should note that even immigrant millennials who reported that they were nonreligious reported proreligion views. In other words, most immigrant millennials believe religion is important to them, even if they do not attend services. There are three main reasons why they believe that religion is important, regardless of attendance or non-attendance: (1) the value of moral guidance; (2) a sense of comfort; and (3) the importance of prayer.

Moral Guidance

Immigrant millennials report that moral guidance is of vital importance to them relating to religion. One immigrant millennial, born in India, shares the following: "I could do without [religion], but there are rules and rules are important. I do not believe in my religion very much. I'm a believer, but I only believe in the good stuff."[8] This young man does not regularly attend services but defers to the rules of his religion for their uplifting moral guidance. Believing only in the "good stuff" probably makes adherence to "the rules" selective; regulations that conform to the social requirements of his diasporic home and his peer community can also provide convenient guidelines. When asked what he thinks about religion, another immigrant millennial, who was born in Iraq, responded: "It is important to believe in something, that you have a goal or something you can hold on to." Although this millennial does not regularly attend church, he expressed that it is important to have a "goal," that is, some type of framework or moral guidance by which to live one's life.

Immigrant millennials report not only that religion morally guides their lives, but also that religion shapes their sense of self. One Turkish immigrant millennial (born in Turkey) explained that religion centers her identity: "Religion is something important. Through my religion I know who I am and without religion you are lost." Religion therefore has a significant influence on the speaker's sense of identity, directly shaping who she is and how she wants to live. In addition, a first-generation Turkish German millennial claimed that religious knowledge provides personal awareness:

> Without religion one cannot know one's direction. In my religion, I am satisfied, and want to know more about this religion and to learn more about God by reading. There are different books and different directions. The Imams teach you about it and that strengthens your consciousness and it strengthens your faith when you get to know it properly. Then you know all the directions and you can give good answers to all questions.

Religion guides this student; it provides "direction" and "strengthens [her] consciousness," ensuring the believer that she will "know all the directions and . . . can give good answers to all questions." An interesting point here is that the speaker does not make a dogmatic point, which complicates common stereotypes about Islam in Germany. The Imams inform their followers about "different books and different directions" but do not indoctrinate them by enforcing a single correct direction. They rather support the believers in a process of becoming aware of "all the directions" and equip their followers with the knowledge necessary to find "good answers" to all the questions they may have.

Comfort

Religion also provides a sense of comfort for millennial immigrants, even if they are not particularly religious: although this young Turkish German woman (born in Germany) left the mosque[9] at age ten and identifies as only a "little religious," she is searching for the comfort religion can provide:

> I believe when I was ten, my family was strictly religious, and it was forced upon me to study Islam, and I don't really know myself which way I want to go, because I'm also very interested in Christianity, that's the thing. That's what I've been trying to find these last years, which way is mine out of all the ways. If it's Islam or Christianity or Judaism, I just don't know and that's why. Let's see what time has to offer . . . I'm looking to find my individual path, which religion I want to be a part of, whether I want to be a part of any religion at all.

Although skeptical, this Turkish German millennial has not completely abandoned religion. She is seeking her "individual path" and differentiates between her religiosity and that of her family. Although she may ultimately turn away from institutional religion, she is still open to finding a religious track, or to seek "which way is [hers] out of all the ways."[10] She elaborates:

> Well, for me, religion is not that important. I could also live without religion, but somewhere I am looking for stability, something to make me feel at ease. And that is why I am looking for the right religion for myself, one that makes me happy, that calms me down. For example, when I visit the mosque, then nevertheless I have this hate inside of me, when I might have argued with my mother or something (laughs)—hasn't happened often, but when I then go into Dschami [Also known as *Jumu'ah or* Friday Prayer or Congregational Prayer, Muslims pray on Fridays in the afternoon at their mosques], then I sometimes still feel hate, but when I visit the church, after I argued with my mother, then not at all. I'm looking for that what makes me feel more at ease. . . . When I walk into the church, then everything inside me is, um, much calmer, I don't know.

This interviewee shares that even if she is only a "little religious," she feels that when she visits church "everything inside [her] is . . . much calmer."

This sentiment suggests that the church brings her comfort. Ultimately, while she may have conflicted feelings about religion, she is nevertheless seeking a religion that provides comfort and puts her "at ease." This Turkish German millennial initially left the church because she felt pressure from her uncles to be religious and therefore felt unable to decide on her own "path." Subsequently, she distanced herself from her family, and with the support of her mother, she aims to "find [her] individual path, which religion [she] want[s] to be part of, or whether [she] want[s] to be part of any religion at all."

A nineteen-year-old immigrant millennial from Egypt also spoke of religion as creating comfort in his life:

> It's about having a good bond with God. You tell what's on your mind, so you'll be happier later. I feel better then. It does not mean that all problems are gone when you step out the church. That also has to do with the person you are. You have to feel good and not mess up.

Although fully aware that his relationship with God does not mean that "all problems are gone when you step out of church," this "good bond" with God helps this Egyptian millennial to be "happier" and to "feel better." This bond is particularly powerful because it allows the speaker to unburden his mind, to confide to a higher authority what he may not be able to share with others, either from his religious community or outside of it. Religion therefore provides comfort through a sense of having someone to talk to beyond the sphere of cross-cultural and cross-linguistic communication between immigrant and host nation.

A deeply religious Turkish German millennial (born in Germany) described her beliefs as follows:

> My faith is everything to me. I think that's right. I think that's logical. Some people say that religion is not right. I can accept that opinion, but I personally think it is logical. I don't think anything happened by accident and that there is a more powerful person who puts everything in order. I can't even imagine that you just disappear after your death. I believe that our Souls still exist after death. When I think of God or of our prophets, I have such warmth in my heart. I'm just fine, and I realize I'm getting better.

Not only is her faith "everything" to her, she feels "warmth" in her "heart" when she thinks of God, and she realizes she is "getting better." Reflecting on this statement (and others cited in this chapter), it is striking how closely the students' thoughts on religion match the experience of being an immigrant. Finding one's own path in life vis-à-vis the expectations of others, feeling lost or fearing loss vs. sensing comfort or looking for warmth, the belief that things must happen for a reason and that there is a larger order or that someone is protecting you—all of these elements described as part of the speakers' religious life could just as easily be taken as reflections on their status as immigrants or children of immigrants. Overall, it appears that religion serves as a major source of comfort in the face of existential insecurity. An immigrant from Bosnia shared that the most important part about her religiosity is

> that someone is protecting us. I had a lot of bad things happening in my life and then sometimes wondered if there really is a God. I am fine now, and I thanked God for giving me the strength. . . . That you have something to hold on to. If you're not doing well, you know there's someone looking after you.

Facing adversity, she thanks God for giving her "strength" and takes comfort in knowing that "there's someone looking after you." God gives this young Bosnian woman the "strength" or resilience to deal with the "bad things" in her life. She feels that God protects her and gives her "something to hold on to," and she subsequently feels deeper existential security from the "bad things" that she cannot control or prevent in her life.

An Italian German (born in Germany) millennial had a similar perspective. When asked about what the most important component of his faith was, he responded: "That you have something to hold on to. If you're not doing well, you know there's someone looking after you." There is comfort that comes from "someone looking after you," someone who provides stability and security for people whose lives have been marked by heightened degrees of instability and insecurity.

A Peruvian millennial also stressed how important religion is and how it brings hope:

> I think that religion is something beautiful and important. People draw hope from religion and it is something that gives them some security. Many people say that religion is an illusion, but I cannot agree. I think that there is something higher, perhaps that is due to my culture. I come from the Andes in Peru and they believe in many mystical things that are not scientifically explainable and I believe in it. I think that religions are right in a way and there is hope and security.

For this Peruvian millennial, religion is "beautiful and important," and "people draw hope from religion" as it gives people "security." While he broadly supports religion, his spiritualty is not beholden to one specific religion but directly connects to Peruvian mysticism.

Prayer affords a direct connection to God that provides immigrant millennials with a consistent source of comfort. For example, a Turkish German female millennial (born in Germany) shared that the most important part of religion is "daily prayers." When asked what prayer does for her, she reported "safety and security." Prayer provides a sense of existential security for this young woman. This "strength" suggests that religion may help immigrant millennials develop resilience for the challenges they face in their host nation. They grapple with reconciling their often highly religious homes with, in this case, a largely secular society; language barriers; discrimination; in many cases, economic hardship; adjusting to the cultural milieu of the host society; disparate family relations; and negotiating a coherent sense of identity. Interviewees even shared that they struggled with their sexuality as they negotiated between their religious and conservative homes vis-à-vis Germany. Moreover, for some immigrant millennials, their transient status as refugees serves as an additional challenge regarding citizenship and nationality.

Many interviewees echoed the sentiment that prayer is the most important part of religion. This finding is discussed in greater detail in the following section.

Prayer

Even if millennials do not attend church or mosque regularly, they still see prayer as a significant part of their lives. Not only is prayer an important ritual practice among immigrant millennials who attend or do not attend services, interviews suggest that it might even be the most important aspect of their religion. For instance, when asked what the most important aspect of their religious practice is, one young woman who regularly attends church noted: "when you pray, it is beautiful." Another young woman who is also a regular churchgoer stated: "I pray every night. That's the most important thing." When asked if she believes in God, another Turkish millennial responded: "It is so difficult to ask that (laughs). On the one hand, yes, on the other hand, no, because there are no tangible pieces of evidence that He exists, but on the one hand if I feel bad and then say a prayer, which I seldom do (laughs), then I do actually feel better somehow." Despite this ambivalent response, prayer plays a significant role in her life because when she feels "bad" and "then say[s] a prayer," she "actually feel[s] better somehow." Prayer connects her to God and is arguably one of the most important aspects of her faith. In that sense, a personal relationship with God or Allah is more important than religious affiliation per se. This personal relationship is strengthened through prayer to God or Allah. One could infer that spirituality is more important than religiosity in general since immigrant millennials tended to reveal that fostering a direct connection to God via prayer, rather than religion per se, is an important aspect of their identity.

A female Turkish German millennial (born in Germany) who is also religious told us that prayer is the most important aspect of her religion: "Prayer is something between God and yourself and there you have a consciousness between God and yourself, and that feels good because you are not alone. You know he always listens to your words. God is merciful, and you know that your prayers are answered." She emphasizes the intimacy and connectedness she feels with God because "prayer is something between God and yourself." Through prayer, this connectedness reminds her that she is not "alone" because God "always listens to your words." She also reports the efficacy of prayer, noting that "your prayers are answered." When asked what the most important aspect of her religiosity is, she responded:

> You pray five times a day to be liberated from sin. So, you cannot be a bad person, because you speak to God in these prayers. These prayers are also spoken so that you don't lose your path and stay with God and, if you mourn, you can ask for help. You're never alone. You know that you can always speak to God. One should not expect this from others, but be directed to God. The evening prayers will be answered by him. Everything has a purpose.

Prayer is an essential aspect that connects her to God, who liberates her "from sin." Prayer morally guides her so that she is not a "bad person." Prayer assists this female Turkish German millennial so that she does not "lose [her] path and stay[s] with God." Coming from a person with a migratory background, this statement implies that you can take your relationship with God with you, that it translates part of an earlier self (for first-generation immigrants) into the new environment or allows the speaker to retain a sense of a family/cultural tradition beyond the culture of the host nation.

She went on to share a particularly personal aspect of her religious development:

> During the time when I did not pray much I was not a good person. I was bad, and I really didn't care. I lied a lot. When I started praying and realizing that this is an important point, I noticed that my behavior changed. I paid more attention to not hurting other people. That I lie less or not lie at all. I test myself now after each day and see if everything has gone well and whether I have crossed any limits of my religion. That I pay more attention to good deeds, instead of doing bad deeds, and that I leave the bad deeds behind me.

This Turkish German female millennial attributes being a good person to her strong prayers. She realizes that due to prayer, "[she] pay[s] more attention to good deeds, instead of doing bad deeds, and that [she leaves] the bad deeds behind [her]." She recalls that when she "did not pray as much [she] was not a good person." Due to her prayers, her behavior "changed," she feels more empathetic for the suffering of other people, and she "lie[s] less or not at all."

Group Ties

The second common theme in our interview findings involved family and group ties fostered through religion. Immigrant millennials find that church or mosque is an important place to preserve community: their family and friends connect through their religious communities, and their culture is strongly expressed through religion. For instance, one young immigrant from Greece, who grew up in a Protestant church and attends church regularly, maintains that "faith means hope; it brings people together." Another woman (born in Germany), who also attends mosque regularly (weekly), found that one of the most important aspects of being involved in a religious community is that "one is accepted and not excluded." Moreover, she reports about her religious community: "You don't feel marginalized there. . . . I feel very accepted and not excluded or so. We in Islam say we are all siblings, brothers and sisters." In other words, in her Muslim community, this young woman feels a sense of personal connection rather than alienation and marginalization. She feels a sense of inclusivity within her religious community when she describes the relationship among its members as family-like, as "siblings, brothers and sisters." When she says that she does not "feel marginalized" in this family of like-mined people, she suggests that she feels more so outside of her Muslim community. It is plausible that she feels alienated as a religious immigrant in Germany. Another woman, who is an Ethiopian German Christian (born in Germany), regularly attends church, reports a similar feeling. Asked why she attends church, she replied: "Because it is beautiful, and you find joy. You meet people from your own country and that's just beautiful." This young woman enjoys being among her co-ethnic peers. What she especially likes about her faith is "being together." Like her, many immigrant millennials deeply value community and a sense of togetherness. Being part of a religious community is "beautiful" and offers a place where immigrant millennials can feel included, rather than excluded.

Another student, when asked why she attends church, responded: "Because of my friends. My parents have never forced me into anything and my circle of friends is religious. If there is a group, it is more fun." When asked what she likes about her faith, she noted: "Being together. We debate about what the Christian faith is and what it stands for." For this young girl, attending church enables friendships and pleasurable encounters, which, in turn, strengthens her religiosity.

Expressing how it feels to be part of a religious community, a female Turkish German millennial noted:

> A nice feeling. You are not alone, you have those people around you who all have the same faith. You can exchange thoughts and never be lonely; even if I live in this [German] culture, I can talk to others about religion. You can get to know other religions and exchange information.

The value of connectedness expressed in these sentiments is reinforced when the woman talks about the role of religion in her life: "To be able to live your religion is a nice thing and it is also nice to see what your friends do for God." The religious actions of her peers become an important part of her own application of her religious beliefs.

A Greek German millennial (born in Germany) suggested similar ideas about religious bonding: "Faith means hope, it brings people together and it's just part of my life. I think there's something above us. You always find the connection to it somewhere." Religion supports a sense of community and togetherness, and it provides a broader "connection" between the daily lives of immigrant millennials and to God.

MIGRANT RELIGION AND A SENSE OF BELONGING: CONCLUSION

Our main research question asks how millennial immigrants negotiate family, community, and difference vis-à-vis their host nation. What we have found was that they value their ethnic communities, which tend to be religious.[11] Millennials who have immigrated to Germany negotiate family, community, and difference by finding value in and connecting with their respective religious and ethnic communities, rather than in connecting with German culture and society at large. Even if millennial immigrants are not necessarily religious, community, family, and culture play a major role in their lives, which explains why the students still value religious community. In other words, even if they are not personally religious, these millennials still recognize and acknowledge religion as an important part of family and community in Germany. With respect to proreligion views, German immigrant millennials believe in prayer, which they find more important than participation in religious rites. Prayer serves as a form of existential security and a sense that someone is "looking out" for them. In addition, religion provides moral guidance, a sense of "rules" and identity as well as a guide to conducting themselves in daily life, both inside and outside their religious communities. One example that illustrates the way religion guides immigrant millennials and helps them navigate daily moral dilemmas is, according to one interviewee, the adherence to telling the truth in all situations. Immigrant millennials report that they connect to their religious communities to foster and nurture their friendships and families. Moreover, they report that within their religious communities—perhaps in contrast to their position in the society at large—they feel "very accepted" and not "excluded."

Religion also serves as a major source of "comfort" or "security." Since immigrant millennials often find their friends and kin within their respective religious communities, they enjoy the feeling of community and "acceptance."

Because immigrant millennials are a young, vulnerable population, religious communities serve as a protective factor against social and economic marginalization and discrimination. Even when immigrant millennials report that they are skeptical of their faith in God or even of their religious communities, they do express that they feel "comfort" when they are in their respective religious communities. They are unable to fully articulate why they feel so—but they do report this sense of "comfort" regardless.

Our research suggests that many immigrant millennials value a relationship with God or Allah. Whether or not they attend church or mosque, they value this personal connection via prayer to cope with existential insecurity. Many of the immigrant millennials we interviewed value community. Since immigrants tend to come from religious families, immigrant millennials recognize that part of connecting to their family and co-ethnic peers means connecting to their respective religious communities. Even though Germany is among the most atheistic countries in the world, religion appears to play a vital social role in the lives of German immigrant millennials. Religiously involved immigrant millennials report that religion helps them negotiate family, community, and difference: prayer helps guide them morally in their daily lives and lends a sense of identity. Religious communities also provide a safe "space" to feel included rather than excluded. This finding suggests that outside their respective religious communities, or secular spaces, they may feel socially excluded and uncomfortable.

With respect to religion and family, immigrant millennials navigate a complex social landscape given that they tend to come from highly religious families; they also navigate a highly secular host nation, in this case Germany. Therefore, although the students interviewed may not necessarily be as religious as their parents or siblings, overall they still largely report prosocial religious views. In other words, immigrant millennials may not even necessarily wholeheartedly possess a deep faith in the theology or metaphysical reality related to their religion, or the social structure of their religious communities. As stated earlier, one immigrant millennial reported a highly ambivalent belief in God, "because there are no tangible pieces of evidence that He exists." Yet, when this respective immigrant millennial prayed, she reported that she felt better. Therefore, the apparent dichotomy of being unsure that God "exists" while still believing in prayer is an intriguing sacred space that some immigrant millennials occupy. Moreover, just because they believe in God does not necessarily mean they also value church or mosque, or church or mosque attendance specifically. This research leads to the compelling question of how generation plays a role with respect to religiosity, and specifically, the intergenerational transmission of religion among immigrant communities. While I have shown that the general differences within immigrant groups lead to friction with respect to the intergenerational transmission of religion, more research is needed to explore this complicated dynamic (see Manalang, "Mostly").

Thus, while they might not necessarily attend services, they still largely believe in God and in the specific value of prayer as a ritual practice that helps them guide their daily lives. Overall, whether immigrant millennials attend church or mosque, they largely express prosocial religious views. These prosocial religious views stem from a deep sense of comfort they report from their "personal relationship with God," strengthened by their "connection" via "prayer," which in turn provides a deep sense of existential comfort in their everyday lives. Moreover, they feel a sense of belonging in their religious communities, since members of their families and their friends attend church or mosque.

Further research should continue to explore how immigrant millennials navigate and negotiate secular spaces through religious community, as well as the unique challenges they face as they attempt to integrate into the host nation. For instance, how do immigrant millennials handle possible discrimination due to their religiosity? One way to infer social acceptance, as opposed to discrimination, is to measure one's comfort with familial proximity. According to the Pew Research Center, over one-third (33 percent) of Germans reported that they would not accept Muslims in their family, though over two-thirds of Germans reported that they would be willing to accept Jews as members of their family (see Diamant). How might religious difference impact immigrant millennials' ability to integrate in Germany? How will their religiosity with regard to a secular society like Germany impact their sense of identity? Finally, how will their religiosity impact their understanding of what it means to be a citizen in the twenty-first century?

Researchers should investigate more closely the intergenerational transmission of religious beliefs among immigrants, intergenerational tension between the children of immigrants and their parents, especially as it relates to religion, and how religion affects civic engagement and political activism. Does religion serve as a basis for empowerment among immigrant millennials? If so, how and in what ways? The project group's forthcoming papers intend to help address these questions.

NOTES

1. This research study is a transnational collaboration among Daniel Stein (University of Siegen), Page Laws and April Manalang (Norfolk State University), and Britta Mölders (Berufskolleg Ehrenfeld, Cologne).

2. Preceding Cologne are the following cities and their percentages of people who are themselves or who have at least one parent born without German citizenship:

Frankfurt am Main (45.3); Stuttgart (40.9); Munich (39.4); Düsseldorf (35.9). According to statista.com, a little over 5 million people claimed a migratory background in North Rhine-Westphalia in 2017 (https://de.statista.com/statistik/daten/stud ie/501577/umfrage/bevoelkerung-mit-migrationshintergrund-in-den-bundeslaend ern-nach-herkunft/).

3. We are conducting a replicate study in the United States that explores the range of religiosity to unbelief among minority millennials. Since it is outside the scope of this paper, we do not explicitly analyze similarities and differences between German and American millennials. See https://research.kent.ac.uk/understandingunbelief/ research/early-career-research-projects/minority-millennials-and-the-rise-of-religiou s-nones-a-comparative-analysis/.

4. For this purpose of this paper, we define "prosocial" as altruism, trust, cooperation, charitable giving, helping, and volunteering.

5. Similar to the United States, Muslims living in Germany are represented by a number of associations, including Zentralrat der Muslime in Deutschland, Verband der Islamischen Kulturzentren, and Islamrat der Bundesrepublik Deutschland.

6. Natarajan focuses primarily on questions of language acquisition; Giessen and Rink address migration in terms of interculturality and transculturality from various social science and humanities perspectives, albeit without any particular interest in religion and the views of millennials; Kulaçatan and Behr propose an extension of the concept of intersectionality to include migration, religion, and gender as identity categories.

7. Heckathorn and Cameron describe the snowball sampling method as follows:

Research begins with a convenience sample of initial subjects who serve as seeds. Sampling then proceeds through network linkages, first from the seeds to the first wave, then from the first to the second wave, and so forth as the sample expands from wave to wave in the manner of a snowball growing as it rolls down a hill. Sampling stops when the target sample size has been attained. The major limitation of this method is that neither the selection of the initial subjects nor the selection of the subsequent waves is random, so the result is a convenience sample—a sample that does not provide the basis for validly inferring from the sample to the population from which it was drawn. (102)

8. Siegen University translated the responses to English.

9. Ethnicity and country of origin do not automatically denote any specific allegiance or belonging to a religious tradition. The chapter focuses more on how the millennials themselves perceive, interpret, and construct their notions of belongingness to the host-nation vis-à-vis religion. Future research will address this differentiation.

10. We will explore the generalizability of this research, or the extent to which the search for orientation outside of traditional social, ethnic, religious, or national contexts functions less as a denial of tradition but as an expression of a willingness to embrace new values is representative of general attitudes among millennials, in follow-up studies.

11. Future research should explore how religiosity among immigrant communities is tied to tradition and the role tradition plays in immigrant adjustment to the host society.

WORKS CITED

Abernathy, Bob. "Diana Eck Extended Interview." Apr. 26, 2002, https://www.pbs
.org/wnet/religionandethics/2002/04/26/april-26-2002-diana-eck-extended-int
erview/11617/. Accessed July 15, 2019.

Bakalian, Anny P., and Mehdi Bozorgmehr. *Backlash 9/11: Middle Eastern and Muslim Americans Respond.* University of California Press, 2009.

Brown, Davis, and Patrick James. "Germany, Religion and Social Profile." *The Association of Religion Data Archives*, 2015, http://52.9.15.250/internationalData/cou
ntries/Country_90_1.asp. Accessed July 15, 2019.

Cadge, Wendy, and Elaine Howard Ecklund. "Immigration and Religion." *Annual
Review of Sociology*, vol. 33, no. 1, 2007, pp. 359–79.

———. "Data Report 2016: A Social Report for the Federal Republic of Germany."
Destatis or *Federal Agency for Civic Education*, 2016, https://www.destatis.de/G
PStatistik/servlets/MCRFileNodeServlet/DEHeft_derivate_00021684/Datenreport
2016.pdf;jsessionid=E5C94A0A9F27899774E66A2BE50E59FF/. Accessed Nov.
15, 2019.

Davie, Grace. *Religion in Britain since 1945: Believing without Belonging.* Wiley-
Blackwell, 1994.

Deutsche Islam-Konferenz. http://www.deutsche-islam-konferenz.de/DIK/DE/Star
tseite/startseite-node.html. Accessed Aug. 23, 2019.

Diamant, Jeff. "How We Measured Attitudes toward Muslims and Jews in Western
Europe." *Pew Research Center*, June 1, 2018, https://www.pewresearch.org/fact-ta
nk/2018/06/01/qa-measuring-attitudes-toward-muslims-and-jews-in-western-eur
ope/. Accessed July 15, 2019.

Ebaugh, Helen Rose, and Janet Saltzman Chafetz. *Religion and the New Immigrants:
Continuities and Adaptations in Immigrant Congregations.* AltaMira, 2000.

Eck, Diana L. *A New Religious America: How a "Christian Country" Has Become
the World's Most Religiously Diverse Nation.* HarperCollins, 2001.

Ecklund, Elaine Howard, and Jerry Z. Park. "Asian American Community Participation and Religion: Civic Model Minorities?" *Journal of Asian American Studies*,
vol. 8, no. 1, 2005, pp. 1–21.

———. "Europe's Growing Muslim Population." *Pew Research Center.* Nov. 29,
2017, https://www.pewforum.org/2017/11/29/europes-growing-muslim-popula
tion/. Accessed July 15, 2019.

———. "Religious Diversity and Community Volunteerism among Asian Americans." *Journal for the Scientific Study of Religion*, vol. 46, no. 2, 2007, pp. 233–44.

Evans, Jonathan. "U.S. Adults Are More Religious than Western Europeans."
Pew Research Center, Sep. 5, 2018, https://www.pewresearch.org/fact-tank/20
18/09/05/u-s-adults-are-more-religious-than-western-europeans/. Accessed July
15, 2019.

Frederick, Marla F. *Between Sundays: Black Women and Everyday Struggles of
Faith.* University of California Press, 2003.

Funk, Cary, and Gregory Smith. *"Nones" on the Rise: One-in-Five Adults Have No Religious Affiliation.* Pew Research Center, Oct. 9, 2012, http://www.pewforum. org/files/2012/10/NonesOnTheRise-full.pdf. Accessed July 15, 2019.

Galvez, Alyshia. *Guadalupe in New York: Devotion and the Struggle for Citizenship Rights among Mexican Immigrants.* New York University Press, 2009.

"Germany and Immigration: The Changing Face of the Country." *Der Spiegel,* Apr. 19, 2018, https://www.spiegel.de/international/germany/germany-and-immigrat ion-the-changing-face-of-the-country-a-1203143-2.html. Accessed Aug. 7, 2019.

Giessen, Hans W., and Christian Rink, editors. *Migration, Diversität und kulturelle Identitäten: Sozial- und kulturwissenschaftliche Perspektiven.* Metzler, forthcoming 2020.

Gonzalez, Joaquin Jay. *Filipino American Faith in Action: Immigration, Religion, and Civic Engagement.* New York University Press, 2009.

Heckathorn, Douglas D., and Christopher J. Cameron. "Network Sampling: From Snowball and Multiplicity to Respondent-Driven Sampling." *Annual Review of Sociology,* vol. 43, no. 1, 2017, pp. 101–19.

Kulaçatan, Meltem, and Harry Harun Behr, editors. *Migration, Religion, Gender und Bildung: Beiträge zu einem erweiterten Verständnis von Intersektionalität.* transcript, forthcoming 2020.

Kurien, Prema A. "Religion, Ethnicity and Politics: Hindu and Muslim Indian Immigrants in the United States." *Ethnic and Racial Studies,* vol. 24, no. 2, 2001, pp. 263–93.

Landeszentrale für politische Bildung Baden-Württemberg. "Flüchtlinge und Schutzsuchende in Deutschland," https://www.lpb-bw.de/fluechtlingsproblematik .html#c51509. Accessed Aug. 8, 2019.

Leal, David L., et al. "Religion and the Political Engagement of Latino Immigrants: Bridging Capital or Segmented Religious Assimilation?" *The Russell Sage Foundation Journal of the Social Sciences,* vol. 2, no. 3, June 2016, pp. 125–46.

Lewis, Valerie A., Carol Ann MacGregor, and Robert D. Putnam. "Religion, Networks, and Neighborliness: The Impact of Religious Social Networks on Civic Engagement." *Social Science Research,* vol. 42, no. 2, 2012, pp. 331–46.

Manalang, Aprilfaye T. "Mostly Catholic or Loose Organizational Affiliation and Intergenerational Immigrant Identity: A Case Study of the Philippine-American Ecumenical Church, United Church of Christ (PAECUSA-UCC) in Detroit, Michigan." *Interdisciplinary Journal of Research on Religion,* vol. 14, article 6, 2018, http://www.religjournal.com/articles/article_view.php?id=129. Accessed July 15, 2019.

———. "Religion and the 'Blessing' of American Citizenship: Political and Civic Implications for Post-1965 Filipino Immigrants." *Implicit Religion,* vol. 19, no. 2, 2016, pp. 283–306.

———. "The Role of Religion and Region in Identity Politics and In-Group Identification: How Does Religion Influence Regionalism among Filipino-Americans?" *Journal of American Studies: Eurasian Perspective,* vol. 1, no. 2, 2016, pp. 111–23.

McRoberts, Omar M. *Streets of Glory: Church and Community in a Black Urban Neighborhood.* University of Chicago Press, 2005.

Mora, G. Cristina. "Religion and the Organizational Context of Immigrant Civic Engagement: Mexican Catholicism in the USA." *Ethnic and Racial Studies*, vol. 36, no. 11, 2013, pp. 1647–65.

Natarajan, Radhika, editor. *Sprache, Flucht, Migration: Kritische, historische und pädagogische Annäherungen.* Springer VS, 2019.

Numrich, Paul D., and Fred Kniss. *Sacred Assemblies and Civic Engagement: How Religion Matters for America's Newest Immigrants.* Rutgers University Press, 2007.

Orsi, Robert A. *The Madonna of 115th Street: Faith and Community in Italian Harlem.* 1985. Yale University Press, 1988.

Park, Jerry Z. "Assessing the Sociological Study of Asian American Christianity." *Society of Asian North American Christianity Studies Journal*, 2009, pp. 57–94. http://www.baylorisr.org/wp-content/uploads/park_assessing.pdf. Accessed July 15, 2019.

Peter Berger. "Postscript." *Peter Berger and the Study of Religion*, edited by Linda Woodhead et al., Routledge, 2001, pp. 189–98.

Pollack, Detlef, and Gergely Rosta. *East Germany: No Signs of a Turnaround.* Oxford University Press, 2017.

Schneider, Barbara, Lisa Hoogstra, Fengbin Chang, and Holly Rice Sexton. "Public and Private School Differences: The Relationship of Adolescent Religious Involvement to Psychological Well-being and Altruistic Behavior." *School Sector and Student Outcomes*, edited by Maureen Hallinan, University of Notre Dame Press, 2006, pp. 73–99.

Smith, Christian, and Melinda Lundquist Denton. *Soul Searching: The Religious and Spiritual Lives of American Teenagers.* Oxford University Press, 2005.

———, Robert Faris, and Melinda Lundquist Denton. *Are American Youth Alienated from Organized Religion?* National Study of Youth and Religion 6, 2004, https://open.bu.edu/bitstream/handle/2144/5/Alienation.pdf?sequence=1&isAllowed=y. Accessed Dec. 1, 2019.

Stepick, Alex, et al., editors. *Churches and Charity in the Immigrant City: Religion, Immigration, and Civic Engagement in Miami.* Rutgers University Press, 2009.

Wagener, Linda Mans, et al. "Religious Involvement and Developmental Resources in Youth." *Review of Religious Research*, vol. 44, no. 3, 2003, pp. 271–84.

Yang, Fenggang, and Helen Rose Ebaugh. "Religion and Ethnicity among New Immigrants: The Impact of Majority/Minority Status in Home and Host Countries." *Journal for the Scientific Study of Religion*, vol. 40, no. 3, 2001, pp. 367–78.

Youniss, James, and Jeffrey A. McLellan. "Religion, Community Service, and Identity in American Youth." *Journal of Adolescence*, vol. 22, no. 2, 1999, pp. 243–53.

———, and Miranda Yates. *Community Service and Social Responsibility.* University of Chicago Press, 1997.

Chapter 15

"Space," "Aliens," and the "Race" to Belong

Changing Geographies and Moving Borders in Europe and the Americas

Geoffroy de Laforcade

The modern world as we understand it today was born when Spain, a society at the crossroads of the Muslim Mediterranean and Renaissance Italy, accidentally encountered, and subsequently conquered, the Caribbean. The growth of Atlantic commerce and gradual evolution of the world-historical "core" from Asia to northern Europe over a span of three centuries coincided with the emergence of the colonial system. It also gave rise to such notions as "Europe" and "the West," as well as ideas about "race," "civilization," "nation," "state," and ultimately to models for the organization of space that we now take for granted. To understand contemporary debates about borders and their crossings, we would do well to acknowledge that "Europe" itself, the so-called "Old World," was as new during the gestation of modernity as were the "Americas" in the eyes of their conquerors. Heritage, it turns out, disinherits and excludes; it is intrinsically dissonant and therefore open to ongoing contestation (cf. Graham et al. 24). Since "much of human history refuses to fall within the confines of nations and national historiographies," Donna Gabaccia asks, how can we "redefine the historical nowhere and the many worlds humans have ever occupied above and below nations and their states?" (15). To quote Paul de Man: "Modernity exists in the form of a desire to wipe out whatever came earlier, in the hope of reaching at last a point that could be called a true present, a point of origin that marks a true departure" (148). The teleological stories we tell ourselves about national and "racial" genealogies of the "West" and the rest, and the representations of culture we deploy to understand our kinship with myths of origins and belonging through the prism of eighteenth-century North Atlantic "modernity," assume patterns of space, time, and movement that merit revisiting.

Both medieval Western Europe and sub-Saharan Africa were comparable economic and cultural peripheries in world-historical terms, an equivalency that clashes with our self-image as the "core" of all things "global." Thus, when David Graeber reminds us that the Abbasid Caliphate, following a ninth-century slave revolt in Basra, began trading in European slaves because they were regarded as more docile than Africans, we flinch. The much-touted hierarchy of "civilizations" crumbles when the "universalizing impulse" of the "Western tradition" is attributed to Islamic expansion: "the intellectual efforts to fuse Judeo-Christian scripture with the categories of Greek philosophy, the literary emphasis on courtly love, the scientific rationalism, the legalism, puritanical monotheism, missionary impulse, the expansion of mercantile capitalism—even the periodic waves of fascination with 'Eastern mysticism'" (339–40). Later, following a pattern begun during the Crusades, in an Iberian region not yet known as "Spain" or "Europe" and imbued with five centuries of African and Arab influences, violent deportations and forced conversions of Muslims (and Jews) accompanied the enforcement of spatial segregation by the ecclesiastical laws of a conquering Catholic Church. Finally, in 1609–1610, a newly centralized monarchy ruled by Philip II of Spain expelled *moriscos* (converts from Islam to Christianity) from Castile, Aragon, and Catalonia, not because of their faith but because of their failure to "assimilate." A new concept of "internal enemy" was born, which rested on the imagined cultural homogeneity of a territorial state and prefigured a vision of the world that would prevail in the conquests of the Americas (cf. Bethencourt 27–31, 141–43).

The term "ethnicity," which we frequently use today to mean "culture" in debates over what assimilation means, was first applied by Latin Christians to pagans and gentiles in the thirteenth century and meant something very different than it had to ancient Greeks, for whom it simply referred to "peoples" (without any assumption of fixity or inherited classification). Similarly, the idea of "race" emerged during the formation and secularization of modernity, an outcome of a complex and gradual becoming of Europe as a cultural and geopolitical entity. Race in medieval times had referred to caste; it also applied to the identification of plants and animals. Over the course of the conflict between Christians and Muslims in Iberia, and subsequently during the Atlantic expansion, "ethnic" in the language of Catholics referred to Muslims and Jews whose sociocultural traditions they associated with impurity of blood. Later it applied to Africans and Indigenous peoples in the Americas in a drawn-out process of designation and classification that asserted the superiority of European peoples over colonized societies. Deployed in the eighteenth century to characterize the condition of women and varieties of human beings, the term "race," by then associated with skin color and an assortment of assumed mental and somatic dispositions, circulated in its current meaning in the nineteenth century as a device to designate a hierarchy of human species under the influence of European scientific racism. It fueled the new ideology of nationalism and became, at the turn of the twentieth century, a marker of the "nation" itself (cf. Bethencourt 6–7). "Once genders, species, and races were identified and classified," Cameroonian philosopher Achille Mbembe writes, "nothing remained but to enumerate the differences between them. . . . From the High Middle Ages to the Enlightenment, curiosity as a mode of inquiry and a cultural sensibility was inseparable from the work of fantasy, which, when focused on other worlds, constantly blurred the lines between the believable and the unbelievable, the factual and the marvelous" (17).

CHAOTIC, UNBOUNDED, IMAGINED NEW WORLDS

We continue to narrate, as we do the creation of modern nation-states, the conquest of "discovered" territories from the sixteenth century onward as an endeavor driven by reason and rationality. It was actually an adventure replete with ignorance, speculation, and superstition. Having conquered the Canary Islands from which the voyages of Christopher Columbus began, a still politically disunited and culturally heterogeneous Spain would invoke the patron saint of the Christian wars against Islam, St. James ("the killer of Moors"), to battle against "infidels" in the "New World." The not-quite-yet Europeans who stumbled on the western hemisphere at the dawn of a new era imagined place and space in mythical and intuitive ways, such as the Seven Cities of Antilia, believed to have been discovered by Portuguese bishops fleeing across the Atlantic from the medieval Islamic settlement of Iberia. The idea gave a name to Columbus's island discoveries of the "Antilles," and it inspired John Cabot's decision to call the shores of New England the "Seven Cities," as well as Francisco Vásquez de Coronado's belief that he had discovered them in the Zuni towns of present-day New Mexico (cf. Weber 24). The name "California" given in the 1540s by Spanish explorers to the west coast of North America came from a legend describing an island where Amazon-like women had sex with men once a year to perpetuate their race. They imagined the new frontier as one of wealthy kingdoms with camels, elephants, and single-horned animals (cf. 44, 46). Franciscan missionaries tasked by the Crown with converting the natives, predicting an impending apocalypse and believing themselves guided by supernatural appearances of the Lady of the Rosary in the form of a bluish light, established missions first in present-day Florida, Georgia, South Carolina, and Alabama before settling in the Southwest (cf. 100).

They opened a seventeenth-century frontier in present-day New Mexico that exported Indigenous slaves to the mining regions of New Spain, facing fierce resistance from the Pueblo peoples and causing a flow of refugees southward to what is now the Mexican border town of Ciudad Juárez, the epicenter, in the eighteenth century, of endless frontier wars with Utes, Apaches, and Navajos (cf. Weber 136–41). Prior to their arrival, however, the present-day states of Utah, Colorado, Arizona, and New Mexico were home to dynamic ancient Hohokam and Anasazi cultures, as well as the Mogollon peoples who extended into what is now the Mexican state of Chihuahua. Anasazi and Hohokam had trade and migration links to ancient Mesoamerica and Chichimeca (on today's northern central Mexican plateau). "There is a perfectly good Nahua word to describe the place of Chichimeca between Mesoamerica and the Southwest: *nepantla,*" Michael Dear writes and continues:

> Nepantla describes the condition of being "in-between." It connotes a bridging between cultures, a border zone or hybrid place where interaction and learning occurs [*sic*]. There may be gaps in the archaeological record, empty spaces in our minds, and no agreement on the extent of this bridging, but the north–south connectivity in the civilizations of the ancient Americas is undeniable. (24)

This "pre-modern" representation of space from the Nahua language is a fitting allegory for zones of encounter in world history across time and continents. Another from the Yoruba tradition, the poetics of which migrated throughout the Americas during the painful begetting of modernity, depicts *orishas* as paths on the journey of life, constantly moving sources of power or *aché*. *Òsun*, the goddess/path of flowing water, draws her name from a source, that of a river, of life, but also of a people (cf. Castellanos 34–35); she is "a metaphor of origins that lacks the fixity and fatalism of land and country" (Sanford 239).

This tradition permeates the Caribbean, which was not only the incubator of modernity in the western hemisphere but also the source of epic struggles to define freedom within it. Its history vividly illustrates how chaotic and unbounded, and fancifully imagined, territory and identity actually have been. Vicente Yanez Pinzón and Juan Díaz de Solís thought Cuba was a continent (cf. Weddle 20–21); chroniclers after them portrayed her as a bridge between the Americas, "The Queen of the Antilles," "The Key of the Gulf," "The Sentinel of the Mississippi" (Kimball 94), and other images conveying historical interaction with the perpetually changing contested ground of the Anglo–Spanish–French imperial frontier. Historical geographer Pierre Chaunu noted that in the age of sail, the time of navigation from Havana to the Mexican port city of Veracruz was roughly equivalent to the journey from the Cuban capital to the Portuguese Azores. Cuba, in this configuration, stood at the very center of the Atlantic economy; more than just an island, it was a strategic gateway between the Iberian/African world and the Indies. In the worldview of early modern transatlantic navigators, any territory between the Andalusian/Canarian ports and Lima, Cartagena, or Veracruz, between Seville and *"Tierra Firme"* (firm land) was an island—not just the Canaries and the Antilles, but also a peninsula such as Florida (cf. 349).

Insularity means different things across cultures. In Sanskrit and Arabic, the word we translate as "continent" in fact expresses the notion of "island," either the Hindu representation of a world of concentric islands surrounding a mountain, or the North African Maghreb seen as an "island" between the Mediterranean Sea and the Sahara desert (cf. Febvre 60, 84). The latter representation of insularity is useful as a heuristic tool for understanding the Caribbean, islands at the crossroads of Africa, Europe, North America, and South America, where the diasporic formation of local and regional identities, having originated in Africa, the circum-Mediterranean, Europe, and Asia, unraveled as a fluid and dynamic historical phenomenon. Created by migrations since ancient times and a crucible of global migrations today, crossroads and laboratory of the modern world, it is allegorically cast by Antonio Benítez-Rojo as a passage, an "island bridge" made "archipelago" by its continental foci, a "cultural sea without boundaries, . . . a paradoxical fractal form extending infinitely through a finite world" (2, 270). For George Lamming, it is an "imperial frontier" (26–27), a collection of "polyglot," "eclectic," "porous," and "absorptive" nations founded by means of geno-cide, the boundaries of which are, in the felicitous phrase of Gordon Lewis, not barriers in the customary sense, but rather "permeable membranes for a massive and constant flow and interflow of groups and individuals" (18). If the symbolic treatment of space is, to quote Marc Augé, "at once an intellec-tual matrix, a social construction, an inheritance, and the first condition of all history, whether individual or collective" (5–6), the question becomes, how did we develop the modern sense of place, territoriality, fixed identities, phys-ical boundaries, civilizational barriers, and bounded national communities?

THE WORLD DIDN'T WAIT FOR EUROPE

As inseparable from modernity as our terms for understanding identity and alterity are, we tend to frame them as an outcome of linear development from core to periphery, the spread of a civilization from its cradle to the previously unknown. That civilization is Europe, of which people living there had no notion for most of history, and whose literati first applied the term "civiliza-tion" to the Hellenistic world in the eighteenth century in order to establish a fictional continuity between classical Greece and Roman Christendom on a post-Reformation path to secularization. Long before Samuel Huntington embraced orientalist scholar Bernard Lewis' "clash of civilizations,"[1] the very word came into use as a discursive strategy by modern imperialists to naturalize the expansion of "Western" civilization and assess how the "barbarians" they encountered could be measured against it, or whether they threatened to corrupt its fabric (cf. Jensen 104–5). Yet Europe itself and its imagined Greco-Roman roots are inventions of the modern era. Neither the ancient Greek world in the eastern Mediterranean nor the vast empire that supplanted the Roman Republic following the Social War, the uprising of slaves led by Spartacus, and the invasion of what would be called "Gaul" by Julius Caesar, created anything like what we would today call "Europe." For French historian Lucien Febvre, the medieval Carolingian kings who did set into motion the emergence of an empire that would become European had no concept of Mediterranean inheritance. Their reign represented an extension of the authority of the Church of Rome to fiefdoms further north and west, and the term "Europe" only entered into common usage to designate their areas of influence in the sixteenth century (cf. 186).

Phoenicians from the Levantine littoral (present-day Lebanon, Syria, and Israel) colonized the shores of the Mediterranean, passing though the straits of Gibraltar to the Atlantic and sailing to Africa from east to west, establishing a "New World" in ancient times during the first millennium BCE (cf. Ball 19–40). "Moorish," Arab and Persian troops settled in regions of present-day Europe, as far as the Danube, during the Hellenistic wars. Families of Phoenician and Arab descent later became Roman emperors—indeed, while Rome was still pagan, Philip the Arab (244–249 CE) became its first Christian emperor, unacknowledged by later apologists of Constantine (cf. 66–84, 94). Meanwhile, early Christianity took root in Aksum (Ethiopia), which conquered ancient Meroe and ruled over today's Yemen and southern Egypt. In medieval times, sailors from what we now call Indonesia settled in the East African coast, linking Africa and Eurasia. Well before the epic expansion of Islam through the trans-Saharan and Indian Ocean trades or the Iberian Atlantic expeditions, Africans settled in Southwest and South Asia, Egyptians and Nubians emigrated to the Great Lakes region (Uganda, Rwanda, and Burundi), and contemporary Morocco, the Red Sea, and the Congo were linked by trade and travel (cf. Manning 49–50). In the Americas, ancient Mayans connected Central America to what is now the American Southwest, through an elaborate trade network in cocoa and jade. California is home to all the principal language families in pre-conquest North America, including the Algonquians, who at the time of British settlement lived in the Northeast—suggesting that Native American mobility, including intercoastal migration, was a feature of their history well before the opening of the Anglo frontier (cf. Kehoe 17). Perhaps none of these ancient societies possessed states, or borders, as we know them today—but neither did, so to speak, "we."

While in the first two centuries of our era much of what we today know as Europe and the Mediterranean world was under centralized imperial control, by the sixth century the western parts of that empire had collapsed into a mosaic of small and localized communities. They were governed by warlords and aristocratic families, some dominated by Anglo-Saxon or Burgundy kings, others by tribal Ostrogoths, Visigoths, and Vandals, and were isolated from the Eastern Mediterranean and North African realms that had been the cradle of Greece and Rome (cf. Jensen 250). Insofar as this primitive medieval world shared a culture shaped by Roman Christianity, it was a Christianity fractured by heresy and schisms. When Muslims, Magyars, and Vikings besieged them, they drew from tropes of barbarism, not of race, to designate their enemies, as would Islamic rulers with Seljuk Turks, Berbers, sub-Saharan Africans, and Christian crusaders. According to Francisco Bethencourt, skin color and other phenotypical traits first emerged in descriptions of the world made by Muslim travelogues, who borrowed from Greco-Roman stereotypes about Africa to make distinctions between the regions they organized and the inhospitable desert and tropical frontier to their south; but there was no self-conscious image of "whiteness" in what we now call Europe. Christians later embraced notions of a separation between culture and nature, humans and animals, organized societies and barbaric desert reaches, imagining monsters and savages in forest and ocean reaches that prefigured their classification of peoples unknown to them prior to the sixteenth century, but they had no sense of fixed territorial boundaries or unified ethnic identity (cf. 17–18).

When in the eleventh century, Sardinia, Sicily, and Corsica changed from Muslim to Christian hands and the First Crusade began, the sedentary, continental polities of the Carolingian world entered into a period of intense interaction with the southern and eastern Mediterranean and Southwest Asia. The stage was set for the incorporation of "Eastern" knowledge and material culture into what would soon become the "West." This gradual transition to a self-conscious European identity was a long and complex period of upheaval and cultural cosmopolitanism, an "age of encounter" between the medieval Christian and Muslim worlds that combined conquest and plundering with the stirrings of cross-cultural scientific, technological, and philosophical dialogue. European polities as we know them today, however, and their representations of internal cultural unity, were still centuries away, as were nationalist narratives of their roots and branches. Modern France, for example, a beacon of this new world, would selectively trace its ancestry to the Christian kingdoms of Roman Gaul, Carolingian kings, and their religious crusades, thirteenth-century state formation under Philip Augustus, fifteenth-century wars against England, mercantilist expansion, absolutist kings, the establishment of modern institutions in the late eighteenth century, and the rise of imperialism in the nineteenth. Apologists for this genealogy assume a long history of "national destiny" to have predated the formation of the state in its contemporary form. At no time during that storied history, however, did the ethnic fragmentation and regional particularisms, or even the cross-border solidarities, within French society disappear. Monarchical or republican unity notwithstanding, it was too diverse a society to acquire an "ethnic" self-definition prior to the rise of scientific racism and colonialism in the industrial age (cf. Crowley 71). It was in the late nineteenth century that the consolidation of a "national" framework took hold in the name of an explicitly universalistic ideology of reason and progress, which cast national kinship in assimilationist terms while dividing colonial societies into racially differentiated subjects.

For Caribbean philosopher Sylvia Wynter, who is also a historian of early modern Spain, the origins of that differentiation lie in the unique establishment by the emergent "West" of an essential distinction between itself and all things preceding it. Early Portuguese navigators had premised their voyages to Africa on the existence of a sea route to bypass the Islamic monopoly on the lucrative gold trade, by circumventing the "torrid zone" that medieval cartography presumed to be an uninhabitable boundary between the Christian world and the fabled "Indies." As the Scholastic order of geographic knowledge crumbled in 1441 with their rounding of the southern African cape—the first "discovery" of the modern age—their settlements along coastal West Africa developed into a mercantile trade network for gold and slaves that lay the groundwork for relations between Christian Europe and the non-Christian peoples of the world. Felipe Fernández-Armesto wrote that the discovery of Neolithic Berber "idolaters" on the Canary Islands validated a symbolic representation of non-European peoples as different and primitive. They became a legitimate target for servitude and evangelization, setting into motion the capture of a disposable, coercible, and unpaid labor force according to a mercantile imperative that commodified human beings in the name of divine providence (cf. 230–43). The Christian Crusades had granted special privileges to vassals of the lords and kings in whose name they were the first to have landed on non-Christian territory and expropriated it. Once the Pope was empowered to adjudicate sovereignty over "discovered" lands, debates ensued over whether the inhabitants of the previously uninhabitable "natural" world were human, and if so, how to understand their place in God's plan. European jurists and theologians addressing the status of newly encountered peoples in the Americas would replace the notion of "idolater" with that of Aristotle's natural slave,

> in order to represent the indigenous peoples as ones who were *by nature different from the Spaniards*. This difference was one expressed in degrees of

rationality, with the symbolic-cultural distance between the two groups being seen as an *innately* determined difference. (Wynter, "1492" 34)

For Wynter, this reversed previous universalistic claims of Christianity and established the premise of the "non-homogeneity of the human species" ("1492" 36–39). As proto-capitalist property relations expanded into the Americas, place, subjectivity, and belonging became increasingly territorialized. Control over land, over a sense of inheritance, who "belonged" there and who did not, was crucial to gaining control over people.

Territorialization ushered in a "new world order" of both constituting and partitioning putative "races," "genders," later "nations," and then "natives" and "migrants" (Ansfield 167). On the one hand, the discovery of human diversity expanded the potential unification of a geographically dispersed but still shared humanity, as aspired to by monotheistic theology and Christian humanism; on the other, the genocidal elimination of much of that humanity became part of the enterprise of extending European territorial claims to exploit and commodify natural resources and labor. The new, ruling mode of subjective understanding contained a distinction between beings, some imagined as human, others less so (cf. Wynter, "Unsettling" 292). The humanist revolution of the fourteenth and fifteenth centuries, the emergence of new sciences, and colonization of the Americas produced a new "descriptive statement" of what it means to be human that is still hegemonic today. Europe's formerly theocentric, Latin-Christian, Scholastic order of knowledge gradually became "modern" by dividing rational whites from irrational African-descended and Indigenous peoples. A new bio-centric representation of economic man, Wynter argues, emerged when bio-evolutionary thinking replaced classical theorationalism in Darwinism's wake. Europeans were narrated eugenically as evolutionarily selected, and their "others" de-selected by the "laws of nature," becoming symbolically constructed as "races" ("Towards" 280). Racialization became a founding principle of modern culture, labeling as "deviant" and inferior not just blacks and Indigenous peoples, but also women, homosexuals, the errant, the poor—Fanon's "wretched of the earth"—who were excluded from the bio-centric concept of what it means to be human (cf. Scott 321). Thus, capitalism regulated, normalized, and legitimated its expansion through an epistemic order that began as theological and evolved into a purely biological description of man. It defined, in binary terms, what is good and evil as what is civilized, evolved, and normatively white, vs. what is dysgenic or "alien." The concrete, material, economic impact of the "new" world upon the "old" would transform that old world from one civilizing project among others—the Christian—to the one, the West, to which all other civilizations were the Other (cf. Wynter, "Unsettling" 300–301).

FRONTIERS OF EMPIRE AND RESISTANCE

An example of how this process played out as an "experience of freedom," to quote Italian philosopher Gianni Vattimo, "a continual oscillation between belonging and disorientation" (8), is the invention of the present-day border between the United States and Mexico. After the struggle between England and France for control of the Ohio River Valley that triggered the Seven Years' War, settlers unleashed a rampage of terror against the Indigenous peoples who had supported the British Crown and won its protection in the form of a boundary drawn to stop westward European expansion. Had the United States not come into being in 1776 and proclaimed the freedom of settlers to establish property rights over lands previously ceded to Indians by the Royal Proclamation of 1763, the western limit, the frontier, would not have reached the Mississippi River, where the Spanish Empire still stood in its way. Indeed, prior to its demise after the Anglo-North American and French Revolutions, Spain had firmly established itself as the sovereign power from California to the Mississippi Valley and the Gulf Coast. Before the nineteenth century, however, there was tremendous political flux on the continent. Patterns of migration within and across sovereignties, the palimpsest of customs, traditions and cultural systems, and quarreling imperial regimes that intersected with mercantile trade systems and forms of usufruct and property of the land, rendered "national" belonging of little attraction in the repertoire of sources of "identity" available to people inhabiting these contested spaces, freely or otherwise (see Smith and Hilton). The 1803 Louisiana Purchase extended the new nation to the Gulf Coast and the Rocky Mountains and opened the floodgates of the western frontier, a notion that entered into usage as the state-sanctioned policy of Indian removal relentlessly advanced. The extension of United States territorial sovereignty also involved an ongoing struggle over African slavery as well as resistance to it, as New Orleans grew into the largest slave market in North America.

Beginning in the 1770s, Spain had subsidized the importation of captives from Senegambia, the Bight of Benin, the Bight of Biafra, and Central Africa, but it had also encouraged the large-scale immigration of free people of color to the Bayou, resulting in the reinvigoration of longstanding creole Fon-Ewe-Yoruba traditions, which were widespread in the Caribbean, throughout the lower Mississippi.[2] The percentage of *libres* in the population of New Orleans at the turn of the century was one in five, two-thirds of them women, during a period that saw the intensification of the city's maritime and commercial interaction with Havana. Spanish legal policies encouraged the manumission of slaves through a negotiated process called *coartición,* in hopes that a large free black population would defend the colony, avert rebellions, fill middle-class urban occupations, and facilitate the integration of new African slaves (cf.

Hanger 107–8).[3] Following the departure of the Spaniards, a million Africans would arrive in New Orleans between 1820 and 1860, as the United States vastly curtailed the privileges of free people of color, restricted manumission, imposed immutable racial hierarchies, and transformed the South from a struggling tobacco and sugar economy to a vast cotton plantation complex stretching from the Carolinas to Texas (see Johnson). New Orleans in the nineteenth century thus served as a base of operations for freedom movements not only within the United States, but also throughout the Caribbean and Latin America. Privateers, smugglers, corsairs, and filibusters from revolutionary Saint Domingue spread the antislavery message throughout the region from bases in eastern Cuba and west of the Mississippi, stimulating the black market, offering refuge to escaped slaves and black political fugitives, even arming expeditions to help Mexican insurgents and maroon communities in Louisiana and beyond (see Bell). These "defiant, stateless, peripatetic" collectivities that operated outside the formal colonial social structure, called "transfrontiersmen" by Franklin Knight (90), contributed to the human, material, and symbolic interconnectedness of the region's porous and perpetually changing boundaries, linking diasporas and defying control, offering a nascent internationalist alternative to socialization by national and imperial slave states.

In the period between the Seven Years' War and the Spanish territory's cessation to the United States, free people of color again emerged in Florida as key players in the shaping of both Spanish colonial and North American frontier policies. Once believed by its "discoverer," Juan Ponce de León, to be an island that extended to present-day Quebec, Florida had long remained a sparsely populated missionary frontier plagued by pirates, natural disasters, and incursions by imperial rivals. The need to defend the western Gulf Coast against French claims to the Lower Mississippi Valley in the years leading up to the founding of New Orleans prompted the establishment of Pensacola in 1699 and San Marcos de Apalache in 1718. By the mid-eighteenth century contraband flowed regularly between Saint Augustine and Cuba alongside the prospering New Orleans-Havana mercantile polygon and its subsidiary networks in Mobile, Veracruz, Galveston, and Campeche. When the treaties of 1763 gave Florida to Britain in exchange for occupied Havana, thousands of Spanish Floridians—many of them Native Americans—flocked to the Cuban capital (see Gold). From there, they launched the Spanish recolonization of Florida at the close of the century, setting the stage for a protracted conflict between Spain and the United States and culminating in a new mass exodus to Cuba in the wake of the US takeover in 1821.

From its very inception as an independent nation, the United States viewed the presence of free blacks in Florida as a permanent threat to plantation owners of the Anglo South. The soaring cotton economy, with its unprecedented influx of Africans through Charleston on their way to the New Orleans slave market, provoked successive government-sponsored attacks on Spanish Florida, leading up to three "Seminole Wars" between 1818 and 1859, in which free blacks were hunted down and routinely forced back into slavery. At stake in this Anglo/US-Spanish rivalry was a 1693 royal proclamation by Charles II declaring all men and women of Florida free, which transformed the peninsula into a sanctuary for Africans from the entire Caribbean and Gulf Coast. In 1738, the Spanish crown granted unconditional freedom to all black fugitives from Carolina and the British colonies of North America and the West Indies (a policy later ended under pressure from Thomas Jefferson). Gracia Real de Santa Teresa de Mose, founded near St. Augustine and governed by a Mandinga captain of the black Floridian militia, Francisco Menéndez, brought Mandinga, Fara, and Arará together with Congo, Carabalí, Guinean, and other African populations, as well as Spaniards and Native Americans in a single frontier town that triggered the wrath of the United States government. People of African descent converged on Saint Augustine from major Atlantic and Caribbean ports, transforming Spanish Florida into an *avant-garde* of freedom struggles everywhere, a place where African, European, and Indigenous societies merged into something unprecedented in the Atlantic world. Jane Landers argues that these "African Creoles" mobilized "linguistic dexterity, cultural plasticity, and social agility" in the defense of sovereignty, religious freedom, antislavery, political representation, and property rights until their mass expulsion to Cuba after 1821 (4; see also Berlin).

In Texas, as well, an assault on laws protecting the rights of black people resulted from a US government-sponsored push by planters to restore slavery through the violent secession of the province from newly independent Mexico, stripping Afro-Mexicans, free blacks who had come to seek refuge, and Native Americans of citizenship and legal rights (cf. Q. Taylor 39–44). In the 1830s, Galveston was the largest slave market west of New Orleans, and in 1848, the Treaty of Guadalupe Hidalgo, followed by the 1853 Treaty of Mesilla (or Gadsden Purchase), formalized the annexation by the United States of all of northern Mexico (Arizona, New Mexico, California, Nevada, western Colorado, Utah, and southwestern Wyoming). Thus was established the first permanent territorial land border in the history of the region. Its policing, however, would await the turn of the twentieth century, after the post-Civil War military "pacification" of remaining Indian nations was complete, after Jim Crow segregation had become law in the South, and after the United States had joined the concert of imperialist powers in the Spanish-Cuban American War. Even in antebellum New England, free people of color suffered from heightened racial prejudice and the triumphant ideology of whiteness, exemplified in Ralph Waldo Emerson's prediction that "the Negro" would eventually "become extinct" in the northern United States (Melish 285). Before him, Thomas Jefferson had believed that "the 'final consolidation' of American liberty wouldn't be achieved until the surface of the continent was occupied by white, English-speaking people, with neither 'blot' nor 'mixture on that surface'" (Grandin 55). Beginning in the age of Andrew Jackson, the notion of "frontier" had come to separate civilization from savagery. As Greg Grandin postulates, "[p]eople of color—enslaved peoples within the United States or dispossessed peoples on its border— helped define the line between proper liberty, which justified self-governance, and ungovernable licentiousness, which justified domination" (64). All of this unfolded alongside the contested emergence of a new form of access to land, resources, and representation, and to modern-day citizenship, which divided people into rightful claimants on the one hand and excluded unfree persons subject to containment and control, on the other. Race was always a key factor in this development. In the 1790s, the US Congress, in its first public definition of citizenship, restricted naturalizations to people deemed "white," a racial requirement that remained in force until 1952 and the McCarran-Walter Act (cf. Jacobson 176–77).

BORDERS AND THE INVENTION OF ALIENS

Immigration to the United States was numerically unrestricted, however, until 1917, with the exception of the exclusion of Chinese in 1882. In 1917, the Asiatic Barred Zone act banned all people from East Asia as well as homosexuals, people with mental disabilities, and anarchists. The Emergency Quota Act in 1921 explicitly targeted anarchist and communist sympathizers, followed by the Immigration Act of 1924, which targeted Jews, Italians, and Slavs from Central and Eastern Europe due to their perceived proclivities for labor activism and political subversion (see Okrent). After World War I had generated millions of stateless persons and refugees, a new nation-state system emerged worldwide based on the strict regulation of migration on the borders. Mexicans, as well as East Asians, were deemed incapable of "assimilating" into EuroAmerican white society, so immigration law invented the concept of "aliens ineligible for citizenship" and new categories of identity based on "national origins."

Mexicans, earlier classified as "white" after the conquest of the northern Mexican frontier and by the 1924 Immigration Act, lost that status when the Census Bureau declared them a separate race in 1930 (cf. Ngai 7–17, 50–55). Subjected to Jim Crow segregation laws in the Southwest, especially in Texas, they became the iconic illegal aliens of the United States, and the targets of the newly created Border Patrol, the goal of which was to "enforce racialized spaces internal to the nation" (64). The 1924 law, Mae Ngai argues, enforced the restriction of immigration long advocated by nativists based on racial and national hierarchies, and established the territorial border as something to be policed, protected through repression, and narrated as immutable (4). In reality, since the time of Mexican dictator Porfirio Díaz's overtures to US capital in the nineteenth century and the convulsions of the Mexican Revolution, and especially after the surge in tourism caused by the 1919 Volstead Act (Prohibition), the borderlands had become a network of integrated and interdependent border towns whose inhabitants were oblivious to the separation. The post-World War II Bracero program, which recruited 4 million Mexican workers to compensate for a labor shortage in the United States, and the subsequent Operation Wetback (1953–1954) that forcibly deported them, grew border towns to the size of cities. These urban centers then underwent industrialization in the 1960s to give low-wage employment to returning laborers in assembly plants (*maquiladoras*) for the production of goods destined to the US market. By 2000, roughly 16 percent of the Mexican population and 21 percent of the US population lived in the six border states of Mexico and the four border states of the US Southwest, respectively (cf. Dear 45–46). Until 2007, when their numbers began to decline, Mexicans were by far the largest population of both legal and undocumented immigrant workers in the United States.

While the designation of "internal enemies" has a long history, the emergence of the "alien" as a legal signifier for persons without citizenship is a contemporary phenomenon. As in the United States, France only began to establish controls over migratory flows in the 1920s and 1930s. The paradigmatic alien in the United States was the Mexican; in France, it was the Algerian. Earlier developments such as imperial expansion, slavery, segregation, nativism, and Asian exclusion preceded the actual enforcement of territorial and racialized borders in the United States. In France, the long history of animosity between the Roman Christian church and Islam, coupled with colonial history and revolutionary, restoration, and republican-era articulations of freedom and assimilation, determined the ways in which "national" and "foreign" would be defined in the age of twentieth-century citizenship. During the French Revolution, assimilation into the Republic was open to all adversaries of monarchy and hereditary privilege; Jews became citizens, and slavery briefly became illegal between 1794 and 1802. The 1804 Napoleonic Civil Code, however, not only upheld the seventeenth-century Black Code and its rigid line of separation between freedom and slavery, but also defined nationality as being determined through kinship (*jus sanguinis*), not birth on French soil (*jus soli*). France underwent a process of imperial decline that contrasts with the expansion of the United States. Its empire had once spanned from Acadia, the St. Lawrence estuary, and the Mississippi Valley in North America, to the French Antilles (including St. Domingue) and Guyana in the Caribbean, and coastal settlements in West Africa and India. By

1814, it had dwindled to Guadeloupe, Martinique, Réunion, French Guyana, and a small territory in Senegal. The conquest of the Mediterranean region of Algeria from 1830 onward was, like contemporaneous annexations of borderlands by the United States, motivated by a strategy to defend against the sights of a competitor (Great Britain) on a strategic trade corridor (the Strait of Gibraltar). It also stemmed from a nationalist desire to reaffirm the glory of a bygone imperial era (cf. Addi 94–95). More to the point, however, France justified the invasion of Algeria as upholding the boundary between European civilization and Islam and preventing the ethnic or religious contamination of the "fatherland" (cf. 95–99). Thereafter, apologists for France's "civilizing mission" couched their rhetoric of universalism in a language that had emancipationist roots in the revolutionary era but remained tainted by colonial separatism (cf. Conklin 254–56).

In 1862, Algerians received the status of "French nationals," but with the specification that they were not equal to those who were born in France itself. This became the 1874 "Code of Indigeneity," which placed colonial subjects below not just French citizens, but other foreigners as well (cf. Blanchard 177). As colonialism soared in the wake of World War I and restrictive legislation emerged to regulate the flow of immigrants into the country, origins, heredity, and race established, as they did in the United States during the same period, hierarchies of citizenship and belonging, which were reinforced in the Vichy era by laws specifically excluding colonial subjects. "Indigeneity" was a status that confined them, geographically and socially, to an "outsider" status from which only a select minority could escape. Cultural identities took on immutable and essentialist forms that intrinsically separated "colonial natives" from "French citizens." The law defined the nation as a natural, exclusive, and spatially barricaded collectivity that conferred rights upon its citizens while limiting access to them by foreigners, even when they inhabited French territories. The promise of political equality notwithstanding, "republican" ideology was as absolutist and hermetic in its imagined homogeneity as the most deterministic discourse of racial belonging, an "abstract communitarianism" centered on the state that conditioned people's "assimilation" to the definitive renunciation of their culture, faith, language, and memory (Balibar, "Le droit" 97–99). During the war for Algerian independence (1954–1962), which set the stage for decolonization worldwide, violence and persecution escalated against Algerian workers who, like Mexicans during the Bracero program in the United States, had been encouraged to work in France; they, too, found themselves massively deported in 1974. Fears that Algerians were socially dangerous and politically subversive were a factor as significant as economic retrenchment, but the belief in an "unassimilable island" of Algerianism threatening the fabric of French national kinship was central to the shift in public policy (cf. Witte

84–88). It marked the birth of "undocumented aliens" by replacing the "flow" of migrants to and from the host nation with a logic of "storage," whereby those who remained entered into an inescapable condition of illegality and exclusion (Morice 128–29).

The irony is that Algerians' ethnic/cultural difference had been encouraged by the state in the tradition of "Indigeneity," which had been thought to guarantee their nonassimilation into French unions and to presage their eventual return to the barbarian shores of the "other" Mediterranean (cf. Castles and Miller 244–45). Before reemerging from the catacombs of late Medieval Christendom as a recurring signifier of radical and menacing difference, the Islamic faith embraced by a mosaic of communities from North and West Africa, Pakistan, the eastern Mediterranean, the Levant, the Comoros, etc., had been practiced in all parts of France since the turn of the twentieth century (cf. Diop 112–20). "That the nation was formed as part of the empire," Étienne Balibar wrote, "means that the empire remains part of the nation for a long time after physical and juridical separation" ("Algeria" 166). Such intertwined cultural frontiers, which have deep roots in history and predate the emergence of policed national borders, challenge the received wisdom of hegemonic national cultures, not by denying the nation itself but by providing historical and cultural alternatives to the foundational narratives of the state. Perennial colonial inheritances remain ubiquitous, however: administrative practices of classification and control; the persistence of labor migration patterns historically woven into threads of French colonial expansion; and cultural obstacles to the achievement of citizenship and equality, as evidenced by recurrent politically charged controversies over the food habits, dress, family relations, belief systems, and other "problematic" signs of failed assimilation. Once restrictions began on all non-European immigration, workers from postcolonial regions found themselves suddenly "undocumented" on a massive scale (they had always been, but it was never before held against them) (Costa-Lascoux 38). The French state preserved, and still exercises today, exclusive possession of the power to integrate foreigners, conceding citizenship to them only if they agreed to become culturally invisible, to forsake their alterity, and embrace "the values of the Republic" (Balibar, "Le droit" 97–99). As in the colonial era, the language of assimilation has served to condition political rights on the transformation of "natives" into cultural clones of their masters, while deferring their "integration" through the public stigmatization of immigrant traditions and cultural practices. All of this has occurred against the backdrop of public debate over the meaning of "national identity" and the hardening of a European-wide border security regime (see de Laforcade, "Broken").

Like the nation-state itself, the novelty of borders and the violence they crystallize is something we tend to forget. Historically, imperial states exercised administrative, military, missionary, and economic control over outlying zones in fluid, perpetually evolving ways. Territorially enforced exclusion, on the other hand, while seldom bereft of porous imperfections, seeks to regulate flows of peoples, commodities, and capital in a manner that consolidates the ability of the state to select the rightful claimants of its regime of rights, and at the same time capitalize on transnational economic networks of exchange. It projects stark insider/outsider oppositions and naturalizes legal, political, and ideological differences while simultaneously provoking their contestation among victims of segregation, criminalization, marginalization, and prejudice. The establishment of detention centers (known as "jungles") from Calais to Ventimiglia and Lesbos, and from Texas to Chiapas is itself a transnational enterprise of control and policing that extends the "borders" of Europe to Morocco, Niger, Libya, and the Sudan, and those of the United States to Guatemala, Honduras, and Haiti. The European Union parks Syrian war refugees in Turkey and seeks to establish "processing camps" in North Africa, while the United States and Mexico cooperate to contain flows of Central American refugees. In all of these theaters, detention and deportation result in the growth of underground human trafficking networks and the criminalization of humanitarian efforts to help undocumented migrants. A highly flexible and disposable global workforce, set into motion by war, social dangerousness, poverty, expropriation, and climate change, but without access to labor and social rights, is subjected to what Reece Jones calls the "Global Border Regime" of the twenty-first century: "The movement of the poor is limited again—just as it was by slavery and indentured servitude in previous eras—through laws that restrict movement based on different classes of people and violence that targets those who disregard the laws" (87). In addition, "an entire privatized industry now capitalizes on the cycle of transporting, incarcerating, hiring, and releasing non-status migrants" (Nail 1).[4]

Yet receiving societies continue to understand immigration as a culturally and economically destabilizing tide that states should endeavor to stem, a kind of disruption in the family. Nineteenth-century élites cast nation-states as mythical kinship communities, in which those élites claimed to fulfill a "parental" role by guaranteeing order, economic security, and social distribution, tapping into the emotional and moral needs of citizens undergoing the disruptive impact of capitalist modernization. Nationalist claims of kinship tend to erode when the state fails to fulfill its developmental promise to "protect," paving the way for the emergence of alternative imagined communities, such as ethnic or regional communities that mimic metaphors of kinship and home in their articulation of an identity dissonant with that of the dominant discourse of national family (see Brown). These representations, channeled by the state in multicultural terms that assume clear boundaries between majorities and minorities, divide and marginalize "others" while, at the same time, demanding their "integration" into a restored national civic community of allegiance, and decrying the disruption of "alien" or unauthorized subjects whose loyalty to the desired cohesive nation undergoes questioning and scrutiny.

The predicament of these so-called "aliens" converges and overlaps with that of "nationals" whose race, culture, social marginalization, mobility, or informal labor arrangements invite suspicions of "foreignness." Saskia Sassen sees this as a consequence of the "incipient unbundling of the exclusive authority . . . over territory, people, and identity" caused by globalization (*Territory* 340). It is a complex and ambiguous negotiation that happens largely inside multiple instances of the national, and is characterized by a "logic of expulsion" (cf. Sassen, *Expulsions*), what Mbembe calls an "imperialism of disorganization" which "leverages practices of zoning to manufacture disasters, and multiply states of exception everywhere" (5). The mass displacement of impoverished and colonized communities resulting from asymmetrical relations of global power, the use of the border as a mechanism of controlling, "othering," and criminalizing flows of migrant labor, and the racialized hierarchy of citizenship that underpins the nationalist state, cast migrants as trespassers who victimize their host society. "The constant imagining of the nation-state—the ideology of 'who belongs'—is best understood within the context of 'border imperialism' and its linkages to the incessant violence of both global and racialized empire and the transnational circulation of capital" (Walia 5–8, 54, 75–76). Mbembe writes:

> The new "wretched of the earth" are those to whom the right to have rights is effused, those who are told not to move, those who are condemned to live within the structures of confinement—camps, transit centers, the thousands of site of detention that dot our spaces of law and policing. They are those who are turned away, deported, expelled, the clandestine, the "undocumented"—the intruders and castoffs from humanity that we want to get rid of because they fundamentally pose a threat to our lives, our health, and our well-being. The new "wretched of the earth" are the products of a brutal process of control and selection whose racial foundations we well know. (177)

EXILIC TRANSGRESSIONS AND NOMADIC CROSSINGS

Thus the Roma peoples of Europe, for example, have become paradoxical outsiders of a "frontier" they historically inhabited. They originated in multiethnic and culturally fluid areas of the eastern Mediterranean, where Phoenicians and Greeks before them had crossed boundaries and expanded cultural horizons. In the early fifteenth century, when Christian navigators were exploring West Africa in an era that was not yet quite "modern," they arrived in Germany, Switzerland, Italy, France, Spain, Portugal, England, and the Netherlands. They partook in the imperial expansion of the "West," migrating to Brazil and Louisiana, before suffering persecution, being classified as a "race" and deemed recalcitrant to "assimilation" in rising western European states. They were then deported to extermination camps in the age of fascism. Nomads perceived as non-whites displaying dubious cultural affinities with the nations they inhabited, uncontained by territorial boundaries, the Roma, people of multiple ethnicities, religious affiliations, languages, and histories, "are no more citizens today, in the minds of most Europeans, than they were when they first presented their letters of penance to the authorities guarding Hildesheim city gates [Germany] in 1417" (B. Taylor 230). In France, they are the targets of police repression and racial violence, and they have been a centerpiece of debates over "national identity" since the 1990s. What they share in common, exclusion and eviction, links them to movements of migrants and refugees for recognition and freedom of movement across national boundaries. Their story prefigures the potential for what Gilles Deleuze and Félix Guattari called "nomadic solidarity" in reference to the concept of "*asabiyah*" developed by fourteenth-century Arab historian Ibn Khaldun,

> based primarily on one's commitment to a group or community without the forced belonging or exclusions of family, state, or other external prodding. . . . Anyone regardless of status, identity, or division can act in nomadic solidarity with anyone else. They do not need to share the same goals, backgrounds, territories, or states; they only need to be able to affirm and believe that their struggles are the same struggle. (Nail 253–54)[5]

Through this "insurgent citizenship," to borrow a concept from Étienne Balibar ("La proposition" 12), "hybrid" and border-crossing political actors exercise their rights via citizenship practices that reflect the central role they play within both the labor market and the larger fabric of social cooperation as workers and communities, even when undocumented and stigmatized as external to mainstream representations of the national "family" (cf. Sassen, *Territory* 294–96). As polyvocal manifestations of cultural hybridity and cosmopolitanism expose glaring fissures in the unitary edifice of the state and its universal claims, the movements they create struggle from a position of liminality to achieve equality and recognition in a society that enforces and ethnicizes their difference.

    In both France and the United States, political discourse invokes the myth of national unity to preserve the "family" of civilized and integrated citizens, and governments enact laws to adjust to the transnational pressures of capitalist globalization without forsaking the state's prerogatives as the guarantor of civil allegiance and cultural heritage. The colonized and marginalized subjects of this homogenizing impetus respond by defying the power of the state and ideologues to determine national pedigree. The marginalized, instead, carve autonomous spaces of activism and horizontal ties of solidarity that prefigure the construction of a new collective agency, diverse in its cultural expressions, hybrid in its appropriation of signifiers of belonging, and unbound in its territorial imagination. A vivid example is the transborder movement *La Otra Campaña* (The Other Campaign) launched by the Zapatistas and communities from southern Mexico and Baja California, which federates, in the spirit of the aforementioned Nahua concept of *nepantla,* Indigenous localities and displaced people throughout Mexico with advocacy groups both north and south, from Guatemala to Los Angeles. *La Otra Campaña* advocates creating transnational solidarity among Indigenous organizations throughout the Southern Americas and grassroots movements of Native Americans, African Americans, Asian Americans, and Latinx in the United States, as well as migrants from a mosaic of origins and nationalities who converge on the border, the historical legitimacy of which they contest.[6]

We are experiencing the aftershocks of the collapse of the imperialist and colonial systems that once structured the modern world, and witnessing their continuation by other means (cf. Smith 19). The modern nation-state mobilized metaphors of kinship to naturalize communities of belonging and logics of exclusion, through a historical narrative of manifest destiny that continually fabricated "aliens" and "others" in order to anchor its inevitability and legitimize its hierarchies (cf. Manzo 219–20). In the nineteenth century, the invention of "civilization," the "people," the "nation," and the "state" in the EuroAmerican regions of the world supplanted divergent or oppositional memories that had existed before, both within and without. Aiwha Ong reminds us that although interconnectedness and mobility across space have once again become the norm, moving peoples today are never entirely free of the discipline and regulation set by state power (cf. 4, 19). Yet the regulatory machinery of states finds itself continually challenged by global mechanisms of production, finance, and communication, by itinerant, "transterritorial" cultural and political solidarities that expose fissures in the power and sovereignty of the bounded territorial frameworks upon which it rests (cf. Carnegie 6). Modernity has never been immune to the existence of exilic spaces, areas of social and economic life in which people strive to escape from capitalist relations and processes, forging subterfuges of autonomy, whether territorial or symbolic, or, in other words, liminal and non-state areas that remain relatively autonomous from capitalist valorization and state control (see Grubacic and O'Hearn).

David Gross wrote that "(m)emory provides a counterweight to the blind power of the actual. It gives us the wherewithal to refuse the given where that is called for. And it allows us to recover and unfold again aspects of the past that, claims to the contrary notwithstanding, are perhaps not yet over and done with" (152). The modern world is "becoming once again what it has never ceased to be in practice—that is, a non-modern world like all the others" (Latour 135). A critical dimension of the creation of exilic or fugitive spaces is the subverting of the very narrative of modernity, which, while premised on universality, in reality has always been parochially Christian, European, and white. Eurocentric history and memory have anchored our representations of the past in a story that naturalizes civilizations, nations, borders, and tropes of alterity (cultural or racial) as if they were predestined to take on the form in which we know them today. It behooves us to recover an appreciation for what James Clifford called "non-Western, or not-only-Western models of cosmopolitan life, nonaligned transnationalities struggling within and against nation-states" (277). In *The Many-Headed Hydra* (2013), Peter Linebaugh and Marcus Rediker famously wrote of the "motley crew" of sailors, slaves, and commoners of all origins, insurgents and dissenters who formed communities of resistance and radical solidarities throughout the revolutionary Atlantic world, across the geographical and cultural spaces created by the expansion of territorial states.[7] When the Franco-Martinican poet Patrick Chamoiseau allegorically evokes today's "unclassifiable" migrant peoples (42), he is projecting onto our contemporary consciousness a similar story of marronage, of exilic transversality, a "counterstance" in the interstices of binary dualisms, which, as Gloria Anzaldúa suggests, require that we disengage from patterns of remembrance and representation that define our racialized and spatially barricaded subjectivities (cf. 78). The migrants of our time, Chamoiseau sings, are the "clandestine banished expelled expurgated exiled desolate wayfaring rowdy refugees expatriated repatriated globalized and deglobalized, desalinated or drowned, seekers of asylum, seekers of all that the virtues of the world lack, seekers of another cartography of our humanities" (42). Édouard Glissant wrote that knowledge is not universal but errant; our "all-world" (*tout-monde*) changes and persists by exchanging, as a "relation," a threading together of archipelagos of difference and thought (*Philosophie* 34, 45, 63)[8]—what Mbembe calls "a thinking in circulation, a thinking of crossings, a world-thinking" (177).

NOTES

1. Samuel Huntington first published *The Clash of Civilizations and the Remaking of World Order* in 1993, borrowing the term "clash of civilizations" from Bernard

Lewis, as found in, for example, Lewis's influential lecture/article "The Roots of Muslim Rage" (60). The "clash of civilizations" remains the paradigmatic vision of world history that predominates in textbooks and political circles. See also Haynes.

2. See Gomez; Hall, *Africans*; Hall, "Formation."

3. See also Montero de Pedro.

4. See also Buxton and Akkerman; O'Connor.

5. See also Khaldun; Deleuze and Guattari.

6. See Pellarolo; Marcos.

7. See Linebaugh and Rediker's chapter "A Motley Crew in the American Revolution."

8. See also Glissant, *Traité du tout-monde.*

WORKS CITED

Addi, Lahouari. "Colonial Mythologies: Algeria in the French Imagination." *Franco-Arab Encounters: Studies in Memory of David C. Gordon*, edited by L. C. Brown and M. S. Gordon, American University of Beirut, 1996, pp. 93–105.

Ansfield, Bench. "Still Submerged: The Uninhabitability of Urban Redevelopment." *Sylvia Wynter: On Being Human as Praxis*, edited by Katherine McKittrick, Duke University Press, 2015, pp. 124–41.

Anzaldúa, Gloria. *Borderlands/La Frontera: The New Mestiza.* Aunt Lute, 1987.

Augé, Marc. *An Anthropology for Contemporaneous Worlds.* Stanford University Press, 1994.

Balibar, Étienne. "Algeria, France: One Nation or Two?" *Giving Ground: The Politics of Propinquity*, edited by Joan Copjec and Michael Sorkin, Verso, 1999, pp. 162–72.

———. *La proposition de l'égaliberté: Essais politiques et philosophiques 1989–2009.* Presses Universitaires de France, 2010.

———. "Le droit de cité ou l'apartheid?" *Sans-papiers: L'archaïsme fatal.* Étienne Balibar, Monique Chemillon-Gendreau, Jacqueline Coste-Lascoux, and Emmanuel Terray. Éditions La Découverte, 1999, pp. 89–116.

Ball, Warwick. *Out of Arabia: Phoenicians, Arabs and the Discovery of Europe.* Olive Branch, 2010.

Bell, Caryn Cossé. *Revolution, Romanticism, and the Afro-Creole Protest Tradition in Louisiana, 1718–1868.* Louisiana State University Press, 1997.

Benítez-Rojo, Antonio. *The Repeating Island: The Caribbean in Postmodern Perspective.* Duke University Press, 1992.

Berlin, Ira. "From Creole to African: Atlantic Creoles and the Origins of Anglo-American Society in Mainland North America." *William and Mary Quarterly*, vol. 53, no. 2, 1996, pp. 251–88.

Bethencourt, Francisco. *Racisms: From the Crusades to the Twentieth Century.* Princeton University Press, 2013.

Blanchard, Pascal. "La France, entre deux immigrations." *La Fracture coloniale: La société française au prisme de l'héritage colonial*, under the direction of Pascal Blanchard, Nicolas Bancel, and Sabine Lemaire. Éditions La Découverte, 2005, pp. 173–82.

Brown, David. *Contemporary Nationalism: Civic, Ethnocultural and Multicultural Politics*. Routledge, 2000.

Buxton, Nick, and Mark Akkerman. "The Rise of Border Imperialism." *Beyond the Border*. ROAR, issue 8, 2018, https://roarmag.org/magazine/border-imperiali sm-europe-africa. Accessed Oct. 1, 2019.

Carnegie, Charles V. *Postnationalism Prefigured: Caribbean Borderlands*. Rutgers University Press, 1985.

Castellanos, Isabel. "A River of Many Turns: The Polysemy of Ochún in Afro-Cuban Tradition." *Òsun Across the Waters: A Yoruba Goddess in Africa and the Americas*, edited by Joseph M. Murphy and Mei-Mei Sanford, Indiana University Press, 2001, pp. 34–45.

Castles, Stephen, and Mark J. Miller. *The Age of Migration: International Population Movements in the Modern World*. 2nd ed., Guilford, 1998.

Chamoiseau, Patrick. *Migrant Brothers: A Poet's Declaration of Human Dignity*. Yale University Press, 2018.

Chaunu, Pierre. *Séville et l'Atlantique (1504–1650)*, vol. 8. Institut des Hautes Études d'Amérique Latine/Paris, 1959.

Clifford, James. *Routes: Travel and Translation in the Late Twentieth Century*. Harvard University Press, 1997.

Conklin, Alice L. *A Mission to Civilize: The Republican Idea of Empire in France and West Africa, 1895–1930*. Stanford University Press, 1997.

Costa-Lascoux, Jacqueline. "L'illusion de la maîtrise, la politique migratoire en trompe-l'œil." *Sans-papiers: L'archaïsme fatal*, Étienne Balibar et al., Éditions La Découverte, 1999, pp. 35–62.

Crowley, John. "France: The Archetype of a Nation-State." *European Nations and Nationalism: Theoretical and Historical Perspectives*, edited by Louk Hagendoorn, György Cspeli, Henk Dekker, and Russell Farnen, Ashgate, 2000, pp. 67–106.

Davis, Christopher. "Exchanging the African: Meetings at a Crossroads of the Diaspora." *South Atlantic Quarterly*, vol. 98, nos. 1/2, 1999, pp. 59–82.

de Laforcade, Geoffroy. "Broken Mirrors: Race, Historical Memory, and Citizenship in 20th/21st-Century France." *Transculturality and Perceptions of the Immigrant Other: "From-Heres" and "Come-Heres" in Virginia and North Rhine-Westphalia*, edited by Cathy Covell Waegner, Page R. Laws, and Geoffroy de Laforcade, Cambridge Scholars, 2011, pp. 76–103.

de Man, Paul. *Blindness and Insight: Essays in the Rhetoric of Contemporary Criticism*. 2nd ed., University of Minnesota Press, 1983.

Dear, Michael. *Why Walls Won't Work: Repairing the US-Mexico Divide*. Oxford University Press, 2013.

Deleuze, Gilles, and Félix Guattari. *A Thousand Plateaus: Capitalism and Schizophrenia*. University of Minnesota Press, 1987.

Diop, A. Moustapha. "Negotiating Religious Difference: The Origins and Attitudes of Islamic Associations in France." *The Politics of Multiculturalism in the New Europe: Racism, Identity and Community*, edited by Tariq Modood and Pnina Werbner, ZED, 1997, pp. 111–25.

Febvre, Lucien. *L'Europe: Genèse d'une civilisation*. Éditions Perrin, 1999.

Fernández-Armesto, Felipe. *Before Columbus: Exploration and Colonization from the Mediterranean to the Atlantic, 1229–1492*. Macmillan, 1987.

Gabaccia, Donna R. "Is Everywhere Nowhere? Nomads, Nations, and the Immigrant Paradigm of United States History." *The Journal of American History*, vol. 86, no. 3, 1999, pp. 1115–34.

Glissant, Édouard. *Philosophie de la relation: Poésie en étendue*. Éditions Gallimard, 2009.

———. *Traité du tout-monde: Poétique IV*. Éditions Gallimard, 1997.

Gold, Robert L. *Borderland Empires in Transition: The Triple-Nation Transfer of Florida*. Southern Illinois University Press, 1969.

Gomez, Michael A. *Exchanging Our Country Marks: The Transformation of African Identities in the Colonial and Antebellum South*. University of North Carolina Press, 1998.

Graeber, David. "There Never Was a West: Or, Democracy Emerges from the Spaces in Between." *Possibilities: Essays on Hierarchy, Rebellion, and Desire*. AK, 2007, pp. 329–74.

Graham, Brian, G. J. Ashworth, and J. E. Turnbridge. *A Geography of Heritage: Power, Culture and Economy*. Arnold, 2000.

Grandin, Greg. *The End of the Myth: From the Frontier to the Border Wall in the Mind of America*. Metropolitan/Henry Holt, 2019.

Gross, David. *Lost Time: On Remembering and Forgetting in Late Modern Culture*. University of Massachusetts Press, 2000.

Grubacic, Andre, and Denis O'Hearn. *Living at the Edges of Capitalism: Adventures in Exile and Mutual Aid*. University of California Press, 2016.

Hall, Gwendolyn Midlo. *Africans in Colonial Louisiana: The Development of Afro-Creole Culture in the Eighteenth Century*. Louisiana State University Press, 1992.

———. "The Formation of Afro-Creole Culture." *Creole New Orleans: Race and Americanization*, edited by Arnold R. Hirsch and Joseph Logsdon. Louisiana State University Press, 1992, pp. 58–87.

Hanger, Kimberly S. "Greedy French Masters and Color-Conscious, Legal-Minded Spaniards in Colonial Louisiana." *Slavery in the Caribbean Francophone World: Distant Voices, Forgotten Acts, Forged Identities*, edited by Doris Y. Kadish. University of Georgia Press, 2000, pp. 102–21.

Haynes, Jeffrey. *From Huntington to Trump: Thirty Years of the Clash of Civilizations*. Lexington, 2019.

Huntington, Samuel. *The Clash of Civilizations and the Remaking of World Order*. 1996. Simon & Schuster, 2007.

Jacobson, David. *Place and Belonging in America*. Johns Hopkins University Press, 2002.

Jensen, Eric. *Barbarians in the Greek and Roman World*. Hackett, 2018.

Johnson, Walter. *Soul by Soul: Life Inside the Antebellum Slave Market*. Harvard University Press, 1999.

Jones, Reece. *Violent Borders: Refugees and the Right to Move*. Verso, 2016.

Kehoe, Alice Beck. *North America before the European Invasions*. 2nd ed., Routledge, 2017.

Khaldūn, Ibn. *The Muqaddimah: An Introduction to History*. Pantheon, 1958.

Kimball, Richard Burleigh. *Cuba, and the Cubans; Comprising a History of the Island of Cuba, its Present Social, Political, and Domestic Condition; also, its Relation to England and the United States*. George P. Putnam, 1850.

Knight, Franklin W. *The Caribbean: Genesis of a Fragmented Nationalism.* Oxford University Press, 1990.

Lamming, George. "Caribbean Labor, Culture, and Identity." *Caribbean Cultural Identities*, special issue of *Bucknell Review*, edited by Glyne Griffith, vol. 44, no. 2, 2001, pp. 17–31.

Landers, Jane. *Black Society in Spanish Florida.* University of Illinois Press, 1999.

Latour, Bruno. *We Have Never Been Modern.* Harvard University Press, 1993.

Lewis, Bernard. "The Roots of Muslim Rage." *Atlantic Monthly*, Sep. 1990, pp. 47–60.

Lewis, Gordon K. *Main Currents of Caribbean Thought: The Historical Evolution of Caribbean Society in its Ideological Aspects, 1492–1900.* Johns Hopkins University Press, 1983.

Linebaugh, Peter, and Marcus Rediker. *The Many-Headed Hydra: Sailors, Slaves, Commoners, and the Hidden History of the Revolutionary Atlantic.* Beacon, 2013.

Manning, Patrick. *The African Diaspora: A History through Culture.* Columbia University Press, 2010.

Manzo, Katherine A. *Creating Boundaries: The Politics of Race and Nation.* Lynne Rienner, 1996.

Marcos, Subcomandante Insurgente. *The Other Campaign: la otra campaña.* City Lights Open Media, 2008.

Mbembe, Achille. *Critique of Black Reason.* Duke University Press, 2017.

Montero de Pedro, José. *Españoles en Nueva Orleans y Luisiana.* Ediciones Cultura Hispánica, 1979.

Morice, Alain. "Le mouvement des sans-papiers ou la difficile mobilisation collective des individualismes." *Histoire politique des immigrations (post) coloniales: France, 1920–2000*, edited by Ahmed Boubekar and Abdellali Hajjat, Éditions Amsterdam, 2008, pp. 125–41.

Nail, Thomas. "Violence at the Borders: Nomadic Solidarity and Non-Status Migrant Resistance." *Radical Philosophy Review*, vol. 15, no. 1, 2012, pp. 241–57.

Ngai, Mae M. *Impossible Subjects: Illegal Aliens and the Making of Modern America.* Princeton University Press, 2004.

O'Connor, Brendan. "Border Profiteers: A Visit to America's Leading Trade Show for State Violence." *The Baffler*, no. 46, 2019, https://thebaffler.com/outbursts/border-profiteers-oconnor. Accessed Oct. 1, 2019.

Okrent, Daniel. *The Guarded Gate: Bigotry, Eugenics and the Law That Kept Two Generations of Jews, Italians, and Other European Immigrants Out of America.* Scribner, 2019.

Ong, Aiwha. *Flexible Citizenship: The Cultural Logics of Transnationality.* Duke University Press, 1999.

Pagden, Anthony. *The Fall of Natural Man: The American Indian and the Origins of Comparative Ethnology.* Cambridge University Press, 1982.

Pellarolo, Sirena. "*La Otra Campaña Transfronteriza*: De-Nationalizing Trans-Border Grassroots Organizing." *Motion Magazine*, Feb. 25, 2007, www.inmotionmagazine.com/auto/sp_trans.html. Accessed Oct. 1, 2019.

Pope Melish, Joanne. *Disowning Slavery: Gradual Emancipation and "Race" in New England, 1780–1860.* Cornell University Press, 1998.

Sanford, Mei-Mei. "Living Water: Òsun, Mami Water, and Olókùn in the Lives of Four Contemporary Nigerian Christian Women." *Òsun across the Waters: A Yoruba Goddess in Africa and the Americas*, edited by Joseph M. Murphy and Mei-Mei Sanford, Indiana University Press, 2001, pp. 237–50.

Sassen, Saksia. *Expulsions: Brutality and Complexity in the Global Economy.* Harvard University Press/Belknap, 2014.

———. *Territory, Authority, Rights: From Medieval to Global Assemblages.* Princeton University Press, 2006.

Scott, David. "The Re-Enchantment of Humanism: An Interview with Sylvia Wynter." *Small Axe*, no. 8, Sep. 2000, pp. 119–207.

Smith, Gene Allen, and Sylvia L. Hilton, editors. *Nexus of Empire: Negotiating Loyalty and Identity in the Revolutionary Borderlands, 1760s–1820s.* University Press of Florida, 2010.

Smith, Paul. *Millennial Dreams: Contemporary Culture and Capital in the North.* Verso, 1997.

Taylor, Becky. *Another Darkness, Another Dawn: A History of Gypsies, Roma and Travellers.* Reaktion, 2014.

Taylor, Quintard. *In Search of the Racial Frontier: African Americans in the American West 1528–1990.* Norton, 1998.

Vattimo, Gianni. *The Transparent Society.* Polity, 1992.

Walia, Harsha. *Undoing Border Imperialism.* AK Press/Institute for Anarchist Studies, 2013.

Weber, David J. *The Spanish Frontier in North America.* Yale University Press, 1992.

Weddle, Robert S. *Spanish Sea: The Gulf of Mexico in North American Discovery, 1500–1685.* Texas A & M University Press, 1985.

Witte, Rob. *Racist Violence and the State: A Comparative Analysis of Britain, France and the Netherlands.* Longman, 1996.

Wynter, Sylvia. "1492: A New World View." *Race, Discourse, and the Origin of the Americas*, edited by Vera Lawrence Hyatt and Rex Nettleford, Smithsonian Institution, 1995, pp. 5–57.

———. "Towards the Sociogenic Principle: Fanon, the Puzzle of Conscious Experience, of 'Identity' and What It's Like to Be 'Black.'" *National Identities and Socio-Political Changes in Latin America*, edited by Mercedes F. Durán-Gogan and Antonio Gómez-Moriana, University of Minnesota Press, 1999, pp. 30–67.

———. "Unsettling the Coloniality of Being/Power/Truth/Freedom: Towards the Human, After Man, Its Overrepresentation—An Argument." *The New Centennial Review*, vol. 3, no. 3, 2003, pp. 257–337.

Index

About the Contributors

Geoffroy de Laforcade (PhD, Yale University) is professor of Latin American, Caribbean, and world history at Norfolk State University. A scholar of the Caribbean, the Southern Cone and the broader Atlantic World, he has published and spoken widely on issues of migration, labor, borders, transnationalism, diaspora, religion, art, and memory, and has coedited *Transculturality and Perceptions of the Immigrant Other* (Cambridge Scholars, 2011), *The How and Why of World History* (2014), and *In Defiance of Boundaries: Anarchism in Latin American History* (2015), which won the Choice Outstanding Academic Title Award in 2017. A native of France, he has also translated books by historians of Europe, Peter Sahlins, Herman Lebovics, and Gérard Noiriel.

Mine Gencel Bek is Mercator Fellow at the Graduate Research Center *Locating Media*, University of Siegen. She was dismissed from her position as a professor in the Department of Journalism, Faculty of Communication, Ankara University, Turkey, with the decree law in February 2017 for signing the petition for peace. She completed her PhD at Loughborough University in 1999. She was a visiting lecturer at MIT Comparative Media Studies, Open Documentary Lab and Civic Media Lab in 2013 and 2014. Her current research and teaching focus on immigration and exile cultures, memory, journalism, peace and trauma, changing media forms, technological innovations, and the use of participatory tools in civic advocacy.

Sarah J. Grünendahl is a North American studies graduate of the University of Bonn; currently, she is a doctoral candidate in political science at the University of Siegen and a research associate at the University of Applied Sciences Düsseldorf. Her dissertation is concerned with political activism in connection with US American war resisters' flight to Canada. The study serves as a lens through which to analyze migrants' adaptation to the destination country, patterns of societal participation, as well as Canada–US relations. In 2014/2015 Grünendahl was a Joint Visiting Research Fellow with the Centre for Global Studies and the Borders in Globalization Project, both housed at the University of Victoria (Canada).

Christopher Hansen holds a bachelor's degree in English-speaking culture and cultural studies and a master's degree in transnational literary science from the University of Bremen. He is currently teaching in the English Department at the University of Siegen, where he also conducts research on the narrative mechanics governing the connections and changes in the transmedial Shared Universes of Marvel Cinematics for his PhD thesis.

Cathy M. Jackson, PhD, is associate professor in the Department of Mass Communications and Journalism at Norfolk State University. She teaches courses on the history of and multiculturalism in the mass media and film. Her 2004 dissertation on Jesse James won the 2005 James-Younger Gang Milton Perry Award for Outstanding Research, in addition to an appearance on a PBS American Experience documentary *Jesse James* in 2006 and a Travel Channel program, *Mysteries at the Museum* (2011). Before pursuing a doctorate at the University of Missouri's School of Journalism, Jackson taught journalism and mass media courses at Johnson C. Smith University in Charlotte, NC. Her career in newspapers included stints as a reporter at the *Flint* (Michigan) *Journal* and the *Tampa* (Florida) *Tribune*. She has freelanced for several publications, including *ESSENCE* magazine, for which she wrote an article that earned her an invitation to appear on the *Oprah Winfrey Show*.

Isabella Karlsson is a PhD student at the University of Siegen and works as a consultant for business communication in an agency in Cologne. Currently, she is working on her dissertation on the role of surveillance and big data in contemporary American dystopian novels. She obtained her master's degree from Uppsala University, Sweden, and taught literary and cultural studies at the University of Siegen.

Andreas Kewes is a postdoctoral researcher at the University of Siegen. He studied political science, history, and geography at the University of Marburg and obtained his PhD in sociology from the University of Erfurt. He works as a lecturer in social work. His research interests include volunteering and turnover intentions (in a research project with Chantal Munsch), flight and asylum, civil societies and social movements, and qualitative social research.

Patrycja Kurjatto-Renard is an independent scholar who was born in Poland but has lived in France since 1992. She earned her PhD from François Rabelais University, Tours, France. Her research focuses on women's studies, African American fiction, Asian American fiction, Native American fiction, immigrant writing, and late-twentieth-century fiction. She has published articles on writers such as Louise Erdrich, Toni Morrison, Gloria Naylor, Amy Tan, Toru Dutt, and has recently worked on Octavia Butler. She is an active member of EAAS, Résonances, CAAR, and MESEA. She is currently employed by the Université du Littoral Côte d'Opale.

Page R. Laws is professor of English and dean of the Robert C. Nusbaum Honors College at Norfolk State University (Ret.). Twice a Fulbright scholar (Germany, Austria), Laws is coeditor of *Transculturality and Perceptions of the Immigrant Other* (2011). She has also written chapters for *Ethnic and Racial Identities in the Media*, eds. Eleftheria Arapoglou et al. (2016); *From Black to Schwarz: Cultural Crossovers between African America and Germany*, eds. Maria I. Diedrich et al. (2010); *Aesthetic Practices and Politics in Media, Music, and Art: Performing Migration*, eds. Dorothea Fischer-Hornung et al. (2010). Laws does occasional reviews for a variety of popular and online publications including *Bright Lights Film Journal* and *Cineaste*. She received her BA from Wellesley College and her MPhil and PhD in comparative literature from Yale University.

Aprilfaye T. Manalang is assistant professor of interdisciplinary studies at Norfolk State University. She trained in the social sciences (University of Chicago, MA) and the humanities (Bowling Green State University, PhD) and ranked as a top ten finalist for the National Hiett Prize in the Humanities, an "annual award aimed at identifying candidates who are in the early stages of careers devoted to the humanities and whose work shows extraordinary promise and has a significant public component related to contemporary culture." A Georg-Bollenbeck (University of Siegen) and Virginia Humanities fellow, Manalang recently received the internationally competitive Early Career Award from the John Templeton Foundation for her ongoing project "Minority Millennials and the Rise of 'Religious Nones': A Comparative Analysis." Most recently, she won the Teaching Faculty Excellence Award, which "recognizes a member of the Teaching Faculty that has advanced the university's mission through outstanding teaching, research, and community service." Her research interests include immigration, transnationalism, sociology of religion, citizenship, race/ethnicity.

Ludmila Martanovschi is associate professor in American studies at the Faculty of Letters, Ovidius University, Constanta, Romania. Her areas of expertise include American Indian literatures and contemporary American drama. Her research as a Fulbright grantee in two US locations led to the publication of *Decolonizing the Self: Memory, Language and Cultural Experience in Contemporary American Indian Poetry* (2009) and *Family Ties: An Introduction to Postwar American Drama* (2012). One of her recent essays appeared in *Women's Life Writing and the Practice of Reading: She Reads to Write Herself*, edited by Valérie Baisnée-Keay et al. (2018). Her latest coedited volume, *Ethnicity and Gender Debates: Cross-Readings of American Literature and Culture in the New Millennium* is forthcoming (2020). She is the Secretary of the Society for Multi-Ethnic Studies: Europe and the Americas (MESEA).

Cassandra L. Newby-Alexander is dean of the College of Liberal Arts, professor of history, and director of the Joseph Jenkins Roberts Center for African Diaspora Studies at Norfolk State University. She has received numerous awards and commendations including the William M. E. Rachal Award for best overall article for 2018 on Sarah Garland Jones in the *Virginia Magazine of History and Biography*, the Distinguished Service Award on behalf of the 400 Years of African American History Commission, the Juneteenth organization's "Junnie" Award for Outstanding Historical Research, and the 2019 Humanitarian Award from the Virginia Center for Inclusive Communities. Her book publications include *Virginia Waterways and the Underground Railroad* (2017), *An African American History of the Civil War in Hampton Roads* (2010), coauthored *Black America Series: Portsmouth* (2003), *Hampton Roads: Remembering Our Schools* (2009), and coedited *Voices from within the Veil: African Americans and the Experience of Democracy* (2008).

Michele Rozga completed her PhD in English at Georgia State University in 2011, after working in performance art that included comedy improvisation and semiprofessional modern dance. She has recently presented at conferences on American poetry and on the teaching of composition, and published poems in a number of literary journals and in an anthology from CityLit Books. Poetry prizes include the Agnes Scott Prize for Poetry and the Southeast Review Prize, selected by Mark Doty. In 2015, she was a semifinalist for the national open poetry manuscript competition at Crab Orchard Review Press in Illinois, and a full-length volume of poetry, *My Adversary Came onto the Windowsill of Another Dream, as a Bluebird*, is forthcoming (2020). In 2017, she took on the position of assistant professor of English at Norfolk State University.

Daniel Stein is professor of North American literary and cultural studies and vice dean for international affairs at the University of Siegen. He is the author of *Music Is My Life: Louis Armstrong, Autobiography, and American Jazz* (2012) and coeditor, most recently, of *Nineteenth-Century Serial Narrative in Transnational Perspective, 1830s–1860s* (2019). His work has appeared in *Popular Music and Society, Southern Literary Journal, European Journal of American Studies*, and *Amerikastudien/American Studies*. He is coeditor of *Anglia: Journal of English Philology,* the *Anglia* book series, as well as a 2013 recipient of the Heinz Maier-Leibnitz Prize for outstanding scholarly achievements (German Research Foundations and Ministry of Education and Research).

Cathy Covell Waegner taught American studies at the University of Siegen until her retirement in 2013. She obtained degrees from the College of William & Mary (BA) and the University of Virginia (MA, PhD). In addition to her work on Native American concerns and authors, including Gerald Vizenor, Stephen Graham Jones, James Welch, and Louise Erdrich, she has published on Toni Morrison and William Faulkner, as well as on the interaction between American and European cultural phenomena. She wrote a chapter for *New Directions in Diaspora Studies* (2018). Waegner coedited volumes on diasporic ethnicities; transculturality and perceptions of the immigrant other; and *Ethnic Resonances in Performance, Literature, and Identity* (2020). She edited *Mediating Indianness* (2015).

Lightning Source UK Ltd.
Milton Keynes UK
UKHW020918191220
375442UK00003B/206